THE ALMOST NEARLY PERFECT PEOPLE

Michael Booth contributes to numerous British and foreign magazines and all of the UK's broadsheet newspapers. He is the author of four works of non-fiction: *Eat, Pray, Eat*, which was nominated for a British Travel Press Award in 2012; *Just As Well I'm Leaving*, nominated for the *Irish Times* first writers award; *Doing Without Delia*, a BBC Radio 4 Book of the Week; and *Sushi and Beyond*, winner of the Guild of Food Writers award in 2010. He lives in Denmark with his wife and children.

MICHAEL BOOTH

The Almost Nearly Perfect People

Behind the Myth of the Scandinavian Utopia

VINTAGE

Published by Vintage 2015
14

First published in Great Britain in 2014 by
Jonathan Cape

Vintage
20 Vauxhall Bridge Road,
London SW1V 2SA

www.vintage-books.co.uk

A Penguin Random House Company

Penguin
Random House
UK

www.global.penguinrandomhouse.com

A CIP catalogue record for this book
is available from the British Library

ISBN 9780099546078

Penguin Random House is committed to a sustainable future for our
business, our readers and our planet. This book is made from Forest
Stewardship Council® certified paper.

Typeset in Dante MT Std by Palimpsest Book Production Limited,
Falkirk, Stirlingshire

Printed and bound in Great Britain by Clays Ltd, Elcograf S.p.A.

To Lissen, Asger and Emil

Contents

THE ALMOST NEARLY
PERFECT PEOPLE

Introduction

Early one dark April morning a few years ago I was sitting in my living room in central Copenhagen, wrapped in a blanket and yearning for spring, when I opened that day's newspaper to discover that my adopted countrymen had been anointed the happiest of their species in something called the Satisfaction with Life Index, compiled by the Department of Psychology at the University of Leicester.

I checked the date on the newspaper: it wasn't 1 April. Indeed a quick look online confirmed that this was headline news around the world. Everyone from the *Daily Mail* to Al Jazeera was covering the story as if it had been handed down on a stone tablet. Denmark was the happiest place in the world. The *happiest*? This dark, wet, dull, flat little country that I now called home, with its handful of stoic, sensible people and the highest taxes in the world? Britain was forty-first on the list. A man at a university had said it, so it must be true.

'Well, they are doing an awfully good job of hiding it,' I thought to myself as I looked out of the window at the rain-swept harbour. 'They don't seem all that frisky to me.' Down below, cyclists swaddled in high-visibility Arctic gear crossed the Langebro together with umbrella-jostling pedestrians, both battling the spray from passing trucks and buses.

I thought back to the previous day's soul-sapping adventures in my recently adopted homeland. In the morning there had been my twice-weekly encounter with the sullen check-out girl at the local supermarket who, as was her habit, had rung up the cost of my prohibitively expensive, low-grade produce without acknowledging my existence. Outside, other pedestrians had tutted audibly when

I'd crossed the street on a red light; there was no traffic, but in Denmark pre-empting the green man is a provocative breach of social etiquette. I had cycled home through the drizzle to find a tax bill relieving me of an alarming proportion of that month's income, having along the way provoked the fury of a motorist who had threatened to kill me because I had infringed the no-left-turn rule (literally, he had rolled down his window and, in the manner and accent of a Bond villain, shouted, 'I vill kill you'). The evening's prime-time TV entertainment had consisted of a programme on how to tackle excessive chafing of cow udders, followed by a ten-year-old episode of *Taggart*, and then *Who Wants to Be a Millionaire?* – its titular, life-altering rhetoric somewhat undermined by the fact that a million kroner are worth only around £100,000, in Denmark just enough to buy you a meal out with change for the cinema.

This, I should add, was long before all those critically acclaimed Danish TV series hit the screens and New Nordic cuisine revolutionised our kitchens, long before Sarah Lund charmed us with her knitwear and Birgitte Nyborg seduced us with her pencil skirts and no-nonsense attitude to right-wing politicians, and long before the recent, seemingly ceaseless wave of Danish mania gripped the world. Back then, I had come to think of the Danes as essentially decent, hard-working, law-abiding people, rarely prone to public expressions of . . . well, anything much, let alone *happiness*. The Danes were Lutheran by nature, if not by ritual observance: they shunned ostentation, distrusted exuberant expressions of emotion, and kept themselves to themselves. Compared to, say, the Thais or Puerto Ricans or even the British, they were a frosty, solemn bunch. I would go as far as to say that of the fifty or so nationalities that I had encountered in my travels up to that point, the Danes would probably have ranked in the bottom quarter as among the *least* demonstrably joyful people on earth, along with the Swedes, the Finns and the Norwegians.

Perhaps it was all the antidepressants they were taking that was fogging their perception, I thought to myself. I had read a recent report which said that, in Europe, only the Icelanders consumed more happy pills than the Danes, and the rate at which they were popping them was increasing. Was Danish happiness nothing more than oblivion sponsored by Prozac?

In fact, as I began to delve deeper into the Danish happiness phenomenon I discovered that the University of Leicester report was not as ground-breaking as it might have liked to think. The Danes came top of the EU's first ever well-being survey – the Eurobarometer – as long ago as 1973, and are still top today. In the latest one, more than two-thirds of the thousands of Danes who were polled claimed to be 'very satisfied' with their lives.

In 2009 there was the papal-like visit to Copenhagen of Oprah Winfrey, who cited the fact that 'people leave their children in buggies outside of cafés, that you aren't worried they will get stolen . . . that everyone isn't racing racing racing to get more more more' as the Danes's secret to success. If Oprah was anointing Denmark, it *must* be true.

By the time Oprah descended from the heavens I had actually left Denmark, having finally driven my wife to the very end of her tether with my incessant moaning about her homeland: the punishing weather, the heinous taxes, the predictable monoculture, the stifling insistence on lowest-common-denominator consensus, the fear of anything or anyone different from the norm, the distrust of ambition and disapproval of success, the appalling public manners, and the remorseless diet of fatty pork, salty liquorice, cheap beer and marzipan. But I still kept a wary, slightly bewildered eye on the Danish happiness phenomenon.

I shook my head in disbelief when, for example, the country topped the Gallup World Poll, which asked a thousand people over the age of fifteen in 155 countries to rate, on a scale of 1 to 10, both their lives now and how they expected them to pan out in the future. Gallup asked other questions about social support ('If you were in trouble, do you have relatives or friends you can count on to help you whenever you need them?'); freedom ('In your country, are you satisfied or dissatisfied with your freedom to choose what you do with your life?'); and corruption ('Is corruption widespread within businesses located in your country?'). The answers revealed that 82 per cent of Danes were 'thriving' (the highest score), while only 1 per cent were 'suffering'. Their average 'daily experience' scored a world-beating 7.9 out of 10. By way of comparison, in Togo, the lowest-ranked country, only 1 per cent were considered to be thriving.

'Perhaps they should ask the Somali immigrants in Ishøj how happy *they* are,' I would think to myself whenever I heard about these surveys and reports, although I seriously doubted any of the researchers ever ventured far outside of Copenhagen's prosperous suburbs.

Then came the final, crowning moment in the Danish happiness story: in 2012, the United Nations's first ever World Happiness Report, compiled by economists John Helliwell, Richard Layard and Jeffrey Sachs, amalgamated the results of all the current 'happiness' research – the Gallup World Polls, World and European Values Surveys, European Social Survey, and so on. And, guess what? Belgium came first! No, I'm joking. Denmark was once again judged the happiest country in the world, with Finland (2), Norway (3) and Sweden (7) close behind.

To paraphrase Lady Bracknell, to win one happiness survey may be regarded as good fortune, to win virtually every one since 1973 is convincing grounds for a definitive anthropological thesis.

In fact, Denmark was not without rivals to the title of peachiest place to live. As the UN report suggested, each of the Nordic countries has its own particular claim to life-quality supremacy. Shortly after the UN report was published, *Newsweek* announced that it was Finland, and not Denmark, that has the best quality of life, while Norway topped the UN's own Human Development Index, and another recent report claimed that Sweden is the best country to live in if you are a woman.

So, Denmark doesn't *always* come first in *all* the categories of these wellness, satisfaction and happiness surveys, but it is invariably thereabouts, and if it isn't number one, then another Nordic country almost inevitably is. Occasionally New Zealand or Japan might elbow their way into the picture (or perhaps Singapore, or Switzerland) but, overall, the message from all of these reports, which were enthusiastically and unquestioningly reported in the European and US media, was as clear as a glass of ice-cold schnapps: the Scandinavians were not only the happiest and most contented people in the world, but also the most peaceful, tolerant, egalitarian, progressive, prosperous, modern, liberal, liberated, best-educated, most technologically advanced, and with the best pop music, coolest TV detectives and even, in the last few years, the best restaurant, to boot. Between them, these five countries – Denmark, Sweden, Norway, Finland and Iceland – could boast the best education system in the world (Finland); a shining example of a properly secular, multicultural, modern industrial society (Sweden); colossal oil wealth, being invested in sensible, ethical, long-term things rather than silly tall buildings or Park Lane call girls (Norway); the most gender-equal society in the world, the longest-living men, and lots of haddock (Iceland); and ambitious environmental policies and generously funded welfare state systems (all of them).

The consensus was overwhelming: if you wanted to know where to look for the definitive model of how to live a fulfilled, happy, well balanced, healthy and enlightened life, you should turn your gaze north of Germany, and just to the left of Russia.

I did more than that. After some years of watching the Danish happiness bandwagon roll relentlessly on from a distance – interspersed with regular visits which, if anything, only served to confuse me more (weather still shitty? Check. Tax rate still over 50 per cent? Yep. Shops closed whenever you need them? Oh yes) – I moved back there.

This wasn't some magnanimous gesture of forgiveness, nor a bold experiment to test the boundaries of human endurance: my wife wanted to move back to her homeland and, despite every molecule of my being screaming, 'Don't you remember what it was actually like to *live* there, Michael?' I have learned from harrowing experience over the years that it is usually best in the long run if I just do what she says.

If anything, the fever for all things Nordic only intensified around the world after I returned to live there. The world, it seemed, could not get enough of contemporary Viking culture: Swedish crime authors Henning Mankell and Stieg Larsson began to shift millions of books, and Danmarks Radio (DR), the Danish national broadcaster, sold three series of its miserablist crime epic, *Forbrydelsen* (*The Killing*), to 120 countries, and even saw it remade for American TV. The company's follow-up, the political drama *Borgen* ('The Castle' – the nickname given to the Danish parliament building), won a BAFTA and a million viewers on BBC4; and even *Broen* (*The Bridge*), a Danish–Swedish crime series, was a hit. (No matter that there was little original about *Forbrydelsen* other than its setting – we had seen tough female cops many times before; no matter that *Borgen* was a third-rate *West Wing*, albeit with better lampshades; or that *The Bridge* was actually really, really rubbish.) Suddenly Danish architects, most notably Bjarke Ingels, were knocking out major international building projects as if they were made out of Lego blocks, and works by artists like Olafur Eliasson were appearing everywhere from Louis Vuitton window displays to the Turbine Hall at Tate Modern. A former Danish prime minister, Anders Fogh Rasmussen, took over as the head of NATO and a former Finnish president, Martti Ahtisaari, won the Nobel Peace Prize. Danish films had a major moment, winning Oscars and awards at Cannes with directors such as Thomas Vinterberg, Lars von Trier, Susanne Bier and Nicolas Winding Refn becoming among the most acclaimed of the current era, and the actor Mads Mikkelsen (*Casino Royale*, *The Hunt*, *Hannibal*) became such a regular figure on Danish and international screens that these days he calls to mind John Updike's famous couplet on a similarly ubiquitous French actor: 'I think that I shall never view / A French film without Depardieu'. And, of course, there was the New Nordic food 'revolution' and the journey of the Copenhagen restaurant Noma from obscure joke to international trendsetter, named best restaurant in the world three times in a row and making its head chef, René Redzepi, a *Time* magazine cover star.

Elsewhere in the region, Finland gave us Angry Birds, won

Eurovision with a band apparently made up of orcs (Lordi) and, for a while at least, mobile phones that took up permanent residence in everyone's inside breast pocket. Meanwhile Sweden continued its domination of our high streets with H&M and Ikea, and of our airwaves with pop producers and singers too numerous to list here, as well as giving us Skype and Spotify; Norway kept the world supplied with oil and fish fingers; and the Icelanders embarked on their extraordinary fiscal buccaneering spree.

No matter where I turned for my news, I could not escape the (Iceland aside) almost exclusively adulatory coverage of all things Scandinavian. If our newspapers, TV and radio were to be believed, the Nordic countries simply could not put a foot wrong. These were the promised lands of equality, easy living, quality of life and home baking. But I had seen a different side actually living up here in the cold, grey north and, though there were many aspects to Scandinavian living that were indeed exemplary, and from which the rest of the world could learn a great deal, I grew increasingly frustrated by the lack of nuance in the picture being painted of my adopted homeland.

One thing in particular about this new-found love of all things Scandinavian – be it their free-form schools, whitewashed interior design, consensus-driven political systems or chunky jumpers – which struck me as particularly odd: considering all this positive PR, and with awareness of the so-called Nordic miracle at an all-time high, why wasn't everyone flocking to live here? Why did people still dream of a house in Spain or France? Why weren't they packing up their mules and heading for Aalborg or Trondheim? For all the crime literature and TV shows, why was our knowledge of Scandinavia still so abysmally lacking? How come you have no idea where Aalborg or Trondheim actually are (be honest)? Why can no one you know speak Swedish or 'get by' in Norwegian? Name the Danish foreign minister. Or Norway's most popular comedian. Or a Finnish person. Any Finnish person.

Few of us visit Japan or Russia or speak their languages but, though you might not be able to name all of their political leaders, artists, or second-tier cities, I'm guessing you would be able to name at least *some*. Scandinavia, though, really is *terra incognita*. The Romans didn't bother with it. Charlemagne couldn't care less. As Nordic historian T. K. Derry writes in his history of the region, for literally thousands of years 'the north remained almost entirely outside the sphere of interest of civilised man'. Even today the lack of interest is deafening. A. A. Gill, writing recently in the *Sunday Times*, described this part of the world as 'a collection of countries we can't tell apart'.

Part of the reason for our collective blind spot – and I am the first to admit that I was quite fantastically ignorant of the region before I first moved here – is the fact that comparatively few of us ever travel in this part of the world. For all its scenic wonder, the cost of visiting Scandinavia coupled with its discouraging climate (not to mention the continuing existence of France) tend to dissuade most from holidaying here. Where is the travel writing on the North? Waterstones' shelves are buckling beneath the weight of Mediterranean memoirs – *Dipsomaniac Among the Olive Groves*, *Extra-marital Affairs on Oranges*, and so on – but no one, it seems, wants to spend *A Year in Turku*, or try *Driving Over Lingonberries*.

One day, while standing for half an hour waiting to be served at my local chemists (Danish *apoteks* are run on a monopoly basis so customer service is not a priority), it dawned on me that, for all the glowing *Guardian* profiles of Sofie Gråbøl (the star of *The Killing*), for all the articles about Faroese knitwear, and recipes for twenty ways with foraged weeds (and I must put my hand up here, I wrote more than a couple of the latter), the truth is that we learn more from our schoolteachers, televisions and newspapers about the lives of remote Amazonian tribes than we do about actual Scandinavians and how they *actually* live.

This is odd because the Danes and Norwegians are our nearest neighbours to the east, the Icelanders our nearest to the north and, in terms of our national character, we have more in common with all of them than we do with the French or Germans: our humour, tolerance, distrust of religious dogma and political authority, honesty, stoicism in the face of dismal weather, social orderliness, poor diet, lack of sartorial elan, and so on. (This versus the emotional incontinence, endemic corruption, banana-skin humour, adolescent temperament, slapdash personal hygiene, exquisite cuisine and elegant tailoring of our southern neighbours.)

You could even go as far as to argue that we Britons are, essentially, Scandinavians. Well, a bit. The cultural links are undeniably deep and enduring, dating back to the infamous first raid on the monastery at Lindisfarne on 8 January, 793 when, as contemporary records have it, 'The harrowing inroads of heathen men made lamentable havoc in the church of God in the Holy-island.'

Viking kings went on to rule a third of Britain – the territory known as the Danelaw – during a period which culminated with that great spell-checker booby trap, Cnut, as undisputed king of all England. Excavations of a ship burial at Sutton Hoo have given plenty of evidence of a Swedish link, too. After they had got the raping and pillaging out of their systems, there is strong evidence that Vikings of various tribes settled amicably among the Anglo Saxons, traded, intermarried and had a major influence on the indigenous population.

They certainly left their mark on the English language. A Norwegian language professor at Oslo University, Jan Terje Faarlund, recently went as far as declaring English a Scandinavian language, pointing to shared vocabulary, similar verb-then-object word order (as opposed to German grammar), and so on. The division of Yorkshire into north, east and west 'ridings' comes from the Viking term for a 'third'; I am guessing that Yorkshire's 'dales' are of Nordic derivation, too (*dal* is Danish for valley); and I have often wondered if northern England's glottal stops are not some kind of linguistic infection from the Danes (who, when they speak, can often sound as if they are swallowing not just most of the consonants in each word, but their very tongues). Then there are some of the days of the week (*Wodin* or *Odin* for Wednesday; *Thor* for Thursday; *Freya* for Friday), and many place names. The Domesday Book is full of Scandinavian names for settlements: any town ending in '-by' or

'-thorpe' (meaning 'town' and 'smaller settlement') was once a Viking settlement – Derby, Whitby, Scunthorpe, Cleethorpes, and so on. I was born near a town called East Grinstead, whose name, I assume, is of Danish origin (*sted* meaning 'place', and a common Danish town name ending); and in London I used to live five minutes from Denmark Hill, a name which stems from a more recent connection, admittedly: it was once the home of the Danish consort of Queen Anne, the Danish and British royal families having been tightly intertwined by marriage over many centuries.

Family words – mother (*mor*), father (*far*), sister (*søster*) brother (*bror*) are all pretty close too, although, sadly in my view, the English never adopted the Scandinavians' very useful *far-far, mor-mor, far-mor, mor-far* method of distinguishing between maternal and paternal grandparents.

'Even today Yorkshire farmers can talk to Norwegian farmers about sheep and understand each other,' Dr Elizabeth Ashman Rowe, a lecturer in Scandinavian History at the University of Cambridge, told me when I asked her about the Viking legacy in Britain. I have heard something similar regarding the ability of the fishermen of Norfolk to make themselves understood by their colleagues from the western coast of Jutland. Rowe also pointed to other cultural links: the influence of Nordic culture on authors ranging from J. R. R. Tolkein to J. K. Rowling, as well as on new age and heavy metal iconography.

The Scandinavian influence has extended further west too, of course. The Norwegian Viking Leif Ericson discovered America around AD 1000. Admittedly, having failed to see the attraction of Newfoundland he promptly turned around and went home again, but Scandinavian efforts to populate North America were more successful 900 years on when 1.2 million Swedes, along with many Norwegians and some Finns, sailed across the Atlantic. At one point in the 1860s, a tenth of all immigrants arriving in the United States were from Scandinavia, many of them ending up in Minnesota, where the landscape reminded them of home. Today there are said to be almost five million Norwegian Americans and as many Swedish

Americans in the States. If it wasn't for them, we wouldn't have Uma Thurman and Scarlett Johanssen.

What makes the current Nordic mania so unlikely is that during the twentieth century the popular cultural influences tended mostly to flow in the opposite direction. Socialise with Scandinavian males of a certain age, for instance, and the conversation will at some point almost certainly turn to the sketches of Monty Python. The women, meanwhile, will share misty-eyed memories of the male cast members of *Brideshead Revisited*, or of their time working as au pairs in London. All will be familiar with *Upstairs Downstairs*, Trevor Eve and *Not the Nine O'Clock News*, and firmly believe *Keeping Up Appearances* is a documentary of English life. Despite their highly advanced education systems, Scandinavians are addicted to *Midsomer Murders*. Give them an ivy-clad Cotswold cottage and a fresh corpse and they are in heaven. Even British cabinet reshuffles make the news in Denmark. I wonder how many British cabinet members could name their Danish opposite number?

Perhaps the vague familiarity, the superficial *sameness*, is one of the reasons that we in Britain haven't really cared to get to know anything beyond fictional representations of the Scandinavians. Also, though stereotypical depictions usually include reference to their sexual liberalism and physical beauty, somehow they still manage to project an image of being pious, sanctimonious Lutherans. It is a neat trick to be thought of as being both deeply hot and off-puttingly frigid, isn't it? And it doesn't help that the Scandinavians are not very forward when it comes to coming forward: they aren't ones to boast. It is against their rules (literally, as we will discover). Look up the word 'reticent' in the dictionary and you won't find a picture of an awkward Finn standing in a corner looking at his shoelaces, but you should.

While I was writing this book, several people – including some Danes and, in particular, many Swedes – expressed genuine bemusement that they would be of the slightest interest to anyone outside Scandinavia. 'Why do you think people will want to know about us?' they asked. 'What is there to know?' 'We are all so boring and stiff.' 'There must be more interesting people in the world to write about. Why don't you go to southern Europe?' It seems Scandinavians tend to regard themselves rather as we do, a bit like bottle banks: functional and worthy, but plagued by an unremitting dullness which tends to discourage further investigation. Industrious, trustworthy and politically correct, the Scandinavians are the actuary at the party, five countries' worth of local government Liberal Democrats, finger-wagging social workers, and humourless party poopers.

So, how do I hope to hold your attention for the duration of this book? The short answer is that I find the Danes, Swedes, Finns, Icelanders, and even the Norwegians, utterly fascinating, and I suspect you will, too, once you find out the truth about how brilliant and progressive, but also how downright weird, they can be. As Oprah would have discovered had she stayed longer than an afternoon, and I have finally, grudgingly, begun to concede, there is so very much more to learn from the Nordic lands – about how they live their lives, the priorities they make and how they handle their wealth; about how societies can function better and more fairly; how people can live their lives in balance with their careers, educate themselves effectively, and support each other. About how, in the final analysis, to be happy. They are funny, too. And not always intentionally, either, which as far as I am concerned is the very best kind of funny.

I dug a little deeper into the Nordic miracle. Was there a Scandinavian template for a better way of living? Were there elements of Nordic exceptionalism – as the phenomenon has been termed – that were transferable, or was it location-specific, a quirk of history and geography? And, if people outside of Scandinavia really knew what it was like to actually live in this part of the world, would they still envy the Danes and their brethren quite so much?

'If you had to be reborn anywhere in the world as a person with average talents and income, you would want to be a Viking,' proclaimed *The Economist*, ever so slightly backhandedly, in a special Nordic-themed edition. But where were the discussions about Nordic totalitarianism and how uptight the Swedes are; about how the

Norwegians have been corrupted by their oil wealth to the point where they can't even be bothered to peel their own bananas; how the Finns are self-medicating themselves into oblivion; how the Danes are in denial about their debt, their vanishing work ethic, and their place in the world; and how the Icelanders are, essentially, feral?

Once you begin to look more closely at the Nordic societies and their people, once you go beyond the Western media's current Scandinavian tropes – the Sunday supplement features on Swedish summer houses peopled by blonde women in floral print dresses carrying baskets of wild garlic and surrounded by children with artfully mussed hair – a more complex, often darker, occasionally quite troubling picture begins to emerge. This encompasses everything from the relatively benign downsides to living among such comfortable, homogenous, egalitarian societies as these (in other words, when everyone earns the same amount of money, lives in the same kinds of homes, dresses the same, drives the same cars, eats the same food, reads the same books, has the same opinion about knitwear and beards, broadly similar religious beliefs, and goes to the same places on their holidays, things can get just a *teensy* bit dull – see the chapters on Sweden for more on this), to the more serious fissures in Nordic society: the racism and Islamophobia, the slow decline of social equality, the alcoholism, and the vast, over-stretched public sectors which require levels of taxation which would be deemed utterly preposterous by anyone who hasn't had them slowly creep up on them over the last fifty years like a deadly tide choking off all hope, energy and ambition . . .

. . . Where was I? Anyway, so, yes, I decided to go on a journey to try to fill in some of the gaps in my Nordic experience. I set off to explore these five lands in more depth, revisiting each of them several times, meeting with historians, anthropologists, journalists, novelists, artists, politicians, philosophers, scientists, elf-watchers and Santa Claus.

The trip would ultimately take me from my home in the Danish countryside to the frigid waters of the Norwegian Arctic, to the fearful geysers of Iceland and the badlands of the most notorious Swedish housing estate; from Santa's grotto to Legoland, and from the Danish Riviera to the Rotten Banana.

But the first lesson before I set off, offered, following a long pause and a deep sigh, by a Danish diplomat friend who had patiently endured a speech by me encompassing much of the above, was that, technically speaking, neither the Finns nor the Icelanders were actually Scandinavians: that term refers to the people of the original Viking lands, Denmark, Sweden and Norway, only. But, as I discovered on my travels round the region, the Finns have reserved the right to opt in or out of the old marauders' club as and when it suits them, and I don't think the Icelanders would be too upset to be labelled Scandinavians either. Strictly speaking, if we are going to lump all five countries together we really ought to use the term 'Nordic'. But this is my book and so I reserve the right to bandy both terms about pretty much interchangeably.

So let us begin on our quest to unearth the truth about the Nordic miracle, and where better to start than at a party.

DENMARK

Chapter 1

Happiness

As the rainclouds finally part to reveal an electric blue, early-evening sky, we venture out of the marquee sniffing the cool, damp air like nervous rescue animals, turning to savour the last warmth of the vanishing sun. It casts a pinky glow which, as the evening continues, transforms into a magical white, midsummer light and, finally, a deep dark blue-black backdrop for a planetarium-style celestial display.

Midsummer's Eve is one of the highlights of the Scandinavian calendar; pagan in origin but highjacked by the Church and renamed in honour of 'Sankt Hans' (St John). In Sweden they will be dancing around maypoles garlanded with flowers; in Finland and in Norway they will have gathered around bonfires. Here in Denmark, in the garden of my friend's summer house north of Copenhagen, the beer and cocktails are flowing. At ten o'clock we gather around a fire to sing '*Vi Elsker Vort Land*' ('We Love Our Country') and other stirring, nationalistic hymns. An effigy of a witch, assembled from old gardening clothes and a broomstick, is burned, sending her – my friend's eight-year-old daughter informs me – off to the Hartz Mountains in Germany.

The Danes are masters of revels such as these. They take their partying very seriously, are enthusiastic boozers, committed communal singers, and highly sociable when among friends. They give good *fest*, as they call it. This one boasts two barmen, two large grills with a variety of slowly caramelising pig parts and, later, there will be the all-important *nat mad*, or midnight snacks – sausages, cheese, bacon and bread rolls – served to soak up the alcohol and see us through to sunrise.

As is often the case, I find the searing anthropological insights begin to kick in around about my third gin and tonic. It occurs to me that this midsummer's party is the perfect place to commence my dissection of the Danish happiness phenomenon, my friend's get-together exemplifying as it does so many of the characteristics of Danish society that I find admirable, and which I believe contribute to their much-vaunted contentedness. As I stand here beside the bonfire's dying embers, I begin to tick some of them off.

One is the mood here in this lush green garden surrounded by high beech hedges, with the obligatory flagpole flying a large, red-and-white Dannebrog at its entrance. Though the drink has been flowing, the atmosphere is relaxed, there are no raised voices, no hints of alcohol-fuelled fightiness.

Then there are the children haring about the place. Danish children are granted what, to British eyes, can seem an almost old-fashioned freedom to roam and to take risks, and it is natural that the youngsters present this evening are as much a part of the party as the adults. They are still haring about as midnight approaches, yelling and screaming, hiding and seeking, buzzing and crashing on Coca-Cola and hot dogs.

Most of the people assembled here will have left work early; not sneaking out 'to go to a meeting', or feigning illness, but straight-forwardly informing their bosses that they will be attending a party an hour north along the coast, and that they will need to leave work early to prepare. Their bosses – if they haven't already left themselves for the same reason – will have been at ease with this. The Danes have a refreshingly laid-back approach to their work–life balance which, as we will see, has had major consequences – both positive (the happiness) and potentially negative (sometimes you do really need to buckle down and do some work: during a global recession, for example). I have met few 'live to work' types in this country; indeed many Danes – particularly those who work in the public sector – are frank and unapologetic about their ongoing efforts to put in the barest minimum hours required to support lives of acceptable comfort. The Danes work almost half the number of hours per week they did a century ago, and significantly fewer than the rest of Europe: 1,559 hours a year compared with the EU average of 1,749 hours (although the Greeks work 2,032 hours so, clearly, this is not a cast-iron measure of productivity). According to a 2011 Organisation for Economic Co-operation and Development (OECD) study encompassing thirty countries, the Danes were second only to the Belgians in the laziness stakes – that's *globally.*

In practice this means that most people knock off at around four or five in the afternoon, few feel pressurised to work at weekends, and you can forget about getting anything done after 1 p.m. on a Friday. Annual leave is often as much as six weeks and, during July, the entire country shuts down as the Danes migrate en masse, like mild-mannered wildebeest, to their summer houses, caravan parks or campsites located an hour or so away from where they live.

More than 754,000 Danes aged between fifteen and sixty-four – over 20 per cent of the working population – do no work whatsoever and are supported by generous unemployment or disability benefits. The *New York Times* has called Denmark 'The best place on earth to be laid off', with unemployment benefits of up to 90 per cent of previous wages for up to two years (until recent reforms, it was eleven years). The Danes call their system *flexicurity*, a neologism blending the flexibility Danish companies enjoy to fire people with short notice and little compensation (compared with Sweden, where jobs can still be for life), with the security the labour market enjoys knowing that there will be ample support in times of unemployment.

More reasons for the Danes' happiness? We must also include this very summer house – a homely, single-storey, L-shaped cabin, identical to thousands of others scattered along the coasts of these islands. These little wood-and-brick hideouts are where the Danes come to unwind in flip-flops and sun hats, to grill their hot dogs and drink their cheap, fizzy lager. And if they don't own a summer house, most know someone who does, or they maybe have a permanent plot in a campsite, or a shed in a *koloni have* (or 'colony garden' – like an allotment but with the emphasis more on sitting with a can of cheap, fizzy lager and a hot dog than toiling among vegetable patches).

This summer house is furnished, like most, with bric-a-brac and IKEA perennials. One wall is lined with well-thumbed paperbacks, there's the obligatory cupboard packed with board games and jigsaws with missing pieces and, of course, a fireplace primed with logs to warm bones chilled from the sea. The floors are bare wood for easy sweeping of sand and grass, and the whitewashed brick walls are hung with art works from the 'School of Relatives' – family members' attempts at oils and watercolours, usually in a fairly grisly *faux naïf* abstract style.

As I said, tonight the alcohol is flowing like the river Jordan. Denmark has a much more laissez-faire attitude to booze than the rest of the region; there is no state-owned alcohol monopoly here as there is in the other four Nordic countries. In Carlsbergland alcohol is sold in every supermarket and corner shop. The Swedes, whose twinkling lights I can see just across the Øresund strait this evening, have long flocked to their southern neighbour to let their hair down and sample what is from their perspective the Danes' louche, fun-loving lifestyle. (Younger Danes, in turn, head for Berlin to get their jollies.)

At the end of the evening a group of us go, giggling, to the beach, disrobe and tiptoe into the waters. It is something I have struggled to adjust to, but nudity is no biggie here and at least by now it is dark. The initial bracing chill as the water reaches thigh-height almost sends me scurrying for my clothes, before I finally pluck up the courage to dive under the surface and, once fully submerged, am reminded once again how surprisingly warm the Danish sea in summer can be.

On evenings such as this it is easy to see why the Danes have come to feel so contented with their lot these past few decades. As long as they can avoid opening their credit card bills, life must feel pretty great as a middle-aged, middle-class Dane. It is hard to imagine how it could be any better, in fact. But things have not always been so rosy in the state of Denmark. To reach this point of heightened bliss, the Danes have had to endure terrible trauma, humiliation and loss. Until, that is, bacon came along and saved theirs.

Chapter 2

Bacon

Once upon a time, the Danes ruled all of Scandinavia. They like their fairytales, the Danes, but this one is true. The Kalmar Union of 1397 was a historic high point for the Danes, with their equivalent of Elizabeth I, Queen Margaret I, ruling a loosely unified Norway, Sweden and Denmark. The union held for over a century until, in 1520, the then Danish king, Christian II, rashly beheaded around eighty Swedish nobles in the so-called Stockholm Bloodbath, something of a diplomatic faux pas. Though Denmark did manage to hold on to Norway for a few hundred years more, henceforth the Swedes would play a far more proactive role in the region's history, mostly by holding Denmark's head in the toilet bowl while Britain and Germany queued up to pull the handle.

There was a brief false dawn for Denmark under the reign of their great Renaissance king, Christian IV – Denmark's Henry VIII, with similar appetites and girth – who oversaw some of Denmark's most ambitious military and architectural projects, funded chiefly via the toll he extracted at Helsingør (Elsinore) from ships entering and leaving the Baltic through the narrow bottleneck there (it was the Panama Canal of the North for a while). Sadly, Christian IV lost a few too many battles, mostly with the Swedes, finally bringing his country to the brink of bankruptcy. He died in 1648, consumed by jealousy at the rise of his Swedish rival, King Gustaf II Adolf. One historian wrote of Christian's funeral, 'Financially Denmark had now sunk so low that, when the most splendid of her kings was finally laid to rest, his crown was in pawn and even the silken cloth which covered his coffin had to be bought on credit.' In contrast, by the time Gustaf Vasa died, battling the Germans (a preoccupation of his later life), he had transformed Sweden into the key power in the region and beyond.

Christian IV was fortunate not to have lived to witness one of the darkest days of Danish loss. By the terms of the Treaty of Roskilde, signed a decade later in 1658, the Danes were forced by the Swedes to relinquish what are today the southern Swedish regions of Skåne, Blekinge and Halland, as well as the Baltic island of Bornholm (the latter was eventually returned and remains Danish). It is easy to forget how Danish these territories once were because, on a map, they appear so clearly to be part of Sweden – the goatee on the chin, so to speak – but up to that point they had always been Danish, and their loss was keenly felt by Copenhagen.

The ensuing centuries were even less kind to the Danes and, I am afraid to say, the English played a pivotal role in compounding their misery. In 1801 a British fleet, with Nelson as second in command, attacked the Danish navy anchored outside Copenhagen to prevent it from falling into French hands. The British returned in 1807 for similar reasons, this time bombarding Copenhagen itself for three days, resulting in the deaths of as many as two thousand locals and the destruction of a good part of the city. This is supposedly the first ever bombardment of a civilian target; really not cricket – even the British media were critical at the time – and, in fact, the attack had the opposite effect of that intended, forcing the Danes into the arms of the French. To this day, if you visit Copenhagen's old university library, halfway up the stairs is a display case in which sits a book with fragments of a British cannonball still embedded in its pages. The book's title is *Defender of Peace* (which is suspiciously apt, I have always thought. Just saying). Though the bombardment of Copenhagen has slipped from the memory of most English people, the Danes still bring up the subject from time to time. 'Well, you were threatening to join sides with Napoleon,' I always try to explain, but it doesn't seem to mollify them.

I can feel myself being dragged against my will into having to explain early-nineteenth-century European geopolitics here, but I shall resist the temptation. Essentially, when the dust settled on the Napoleonic wars and everyone had swapped sides at least once, Denmark discovered that it had lost Norway to Sweden in yet another of those dratted treaties, this one signed in Kiel in 1814.

How the Danes must have come to dread treaty-signing time. Another, signed later during that, for them calamitous, century, would finally denude Denmark its troublesome territories, Schleswig and Holstein, the Danes having been forced to abandon their thousand-year-old defences, the Danevirke, to the Prussians in 1864. (Again, I'd love to go into this in more detail but, as Lord Palmerstone famously said, 'The Schleswig-Holstein question is so complicated, only three men in Europe have ever understood it. One was Prince Albert, who is dead. The second was a German professor who became mad. I am the third and I have forgotten all about it.') Suffice it to say that, at one especially low point in the negotiations, the Danish king even mooted the idea of Denmark becoming part of the German Confederation and, when that was rejected, offered Iceland instead. But Bismarck was an all-or-nothing kind of guy, and so both duchies became for ever German, and Denmark's borders were redrawn once more.

With Schleswig and Holstein gone south, Denmark had lost roughly a third of its remaining land area and population, and by some estimates as much as half of its potential income. Over time, it would also lose its small colonies in India and the West Indies, and even the Faroes voted for autonomy. Thank goodness for Iceland, I hear you cry. But eventually the slender thread of a shared monarchy linking those two nations was also severed by that most unlikely of liberators, Adolf Hitler: when his army invaded Denmark in April 1940, it inadvertently relieved Iceland of its Danish head of state.

Denmark and Germany had signed a pact of mutual non-aggression a year earlier, but the Danes had effectively extended an open invitation to the Nazis to invade when they decided to leave many of their military posts unmanned for seven months of the year. The Danish Nazi Party had grown in strength, thanks largely to support from farmers and landowners, and now had representatives in parliament; the Germans rightly assumed that the Danes would be reluctant to retaliate and risk provoking a bombardment similar to the one they had endured in 1807.

There was little resistance to German occupation for the first three years or so, indeed, both the Danish king and prime minister at the time criticised the nascent Danish underground when they occasionally carried out minor acts of sabotage. Unlike the Norwegians, who resisted with great courage and ingenuity (greatly aided by their mountains and climate, admittedly), Denmark had little choice but to submit to life as a pliable German satellite. Some have gone as far as to categorise the Danes as German allies, as they supplied much-needed agricultural produce and even troops to fight on the Eastern Front and in Berlin during the Second World War. Churchill called the country 'Hitler's pet canary'.

It would be surprising if this long litany of loss and defeat had not had a lasting impact on the Danes, but I would go further. I suspect that it has defined the Danes to a greater extent than any other single factor – more than their geography, more than their Lutheran faith or their Viking heritage, more even than their modern political system and welfare state. You see, in a roundabout way, Denmark's losses were her making.

Their greatly reduced circumstances bound the Danes together more tightly as a tribe than any of the other Nordic countries. As historian T. K. Derry writes (about the accession of Norway to Sweden), 'The Danish king and people resigned themselves to the loss . . . as a common misfortune which drew them together in a desire to avoid all further changes.' The territorial losses, sundry beatings and myriad humiliations forced the Danes to turn their gaze inward, instilling in them not only a fear of change and of external forces that abides to this day, but also a remarkable self-sufficiency and an appreciation of what little they had left.

No longer the great European power it had once been, Denmark withdrew, mustered what few resources remained within its much-reduced boundaries, and decided never again to have ambitions in that direction. What followed was a process of what you could call 'positive parochialisation'; the Danes adopted a glass-half-full outlook, largely because their glass *was* now half full, and it is an outlook which, I would argue, has paved the way for the much-trumpeted success of their society to this day.

Of course there are many factors which combine to form a national psyche, and I am being reductive to make a point, but this parochialist urge towards insularity and its accompanying national romanticism is a defining element of Danishness that is epitomised by a saying that every Dane knows by heart to this day:

Hvad udad tabes, skal indad vindes.
(What was lost without will be found within.)

The line was originally written by the author H. P. Holst in 1811, but it obtained greater purchase when it was adopted by the Danish Heath Society, which interpreted it, quite literally, in its work to reclaim coastal land by draining sandy territories in Jutland. So successful was the society at this that, by 1914, Denmark had effectively replaced the hectares it had lost to Germany with fresh, farmable arable land.

But Holst's declaration also encapsulates what turned out to be the Danes' great cultural 'Golden Age', a mid-nineteenth-century period of increased social mobility and artistic blossoming that saw the son of a washerwoman, Hans Christian Andersen, publish his first fairy stories and go on to become one of the first genuinely world-famous figures; Søren Kierkegaard write his groundbreaking existentialist works; and the great classical sculptor, Bertel Thorvaldsen, along with painters like C. W. Eckersberg and his pupil Christen Købke, and the Royal Ballet master August Bournonville, contribute to a great flurry of artistic activity within Denmark at the time. The Danes embraced the works of these genuinely world-class artists almost as a consolation for the painful losses of the era. They were learning how to do what they still do best: to be grateful for, and make the most of, the resources available to them; to cherish the simple pleasures of community; to celebrate their Danishness; and, above all, avoid annoying the Germans.

Anne Knudsen is the editor of the Danish national broadsheet newspaper *Weekendavisen* and one of the country's leading political and social commentators. When I met with her in her office in central Copenhagen, she talked me through her timeline for the establishment of this modern notion of *danskhed* – or 'Danishness'.

You had the loss to Sweden in 1658, and the bombardment by the British in 1807, and the loss of Norway in 1814, but at that time the people in Jutland didn't know what people in Zealand thought about any of this. Of course the bombardment affected the bourgeoisie and the military, but they were centred on Copenhagen; and the loss of Norway was felt more in Aalborg, which had been Denmark's second city, was very wealthy, and lost about 75 per cent of its trade. But still it was only really a very small group of people who had any opinion. The development of a Danish national consciousness really started from the constitution in 1849, so it is from here that you can first talk about 'the Danes' in any cohesive sense, really. Soon afterwards there was this disastrous war in Schleswig and that really created a common ground for all Danes. The party that lost that war set out to explain that we were all the better for being so small, and the Social Democratic Party continued this world view. Elsewhere, Social Democracy was firmly based on progress, industry, modernity, but in Denmark it was about the *koloni have* [those cosy allotment zones].

In other words, while the Swedes forged forwards with their great modernist, progressive social agenda, the Danes retreated, seeking refuge in their parochial, National Romantic vision. Parochialism

remains the Danes' defining characteristic,* but their radically recali-
brated sense of identity and national pride has created a curious
duality best described as a kind of 'humble pride', though many
often mistake it for smugness.

Let me explain. Assuming that you know nothing about their
country, within the first five minutes or so of meeting a Dane they
will usually say something along the lines of 'This is just a little land.
We are only a little over five million people; we're pretty much all
the same.' They will probably add that they have no mountains or
waterfalls, and that you can cross their country by car in four hours.
But after a while – it can take anything from five minutes to a year,
depending on the Dane in question – you will begin to detect the
steely pride beneath the 'aw shucks' surface humility. That's when
they might casually mention their world-leading wind turbine
industry, the absence of poverty in Denmark, their free education
and health systems, and generous benefits. They will tell you how
they are the most trustworthy and equal people in the world,
how they have the best restaurant in the world, and, yes, the Vikings
will probably crop up as well.

A double-page spread in the newspaper today epitomises this
schizophrenic self-image. On one page is a cartoon depicting Chinese
businessmen looking at a map of the world. One of them is saying,
'Denmark? Where is it exactly? Can you get me my glasses?' – a
reference to the fact that the Chinese have invested less money in

---

* A good example of this is Danish news coverage. Generally, not a lot
happens in Denmark, but this doesn't stop the news editors putting whatever
has happened in Denmark at the top of the agenda, regardless of events elsewhere
in the world. I was once so infuriated that the national radio news, in the aftermath
of the Japanese tsunami and at the commencement of the Libyan Civil War, was
running as their lead item a story about how some tenants of rented properties
might not be aware that their home contents insurance could assist them in claims
against high rents, that I rang the news editor to ask what they were thinking.
'Well, we didn't think there was much new to say about Libya,' he told me, a
little embarrassed.

Denmark than in any other European country. On the opposite page, meanwhile, is a headline which reads, 'Thorning Can Put Pressure on China', which is about how the Danish prime minister is going to tell the Chinese leadership a thing or two about their human rights record during an imminent visit to Beijing – I bet they were quaking.

The Danes have a deep and justifiable satisfaction born from the knowledge that they have built, from relatively unpromising foundations, arguably the most successful society on the face of the earth. The 'arguably' is mine. To the Danes, there is no argument.

An important building block for this success was Denmark's Great School Commission of the mid-nineteenth century, which laid the foundations for one of the first free nationwide primary school systems in Europe. It was followed within thirty years by the Folk High Schools, founded by the poet, theologian and fervent anti-German N. F. S. Grundtvig (still a great national hero; Denmark's propagandist-in-chief). Other key moments in Denmark's recent history include the country's peaceful move towards democracy when the king renounced his absolutist powers with the constitution of 1849, and the all-important agricultural cooperatives that emerged soon after. When corn prices crashed because of cheap US imports, these cooperatives meant that Danish farmers were able to turn from arable production to pig-farming virtually overnight. Then someone realised what type of streaky bacon the British preferred for breakfast, figured out a way to standardise pork production to meet that demand, and the Danish labour force found its true calling.

They have never looked back: today, the Danes are the world's leading pork butchers, slaughtering over 28 million pigs a year. The Danish pork industry accounts for around a fifth of all the world's pork exports, half of domestic agricultural exports and over five per cent of the country's total exports. Yet the weird thing is, you can travel the length and breadth of the country and never see a single sow.

My own ignorance of Denmark was almost total before I started coming here a decade and a half ago so, before we attempt to divine the secrets of the Danes' success in greater depth, I am going to

take a moment to fill you in on some of the aspects of contemporary
Danish life that I believe make it such a wonderful place to live, but
of which you might not be aware. It is a bit random but bear with
me, I think it gives a good overview:

- The landscape of southern Funen (Fyn), which undulates like
  a reclining nude.

- The pleasantly woozy feeling after a lunch of pickled herring
  with red onion on rye, a Tuborg and an icy schnapps.

- *Flødebolle* – a chocolate-covered Italian meringue with a wafer
  base (a bit like a Tunnock's teacake. Sometimes they have a
  marzipan base, but those are to be avoided).

- There's parking.

- The view from the room which houses the numismatic collection
  at the National Museum of Denmark (the Nationalmuseet)
  looking across to the royal stables at the rear of Christiansborg
  Palace, the Danish parliament building.

- The word *overskud*, meaning a kind of surplus of energy. As
  in, 'I can't cut the lawn now, after that great big boozy lunch
  I simply don't have the *overskud*.' I don't know how I managed
  without this word for so many years. *Smask* is another great
  Danish word: it's the annoying noise some people make when
  they eat, say, an apple, or breakfast cereal, or when radio
  presenters have dry tongues.

- The bittern that is honking like a foghorn outside my window
  as I write this.

- The fact that I once saw the Danish prime minister on a pre-
  election walkabout in Copenhagen, on the equivalent of Oxford
  Street, and no one was paying him the slightest bit of attention.

- Arne Jacobsen's petrol station on Strandvejen, the most elegant
  petrol station in the world.

- The TV series *Klovn* – a Scandinavian *Curb Your Enthusiasm*, only far ruder.

- A visit to Bakken, the old amusement park to the north of the city. It is the best way I know of travelling back in time to 1968.

- Babies left sleeping outside cafés; a perfectly normal occurrence throughout the country and one which happens in all weathers. (The former US housing commissioner, Catherine Austin Fitts, once came up with something called the Popsicle Index, which ranks countries according to the percentage of people in a community who believe that their children can safely leave their home, walk to the nearest possible location to buy an ice lolly, and walk back home again. Denmark must surely rank at, or near, the top of this index.)

- The word *Pyt*. A dismissive exhalation which roughly translates as 'Let it go, it's not worth bothering with.' Midsummer party threatened by rain? *Pyt med det!* ('*Pyt* with that!')

- They sell wine and beer in cinemas, and you are usually allowed to take it into the auditorium with you. Is there any greater litmus test of a civilised society?

- The actor Jesper Christensen (Mr White in *Casino Royale*), upon whose wry, weary face is etched all the tragedy of the world.

- The hollyhocks that spring up from between the cobbles of Christianshavn, the canal quarter of Copenhagen.

- The rainbow of grey in a Hammershøi interior.

- The Lego Death Star.

Do great confectionary, pickled herring and complex modular construction toys amount to the recipe for human happiness? Probably not (although for me, yes). There is more to Denmark's success and the enduring, Olympic-gold-level happiness of its people. Much more.

Chapter 3

Gini

Back to the summer-house party. Perhaps the most striking aspect of my friend's midsummer get-together is the socio-economic mix present here this evening, which is far broader than I would expect to find at a similar get-together back home. So far I have chatted with a gynaecologist, a wine writer, a member of parliament, a few theatre people (the host is a singer) and several teachers (there are *always* teachers), but also craftsmen, cooks, a baggage handler and many, many public sector workers, including a nurse, a civil servant and a museum administrator. Over there is Danish television's golden girl, a presenter of the evening show; she's talking to a roofer. Behind me is a member of parliament earnestly debating Denmark's chances in some or other handball tournament with the man who grows the strawberries in these parts.

The Danes do seem to have an uncommon facility to get on with each other regardless of age, class or outlook. Egality comes easily to them. One of my most cherished memories of this inclusiveness is of a friend's fortieth birthday party where his octogenarian grandmother was seated next to the country's most notorious rapper, and the two spent a jolly evening chatting together.

It helps, of course, that Denmark is essentially one giant middle class or, as the Danes would have you believe, effectively classless. The creation of this economically and gender-equal society has driven much of Denmark's social and economic development over the last hundred or so years. One very well known Danish quotation sums this up – it is another line, like Holst's 'What was lost without . . .', that every Dane knows by heart, and was written by N. F. S. Grundtvig:

Og da har i rigdom vi drevet det vidt, når få har for meget og færre for lidt.

(And we will have made great strides in equality, when few have too much and fewer too little.)

It sounds like some kind of utopian fantasy but, by and large, the Danes have succeeded in achieving it. As historian Tony Hall writes in *Scandinavia: At War with Trolls*, Grundtvig's Folk High Schools were founded on the principle of 'teaching them, whenever feasible, that regardless of their social rank and occupation, they belonged to one people, and as such had one mother, one destiny and one purpose'. The result is that, according to the *New Statesman*, 90 per cent of the population [of Denmark] enjoy an approximately identical standard of living.' This striking economic equality lies not only at the core of the happiness and success of the Danes but of the people of the Nordic region as a whole. To find out why, we must take a brief detour to northern Italy at the end of the nineteenth century.

The Italian scientist Corrado Gini was born into a wealthy land-owning family in Treviso in 1884. Gini was an academic prodigy; by the age of twenty-six he was head of statistics at Cagliari University. A cold, hard-working, autocratic figure, he befriended Mussolini early on in his career, becoming head of Il Duce's Central Institute of Statistics. By the time he died, Gini was widely judged to be the greatest Italian statistician of all time, credited with paving new ground in the fields of demography, sociology and economics.

Improbably, considering his background, it is thanks to Gini that we have what many believe is the single most revealing piece of evidence – statistical or otherwise – for the root cause of Nordic exceptionalism, not to mention the most helpful guide to answering the ultimate secular question of our age: how to be happy.

This is the Gini Coefficient, a statistical method for analysing the distribution of wealth in a nation, which he introduced to the world in 1921. The Gini Coefficient quantifies how large a percentage of the total income of a society must be redistributed in order to achieve a perfectly equal distribution of wealth. It remains to this day a brilliantly concise way to express the inequality of a group of people as a simple figure (although technically, I am told, it is not actually a coefficient, but let's leave that discussion to people with dandruff and elbow patches).

The Gini Coefficient of a country is divined by mapping the degree to which the range of wealth of its people diverges from a point of total equality (i.e., where everyone is as rich/poor as everyone else), the latter represented on a graph as a 45-degree diagonal line. The divergence from this zero line is charted by what is known as a 'Lorenz curve', which traces the dispersal of income or wealth in the society in a beautifully succinct parabola of poverty and wealth. Between the curve and the diagonal line is a space which is converted into a ratio, usually expressed as a fraction. The closer a country's Lorenz curve is to the 45-degree total-equality line, the closer the Gini Coefficient will be to zero, and the more equal it will be; the more the curve bows away from that diagonal, the closer the figure will be to 1, indicating a greater distance between the haves and the have-nots in that particular society.

If, due to what would surely have to be an exceptional set of extenuating circumstances, you are not able to join me on the fascinating, insightful, hilarious and at times deeply moving journey through the Nordic region on which we are about to embark* and are only able take away one nugget of information from this book, it might as well be this: according to much of the prevailing anthropological, political, sociological and economic thought, from eminent figures such as Nobel-Prize-winning economist Joseph Stiglitz, author Francis Fukuyama and organisations as august as the United Nations, the Gini Coefficient is the silver bullet which goes directly to the heart of not just how equal a society is, but how happy and healthy its people are likely to be. It is, if you like, the very sum of human happiness.

The most talked about, and politically influential, treatise on the subject of Gini-measured equality was published in 2009 by

---

* Are you sure? There's lots of really great stuff coming up about sex, violence, alcohol and Nazis.

epidemiologists Richard Wilkinson and Kate Pickett. In *The Spirit Level: Why Equality is Better for Everyone*, Wilkinson and Pickett use statistics from sources such as the World Bank and the UN to compare twenty-three of the richest countries in the world and – they claim – to clearly, methodically and irrefutably prove why more equal societies are simply better in every way, shape or form than unequal ones.

Through page after page of their trademark graphs, Wilkinson and Pickett sledgehammer home their argument: that greater income inequality has a direct correlation to just about every social problem we face in the West, from obesity to crime, drug abuse, mental illness, depression and stress. Crucially, it isn't the *absolute* levels of poverty and wealth that are the issue, but the *differentials* in income levels from the lowest to the highest in each country which are the crux of the matter. So, while notions of poverty differ greatly between, say, the UK and Cambodia, the fact that more people have a dishwasher in the former, for instance, is by no means a guarantee that crime rates will be lower and people will be happier or healthier. As the *New York Times* pointed out in its review of the book:

> The US is wealthier and spends more on health care than any other country, yet a baby born in Greece, where average income levels are about half that of the US, has a lower risk of infant mortality and longer life expectancy than an American baby.

In virtually all of Wilkinson and Pickett's graphs the most drastically unequal countries – the US, the UK and, oddly, Portugal – the countries where the top 20 per cent earn up to nine times that of the lowest 20 per cent, are invariably at the *Shameless* end of the social problem spectrum, while the most equal societies are the least afflicted by almost all categories of social malady.

Their most radical conclusion is that inequality breeds stress among poor and rich alike; the more unequal a society, the less benefit is obtained from an individual's wealth. The stress of inequality does not just breed envy, it is not just about coveting your neighbour's ox/Audi A8. Inequality breeds depression, addiction, resignation, and physical symptoms including premature aging, that affect the *entire* population. In other words, the well-being of individuals, rich or poor, is mutually dependent. Living as a richer person among the poor is very stressful. It heightens your competitive consumption (tellingly, the amount a country's corporations spend on advertising increases in relation to economic inequality as people become more susceptible to, and dependent on, the allure of advertising messages), and you never know when the rabble are going to try and snatch your wealth away from you.

The equality argument is highly persuasive, though not without its critics, whom we will meet in a while. For now, there is one glaring anomaly that I can see: if this theory of economic equality leading to societal success is true, then the happiest country in the world should also be the most economically equal. But that is not the case. Though the global Gini rankings of the world's countries do change from year to year, the top spot is usually held either by Sweden – as is currently the case and has been for a couple of years – or that honorary Nordic country, Japan.

Denmark, the happiest country in the world as judged by a wide range of researchers, institutions and Oprah Winfrey, over many decades, is usually around fifth or sixth on the list, the lowest of all the Nordic countries. If Gini is the best indicator of income equality, and if income equality is the key ingredient for a social utopia, then how come it is the Danes, the southernmost members of the Nordic clan, the ones with the highest taxes, the most meagre natural resources, the worst health, the most ignoble history, the very worst pop music and the weakest economy, who are so regularly held to be the happiest people in the world, and not the more equal and, by most parameters, the much more successful Swedes?

I wondered what to make of this, so I rang Richard Wilkinson.

'Well, my answer is going to be a little bit disappointing,' said Professor Wilkinson with a sigh. 'I don't really think measures of happiness internationally are necessarily very dependable. For instance, for an American to say they are not happy sounds like an admission of failure, but for a Japanese person it sounds like bragging to say they are, so I think one has to be very careful. We find there are systematic problems with subjective measures related to inequality. How people use the word "happy", for instance, or how they present themselves. I don't think these surveys mean nothing, but I wouldn't put a great deal into them. All of *our* measures are objective, like death rates, obesity and so on.'

He is right, there are obvious flaws in these happiness surveys. Happiness is subjective and clearly tricky to quantify, plus, as Wilkinson points out, notions of happiness differ depending on whom you ask. Happiness probably does conform to roughly comparable parameters among the people of the Nordic countries, but it probably won't mean the same to a Bolivian or a Tutsi. There is a risk of cultural bias, not just from the people answering the questions, but from those asking them: one can't help but notice, for instance, that when the Swiss measure international happiness they report that more direct democracy is the key (as, say, just for instance, in the direct democracy they have in their cantons). When others have sought to remove simple measures of wealth as a factor in happiness – as in the New Economics Foundation's Happy Planet Index – countries like Vanuatu and Colombia have topped out as the happiest on earth, which is patently preposterous. Does anyone even know where Vanuatu *is*?

It has also occurred to me that it might well be the case that these kinds of polls become self-perpetuating. The Danes are now well aware that the world considers them to be the happiest people, so perhaps this knowledge, along with the pleasure and pride they justifiably feel in having such a reputation, influences the way in which they respond to these quality-of-life surveys. Just a thought.

According to Wilkinson and other experts in this field, such as University College London's epidemiologist Michael Marmot (the world leader in research into inequalities of health), you get a much more accurate picture of people's well-being – as distinct from, and slightly easier to quantify than, their happiness – by analysing the state of their health, than you get from asking them if they feel happy, or satisfied, or content, or any other such subjective measure.

Unfortunately, the Danes score notably badly in terms of their health. According to a recent report from the World Cancer Research Foundation they have the highest cancer rates in the world (326 cases per 100,000 people, compared with 260 in the UK, in 12th place). They also have the lowest average lifespan of any of the Nordic countries, and the highest levels of alcohol consumption, ahead even of the famously boozy Finns.

'Yes, the Danish health statistics are quite bad – they're a bit of a puzzle to most people,' chuckled Professor Wilkinson. 'People suggest it is the high levels of smoking that's doing it. There is an enormous gulf between these happiness surveys and actual health. Why take these simplistic measures of happiness when we have objective measures of well-being?'

I asked the professor to indulge me on the happiness question just a little longer. In terms of the Nordic countries, I had a hypothesis, I said. Could it be that, once a society achieves a certain high level of equality, beyond that point greater equality merely leads to diminishing happiness returns? As has been proven with measures of wealth, once people have enough equality to cover their basic needs, greater equality does not necessarily result in corresponding increases in happiness. Could this explain why the Danes were judged to be the happiest people on earth, even though they were not the most equal?

'Colleagues at Harvard think there might be a levelling-off in terms of some health aspects,' said the professor. 'But if you look at our graphs, where we put all our sources together in terms of all health and societal problems, there is no sign of it levelling off at the other end. It is a linear relationship. My view is that we don't know what happens if you get more equal than Sweden.'

Ultimately, for Wilkinson, Gini was all ('It is much the most powerful tool at a government's disposal.') Far be it from me to disagree with such a distinguished academic, but I was not so sure that the Gini Coefficient was the be-all and end-all. I could not quite shake the suspicion that, once a society reaches a certain level of income equality, other factors take on a greater importance in determining how happy the people are.

And I was beginning to think I had a good idea what those factors might be.

Chapter 4

Boffers

'Scaramouche, scaramouche . . .' Four hundred pairs of eyes flick our way as we squeeze through the door into the high school hall, and then flick back to their notes. 'Will you do the fandango?'

My wife, who knows her way around a choir, immediately locates the soprano group and disappears into the crowd. I have no idea whether I am soprano, tenor or castrato so I nod along with the music, try to look as if massed choirs are my natural habitat, edge over to a vacant seat, and begin to mouth along to the words.

I am not a joiner. Some have gone as far as to call me a hermit, which is a little unfair, although it is true that there are few evenings out that can compete with a Larry Sanders box set, a box of Jaffa Cakes and a squashy sofa. In contrast, the Danes are arguably the most sociable people on earth. According to the Danish think tank Mandag Morgen, they belong to more associations, clubs, unions, societies and groups, and have larger social networks, than any other nationality – 43 per cent of over-sixteens belong to something or other. On average, each Dane has 11.8 people in their personal network, compared with 8.7 per British person. There are 83,000 local and 3,000 national societies and associations in Denmark – on average every Dane belongs to three. Over a third belong to a sporting club or association. These range from your common-or-garden leisure-orientated groups – the Bittern Spotters Club, say, or the Danish Flødeboller Association – to the still-powerful trade unions, which have a combined membership equivalent to a quarter of the population (1.25 million people). Support for all these groups is enshrined in Danish law – the *Folkeoplysningslov*, or General Education Act – and local authorities provide all manner of assistance, funding and premises for free, provided the association is properly organised and registered.

Right now, the Danes are especially preoccupied with role playing – dressing up like Gandalf or elves and acting out violent narratives deep in the woods with their foam 'boffers' (the name given to role-play weapons). There are also 219 folk dancing clubs in Denmark, but do not worry, as with the pigs, you very rarely see them.

Crucially, like my friend's Midsummer's Eve party, Danish clubs and societies tend to draw their members from across the class spectrum. One friend's weekly indoor hockey club, for instance, includes a factory worker, a doctor, several middle-management types and a forester in its members. Another friend's Wednesday football game in Parken (the park beside the national stadium) draws public sector workers, graphic designers, shop workers and a spin doctor; and a pub quiz team of my acquaintance boasts two academics, another spin doctor (they are something of a plague in Copenhagen), a shop assistant, and a dashing, award-winning English journalist of the very highest calibre.

These clubs, associations and societies are one manifestation of the Danes' remarkable social cohesion. They do seem to be very much more *tilknyttet* or 'tied together' than the rest of us. You will be familiar with the concept of 'six degrees of separation' – the idea that the world's population (or Kevin Bacon's co-stars) can be joined together by six relationships. In my experience, between Danes, the degree of separation is three, perhaps fewer. When two Danes who do not know each other meet at a social gathering they will take, on average, no more than eight minutes to discover either a direct mutual acquaintance, or at the very least a friend-of-a-friend connection (I have actually timed this). More than three degrees of separation is genuinely rare.

The Danes' fondness for clubs and associations is shared by their Nordic neighbours. The Swedes have an even greater trade-union membership and in their spare time are particularly keen on voluntary work: they call this instinct for diligent self-improvement *organisationssverige* or 'organisation Sweden'. The Finns are famed for their after-work classes, particularly their amateur classical musicianship and fondness for joining orchestras, while the Norwegians' love of communal outdoor pursuits, most famously cross-country skiing, is one of their defining characteristics.

It seems logical to conclude that this social cohesion is closely linked to another factor that is often cited when talk turns to the Danish happiness phenomenon: their extraordinary levels of trust. All of the Nordic countries have high levels of trust, but the Danes are the most trusting people on the planet. In a 2011 survey by the OECD, 88.3 per cent of Danes expressed a high level of trust in others, more than any other nationality (the next places in the list were filled by Norway, Finland and Sweden respectively, with the UK a creditable 10th, but the US way down in 21st out of 30 countries surveyed). In the same OECD survey, 96 per cent of Danes said that they knew someone on whom they could depend in times of need. The Danes even trust their politicians, one measure of this being their 87 per cent general election turnout. Other surveys show that Denmark is one of very few countries in which trust levels have maintained an unbroken upward trajectory for the last half-century. And Transparency International's annual Corruption Perception Index currently ranks Denmark and Finland as the least corrupt countries in the world, with Sweden and Norway following closely behind.

As anyone who has lived in a city knows, anonymity breeds a lack of responsibility and trust, so it seems logical that the greater the number of people who know each other, or are able to identify one another, will have the opposite effect, as is the case with the tightly knit Danish tribe. One example of how this affects the way in which the Danes behave to one another is that, when I first moved to Denmark, whenever I had a Dane in my car and was given, I thought, good cause to sound the horn at another road user or pedestrian, my passenger would invariably squirm uncomfortably. 'What if they *know you*?' they would hiss. It is a small example, admittedly, but I am convinced that high levels of interconnectedness must have an impact on everything from crime rates to levels of altruism – there being a greater chance that a supposedly altruistic gesture will be spotted and broadcast.*

It can be no coincidence that the happiest people in the world are also the most sociable and the most trusting, but I wanted to find out more about the connection between these three archetypal elements of Danishness, which is why I have allowed myself to be persuaded by my wife and children to join this residential choir week, held over six days every summer in the idyllic southern Jutland town of Tønder, close to the German border. I want to experience for myself, first hand, what kinds of benefits the Danes enjoy as a result of their collective approach to life – from their so-called 'third sector' activities. For what could be more communal in this most communal of countries than gathering together to sing popular tunes from the seventies and eighties?

The plan is that, from our (late) arrival on Sunday afternoon we will spend the next five days rehearsing a programme of around ten songs which we will then perform at a concert for the public on Friday night. It turns out that most of the choristers are staying in the same youth hostel, so we will all eat together three times a day and spend the evenings singing other popular Danish folk songs and hymns. Just for fun.

Some might see this as a blessed opportunity to live the Danish communal dream but, in fact, the whole week is so far beyond my comfort zone (I'll explain more about this in another chapter, but

---

* The only strange anomaly in this regard is civic manners, an area in which the Danes – and indeed, all the Nordic peoples – suffer an epic fail. They often seem fantastically rude from an English perspective. Someone once explained this to me as a kind of 'perverse egalitarianism', as in, 'I am just as important as you, so I have every right to barge my shopping trolley into yours to get by,' but I don't think I will ever properly come to terms with the Scandinavians' brutal rudeness (and the Swedes are the worst offenders, as we will discover). Oh yes, and they use the word 'fuck' indiscriminately – in adverts, children's books, church, wherever – much to the chagrin of Americans and my mother.

'youth hostel' and 'hymns' offer a reasonable clue), that it is virtually an out-of-body experience. My fellow choristers – this year a
record-breaking attendance of four hundred – are almost entirely
late-middle-aged or elderly, exclusively white, and mostly, it turns
out, Danish public sector workers. I don't have that much in common
with them, which is no criticism and, I hasten to add, my loss, not
theirs. Actually, my disconnectedness is quite helpful, as it has
allowed me to view the proceedings one step removed, and I soon
realise that I have chanced upon a serendipitous metaphor for the
cohesion, high trust and collectivism of the Nordic model. It may
sound obvious to anyone who has sung in a choir before, but I am
quite struck by the way individual members strive to sing together
in one voice, safe in the knowledge that, should they lose their key,
struggle with the tempo, or fumble the lyrics, they can lean back
and let the others carry them to the safety of a familiar chorus.
These four hundred people have gathered here from all over
Denmark because they love to sing, but more importantly, they love
to sing *together* and it is easy to understand why. Singing in a choir
gives a salutary and surprisingly moving lesson in the power of the
group; the massed voices weave together helix-like, lifting the collective heavenwards on thermals of community and trust. It is social
capital, to an Andrew Lloyd Webber soundtrack.

How does the trust fostered by these kinds of social activities
manifest itself in the rest of Danish society? 'Do Danes really leave
their bikes unlocked?' I was once asked by a British radio interviewer with an especially rose-tinted view of the region. Not in
Copenhagen they don't, but it is true that, out in the countryside,
front doors, cars and bicycles are often left unsecured. If you drive
around the country lanes you will find fruit and vegetables on sale
in stalls to be paid for via honesty boxes and, as I have mentioned,
people do leave their kids sleeping in prams outside cafés and
shops, even in the cities, and they let their children commute to
school alone, often by bicycle, from as young as six or seven years
old. But beyond these few examples, I had to admit, I couldn't
really come up with much more evidence that the Danes were

any more trusting – or, by implication, trustworthy – than the rest of us. After all, one encounters honesty boxes in rural England, too, and you need only open a Danish newspaper to find plenty of stories about Danish swindlers, smugglers, crooks and fraudsters. (In fact, when talking all this over with my Danish publisher, he said that it was the *Swedes* he really trusted the most, 'They simply don't have the imagination to lie or cheat,' he said.)

I grew curious: how do you actually measure trust in a society? It turns out to be remarkably simple.

'You ask people, "How much do you think other people in your country can be trusted?"' associate economics professor Christian Bjørnskov of Aarhus University told me when I met him in the dimly lit back room of a café in the centre of Denmark's second city one blustery spring afternoon.

For example, the EU's Eurobarometer asks: 'Generally speaking, would you say that most people can be trusted or that you need to be very careful in dealing with people?; the answers are given on a scale of one to ten. From the answers given you can indirectly argue that the Danes are not only the most trusting, but also, Bjørnskov said, the most trustworthy, because the 'people' in the question are, by definition, other Danes (just as they are other Americans when Americans are asked the same question).

Bjørnskov, an expert in the fields of social trust, subjective well-being and life satisfaction, told me about some other, highly revealing experiments that had been carried out in the field. 'Back in the nineties there was an experiment done [in 1996, by *Reader's Digest*] where wallets were left around in various cities and they counted how many were returned. And the cool thing is that in the places where more people say they can trust others, the more wallets were returned. I think they did an experiment with about forty wallets and the only two countries where all forty were returned were Norway and Denmark. I thought it was too good to be true, but TV2 [a Danish TV channel] did the same experiment again four years ago in Copenhagen Central Station, and they literally could not even leave the wallets – people would instantly pick them up and come running after them, so they had to give up!'

According to Bjørnskov, trust doesn't just have an intangible, feel-good, socially cohesive impact on a society; as well as the warm, *Little House on the Prairie* glow you experience paying for your asparagus via an honesty box, trust also contributes measurably to Denmark's economic success. By his calculations, Danish trust saves the justice system 15,000 krone (£1,500) per person per year, for instance; others believe that as much as 25 per cent of the economy can be accounted for by social capital. That's a fairly sizeable proportion of GDP. Enough, say, to cover the cost of a rather large welfare state.

The theory goes that, if there is trust in society, then its bureau-cracies will be more straightforward and effective – the cost and time of transactions between companies will be reduced and less time will be spent paying lawyers to draw up costly contracts, and in litigation. A handshake is free. Anyone who has tried to conduct business in France or America will have soon become aware of the massive inconveniences involved with living in a society where the default setting is to assume the other person is trying to pull your trousers down. Danish companies are freer about sharing knowledge and divulging secrets to one another; this has been cited as one of the reasons why, for instance, the wind turbine industry flourished here in the 1970s, ultimately becoming the world leader.

Bjørnskov also claims that education is more effective in societies with higher levels of trust because the students trust their teachers and each other more, and are thus able to concentrate better on the business of learning. Higher-skilled industries fare better too – the more skilled a job is, the more difficult it is to check up on whether an employee is carrying out his or her duties as they should be, and so trust becomes that much more important. It is tricky and costly to check that high-level consultants, architects, IT technicians or chemical engineers are working as they should, so trust becomes that bit more important, which is one reason why high-trust societies such as Denmark, Finland and Sweden, excel in advanced industries like phar-maceuticals and electronics and attract foreign companies operating in these fields. 'If you talk to German businessmen, that's what they see in us,' said Bjørnskov. 'They have realised that it is cheaper to employ highly skilled workers here.'

But where do these trusting tendencies come from? Do high levels of trust and an overriding flock instinct lie deep in the psyche of the Danish? Is their collectivist approach a legacy of the painful diminishment of their territory and power over the last five hundred years – a symptom of Holst's 'What was lost without', parochialised approach to life? Or is it something more recent – a hallmark of the welfare state, high taxes and economic equality?

This, it turns out, is the million-krone question.

Chapter 5

Chicken

Which came first, the chicken or the egg? That's easy. Allow me: the chicken evolved into an egg-laying bird from some other kind of egg-laying creature, probably a fish. Sorted. Done. Finding out which came first, Denmark's high trust levels or its social cohesion, is a far, far knottier conundrum.

Does social cohesion generate trust because it brings people together in a shared goal or interest, or is trust a precondition for people gathering together in the first place? After all, if you don't trust someone, you are hardly likely to want to spend Friday evenings line-dancing with them, are you?

I suspect trust and social cohesion are so inextricably intertwined and mutually reinforcing as to be indivisible. One thing I do know about trust is that it does not appear to have much to do with the absolute wealth of a country. If this were the case, why is relatively poor Estonia in seventh place on the OECD's trust index, while far more prosperous South Korea and the US are in the bottom quarter of the list? Another theory used to be that wealthy people are at less risk financially and so trust people more. But if this is true then why is super wealthy Brunei a lowly forty-fourth place on Transparency International's Corruption Perceptions Index?

It turns out that explaining the reasons for Denmark's trust, social cohesion and, ultimately, the happiness of its people, is the most politically divisive discussion in the country right now, encompassing, as it does, highly polarised political beliefs regarding everything from immigration through tax, class and equality to, yes, even the Vikings.

Divining the cause of Danish happiness has created an uncharac-teristic schism in this ordinarily consensus-orientated society. In simple terms, in one camp are those who believe that the source of Denmark's remarkable trust and social cohesion, and by extension also its happiness, is the country's economic equality – let's call this group the 'Ginis'. Naturally, the Ginis are the cheerleaders for the Danish welfare state model, which they believe plays a central role in redistributing the country's wealth fairly via taxes. Having read Wilkinson and Pickett's arguments, I too assumed that this was the main explanation for high trust levels in Denmark – inequality breeds ill-feeling, resentment, envy and mistrust so, naturally, equality would have the opposite effect. I had even begun to feel happier about handing over more than half my earnings to the government in the form of taxes. It was comforting to think that my immediate financial loss, no matter how painful it might feel at the time, would be society's, and therefore, indirectly, my, gain.

On the other hand, you have those of a more monetarist, centre-right persuasion – including Aarhus University's life-quality economist, Christian Bjørnskov, it turns out – who argue that the Danes have always had high levels of trust and social cohesion, and that these date back to long before the advent of the welfare state. Top of this camp's agenda is the downscaling of Denmark's welfare state, which they feel has become unsustainable, and the reduction of Denmark's taxes; they place less emphasis on economic equality and more on motivating society's wealth-generators to improve Denmark's poor productivity growth.

This second camp argue that, far from creating the economic equality that Denmark and the rest of Scandinavia enjoy today, the region's welfare state systems were actually founded on a broader social equality, which existed long before the public sector and high taxes. Bjørnskov claims that research into pre-war trust levels shows that the Danes have always been a trusting people and that trust and social cohesion prepared the way for the welfare state, and not the other way round. 'If you want to redistribute wealth, then it is easier in a high-trust society because you believe that the money will be distributed well to deserving people. We've always had trust and this trust is the cornerstone of the welfare state,' he told me.

'Yes, today Denmark has low inequality and the greatest happiness, but if there was a correlation you would also expect it to be true for other countries with low inequality. But it's not.'

Bjørnskov claims that Wilkinson and Pickett's famous graphs, which purported to demonstrate direct correlations between inequality and numerous social ills, omit key countries which do not fit in with their hypothesis: 'They include South Korea, but not Taiwan. Slovakia, but not the Czech Republic. If you included these countries, then the graphs would resemble a perfect cloud [instead of a simple, linear correlation]. It is a conjuring trick. Nobody took that book seriously in Denmark.'

I had to admit, it had puzzled me that, while Japan is one of the few countries whose Gini Coefficient matches those of the Nordic region, it still only ranked a mere sixteenth on the OECD's trust index; the Japanese were equal yet still did not trust each other. And we know that, while the Danes' income equality has actually *decreased* over the last two decades, their trust levels have continued to *increase*. Both of these factors seemed to undermine the theory that economic equality fosters high levels of trust.

So, if Denmark's trust and social cohesion were not created as a result of the welfare state spreading everyone's money around equally, providing equal educational opportunities, free health care and so on, what were their origins?

Chapter 6

Vikings

'We have indeed heard tell of the splendour of warrior Danes in days gone by, of the kinds of that nation, and of how their high-born men achieved deeds of valour.'   *Beowulf*, anon.

The warrior Danes have gathered together at either end of the battlefield in two rowdy circles, raging and baying like animals. They are huge, these men, beasts in their skins, leather and chain mail. They clutch pikes and axes and the blades of their mighty swords glint through the mist. I am some way off, but the incitements of their leaders carry on the chilly breeze as they rouse the ranks for battle and, if need be, death.

'Do you want some ketchup?'

'No thanks, it's fine like this. Thanks.'

I tuck into my spit-roasted wild boar sandwich, bought from one of the many market and craft stalls set up nearby, and wince as, a minute or two later, the two armies hurl themselves across the grassy ramparts and collide in an almighty clatter of wood and iron. Pointed weapons thrust out of the melee at alarming angles; the armies look like two giant, brawling porcupines.

'They'll have someone's eye out,' I think to myself. Actually, the other day they very nearly did: 'We've had all sorts of accidents. Mostly broken fingers and arms, but there was a guy last year who got hit across the eye. It was pushed back into its socket, but luckily it popped back out overnight.'

I am chatting to Mike, a guide here at Trelleborg, one of Denmark's largest Viking sites, in western Zealand. We are watching a re-enactment of the kind of battle fought by the man who built this impressive circular fortress in AD 980, the legendary Viking king Harald Bluetooth (of wireless technology fame, which was invented in Scandinavia).

The Danes are highly enthusiastic historical re-enacters and, naturally, they gravitate to an era (*the* era) when they reigned supreme: the two-hundred-or-so-year period from the late eighth century when Vikings terrorised a good part of Northern Europe, ruled parts of Scotland and Ireland, rattled the gates of Paris, and discovered North America. This was the time of warrior kings like Bluetooth, Sweyn Forkbeard, and King Cnut the Great, who used the strategic location of their homeland – within striking distance of modern-day Germany, France and Britain – together with their recently developed fast, agile ships, to make devastating lightning raids on unsuspecting Christians across what is new Europe. And, yes, as countless Danes have reminded me over the years, they also ruled eastern and northern England (although, as I keep having to point out, their rule lasted less than thirty years in total and Yorkshire was mostly swamp at the time).

I am here because, according to some, the Vikings are the best bet as to the source of the Danes' remarkable egalitarianism. For those who argue that high taxes are a disincentive to hard work, that they stifle ambition and innovation, that the welfare state encourages a feckless underclass of spongers, and that social democracy is one step removed from communism, it is far more satisfying to point to history, and even genetics, to explain the Nordic miracle.

'You hear those famous stories about the Vikings attacking Paris in the 800s,' Bjørnskov had told me. 'And a Parisian coming out with a white flag or whatever and asking to speak to their king. The Vikings are supposed to have roared with laughter and said, "But we are all kings here." We didn't use to think trust and equality went that far back [to the Vikings]. We used to think there was this link between trust and the welfare state, that trust was something that could be changed, was malleable, and that the welfare state created it, but I don't believe that now. The welfare state didn't really start until 1961, but trust levels were high in Scandinavia long before that.

If you want to explain where those trust differences [between the Scandinavians and other countries] come from, you have to go back to at least the nineteenth century.'

When you visit a Danish company and can't tell the CEO from the office clerk, that's Viking egalitarianism at work. When you see women leaving their babies sleeping in prams outside cafés, that's Viking social trust. When the Danish prime minister can walk the streets of Copenhagen with few turning a head, that's a Viking attitude to class and leadership. Or that's the argument.

Unfortunately, it is not as straightforward as that. At least, not if you ask Mike the Trelleborg Viking guide. 'It is a myth that there was no class society then. Oh no, there was lots of conflict,' Mike, dressed in a woven wool tunic and sturdy leather boots, tells me. 'There was the *store mand*, which literally means the "Big Man", the ruler; then the middle-class farmers; then the slave class, the thralls. If you were rich and had a big farm then you could build a retinue and power.'

In other words, of course the Vikings had kings but, in terms of trust, it is also true that the Vikings had a strict code of honour, which you could argue finds an echo in the high levels of trust in Danish society today. 'One of the fundamental elements of Viking-age society was honour,' Dr Elizabeth Ashman Rowe told me. I had telephoned her after coming home from Trelleborg, more confused than ever about the Danes' Viking inheritance. 'It was like a credit rating. Every action you took would have real-life repercussions, practically every interaction could affect your standing. Valour and honour were especially valuable to men because they were a measure of who you could trust, who your daughter could marry, and so on.'

But the Vikings were also ferociously violent, immoral renegades, famed for their brutal attacks, rapes and murder: contemporary Danes not so much.

'Well, yes, they were pillagers and marauders, but obviously it was a violent age, those were the times. But they were also very law-abiding. The English 'word for law comes from Old Norse,' Rowe said, adding that cooperation and a spirit of community were extremely important in the harsh northern lands. 'There are many instances of people working together because they could not survive alone. You needed friends and allies, and that community and solidarity shows up very early with reciprocity, gift giving cementing personal relations.'

Back in the Aarhus coffee shop, Bjørnskov was sticking to his line that even if Danish trust levels didn't go all the way back as far as the Vikings, they did at least predate the welfare state. As evidence, he cited his ability to predict trust levels in American states based on where their immigrants had come from over the last 150 years. There are, it turns out, high levels of trust in those states, such as Minnesota, that received a large number of immigrants from Scandinavia in the mid-nineteenth century (i.e. pre-welfare state), and low levels of trust in those that welcomed, say, Greeks and southern Italians.*

'Whoa, there,' I said, placing my elderflower cordial on the table. 'This is heading into fairly dodgy territory, isn't it?'

'Yes, it is so sensitive,' agreed Bjørnskov, looking around rather anxiously, as I now realised he had been doing since we started discussing the subject. 'And I don't like it because it means it is really difficult to change things.'

'Wait, though,' I said, suddenly relieved. 'If your theory is true, then Sweden, which has had far higher levels of immigration from supposedly "untrustworthy" non-European countries, would have

---

* This calls to mind a famous Milton Friedman anecdote. 'In Sweden we have no poverty,' a Swedish left-winger had boasted to him. Friedman, no enthusiast for state-imposed equality, replied, 'That's interesting, because in America, among Swedes, we have no poverty either,' the inference being that the success of Swedish immigrants to the States was cultural or genetic and nothing to do with Sweden's social democratic policies. What Friedman conveniently ignored, of course, was the disposition of those Swedes who left Sweden in the nineteenth century, who were, by definition, notable self-starters, which presumably muddies things somewhat.

much lower levels of trust than Denmark, and ultimately be a much less successful country. But it's not.'

Bjørnskov pointed out that immigration had happened gradually in Sweden, which had helped keep trust relatively unaffected, and that it was very difficult to conduct research in areas with large immigrant communities, like the infamous Rosengård housing estate in Malmö. 'You can't even go there if you are a policeman, so crime and things like that are under-reported. In fact trust levels *are* a little lower in Sweden, but what we do see is that immigration doesn't actually change trust level because if you ask immigrants, 'Do you trust most people?' most of the people around them are Swedes in Sweden, or Danes in Denmark.

'I know it is politically incorrect to say these things, and it doesn't help to have to say that, if you come here, you have to get used to Danish society, but it pushes us to dig even deeper for evidence. What you do find is that you can't just talk generally about "immigrant groups". For instance we have observed that Iranian immigrants have much more trust in Danes than in other Muslim immigrant groups, because Iranians define themselves as Persians, not Arab Muslims. We are now realising that you will probably want to know where a Turkish immigrant comes from: if he is from the coast or from Istanbul, where trust levels will be more like they are in Greece [in other words, not terribly trustworthy]. And there are major differences between French-speaking Quebec and English-speaking Canada.'

Aside from the troubling racial stereotyping, the branding of some nationalities as less trustworthy seemed to me to be dubious for so many other reasons, not least the nagging suspicions that, as with happiness, presumably notions of trust are different in different countries, and that the happiness surveys always seemed to be slanted toward Nordic notions of what is trustworthy or not. Plus it is worth re-stating that Canada and Sweden both score very well in terms of trust, yet both have high immigrant populations.

As for the Vikings, they rampaged, raped and pillaged, had slaves and kings, and wrote epic, boastful poems about themselves. None of this can be said of their modern descendants (aside from the kings, with whom we will deal later). It seemed a little too convenient that the Scandinavians had inherited only the positive traits of their forefathers. And but still, I had to admit that my faith in the value of wealth-distribution had been slightly shaken.

My next meeting was with Ove Kaj Pedersen of the Copenhagen Business School, one of the most respected political scientists in the Nordic region. He has taught at Harvard, Stanford, and the universities of Stockholm, Sydney and Beijing. As he was an economist, I expected Pedersen to have a centre-right, liberalist approach to all this, but I could not have been more wrong.

The new Copenhagen Business School building is the closest thing I have ever seen to one of those idealised architect's models. Students lounged in perfectly mixed race- and gender-clusters on landscaped, manicured lawns, or walked in twos and threes, or cycled by on gearless racers. It was fabulous. Like *Gattaca*. Unfortunately, as I discovered at reception when I rolled up precisely one minute before our scheduled appointment, this was not where Pedersen's office was located. That was twenty minutes' walk away in a handsome stucco villa at the end of a quiet cul-de-sac in leafy Frederiksberg. I arrived sweaty and flustered, but Pedersen immediately put me at ease, both personally and with regard to the Danish system.

'Nah, bullshit. That's absolute bullshit,' he laughed when I asked him about the Viking inheritance theory. 'Absolutely it is because of the equality and our tax rates and the welfare state. The trust is based, on my understanding, on the welfare state, period. You trust your neighbour because you know your neighbour is paying tax just like you are, and when that neighbour gets sick, they get the same treatment as you, they go to the same school. That is trust: that you know that, regardless of age, sex, fortune, family background or religion, that you have the same opportunities and the same safety net. You don't have to compete with your neighbour, or be envious of your neighbour. You don't have to cheat your neighbour.

'The welfare state is the most important innovation of any

country in the post-war period. Before it, Denmark was split between 25 per cent with the highest income, 25 per cent at the bottom: now we have 4 per cent at the top and 4 per cent at the bottom.'

I had met many Danes like Pedersen before, usually of his generation and perhaps a little oversatisfied with what they had achieved, but he was not without his doubts concerning the direction in which his country was going: 'I see a major problem in Denmark at the moment. We are in the midst of a historical process. We can go from the traditional, Nordic, egalitarian welfare state to a more Continental French or German one based on a two-tier society – those working, and those outside the labour market. [The Right] sees no problem in the Continental model, with the inequality that brings, but I do. It is a big fear for me that the traditional model will go down the drain, like in Britain, because that will pose problems for social capital and trust, and bring higher crime, and so on. Our comparative advantages in these areas will disappear, and the only way we can beat Germany is by having an even more equal society.'

But the truth is, Denmark is no longer the classless society Pedersen and others on the Left claim it to be. The proportion of the Danish population considered to be below the poverty line has almost doubled, from 4 per cent to 7.5 per cent, over the last ten years. The elite are increasingly congregating in residential ghettos, almost all of them in and around Copenhagen. (Telltale signs that you are in one include a: a branch of Sticks 'n' Sushi and b: swarms of Fiat 500s.) The upper-middle and upper classes are increasingly sending their children to the same schools, too, and, according to national Danish newspaper *Politiken* the tendency has doubled since 1985. More generally, economic inequality has been increasing since the mid-1990s to the point where, according to the OECD – and rather at odds with Pedersen's interpretation – the top 20 per cent of Danes earn more than three times as much as the bottom 20 per cent. That is still better than in the UK where they earn six times as much, but it is far from an equal society.

I can, though, see why foreigner visitors might think Denmark is classless, particularly if their impressions are gathered either from a long weekend in Copenhagen, or a few episodes of *Borgen*, but travel more widely in the country, or spend some time learning the signifiers of Denmark's social classes, and the strata become all too clear.

I have had the mixed blessing of meeting several members of the Danish landed gentry over the years, and can confirm that – with one or two exceptions – they are just as weird and arrogant as the British variety and as numerous in per capita terms, too, I suspect (the Danish countryside is lousy with minor castles and manor houses). But perhaps more representative polar opposites of Danish socio-economic extremes are the 'Whisky Belt' Danes and the 'Rotten Banana' Danes. The former live on Denmark's 'Gold Coast', Strandvejen (the Beach Road), a ribbon of lavish villas, modernist bungalows and sea-view apartment blocks, many of them designed by Denmark's legendary post-war architects (the aforementioned 'most beautiful petrol station in the world', designed by Denmark's master builder Arne Jacobsen is here). Strandvejen stretches twenty or so miles north from the prosperous suburb of Hellerup and boasts great beaches, Michelin-starred restaurants, Jacobsen's famous Bellavista housing complex, the forested deer park of Dyrehaven and, further north, the loveliest art museum in Scandinavia, the Louisiana Museum of Modern Art.

Strandvejen's fishing villages and Hamptons-esque waterfront mansions are home to Denmark's elite – its movie stars and directors, big-time lawyers, bankers, hedge funders, sports stars, CEOs and IT entrepreneurs. Property prices are piffling in UK or US terms, averaging a million or so pounds, rising to perhaps three million at most, but for Danes Strandvejen is a symbol, either of everything they might allow themselves to aspire to when they are sure no one else is looking, or of a vulgar and reprehensible anomaly in an otherwise modest and egalitarian society.

And who are the Rotten Bananas? This is a recent media term used to describe a great, crescent-shaped swathe of the country which is plagued by high unemployment, low wages, crumbling infrastructure, poor health care and underperforming schools. It runs from northern Jutland south along the west coast, before curving east across the island of Funen and ending with the southern islands of Lolland and Falster. Also referred to as *udkantsdanmark* ('outlying', or 'peripheral' Denmark; the hinterland), the Banana is mostly rural and actually encompasses the majority of Denmark's land mass, bar its two main cities – Copenhagen and Aarhus – and North Zealand.

These Danish provinces are dying a slow death caused by a constant flow of the young and the educated towards the cities, and of the unemployed and the elderly in the other direction. It is a decline which successive governments have failed to stem, despite throwing disproportionate amounts of public money at the problem.

'Yes, I do see differences,' conceded Pedersen, when I brought this up. 'But these are not dramatic ones. I have lived in Manhattan, I travel to Beijing and everywhere else. We aren't *that* poor. They will never lack anything to eat. In Denmark poverty is a lack of two televisions!'

But I wasn't so sure. The often striking imbalance in employment opportunities, transport provision, public services, cultural offerings and, well, just nice stuff to see and do between Copenhagen and the rest of the country seemed self-evidently unhealthy.

There are also fears that, in terms of both healthcare and education, Denmark is becoming a two-tier country. More and more Danes who can afford it are turning to private healthcare – 850,000 at the latest count – and poll after poll show that, though they have the largest per capita public sector in the world, the Danes' satisfaction levels with their welfare state are in rapid decline. It is probably true that they have especially high expectations given the amount of money they contribute to it, but in one survey by management consultants Accenture only 22 per cent of Danes thought their public sector did a good job.

Looking to the future, of greatest concern is the gulf that exists in school performance depending on whereabouts in the country you are educated. A recent survey carried out by *Politiken* revealed that students at Ishøj Gymnasium ('gymnasium' is the name the Danes give their secondary schools), in a predominantly working-class and immigrant area south of Copenhagen, scored an average of just 5.4 out of 12, compared with 7.7 in one school in the more affluent North Zealand. (The national average is 6.9).* This imbalance of educational opportunity strikes at the very heart of Denmark's future equality.

Denmark is not alone in this trend. Finland faces similar challenges, and urban migration has been even more starkly felt in Sweden where almost 40 per cent of the population now lives in the three main cities – Gothenburg, Malmö and Stockholm. These days, large areas of northern Sweden are depopulated, derelict and largely devoid of any civic presence. There are two reasons for this: firstly, Sweden is a much less densely populated country (it has over ten times the land mass of Denmark but less than twice the population), and secondly, the drive towards industrialisation has been far stronger in Sweden over the last hundred years. Only Norway seems to have bucked the trend, its colossal oil wealth and a long tradition of decentralisation from Oslo – the right to receive a variety of services wherever you live in the country is enshrined in law – have helped keep its provinces relatively well populated and with reasonable infrastructure.

'We should have it easier because we are such a small country, but it isn't small in our heads,' Torben Tranæs, head of the Rockwool Research Foundation, an independent social research body (funded, bizarrely, by an insulation manufacturer), told me when I met him in his Copenhagen office. He believes that a lack of labour-force mobility lies at the heart of Denmark's provincial problem. Ironically, for this enthusiastic cycling nation, the Danes do not like to get on their bikes – in the Tebbitian sense – to look for work.

---

* Oddly, and for reasons which no one has ever been able to explain sufficiently to me, the '7-step' Danish school-marking system runs from -3 to 00 (non-passing levels), then 02, 4, 7, 10 and finally 12 as the top score.

'There's lots of talk in the media about how young people can't get apprenticeships, but then you discover that companies can't actually get enough young people to come and work for them because the companies aren't located in Copenhagen or a big city,' Torben explained. 'There are a lot of people around the world who would give their right arm for a job at Danfoss [a manufacturer of thermostats located in a not terribly exciting part of Jutland] but you hear many young people talk as if it is extremely unjust that they be required to move away to get a job. It also works like that with professors – you would rather stick with an associate professor post in Copenhagen than take a professorship in Aarhus. I think that's terrible. It is a real challenge to make sure that there is a modern standard of jobs and welfare all around Denmark.' Christian Bjørnskov agreed: 'You have these areas where no one works. People won't move to get work. I grew up in south-west Jutland and it is a major problem getting doctors to move there. Danes are not mobile.'

It is true that the Danes are not the most adventurous of people. Some might backpack around South-East Asia or South America in their twenties, but they tend to stick closer to home thereafter. As we've seen with the annual summer-house exodus, many are quite happy to go on holiday an hour away. Come July they clamber aboard their Citroën Berlingos and head to their wooden houses on the coast, and that'll do them. There is the sense that the world exists within a tankful of petrol and there is no need to venture any further.

'I don't think it's possible to change. Urbanisation has happened everywhere industrialisation happens,' Martin Ågerup, head of the centre-right think tank CEPOS told me when I met him in his office in Frederiksstaden, central Copenhagen. 'Nowhere in the world is the trend going the other way. People want to live in cities, they want to move from the countryside close to cities. You want to stop that or reverse it? Well, the costs of that are quite high and I don't think they are worth paying.'

Ågerup was not the only Dane I met who was also prepared to

go on record as saying he would be happy to see further increases in economic inequality in his homeland. Another who shares his view is the Danish People's Party's EU parliament member, Morten Messerschmidt, one of the country's most polarising right-wing politicians (frankly, he's loathsome), who has spoken out against 'equality fascism' and what he sees as the blinkered ideological drive for an equal society.

Ågerup is not nearly as extreme as Messerschmidt, but as we were talking I looked over his shoulder and caught sight of a photograph on the wall of his office. In it he beamed proudly as he stood beside a familiar woman in a blue dress. It was Margaret Thatcher.

'So Martin,' I said, turning back to my interviewee. 'Let's talk about tax.'

Chapter 7

72 per cent

If you wanted to sum up each of the Nordic lands in a single statistic, one peremptory and reductive yet insightful factoid, what would they be? In Iceland, it would probably be the size of the population, which tells you just about everything you need to know about the windswept and frozen island's appeal over the centuries as well as providing a fairly strong clue about how the financial misadventures of recent years came to pass. In Finland my gateway fact would be a list of the three most popular prescription drugs (no skipping ahead). In Sweden it is probably the size of its immigrant population; in Norway, the gargantuan size of its oil-revenue wealth fund.

Denmark's defining statistic has to be its tax rate. The Danes have the highest tax rates in the world, both direct and indirect. They pay the most for the goods in their shops (42 per cent more than the European average – more even, in some cases, than the Norwegians), the most for their cars, the most for their meals in restaurants (up to 150 per cent more), and it is all because of their taxes. In Denmark, books are luxury goods. And don't get me started on the cost of decent cheese.

How does the Danish government get its hand on the electorate's money? Let us count the ways.

There is income tax, for a start, which ranges from a *base rate* of 42 per cent (in the UK it is 20 per cent) up to the top level of 56 per cent.

On top of that is a 'church tax' of a little over 1 per cent (it is optional, but the majority pay it because it's a bother opting out), and something called *ambi* (*arbejdesmarkedsbidrag*). I have yet to fully understand what *ambi* actually is or whose pocket it goes into, but together they bring the top level of direct tax up to as good as 60 per cent.

If you own your home you can probably wave goodbye to around 5 per cent of what's left to property taxes. According to a recent report by Deloitte, if you take into account loan costs, water rates, heating, repairs, and so on, the Danes pay 70 per cent more for the cost of owning a home than the European average. If they use electricity, the government adds 76.5 per cent to the bill.

If you buy a new car you can count on adding 180 per cent on top of the car's purchase price (which is why mine is fifteen years old and smells funny). Petrol (75 per cent) and road taxes (around £600 per year) are also among the highest in the world.

VAT (called 'MOMS' in Denmark) is 25 per cent and levied on everything you buy, including food and children's books, although not newspapers.

And they haven't stopped there. A couple of years ago the government attempted to introduce a 'fat tax' on products like bacon and butter that it deemed deleterious to its citizens' health. Unfortunately, many Danes simply drove to Germany and Sweden to buy such products, and the tax was repealed. Meanwhile, though Denmark's magnificent road and rail bridges to east Sweden and between the Danish islands of Zealand and Funen were paid for long ago, there is still a charge to cross them of almost £30, one-way, which is a kind of tax in itself.

Thus the total direct and indirect burden on the Danish tax payer ranges from 58–72 per cent. Put another way, the Danes are allowed to decide the fate of one-third of the money they earn. Put it yet another way: in Denmark, even if you work in the private sector, you work for the state up until at least Thursday morning.*

And, in case you are wondering, Danish wages are not correspondingly excessive: the country ranks sixth in the OECD's most recent figures for gross income, behind the likes of Ireland and the US; it's not as if the Danes aren't feeling the pinch when they count what's left at the end of the month.

---

* In Danish, the word for tax (*skat*) also means 'treasure' and 'darling'. Meanwhile, the word for poison (*gift*) also means 'married'. After all these years, I still do not really know what to make of this.

So you can see why the Danish economic liberalists feel they have a case for tax reductions. Except for one really strange thing: no one else really complains about the taxes in Denmark. They do whinge a little, but when it comes down to actually doing something about it and *changing* the tax rates, the Danes have been remarkably reluctant to vote in favour. Denmark has seen anti-taxation political parties come and go since the early 1970s, yet none of them has achieved any lasting success based on that manifesto. Currently, tax reduction is the Liberal Alliance party's battle cry, and they won a measly 5 per cent of the vote at the last election. I can think of several countries where the politicians would end up with their heads on pikes if they tried to nab 60–70 per cent of their elector-ate's income, but the Danes are remarkably chilled about the amount they pay in tax. They might roll their eyes a little when the subject is raised, and perhaps indicate with a shrug or one raised eyebrow that they wouldn't be *averse* to rates dropping, just a *little*, but only as long as the sick and unemployed are still cared for, the hospitals and schools have adequate funding, and the all-important safety net remains in place.

'It is true,' centre-right think-tanker Martin Ågerup conceded with a sigh when I put this to him. 'Lower taxes have not been the great vote-winner that you would expect of the country with the highest taxes in the world.' For many Danes, their tax burden seems to be the ultimate symbol of collective sacrifice.

As well as being the editor of *Weekendavisen*, Anne Knudsen – who kindly filled us in on the timeline of Danishness earlier – is a trained anthropologist. She has spent many years studying what makes Danes tick, with a particular interest in their welfare state. She expressed her concerns about the size of Denmark's public sector to me, and had a theory about the Danes' relationship to their tax burden.

'It is a matter of pride to say, "I pay a lot of taxes,"' she told me. 'It's a status gesture, like giving alms. It is why you get 30 per cent of people who live in Østerbro [home to Copenhagen's bourgeois bohemians] voting for Enhedslisten [Denmark's most left-wing main-stream party].'

This chimes with a fascinating theory expounded by a Danish friend of mine, the science writer Tor Nørretranders. In his 2005 book *The Generous Man*, Nørretranders explains how demonstrations of altruism or displays of excess among both animals and humans are driven by an evolutionary imperative: the peacock shows how strong it is by displaying its burdensome excess of plumage; the hedge-fund manager demonstrates how successful he is by frittering a preposterous amount of money on a Bentley. Perhaps, in their way, the Danes are showing the rest of the world, and each other, how much of an *overskud* – that useful Danish word for a surplus or excess – they have by paying their exceedingly high taxes, and gladly. 'This is how successful I am,' the Danes are saying. 'This is how successful our society is – 72 per cent is no problem for a wealthy, high-achieving people such as us.'

Well that's one theory, but are the Danes really as selfless and altruistic as that? Are they really getting value for their tax kroners, or are they the victims of a crafty political sleight of hand?

In their 1980 free-market opus *Free to Choose*, Milton and Rose Friedman detailed the four ways in which money can be spent in what they saw as a descending order of fiscal responsibility:

1) You spend your money on yourself.
2) You spend your money on other people.
3) You spend other people's money on yourself.
4) You spend other people's money on other people.

The clear implication was that, the closer you got to the fourth model, the more irresponsible the spending would be, but – not for the first time – the Danes disagree with the Friedmans. The Danes' willingness to hand over great chunks of their earnings for the good of society would appear to imply two forces at work.

The first is that the Danes trust that their government will spend their money wisely. 'The explanation of the Danes' willingness to pay tax is not that we are an especially unselfish people,' Professor

Christoffer Green-Pedersen of Aarhus University told a Danish newspaper recently. 'But that they feel that they are getting something of value in return – for example, well-functioning schools and hospitals. Tax is seen as a price worth paying.'

The second explanation is that the Danes are tremendously publicly spirited people who think only of the next incubator or school computer as they toil at their respective coalfaces. Certainly, poll after poll show that, in the eventuality of a government surplus, most Danes would rather see it spent on improving welfare than on tax cuts. And this, remember, in a country which, depending on where you go for your statistics, and how those statistics are compiled, already ranks between the highest and third-highest in the world in terms of public spend of GDP per capita (between 26 and 29 per cent).

Perhaps the Danes somehow instinctively understand the value to all levels of society of economic equality, as laid out in *The Spirit Level*. Or could there be another, more self-interested explanation for their contentment with their vast public sector? There is, I'm afraid. And it is a blindingly simple one.

Over *half* of the Danish adult population – as much as two-thirds according to some estimates – either works in the public sector or is financially supported by it in the form of benefit payments. The idea, then, of the Danes voting for a reduction in the size of the public sector funded by tax cuts puts one in mind of that long-mooted turkeys vs Christmas referendum. The majority will always vote for the status quo because their livelihood depends on it. The Danish economy is, in essence, one giant circle jerk funded by a slowly decreasing, but increasingly beleaguered, private sector.

As well as this, the Danes have a couple of other dirty little financial secrets they would probably rather the rest of the world didn't know about that further cast their apparently saintly acceptance of high taxes in a more questionable light.

The first is that the Danes are highly enthusiastic shoppers on the black market. Torben Tranæs's Rockwool Foundation Research Unit recently published some headline-grabbing statistics regarding the black market in Denmark. According to its survey, more than 50 per cent of Danes reported purchasing goods or a service in the previous year without any tax being paid, while another 30 per cent admitted they would have liked to if only a decent offer had come their way.

'That's over 80 per cent,' marvelled Tranæs when I met him in his office in central Copenhagen. 'Almost everyone! But it's not a double standard. I call it "advanced morals". People believe that, because they do a job and pay their income tax, then it is okay to come home and [if they are a plumber] help their neighbour fix their sink and get 100 kroner.'

Ove Kaj Pedersen of the Copenhagen Business School was surprisingly relaxed about the Danish black market. 'We have a very specific type of black market, which to some extent is known about and allowed. If we wanted to get rid of it we could very easily, but you would destroy probably the basic part of the private service sector because they couldn't survive. And the private service sector is the biggest problem in Denmark at the moment because it is made up of very small companies, five to seven employees, no more than twenty people, and you could easily destroy them by wiping out the black market' [76 per cent of Danish companies have fewer than nineteen employees].

In other words, the politicians turn a blind eye to public sector workers' and benefit claimants' tax-dodging for the greater good of the Danish private sector, which in turn is paying those public sector workers' salaries or claimants' benefits. It is a very pragmatic, actually very Scandinavian solution of a kind which can also be seen in Sweden, Norway and Finland.

The second curious anomaly about these supposedly careful, parsimonious Lutheran Danes is their gargantuan, world-leading private debt levels. Though Denmark's national debt is relatively modest at half the EU average, according to a recent IMF warning, the Danish people have personally indebted themselves up to their Gucci glasses. Today, Danish households have the highest ratio of debt-to-income of any country in the Western world: the Danes owe, on average, 310 per cent of their annual income, more than double that of the Portuguese or Spanish, and quadruple that of the Italians. An astonishing figure, yet something rarely discussed in the Danish media or at Danish dining tables. And, of course, this doesn't stop the Danes from sucking their teeth at those devious, lazy, 'live for today' Southern Europeans.

The Danes' debt levels are partly a result of the former Venstre party government's introduction of calamitous interest-only mortgages in 2003.* This helped fuel a property boom over the following couple of years that saw the value of some properties rise by as much as 1,200 per cent; many home-owners borrowed large amounts against their newly released equity. (Today over half of all home loans are of this 'never-never' variety.) This was all fine as long as the value of the properties continued to soar, but then came the inevitable bust; house prices plummeted from 2008 onwards, leaving many with negative equity. Today, just about the only people in Denmark who are solvent are the pensioners who paid off their mortgages before the interest-free loans were introduced; the massively indebted thirty-to forty-year-olds are, I believe the correct economic term is, 'screwed', not least because the Danes' productivity has never come even remotely close to keeping up with their spending. Something, eventually, has to give.

Perhaps more worrying than their debt is that fact that the Danes are as reluctant to save as they are enthusiastic about borrowing: a deadly combination. 'Why should you save if everything is paid for by the State? I pay all this tax money, so I don't have to save,' is how Ove Kaj Pedersen explained the Danes' approach to saving. His compatriots save the least of any Western nation: 1 per cent of their annual income compared with the 5.7 per cent average in other Western countries. Still, Pedersen seems unperturbed: 'The Danes have the biggest pension funds in the world, so the pensions are guaranteed. It doesn't bother me because the debt is covered by that saving. It is a problem but it has no influence on the next generation, not like in Greece or the US.'

---

* Confusingly, Venstre translates as 'left', but this is in fact Denmark's centre right party, the rough equivalent of the Conservatives.

As I left Pedersen's office, and walked down his leafy Frederiksberg street lined with grand villas, a thought struck me. Could the Danes' 'live for today' approach to saving and borrowing actually be another facet of their happiness? To an economist, or even a financial retard such as myself, their approach to borrowing and spending appears near-suicidal, but will the Danes have the last laugh regardless? You can't take your money with you, as they say, but neither do your debts accompany you to the afterlife. The Danes certainly have a carefree approach to living in the red but might they actually be the ones with the right attitude to their banks' money? It's not as if the banks have been paragons of probity these last few years, so why should their customers behave any differently?

Still, it is a paradox that, while the Danes claim that they gladly give their cash to the government with one hand, the other is either online applying to borrow more to pay for their nice German cars, Bang & Olufsen TVs and occasional holidays to Phuket, or slipping a bulging brown envelope to a Polish builder.

It turns out that they have a track record here. In 1694 the English ambassador to Copenhagen, Robert Molesworth, wrote in his memoir *An Account of Denmark*:

Denmark is a country which is plagued by terribly high taxes. The result is that everyone does what they can to cheat on their taxes . . . From the whole I conclude that there is a moral Impossibility all these Taxes and Impositions should continue. The weight of them is already so great that the Natives have reason rather to wish for, than defend their Country from an Invader; because they have little or no Property to lose.

It seems the Danes are behaving to type every bit as much as the Greeks, yet somehow their image remains untarnished. And for that, at least, you have to admire them.

Chapter 8

Hot-tub sandwiches

It is odd, isn't it, that a nation of people famed for their laid-back approach to life, for being moderate and concensus-driven, so relaxed and easy going, are in fact such economic extremists: welfare state extremists, borrowing and debt extremists, tax extremists, (low) working hours extremists, and so on.

One would *assume* that the country with the highest tax rates, some of the highest public-sector spending in the world, and a welfare state which has grown at a rate of about 2 per cent every year for the last three or four decades, would have equally exceptional public services, the best hospitals, the best transport system and the best schools, right? As well as being the happiest people in the world, the Danes should also score at the top – or at least very highly – in these more tangible, statistically verifiable fields, no?

But cold statistics don't always cast Denmark in such a glowing light. In general terms, the United Nations Human Development Index, which assesses how developed a nation is based on such things as life expectancy, literacy and gross national income per capita, places Denmark in sixteenth place, below countries like Ireland and South Korea and all the other Nordic countries save for Finland.

More specifically, the Programme for International Student Assessment (PISA), the most widely accepted international ranking list for school standards, takes a particularly dim view of Denmark's education system. Its most recent report, in 2009, placed Denmark in the bottom third of the top 30 countries in most of the key categories, below even Britain in the sciences, which is really saying something (in contrast to Finland which is invariably at, or near, the top).

'Who cares?' said Ove Kaj Pedersen when I put Denmark's poor PISA performance to him. 'PISA is measuring something that doesn't really count in the Danish situation. If you take our social skills, the way of collaborating, empathy, the ability to work in teams, Denmark comes in number one.' Pedersen – who I think it's fair to say might have a bit of an agenda, having been chairman of the board of education in Denmark for many years – pointed out that in modern Denmark, with its profusion of small or medium companies with their flat hierarchies, these social skills were far more important than high scores in 'the three Rs'.

Shortly after Pedersen and I spoke, some or other Danish university published a report rubbishing PISA's methodology. It simply wasn't true that Danish children drastically under-performed compared with the rest of the world, it claimed. PISA hadn't done its sums properly. Unfortunately, shortly after *that*, Danmarks Radio – the Danish equivalent of the BBC – screened a fascinating four-part documentary series comparing a Danish class of sixteen-year-olds with a Chinese class of the same age in four categories: maths, creativity, social skills and English. I think it's fair to say that most Danes would have expected the Chinese students to do better in maths, but for the Danish children to have better social and creativity skills, and be better at English. As it turned out, the series sent major shockwaves through the Danish education system, the viewing public and the government when the Danish kids were roundly bested by the Chinese in the first three categories. Only in their English skills were the Danes superior. (None of this helped the Danish teaching unions who, at the time, were arguing against increasing the number of hours spent teaching, despite the fact that they spent fewer hours actually teaching than teachers everywhere else in Europe. They lost that argument.)

My own, fairly limited, experience of Danish public services has been patchy over the years. In terms of the Danish health service, the birth of one son was a state-of-the art experience with a fabulous midwife, a hot tub and sandwiches; the birth of the other was borderline third-world, with uninterested midwives mooching in and out of the delivery room as if they were checking on gently simmering stew, and a bit of a panic at the end. Other than that, I have no great first-hand knowledge and only anecdotal reports which range from high praise to terrifying tales of incompetence – in other words, pretty much just like any other national health service.

Actually, I did have one telling experience recently, which relates to the significant cuts to provincial Danish health services. My youngest son had something in one of his eyes, so we took ourselves off to the nearest accident and emergency department, which was about thirty miles away. The waiting room was packed and I led my son, who was holding his hands over both his eyes for emphasis, to the only free seat beside a fantastically obese, tattooed family who had brought their equally barrel-shaped dachshund along for the trip ('Is obesity an emergency?' I wondered idly as I queued at reception. In their case, I decided it probably was.)

When I finally reached the end of the queue I was told that a doctor would not be able to see my son as I had not made an appointment. This was a new one on me: an appointment for an emergency? It was a recent cost-cutting measure, the receptionist sighed, designed to streamline the system.

'Oh, sorry! Next time I'll be sure to ring ahead, before anyone injures themselves,' I chirruped politely, as I led my blinded son from the premises.

Equally surprising, given the proportion of their wages they hand over for such services, Danish people have to pay for visits to the dentist and the optician, as well as for their prescription medicines (which are more expensive than they are in the UK). They also have to pay most of their physiotherapy and psychology costs – both of which are free in the UK. Even the ambulance service is privatised. Perhaps it is a result of all this that the Danes are very much the unhealthy sibling in the Nordic family with, as we've seen, the highest rates of cancer, the lowest life expectancy (78.4 years), and among the highest levels of alcohol consumption in Europe. They would also appear to be addicted to sugar, consuming more sweets per capita than anyone else in the world (7.81kg per year). They are also, perhaps less surprisingly, the largest consumers of processed pork products in the world, a subject about which there have been several health warnings in recent years (according to one source I found, the Danes eat 65kg each of dead pig per year). They have also proved reluctant to wean themselves off their nicotine habits, largely, I suspect, because they have an important tobacco industry, along with a much-loved, and long-lived, queen who is a prominent smoker. Smoking was only banned in Danish schools in 2007.

As for the Danish education system, obviously I did not pass through it myself, but my children are doing so at the moment. Initially, they attended a *folkeskole*, or state school. The Danish state's *folkeskoler*, which date back to the early 1800s, are a key element of their national identity, not to mention their enduring equality. As Villy Søvndal, the former leader of the Socialist People's Party, once put it: 'The *folkeskole* is the best example of a genius institution which gathers children from different social levels and, in doing so, binds our society together.' It is rare that I find myself agreeing with Søvndal (a supposedly old-school lefty whose principles were promptly discarded the moment he got his ministerial limo) but he is right when he says that the *folkeskoler* are a key element in fostering Denmark's social cohesion. But, as with the British comprehensive system, there is a growing concern that the schools tend to sacrifice the potential achievements of the higher-performing students for the better good of the middle and lower achievers: the level of instruction is brought down to include the least able, testing is frowned upon, and, though I realise I sound like a reactionary old fart when I say this, there does seem to be a little too much emphasis on social skills at the expense of actual learning.

We ended up moving our children to a *privatskole* where there was more emphasis on things like stopping the children from hitting each other over the head with chairs. (I should point out, Denmark's private schools receive financial support from the state, with parents paying top-up fees amounting to a fraction of those of the British private sector.

The more I thought about the often parlous state of Danish public services – the rail system, which is virtually bankrupt, the under-performing hospitals, the almost comedically poor schools – I began to wonder whether the reason the Danes still feel they are getting value for their tax kroner is because they don't actually have all that clear an idea of where their taxes are being spent. A while ago a member of parliament for the Liberal Alliance (the right-wing, liberal economic party) suggested that all public spending should be detailed on individuals' tax returns so that Danes could see how much of their tax money went on education, how much on defence, and so on. This doesn't seem too revolutionary an idea to me, yet, perhaps unsurprisingly, there was an outcry in parliament and the proposal died a death. But would it be such a bad idea? Where *is* all that tax money going?

'Activation of the unemployed is around DKK20 billion. We have a fairly expensive childcare system, and then of course there are the transfer payments,' said Martin Ågerup, referring to the hundreds of millions of kroner spent on pensions, unemployment and sickness benefits, child and housing support, and student grants. A million Danes receive housing benefit, he said, and the pensions pot is essentially bottomless.

If I can return to my choir metaphor for a moment, as I discovered during the twiddly bits of 'Bohemian Rhapsody', when you are but one singer in a choir of hundreds, it is really quite easy to contribute nothing yet remain part of the group. Switch off and mouth the words and no one will call you out because they are too busy concentrating on how they are sounding. It is easy to coast.

There is a growing feeling that too many Danes have been doing just that for too many years. The most high-profile case in the media recently concerned 'Dovne Robert' (Lazy Robert), a well-educated, physically able man in his thirties who has been signing on for the dole for over eleven years, playing the system like a maestro with his Stradivarius. There was a predictable outcry, which does seem to have moved the debate forward a little, but Robert now makes a nice living as a media figure so is, essentially, still unemployed.

Surely Denmark is going to have to bite the bullet and endure the kind of far-reaching and controversial reforms the Swedes were forced to implement following their banking crisis of the early nineties, and from which they emerged by far the stronger economy. The Danish public sector and tax levels cannot continue to grow. As is happening throughout the Western world, its population is aging, the working-age population is diminishing, and the birth rate is at a twenty-year low. The only question is, which politician or political party is going to have the *cojones* to take what will be hugely unpopular, but necessary, decisions?

The Danes, it seems, have some very difficult choices ahead, choices which could have direct consequences not just for their long-term economic stability, but also for their much-vaunted happiness. Or do they? Perhaps the rampantly individualistic, child-of-Thatcher, 'greed is good' atmosphere prevalent in Britain during my childhood has blinkered me to the collectivist benefits of a society such as Denmark's. After all, who has greater poverty, more crime, greater inequality and Jeremy Kyle – the Danes or the British? Who is the happier? It was time to hear the argument for the Danish model, from one of its most prominent proponents.

Chapter 9

The bumblebee

It all looks so very familiar, but I can't quite put my finger on why. I have never been inside Christiansborg Palace, the Danish parliament building, before, yet I am experiencing an almost overwhelming sense of déjà vu.

I have arrived early in the morning and made my way, untroubled, past the virtually non-existent security system. Something on my person sets off a metal detector, but there is no one here to stop me, so I continue through to reception. It all seems remarkably relaxed for a country that has experienced a number of terrorist threats, and actual attacks, in recent years.

After a lengthy wait in a windowless holding pen – during which things get so boring I have plenty of time to ponder why the Danish welcome sign, *Velkommen til Folketinget*, does not have an exclamation mark, but the English translation 'Welcome to the Danish Parliament!' does – a tall women in a smart suit arrives and I follow her up a broad, palatial flight of steps and along some imposing corridors before, finally, I am shown into a high-ceilinged office the size of half a football pitch, furnished with classic Danish chairs and tables, and large abstract oil paintings.

My skin prickles. I *know* this place. I have *been* here. And then, as the grand old man of Danish politics, chief architect of Denmark's tax policy for many years, current speaker of the house and chairman of the ruling Social Democrats Mogens Lykketoft enters the room, it suddenly dawns on me why I feel this way.

'*Borgen!*' I exclaim gesturing around the room. Lykketoft frowns and looks slightly concerned. 'I was just trying to figure out why this all seems so familiar. It's because of *Borgen*, the television series.'

Borgen is the Danish TV series featuring fictional female Danish prime minister Birgitte Nyborg, and is filmed in a replica of Christiansborg. It has been a major hit on British and US television, as well as, of course, here in Denmark, where half the population tuned in to watch on Sunday evenings, its storylines uncannily presaging the election of Helle Thorning-Schmidt as the country's first female PM. Lykketoft, who, I suppose, is a kind of real-life version of the older, dishevelled man who councils Nyborg on how to handle the cut and thrust of minority government politics, continues to regard me warily as he sits down.

Active in Danish politics since the 1960s, Lykketoft was there, or thereabouts, when most of the key decisions that shaped contemporary Denmark were made, not least those that have seen the tax burden double from 25 per cent of GDP in 1960 to its current world record of just under 50 per cent today.

He recently published a pamphlet, *The Danish Model*, which highlights the many economic and labour policies he has helped to introduce since he entered parliament in 1981. The pamphlet seeks to explain Denmark's so-called 'bumblebee' economy: conventional economic thinking has it that this high-tax, large public-sector model ought to stifle growth, innovation and competitiveness. It should not work but, just as the laws of physics tell us that the heavy, unaerodynamic bumblebee shouldn't be able to fly, both bee and economy remain airborne regardless.

'The driving motivation was to create a society that was competitive, with high growth and high employment, but that also had fewer differences between people economically than in most other countries in the world, with more harmony, more social security,' Lykketoft, now in his late sixties and these days no longer sporting his once-trademark goatee, tells me. He sips his coffee and unwraps a sweet from the dish on the low table between us. 'The Danish model of redistribution – of money and qualifications – has opened up to many more people than in the US or Britain the chance to make a decent living, to explore their own potential. We have been trying to demonstrate to all the sceptics of neo-liberal origin that this bumblebee can fly.'

According to Lykketoft, Denmark's post-war success was due to the redistribution of wealth and flexibility in the job market, supported by generous benefits. 'We are more flexible than other European countries.' He starts to bang the table for emphasis. 'We had an *obligation* to make sure that people were *not impoverished* when they lost their *jobs* and that they were *helped* to get new *jobs*. This goes hand in hand with the ability we have had to create a more qualified workforce.'

Does he not accept the Right's argument that taxes are a disincentive to work, to innovate, to take risks? Naturally, he does not. When one looks at middle-class disposable income in the US and Denmark, once things like childcare and health insurance are taken into consideration, they are on a par, he says. In Denmark you get all these things for free – 75 per cent of childcare costs are paid for by the State, along with health care, of course, and much elderly care – while in the US you pay lower taxes but then have to pay for these services. It is merely a matter of at what stage you pay for them.

'The real difference is that those who have a high risk of being ill or unemployed are better off in our system, and those who have a very high income are not. They are better off in other parts of the world. But does that mean that those high achievers, highly skilled people, migrate from Denmark to avoid tax? That's the real question.' Skilled politicians rarely ask questions to which they do not already have answers, and Lykketoft has one. There is no evidence to support this, he says. The wealth generators are staying in Denmark, there is no brain drain.

Now, brain drains are rather tricky to quantify but, from what I've seen and heard, New York and London are full of creative, ambitious Danish émigrés. A few years ago the *New York Times* ran a story with the following headline: 'Denmark Feels the Pinch as Young Workers Flee to Lands of Lower Taxes', and the Confederation of Danish Industry has complained regularly over the years that high taxes are driving talent overseas.

I also mention the country's poor PISA performance, the

complaints about the health service, and point out that Denmark's public rail company, Danske Statsbaner (DSB), has recently skirted with bankruptcy. Is Lykketoft happy with what the Danish tax payers receive for their money?

'There are certain corners of the public service where there is a deterioration,' he concedes, carefully. 'There are dysfunctionalities, of course, but we are catching up.'

I point out that Sweden's economy is doing significantly better than Denmark's, and has been doing so for many years. Denmark is slowly sliding down the BNP charts while Sweden is holding its own. The *Washington Post* has called it the 'Rock Star of the Recovery', and a recent special feature in *The Economist* about how great the Nordic region is doing was really mostly about Sweden. Yet, in contrast to Denmark's supposedly agile, responsive *flexicurity* system, with its relaxed labour laws and generous benefits, Sweden has much stricter employment legislation, with lower benefits but much greater job security (as I understand it, a Swedish employee would have to be caught defecating on the CEO's desk while setting fire to the blueprints for their groundbreaking new product to merit the first written warning of the five required for it to go to arbitration, and even then, the tea lady would have to give her consent to his sacking). Meanwhile, Sweden is fourth in the World Economic Forum's latest Global Competitiveness Index, while Denmark has plummeted from eighth to twelfth in just a year (from a high of third place a few years back). According to OECD predictions, Denmark is predicted to have the lowest BNP per person in all of Northern Europe, while Sweden will remain in the top 10. Many would point out that the key to Sweden's success is that it slashed taxes, greatly reduced its public sector, and underwent a massive privatisation programme in the 1990s. Denmark is only just now beginning to be forced to consider such reforms.

Lykketoft disagrees.

'Yes, but they have taken advantage of devaluation during the financial crisis and they have sold their large stock of public companies, and that cannot continue.' In other words, according to

Lykketoft, Sweden's recent economic performance is based on external factors, and the selling of the family silver.

I like Lykketoft. He is one of the most well-thought-of politicians in Denmark, respected by all sides of Denmark's kaleidoscopic political spectrum. But I can't help feeling he has his head, if not buried in the sand, then at least sporting some nice, noise-cancelling headphones.

Beyond questions of fat taxes, incubators and high-performing Swedes, the overriding concern for many observers of the Danish economy is its pitiful productivity levels, which have been lagging behind the European average since the mid-nineties. There have been public commissions, endless newspaper columns and TV debates on the subject, but no one really knows why the Danes aren't making as much use of their working hours as the rest of us.

Torben Tranæs at the Rockwool Research Fund believes he might have discovered why. 'This is confidential, we are having a press meeting later this month,' he had told me. 'But we have carried out some data collection. We have had people register what they do every 10 minutes so we can see how much they are working compared to how much they say they are working. It shows that, though people say they are working more, actually [the amount they work] is decreasing.'

What Tranæs appeared to be saying was that, a) the Danes were lazy and b) they were lying about it. Fittingly, for the home of Hamlet, it turns out that the Danes are heroic procrastinators. During any given working day they will do their utmost to find something, *anything*, with which to occupy themselves as long as it is not productive work.

'They [the Danes they surveyed] were telling us, "Okay, *normally* I work this much, but this week I had this thing at my kid's school."' The excuses were endless – tending to sick children, dental appointments, anything. And the higher up the job scale, the worse it got: the CEOs were the most indolent of the lot. Tranæs continued:

'There are many elements to this productivity thing, but I think that just not hanging in there as much as we used to do is a major one.'

Of course, those on the right point, again, to Denmark's high taxes as an explanation for low productivity: why work harder when you will only be taxed more or even take your earnings up to the top rate? 'We have alcohol and fat taxes as a disincentive to drink and eat fatty foods,' says Martin Ågerup. 'So it seems logical that income taxes will have the same effect. Look at Sweden. They lowered marginal taxes in Sweden quite a lot in the early nineties and they found that people worked more and were paid more per hour.'

Mogens Lykketoft was having none of this talk of taxes as a disincentive. 'Well it was very few years ago that we were one of the three most competitive countries in the world,' he countered, although he did concede that productivity was a problem. But, he said, rather than the Danes' laziness being the explanation for their low productivity growth, Denmark had simply become a victim of its own success. The government had been so successful in activating such a large proportion of the working population (during the good times at the turn of the century, there was virtually no unemployment) that it had engaged the least productive members of society, consequently bringing down overall productivity. I suppose this might once have been the case but the truth, I suspect, is that the Danes have had it so good for so long that they have simply lost the will to fight. Another report, published in June 2013 by the government's statistics department, no less, revealed that the Danes were working *even less* than previously thought – fewer than 28 hours a week.

'There seems to be an inconsistency between how much we want to work, and how much we want to have of the public sector,' is how Tranæs had put it to me. 'I don't think the Danes have a preference to work as much as they should, in order to support the [scale of] welfare state that they want.' One can't help feeling that reducing taxes even just a tad – say, to Swedish levels – and cutting back on the transfer payments and, for example, defence spending (after all, one can't help wondering, given its track record, what exactly the Danish military is *for*) might help turn all this around and provide an incentive for the Danes to spend a little more time at their desks, and a little less time at the hairdressers.

Nevertheless, as I was leaving Lykketoft's office, a chilling thought suddenly occurred to me. Looking ahead, might he actually be in favour of *raising* taxes at some point in the future?

'I would never be able to be quoted on this,' he said (as far as I was concerned, the whole meeting was on the record). 'But I think we will have at least to change the tax system even more in order to put taxes on resources.'

People of Denmark, you have been warned.

Chapter 10

Denim dungarees

It was time to see some more of the fabled Rotten Banana. Could it really be as provincial and unsophisticated as my condescending cosmopolitan Copenhagen friends claimed? I packed an overnight bag, climbed aboard my geriatric car and headed west, crossing the mighty Storebælt Bridge – always a nerve-wracking experience given the playful crosswinds – and arriving on the island of Funen (*Fyn*).

Hans Christian Andersen was born in Funen in 1805 and left as soon as he was able. Not much has happened since and, for many Danes, the island is little more than a stepping stone between Copenhagen and the Jutland Peninsula (*Jylland*). I think that's a shame. Once you adjust to the slower pace of life here, the countryside is quite charming, especially in the south of the island, with its Teletubby fields, magical beech forests and beaches. Funen has not been quite so ravaged by industrial agriculture as Jutland and Zealand have, so the fields are smaller and there is some excellent produce to be had in the summer; a drive along the backroads in spring or summer offers plenty of opportunity to stock up on fresh peas, new potatoes, strawberries and asparagus, while autumn brings apples, plums and cherries. Americans would call these fruits and vegetables 'heirloom', but to the *Fynboer*, it's just the stuff they eat with the seasons.

As with the rest of the Rotten Banana, Funen's population is declining in size and increasing in age. You drive through village after village of drab, cinder-block houses, many semi-derelict, without seeing a soul. The bakeries have closed, the butchers have disappeared, the grocers are gone, all retail activity is now focused on the supermarkets, in their charmless out-of-town warehouses, which siphon the life out of otherwise attractive, historic villages like Faaborg.

I know this part of Denmark well, as this is where my parents-in-law live, so I press on for Jutland.* I know Denmark's peninsula less well, largely because every time I have visited I have departed shortly afterwards wondering why I ever went there in the first place. Jutland is windy and smells of manure. The people remind me a little of Yorkshiremen: blunt and chippy, mistrustful of Copenhageners and their fancy ways, and perhaps a little narrow-minded. The men wear denim dungarees and ride farty little motor scooters. The women, it has to be said, are staggeringly beautiful (particularly in Aalborg, for some reason), but Jutland offers little by way of cultural entertainment or natural beauty that you can't get on Zealand. (Aside that is, so I'm told, from a brothel where those with a taste for, let's call it, 'pleasures of the fur', can indulge.)†

I felt it might be time for a reappraisal of Jutland, to give it another chance. After all, Jutland has Denmark's best beaches, its highest point (an admittedly modest mound called Møllehøj, at 560 feet just over half the height of the Shard) and Legoland. It is also home to Denmark's answer to Stonehenge and the Pyramids of Giza combined, the Jelling stones, my first stop.

---

* I ought to make it clear that I did not press on *because* Funen is where my parents-in-law live.

† And it's legal. Denmark is the only country in Europe, quite possibly the world, where bestiality is not a criminal act due to fears that legislation would expose pig farmers to prosecution when they artificially inseminate their sows. According to a TV programme I once watched on the subject – for research purposes – an estimated 7 per cent of Danish men have had sex with an animal. (The figure came from one of Denmark's leading vets interviewed on the programme, *Danmark Ifølge Bubber*, broadcast during prime time on Denmark's main commercial station, TV2, and also happened to be presented by a much-loved children's TV personality.) The next time you see the Danish national team playing football, consider this: there is a good chance at least one of them has shagged something with four legs.

It is an unwritten rule that every Dane must visit the Jelling stones at least once in their life. They are two stones, tenth-century memorials: the oldest erected by King Gorm the Old in memory of his wife, Thyra; the second by Gorm's son, Harald Bluetooth. This second stone commemorates not just a king, but also the transition of his kingdom from pagan worship to the arrival of Christ's teachings and, in a sense, the birth of Denmark itself, as it bears the first written mention of the country's name.

Danish flags were fluttering throughout Jelling on the sunny spring morning I arrived there, as I suspect they do every day in this archetypal Danish village. Housemartins screeched and swooped above the gravestones and the smell of freshly mown grass completed the idyllic scene. In the well-appointed visitor centre across the road from the churchyard where the stones stand, they were selling the usual Viking tat – bottles of mead, paper napkins decorated with runes, CDs of Templar music – while an exhibition charted the various, largely fruitless archaeological excavations which had taken place there. The Danes have been searching for royal remains among the Jelling stones for centuries, but only ever seem to find Obelix-style menhirs.

Over in the churchyard I stood for a while looking at the stones themselves. For a long time Gorm's stone lay slumped against the church and was used as a bench. Today, now a cherished totem of the birth of Denmark, it resides in its own climate-controlled glass case to protect it from the elements. Both stones – one not much bigger than a postbox, the other about twice that – are decorated with faded runic inscriptions that were once coloured blue and red. They have been eroded by the wind over the centuries so that their inscriptions now look much like the ones convicts make on their cell walls to count off the days of their sentences. The runes also feature the first depiction of Christ found in Scandinavia: he is shown with branches wrapped around his body, in the pagan style. Thus, the Jelling stones are not just an early royal public-relations stunt (neither Gorm nor Harald were in fact kings of 'all' Denmark, but this was the image they wanted to project); they are also the first recorded references to the one social force that, though these days it is almost a taboo, would come to define the societies of the North more than any other. Though the Nordic people have largely grown out of religion, boasting the lowest church attendance of all the Christian countries, and though its impact on society today is little discussed, their particular form of Christianity, Lutheranism, has been a formative influence on the Nordic psyche and remains fundamental to the way people here behave and relate to one another.

In a sense, then, you could claim that the Jelling stones are memorials to the beginnings of Nordic exceptionalism itself. It was the arrival of Christianity – at that time, of course, Catholicism – which kick-started the long, slow process towards the civilisation of the Vikings, bringing to an end some of their less edifying practices – the polygamy, the use of slaves, blood feuds, and so on. Over the following centuries, the Church steered the development of the arts and literature across the region and the monasteries became the main seats of learning, with some bishops – like Bishop Absalon, the founder of Copenhagen – becoming as powerful and bloodthirsty as any king. And then came Martin Luther's church-door antics.

In Scandinavia, the Reformation was a more important cultural and social force even than the Renaissance. As T. K. Derry writes in his magisterial history of the region, 'After the passage of three and three-quarter centuries, the view of religion which was shaped in Germany still received an ampler recognition in Scandinavia than in its homeland.' Something deep within the Scandinavian psyche embraced Lutheranism to a far greater extent than it was in the land of its birth; Luther's teachings – and their spin-offs, Calvinism and Pietism – gained a deeper purchase here, perhaps because the population had a more independent streak and tended to live in poorer, more isolated communities (Protestantism being less interested in overt displays of worship than Catholicism, and more about the individual's inner conscience – that's my theory at least). It also helped that the then Swedish king, the mighty Gustav I, became an enthusiastic adherent of Lutheranism for his own, mostly political, motives, and what GI wanted, GI got.

Once Luther had challenged the Catholic hegemony there was no looking back, at least as far as the Scandinavians were concerned. Catholicism was virtually eradicated within a few decades. Both the Danish and Swedish kings embraced the new doctrine, although the older faith still had a relatively easy ride compared with the persecution it suffered elsewhere in Europe. In 1527 the Danish king, Frederik I, proclaimed that his people should be free to worship in which ever way they pleased, 'For His Grace is king and judge over life and property for his realm, not over the souls of men.' (That said, in Iceland, then still a Danish domain, non-attendance of Lutheran services was still punishable by flogging.)

But in the late twentieth century secularism replaced Lutheranism with similar ease and all-encompassing effect, at least in the urban centres of Scandinavia. These days Lutheranism can sometimes appear about as popular as bear-baiting, not least if the church-attendance figures are anything to go by: they are now down to around 2.5 per cent throughout the region.

How then, I wondered, does the influence of Lutheranism manifest itself, if at all, in Scandinavia these days?

Chapter 11

Bettina's shoes

Aksel Nielsen was a sensitive and sickly child who grew into a weak and stunted young adult. The son of a smith, he was born in 1899 in the somnolent North Jutland town of Nykøbing on the island of Mors. He received a rudimentary education at the local school until, at the age of seventeen, he went to sea on a schooner bound for Newfoundland.

This was the first of many flights from reality upon which the bookish Aksel would embark during his life: the next came just a few weeks later on the other side of the Atlantic, where he jumped ship. But, with the world now at war, Nielsen's habit of scribbling secretively in his notebooks late at night in his bunk bed, combined with his strange accent and inability to speak English, aroused suspicion. His workmates began to think he might be a German spy. Once again he fled, this time back to Denmark, via Spain, working his passage on a ship.

Back home in Nykøbing, few were pleased to see Aksel. His parents had not been happy about him leaving in the first place, and the fact that he had jumped ship compounded their disapproval. But in fact his North American escapades were to prove his making. At the age of twenty-four, following numerous rejections, Nielsen's fictionalised version of his Newfoundland adventures was finally published as *Stories from Labrador*, under a newly acquired surname, Sandemose, taken from a place close to his Norwegian mother's home town. More books followed, blending fiction and fact in a style critics have likened to Joseph Conrad's, albeit interspersed with long, rather worthy essays.

There would be yet more flights in Sandemose's life. The next was to Norway, where he fled in 1930 with his wife and three children following various financial misadventures, including selling the rights to his next book to two different publishers (I did kick myself when I heard about this). During the Second World War he ran away again, this time to Sweden, following a peripheral involvement in the Norwegian resistance movement. This amounted to little more than sharing a beer or two with actual resistance members, but they grew fearful that Sandemose wouldn't be able to keep his mouth shut and so persuaded him to cross the border to their neutral neighbour. Back in Norway, in 1945 having left his wife and three kids, he fathered twins with another woman.

By all accounts, Sandemose was a deeply unpleasant man, an untrustworthy, amoral fantasist. One of his sons would later accuse his father, variously, of paedophilia, incest, cruelty to animals and bigamy, while the alleged murder of a Norwegian man has also been added to the charge sheet against him. I recently noticed Sandemose's portrait on the tail of a Norwegian Air 737, one of a series of 'Norwegian' heroes featured on the tails of the company's planes. He makes for an unlikely corporate icon, it has to be said.

Sandemose's works are little read these days, except, that is, for a small fragment of one novel, *A Fugitive Crosses His Tracks*, that was published in 1933. The book is a thinly veiled *roman-à-clef* about the people of Nykøbing, in the book renamed 'Jante'. It caused a storm of controversy, satirising life in small-town Denmark as being ruled by pettiness, envy, backbiting, gossip, inverted snobbery and small-mindedness. Naturally, the book generated some especially indignant spluttering in Nykøbing, exposing as it did the mean-spirited behaviour of its residents, many of whom were easily identified.

The fragment of *A Fugitive* that has come both to define and to torment the Danes is a list of rules by which the residents of the fictional town of Jante were said to abide. These rules set out the Law of Jante (*Janteloven*), a kind of Danish Ten Commandments, the influence and infamy of which have spread beyond their home country throughout the Nordic region.

These are the rules of Jante Law, the social norms one should apparently be aware of if one is planning a move to the North:

You shall not believe that you are someone.
You shall not believe that you are as good as we are.
You shall not believe that you are any wiser than we are.
You shall never indulge in the conceit of imagining that you
    are better than we are.
You shall not believe that you know more than we do.
You shall not believe that you are more important than we are.
You shall not believe that you are going to amount to anything.
You shall not laugh at us.
You shall not believe that anyone cares about you.
You shall not believe that you can teach us anything.

Knowing even just a little of their author's biography, one would think it easy to dismiss these rules as the products of a somewhat unbalanced mind, an irrelevance. But the truth is, Sandemose really nailed the Danes. And not just the Danes: Jante Law sent ripples of recognition beyond Denmark – the Norwegians are all too familiar with them and, as we will hear, they act as an even more powerful normalising force in Sweden. Yet raise the subject of Jante Law with Danes today and there will likely be some eye-rolling and a deep sigh or two. You will be told that the phenomenon has died out, that Sandemose's satire is no longer relevant, a throwback to a time when most Danes were peasants. Even Queen Margaret condemned it in a New Year's speech back in the eighties, they'll say. These days, Danes are proud of their achievements, happy on behalf of others who enjoy success in life, and do not themselves hold back on exhibiting their success. Wait a while, though, and the examples of 'friends' or 'relatives' who have suffered from the tyranny of Jante Law 'out in the provinces', will be shared. This kind of suffocating social conformity might still exist somewhere out there in darker Denmark, they will eventually concede, but not in Copenhagen. The Danish capital is far too globalised and its citizens far too individualistic, what with their social media, reality TV, and rampant US-style consumerism.

My experience has been that Jante Law operates everywhere in Denmark on some level or another, but it is true that it is harder to spot amid the cosmopolitan whirl of the capital. Certainly, I know from speaking to people who have moved away from Jutland that Jante Law still underscores attitudes and behaviour to a greater extent on the Danish peninsula, and along the yet more insular, traditional west coast in particular. Sitting next to a woman at a dinner party recently, she had explained how stifling she found the attitude in her home town. 'On the west coast, anyone who even slightly broke with convention, or showed that they had any ambition, was frowned upon,' she told me. 'People really didn't like it. Everyone knew your business, everyone had an opinion about what you should be doing. I had to get away. I came to Copenhagen as soon as I could, and don't often go back. It is common to have such feelings about one's home town, I suppose, but they do often seem to be particularly keenly felt by people from Jutland.

But what of Nykøbing itself? What signs of Jante Law's existence would I find if I were to visit its home town, I wondered? Was Nykøbing Mors, to give it its full name, as small-minded and mean-spirited as Sandemose had made it out to be? Did its people suppress their hopes and dreams, hold each other back, not allow themselves to 'think they were anything'? And if so, would I be able to see any evidence of this?

As I drove into Nykøbing I was on red alert for any traces of Jante Law. My first thought as I passed the town sign was, could its very name be an indication of Jante Law at work? The 'Mors' is added to Nykøbing to differentiate it from other Nykøbings in Denmark. Why could they not stand proud as *the* Nykøbing and let the others fight to differentiate themselves? In truth, though, I hadn't for one minute expected to find concrete evidence that Jante Law was alive and well in Nykøbing in the early twenty-first century but, just to make sure, once I had parked the car down beside the still, dark waters of the Limfjord, I took a quick stroll up the high street before my appointment at the library.

Nykøbing's high street looked much like every other provincial Danish high street, at least at first glance. There was a book/gift store with birthday cards on a revolving stand outside, some mid-range men's clothes shops selling the usual dark jeans, polo shirts and three-buttoned jackets that Danish men favour for just about every occasion, a hairdresser's, tobacconist's and wine store, a pub and a pharmacy. All typical small-town stuff. It was only as I walked back down the street and looked again at the names of the shops that I noticed something curious. My heart sang! The shop names! They were quite extraordinarily prosaic, almost aggressively mundane or, as the Danes would say, *tilbageholdende* (back-holding, or 'reserved'), devoid of even the slightest suggestion of promotion or branding.

The hairdresser's was called, baldly, 'Hair'. The pub was called 'The Pub'. The shop that sold clothes and shoes ventured to grab the attention of passers-by with the razzle-dazzle name 'Clothes and Shoes'; the bookshop was *Bog Handler* or 'Book Dealer'. Clearly affronted by its neighbours' shameless self-promotion, one retailer had simply taken to naming itself 'No. 16'; another, clearly wary of accusations of hubris, had plumped simply for *Shoppen*, or 'The Shop'. These retailers were not merely lacking in marketing skills, they defiantly renounced all conventional notions of salesmanship.

Only one shop dared to break free from the herd and boldly proclaim the eponymity of its owner and risk standing out from the Nykøbing retail crowd: 'Bettina's Shoes'.

'Watch out, Bettina,' I thought to myself, as I carried on down the high street. 'They aren't much for that kind of showboating in these parts.'

At the library I asked Bent Dupont, chairman of the Aksel Sandemose Society, whether he felt Jante Law was still evident in Nykøbing or Danish society (all the while stroking my camera, knowingly).

'No, no, it was relevant in those days when Sandemose wrote it, but not today,' Dupont, a kindly retired teacher-type with round glasses, told me. 'The Jante Law he wrote about, where everyone holds everyone else down, and each believes the other is in cahoots with the rest of the people around them, the "You shall not think you are anything" attitude, is dead. The only place it still exists is in the Danish media. It's used by celebrities, writers, film-makers, sports stars. Take Bille August [the Danish Oscar-winning director]. When he directs a bad film and then gets bad reviews, he always says, "Oh, that's Jante Law." If anything, these days we have positive Jante Law – "You *shall* think you are something."'

Silently, I turned on my camera and cued up the photos I had taken of Nykøbing's high street. Dupont flicked through them, a smile slowly spreading across his face, until by the end he was – to my great relief – laughing. 'I get your point. I can see there is an element of people holding back there,' he said.

To be fair to Dupont, most Danes would claim that the Jante Law attitude is in decline. I did sense its influence more when I first started to visit Denmark many years ago, probably because I was young, ambitious and somewhat arrogant. I hadn't yet learned the mysterious code of the Danes, whose outward similarities to the Brits, I soon discovered, masked far deeper differences. Over time I have probably also gravitated away from Danes with Jante tendencies – as one does from people with whom one has little in common – but I do still sometimes come up against traces of it when I venture outside my social circle, where it typically manifests itself in the form of confusion-verging-on-mild-scorn when I try to explain what I do, or have done, for a living. From time to time I have been lucky enough to travel with my work, to stay in extravagant places, eat indulgent meals and drive expensive cars, but I tend to tone down recollections of those elements of my life when talking to Danes I don't know very well. It only causes confusion and upset.

Some recent examples I have encountered of Jante Law at large: there was the friend who bought a new Mercedes and was forced to endure 'Did anyone order a cab?' jokes for some time afterwards from his brother (the same model was used by Copenhagen's taxi companies); another friend whose wife ruled out a house purchase because the house in question, though in fact a little cheaper than the others they had viewed, had a modest swimming pool, and a swimming pool was deemed de trop. 'We don't need a swimming pool,' she had said. 'What would we need a swimming pool for?'

One friend of mine, the newspaper columnist Annegrethe Rasmussen, sparked a recent Jante Law debate when she wrote about her experiences of coming home from Washington DC, where she lives, and telling her friends about her son's performance at school. 'As a kind of quick way in to the subject,' Annegrethe told me shortly after the column was published, 'I said, "He's doing really well, he is number one in his class." And the table went silent.' Though she is Danish, and so should have known better, she realised immediately that she had breached the code. 'If I had said he was great at role-playing or drawing it would have been fine, but it was totally wrong to boast about academic achievement.'

'Jante Law is just as normal as the law of gravity,' newspaper editor and anthropologist Anne Knudsen assured me. 'You find it everywhere, especially in peasant societies, and back [in Sandemose's day] there were peasants peasants peasants all over the place in Denmark. This kind of ideology became the State ideology when democracy was established in the country [in 1849] and it got a second life with Social Democracy, and all of this was transmitted from generation to generation by propaganda and by a unified school system.' She added, 'But, you know, the envy part is not the important part. The important part is the inclusiveness: we want to include you, but that is only possible if you are equal. It's what peasants do.'

I opened a newspaper to see if I could spot signs of Jante Law in action today and, what do you know, there was a story about the Swedish Tetra Pak heir Hans Rausing's drug-fuelled downfall: the gloating headline reads 'His Billions Could Not Save Him'. Another concerns the bankruptcy of a flamboyant Danish businessman from a humble background who amassed a collection of snazzy cars and foreign homes and made the mistake of parading them in the media over the years. Again, the article is dripping with Jante revenge, detailing the luxuries he has had to give up: 'Three years ago he told this newspaper proudly of his Bugatti, his Lamborghini and the Porsche he was about to buy,' the article read. 'Now he has run dry of cash.' All newspapers, wherever they are in the world, relish a good downfall, but the Danes do seem to love them just that little bit more.

Jante Law moves in mysterious ways. Some Danes are exempt from it: the most glaring anomaly is their royal family (which we will return to), but successful artists are generally approved of, although it is preferred that they come from a solid middle- or working-class background and consistently demonstrate that their achievements have not changed them in any way. And actors or directors must express their disdain for the hullabaloo of the red carpet, and stress that they shop in Netto and change nappies like everybody else.

Success in, or the accumulation of wealth from, less obviously artistic fields is harder for the Danes to process. The chef René Redzepi of Noma has told me of being spat at in the street and ordered to 'go back home' (his father is Macedonian) by fellow Danes, most notably after a documentary about his restaurant (named the best in the world three years in a row by a British catering trade magazine) aired on Danish TV. The Danish media called his team at Noma the 'seal fuckers' when they first began to serve their revolutionary New Nordic cuisine. Who did they think they were to be meddling with traditional Danish food? The Danes also seem to begrudge the wealth earned by sports stars (the fact that many become tax exiles doesn't help, of course), and have mixed feelings about the adulation of pop singers, too.

I have often wondered about the pre-Sandemose roots of Jante Law. After all, Sandemose claimed merely to be observing existing Danish traits, so those tendencies must already have been present. Professor Richard Wilkinson had told me that people from more egalitarian societies have less need to show off, so perhaps that is where Jante's roots lie: the Danes are especially scornful of people who boast because they prize equality so highly. 'Hunter-gatherer societies – which are similar to prehistoric societies – are highly egalitarian,' Wilkinson had said. 'And if someone starts to take on a more domineering position they get ridiculed or teased or ostracised. These are what's called counter-dominance strategies, and they maintain the greater equality.'

Or could it be that their Lutheran heritage means the people of the North still baulk at success in frivolous, individualistic or elitist pursuits, and frown upon conspicuous displays of wealth? Though the Danes limit their church attendance to the big-ticket events only – Christmas, weddings, christenings – and churches are closing across the country on an almost weekly basis, Christianity still plays a central role in notions of Danishness and how Danes should behave. Unlike Sweden, there is no separation between Church and State in Denmark and, after some years off the curriculum, religion is once again a compulsory subject in schools.

Perhaps this is why working hard to get rich and then exhibiting your success is still very much disapproved of. Danish tycoons and captains of industry are rarely role models here. The late shipping and oil magnate – and probably the wealthiest non-royal Dane of all time – Mærsk Mc-Kinney Møller was respected but neither loved nor a role model. Møller wisely chose not to display his wealth too gratuitously. According to the Mærsk Corporate Communications department, he also abided by a strict work ethic, attending meetings well into his nineties, bringing a packed lunch with him to work, and climbing several flights of stairs to his office every day. Together with many generous donations to public works – he paid for Copenhagen's opera house, among other projects – this seemed to help him avoid much of a Jante Law backlash.

What is the foreigner to make of Jante Law? How does one negotiate its boobytraps and trip-wires? There are two approaches to take: one is to play the stupid foreigner card, proceed as you would at home and feign obliviousness to the frowns as you sail through Danish society boasting of your successes and acquisitions.

Or you can keep your head down, your socks up and your nose clean. Becoming a teacher would help.

Whichever route you choose, to live at ease in Denmark and assimilate with the Danes it pays to be alert to Jante Law. But I am afraid there are two other key social phenomena you are going to have to get to grips with if a life in Denmark beckons.

Chapter 12

Dixieland

Alongside Jante Law, there are two other prime drivers of Danish conformism – *hygge* and *folkelig*. They are tricky to translate: the former is a deceptively relaxed and informal, uniquely Danish form of cosiness or conviviality, which is actually highly codified, with strict social rituals that exercise a relentless, tyrannical pressure to conform; the latter is a kind of broad-based cultural populism that pervades a good deal of Danish mainstream culture and, in a kind of reverse-Midas effect, turns everything it touches to cack.

Let us start with *hygge*, for the Danes prize it more than ambergris and stardust. While it is true that you can often simply substitute the word 'cosy' for *hygge* * – 'Didn't we have a *hyggelig* time at the pub quiz yesterday?' 'Aren't those candles *hyggelig*?', and so on – the closest available English translation still fails to encompass the full import of the word. Then there is the word *uhyggelig*, which doesn't, as you would expect, mean un-*hyggelig* (for that you would say *ikke hyggelig*, or not *hyggelig*), but instead means anything from 'spooky' or 'scary' to 'unnecessarily confrontational', 'suspicious', or 'uncanny'. Unemployment figures might be said to be *uhyggelig*, for instance; I don't think I have ever heard statistics defined by whether or not they were cosy.

In theory you can have a *hyggelig* experience with anyone, anywhere and at any time; and you can have it with an almost limitless number of people at once; you can even *hygge* yourself, although that always seems somehow deviant to me. *Hygge* need not cost a

---

* Or, if you are German, *gemütlichkeit*, or Dutch *gezelligheid*.

penny. It is entirely democratic and egalitarian, open to all (assuming, of course, you understand the rules, for which it is necessary to either be Danish or have had extensive tutoring from a benevolent Dane). And then there is *råhygge*, literally 'raw *hygge*', the especially intense form – *überhygge*, if you like. You'd better know what you are doing if you dabble with *råhygge*, I can tell you.

Upon initial acquaintance, *hygge* would appear to fall into the 'what's not to love?' column of Scandinavian social mores, conjuring as it does visions of free-flowing wine, open fires, candlelight and good times. *Hygge* requires equality of participation (it is decidedly *uhygglig* for one person to hog the limelight), and is predicated on the participants living in the moment ('Isn't this barbecue *hyggelig* [the barbecue that is happening right here, right now]?'). As ethnographer Stephen Borish wrote in his analysis of the phenomenon, 'It depends on the complete and positive participation of all present in the encounter . . . an evenness of flow, a sustained back-and-forth dance of involvement that encourages, and even demands, this level of participation . . . the achievement of these goals is made possible by a range of positive social skills, including teasing (a national pastime), quick repartee, the telling of stories and jokes, patience, sensitivity, and the ability to be an enthusiastic audience as well as a performer.'

But I am afraid to say that over the years I have come to detest *hygge* somewhat. It wasn't the cheap, fizzy beer (how did they *ever* have the nerve to claim it was 'probably the best'? It's like claiming Sunblest is the best bread), the curried herring or the communal singing in which the Danes inevitably indulge when more than two of them gather together and which can drag out a formal Danish dinner to interminable lengths,* that ultimately turned me against *hygge*; it was more *hygge*'s tyrannical, relentless drive towards

---

* Oh, the number of festive occasions where I have sat patiently awaiting dessert as midnight strikes and yet another aged aunt hands round the photocopied lyrics to a popular song, which she has rewritten to incorporate humourous references from the celebrant's life.

middle-ground consensus; its insistence on the avoidance of any potentially controversial topics of conversation; its need to keep things light and breezy – the whole comfortable, self-congratulatory, petit bourgeois smugness of it all.

As Danish anthropologist Jeppe Trolle Linnet once wrote, 'When people *hygge*, they engage in a mutual sheltering of each other from the pressures of competition and social evaluation.' In this way *hygge* can seem like self-administered social gagging, characterised more by a self-satisfied sense of its own exclusivity than notions of shared conviviality. Linnet also wrote that *hygge* 'acts as a vehicle for social control, establishes its own hierarchy of attitudes, and implies a negative stereotyping of social groups who are perceived as unable to create *hygge*.' The inference here is that only Danes really know how to have a properly *hyggelig* time; pity those poor foreigners with their la-di-da cocktail parties, their gladiatorial dinner-party discussions, and sophisticated soirées. Similarly, British anthropologist Richard Jenkins has described *hygge* as 'normative to the point of coercive'.

That was my experience when I first arrived in Denmark. I soon discovered that playing devil's advocate to stimulate discussion is unwelcome, for instance, as is spirited debate on political and social issues. Such things make the Danes shift their buttocks awkwardly. I am exaggerating a bit, I'll admit, but it is true that the Danes do not generally appreciate the ding-dong of heated discussion when they gather socially. They much prefer to occupy themselves with the nitty-gritty of where the wine was bought, how little it cost, and whether the bottle they are currently drinking is better than the last one.

I am not alone in this view. 'We in Sweden ridicule the Danes for their insularity and their so-called *hygge* – just have a cosy time with your family and friends,' one Swedish academic told me. 'There are some sociologists who have looked at Danish xenophobia and racism and they refer to *hygge* and how the Danes like to put up fences between themselves and the rest of the world and draw back and be comfortable and cosy.'

This overarching desire to foster an unchallenging, informal, *hyggelig* atmosphere chimes with my post-colonial 'drawbridge theory' – the 'What was lost without . . .' way of valuing what little cultural and economic capital Denmark had left after the loss of its empire, and the way in which the country turned its gaze inward. The need to cling together, to identify shared values and stick resolutely to them regardless of prevailing winds or fashion, could well have its roots in the history of Danish territorial loss. They clung together on their flat little life raft, and soon learned not to rock the boat. *Hygge* is a highly effective way to skirt controversial topics, or sweep unhappy memories under the carpet – 'Okay, all right, so we had Norway and Schleswig-Holstein and lost it all, but do we really need to talk about it? How about another bottle of Amarone? Aunty Inge: a song!'

The Danes pride themselves on their informality: the men rarely wear ties, teachers are on first-name terms with their pupils, Danish politicians cycled to parliament long before it was a fashionable cause. Yet, like every other race on earth, they still have their social rules and formal procedures. Even when the Danes appear to be at their most informal, often it will be a highly ritualised informality. In fact, this is when the foreigner should be most on his guard, because this is when the traps are set: the beer may be poured, but wait for the host to lift their glass and say *skål* before you taste it; there may be rye bread and salmon on the same buffet, but the salmon always goes on white bread; and, please, don't ask what Great Uncle Oluf did during the war.

Christmas is the most ritualised event of the Danish calendar. You could write a whole book about Danish Christmas traditions (and, my Danish publisher told me with a weary sigh, many have); from circling the tree singing carols, via the 'almond game' (in which an almond is concealed deep inside a gigantic rice pudding, all of which must be eaten before the winner reveals they have the nut in their mouth), to joining hands to form a chain, then running through every room in the house singing '*Nu er det jul igen*' ('Now it is Christmas again'), and so on. The Danes have put in serious training to perfect the Christmas experience and, to be fair, even a toxic old humbug like me can't help but enjoy it.

There are many other special days in the Danish calendar: *Sankt Hans* we have already encountered; there is also *Fastelavn* (Shrovetide) when they beat a cat with a stick (or, at least, they used to; now they whack a barrel filled with sweets); *Store Bededag* (Great Prayer Day), a random religious holiday that falls on the fourth Friday after Easter; and something called *Mortensaften* (I never have been able to figure out what this is, but it is in November and they eat a duck). Then there are all the various anniversaries and birthday parties which, with their sit-down meals, speeches, songs and toasts, tend to adhere to a strict template (for a good idea of what this involves, I direct you to the film *Festen*, although not all Danish parties feature impromptu revelations of incest and suicide), as do weddings, christenings and confirmations – the latter a fast-growing industry of their own.

Thinking about it, you could argue that the Danes have developed complex rituals and social signifiers that are every bit as impenetrable to outsiders as those of, say, the Jains in India, or Hasidic Jews: from the order in which you tackle the *kolde bord* (the Danish equivalent of a smorgasbord, or lunch buffet), to the way you introduce yourself to fellow guests at a party, or how you discuss your children's performance at school.

As for *folkelig*, I have an even less ambiguous relationship to that: I loathe it. I loathe its whole Dixieland-jazz-in-a-beer-garden forced bonhomie; its lowest-common-denominator, often xenophobic humour; the assumption that all people require from their entertainment is to be anaesthetised by the lazy pastiche of the ever-popular summer review shows ('Look, a man dressed as the queen!'); and all they want from the caterers is industrial beer and processed pork products. But that's just me. Lots of people like it, and I acknowledge that I am a hateful snob.

Folkelig pervades a great deal of Danish popular culture and life. One must remain vigilant at all times if one is to have any hope of avoiding it. I failed to do this when I agreed to attend the residential choir week in Jutland I mentioned earlier. This was the single most intense period of exposure to *folkelig* I have ever experienced in my time in Denmark, involving six days singing popular hits of the seventies and eighties together with four hundred retired public-sector workers. By midway through the second day I was experiencing a profound identity crisis; by the third day I was making plans to leave Denmark for ever; but by the fourth day I had become strangely becalmed by the easy-listening arrangements and collectivist atmosphere.

As Friday's concert grew nearer, nerves began to fray slightly, but voices were never raised and our endlessly patient choirmasters coaxed and cajoled us across the finish line with just a few notes missed and the odd line dropped. There were no rows or diva-like tantrums.* In the evenings of the choir week, after rehearsing all day, we would reassemble in the wake of a meal usually featuring some meat, boiled potatoes and thick brown sauce of indeterminate origin and eaten at long tables in the school cafeteria with a plastic beaker of warm Chilean Cabernet Sauvignon, to sing Danish folk songs and hymns, the lyrics of which spoke of the Danish seasons and countryside, community and fellowship, death, and loss, in tones that were fond and ironic, modest yet proud.

Many of them had been written by Benny Andersen, the great

---

* This is not strictly true; there was one – from me. At the conclusion of his specially arranged 1980s medley, one of the choirmasters had included two lines of rap from Grandmaster Flash's 1982 hit 'The Message', to be spoken in a 'forceful' style by the basses and tenors. I pointed out that in the line 'Don't push me 'cos I'm close to the edge', you pronounced it 'th*e* edge', not 'th*ee* edge', or, at least, that's how Mr Flash had rapped it. But a 65-year-old ex-English teacher in the bass section was having none of it and rallied the rest of the section behind him. The correct pronunciation was 'th*ee* edge' he said, crossing his arms and shaking his head in disgust. I persisted, pointing out that my version was both more authentic and had a more percussive impact. The choirmaster agreed, but the elderly ex-teacher and his bass cronies stubbornly sang his version throughout the rehearsals and in the final concert, amid a mutual crossfire of glares.

Danish folk poet, now eighty-three years old. Andersen even turned up in person for an evening in his honour, during which we sang his wry, bittersweet songs about Denmark ('This little, neurotic land of smiling crazy people,' is one of his best-known lines) and listened to reminiscences from his career. Andersen is an important cultural icon to these people, and at the end of his appearance the ladies of a certain age were false-starting each other to be the first to give him a standing ovation.

I feel a bit of a heel being critical about the kind, good-natured, gentle folk who attended the choir week in Tønder. It is easy to mock their Gary Larson aesthetic (sandals with socks, cut-down denim shorts with their shirts tucked in, and so on), and their Ned Flanders sensibilities. In truth, a more contented, kind, honest, community-minded group of people you could never hope to meet. The problem was that, for a cynical misanthrope such as myself, *folkelig* has much the same effect as Kryptonite on Superman, or water on the Wicked Witch of the West. I become weak and confused, and begin to question who I am. Prolonged exposure to *folkelig* undoes me, smothers me, suffocates me. It's because I am bad.

One particularly visible manifestation of *folkelig* which can be especially discordant for visitors is that central ornament of the *folkelig*, or *hyggelig* occasion: the Danish flag, the *Dannebrog*. The Danes genuinely believe that they have the most beautiful flag in the world, and will hoist it given the slightest opportunity – birthdays, funerals, anniversaries, any old social event. Flags are used to decorate gift-wrapping paper, to grace birthday cards and are stuck in cakes and buffets. Richard Jenkins cleverly deduced that a *Dannebrog* flying on a Tuesday often signifies a twenty-fifth wedding anniversary, because 'allowing for leap years, the twenty-fifth anniversary of any original matrimonial Saturday will fall on a Tuesday'. He claimed that the Danes spend up to DKK60 million (£6 million) a year on flags. Various rituals and rules attend to the use of the *Dannebrog* – it must never be allowed to touch the ground, must be lowered before it gets dark, and so on. It stirs the Danes' collective hearts and can genuinely bring tears to their eyes to see the *Dannebrog* fluttering in the breeze, or painted on a child's face – as I said, I remember my mother's horrified look when my wife wheeled in the cake for my son's first birthday and it was crowned with a ring of Danish flags, and the bewilderment I felt when my in-laws telephoned to tell me they had raised their flag in their front garden on the occasion of my own birthday (virtually every Danish home, summer home and even children's Wendy house has a flagpole outside).

From a British perspective, the Danes' enthusiasm for their flag can be quite unsettling – like finding out a much-loved friend votes for UKIP. When you spot the *Dannebrog* on the packaging of innumerable products in Danish supermarkets (everything from potatoes to washing-up liquid), or flying from buses on the occasion of some or other minor royal's birthday, it can sometimes seem like the entire country has been set-designed by Leni Riefenstahl. But the truth about the Danes' love of their flag is not as sinister as first impressions might have you believe. Though the *Dannebrog* has been slightly tainted in recent years by the Danish People's Party's xenophobic nationalism (a while back they attempted to pass a law to put the Danish flag on car number plates, but failed), the Danes do not see their flag-waving as a nationalistic gesture. It's just, well, *hyggelig*.

'Other countries love their flags,' a Danish dinner guest protested to me recently. 'Look at the Olympics!'

'Yes,' I said. 'That's true. But the French don't hoist the *Tricolor* on the cat's birthday.'

Richard Jenkins has written about the Danes' curious attachment to their flag in his book *Being Danish: Paradoxes of Identity in Everyday Life*. He doesn't see it as wholly negative.

'Not all nationalism is bad, for a start,' he told me over the phone from his home in Sheffield. 'The point is, the Danes use their flag in lots of different ways. It is *the* most complicated flag in terms of its use. Over the last 150 years it has become identified with happiness and good times, celebration.'

Jenkins's interest in the *Dannebrog* was initially piqued when he arrived at a Danish airport for the first time and saw, as is often the case, crowds of Danes waving the Danish flag to welcome home their friends and families.

'I wondered what was going on. Had there been a member of the royal family on the plane and I had missed them?' he said. He thinks that the Danes are such ardent flag-wavers because, as a small country with Sweden and Germany for neighbours, they have a much greater need to express their national identity and, if anything, they are growing even more attached to the *Dannebrog*. 'It has steadily become ever more visible as a marketing device and decoration,' he writes, noting that, despite this, the Danes were surprisingly blasé about seeing it being burned in the streets of Damascus during the Mohammed cartoon crisis of 2005, perhaps because they weren't real *Dannebrogs* and it wasn't Danes who were doing the burning.

Jenkins also recalls seeing a display of bananas in a supermarket bedecked with Danish flags. The flags were simply to draw the attention of shoppers to a special offer, 'But I was a bit perplexed. I thought to myself, "They don't grow bananas in Denmark."'

Chapter 13

Pendulous breasts

After taking in the Jelling stones, I continued my exploration of the Rotten Banana, driving west across Jutland through forests of Christmas trees, past fields filled with purple lupins, grazing cows (the pigs remaining hidden away in prisoner-of-war-type sheds) and gigantic wind turbines. I passed through small towns with the same chain stores, the same kebab shop, about ten banks and always a charity shop or two – the Rotten Banana is awash with charity shops. There would be a bakery selling the same rye bread and pastries (the Danes don't call them 'Danish pastries', by the way, they are *weinerbrød*, or Vienna bread, after the city in which the style of baking was invented), and each town would, without fail, have a piece of civic art, usually, for some reason, a sculpture of a fat woman, or small fat figures climbing on a boulder.

You find this kind of body-dysmorphic sculpture all over Denmark; there are even entire galleries full of such *folkelig–hyggelig* 'art' in Copenhagen. The most strikingly unattractive example of what I came to think of as the 'Comedy Fatty' school of art is in *Ringkøbing*, which I passed through on my drive up the west coast: here, on the harbourfront of this otherwise very pretty fishing village, stands a statue of a fat, naked Western woman with pendulous breasts, sitting on the shoulders of an emaciated African with cartoonish big lips and a loin cloth. She holds scales of justice but, just in case you don't get the message, a small plaque informs you that the piece is called *Survival of the Fattest*, and that 'it has been exhibited at several international NGO meetings'. Ah, NGO art. Ironically, *Survival of the Fattest* stands literally within sight of several outdoor harbourfront restaurants whose menus consist mostly of stuff that's been dropped in vats of hot oil.

Through more forests and fields and past more windmills I drove on endless straight roads. Just outside of a small town called Brande, at the very moment when the monotony of Jutland was really beginning to get to me, I passed on my left, in the midst of the trees, a cathedral-sized Hindu temple replete with multicoloured, god-encrusted ziggurat. I screeched to a halt, reversed, and jumped out, standing for a good couple of minutes taking in this extraordinary mirage.

This, it turned out, was the Sree Abirami Amman temple, the spiritual focal point for the several thousand Tamil refugees who came to Denmark from Sri Lanka in the 1970s. I walked inside the entrance hall. The smell of sandalwood and jasmine was intense, transporting me back to India. As I peered in through the inner glass doors into the temple proper, a young woman wearing a thick winter coat over a green and gold sari approached me, smiling.

She explained that the temple was overseen by a priestess, Sri Abirami Upasaki, or 'Amma', who performed daily rituals at 1 p.m. and 7 p.m. As it was nearly 7 p.m., she invited me to stay and watch.

Soon after, a petite woman, swaddled from head to toes in orange robes, emerged from an old thatched cottage in the shadow of the temple and shuffled towards us. This was Amma. She glanced at me and then carried on inside, followed by a small middle-aged man, who smiled and nodded.

'Have you eaten any meat today?' he asked.

I had, I said. 'A really great hand-cut steak tartare in a bistro in . . .' I began to enthuse about the meal. He held up his hand: 'Then you may not enter the temple.'

This was a vegetarians-only performance, so I watched through the glass doors of the temple as Amma waddled around in a cloud of incense, ringing bells, performing blessings and saying prayers, all the while being filmed by the younger woman for their daily online streaming service.

Apparently, Amma has cured all manner of maladies, from

infertility to cancer. She diagnoses ailments by rolling a lime over the patient, then slicing the fruit in half, curing whatever she finds by anointing them with holy water.

'Does it really work?' I asked the young woman.

'Sometimes it works. She has made miracles. I have seen people come here mad, they were not in our world, and leave normal and healthy, now married with kids.'

Even more remarkably, every 31 December, during a ceremony held at midnight, blood pours from Amma's mouth, her face turns blue or black, and marks appear on the palms of her hands. After that evening's – less eventful – ceremony, I talked a little with Amma, a shy woman who spoke heavily accented Danish in a virtual whisper.

She came to Denmark, from Jaffna in 1974, when she was nine, she told me. I asked her about her first impressions.

'I loved it,' she said. 'It was so peaceful, the people were so sweet.'

She received her energy from God and transmitted it through her hands, she explained. She also gave advice to pilgrims, many of them Danes. I wondered if Amma had heard the theories about why the Danes were so happy.

'Yes, they are happy. They are not so busy. A little less stressed. Lovely,' she said.

And with that, she bowed slightly and shuffled off to her little thatched cottage.

From the temple I drove across to Jutland's west coast which, with its vast sandy beaches, tempestuous surf and sprawling favelas of summer houses, draws tens of thousands of Danish and German holidaymakers every summer to places like Blåvand and Søndervig, with their old-fashioned seaside vibe, shops selling inflatable boats and fishing nets, soft ices, and so on. I felt a twinge of nostalgia for the British resorts of my childhood. All along the coast, thatched holiday homes nestled in the bosom of grassy dunes, like Hobbit houses sheltering from the ceaseless gales.

I followed the coast road north until, without warning from my GPS, it ended abruptly at the Nissum estuary. Getting out of my car to stretch my legs, an immense gust of fishy stink hit me from the huge seafood-processing plant a few hundred metres away. I chatted with a man who was also waiting for the small roll-on, roll-off open-air ferry, which we could now see slowly chugging towards us from the other side of the inlet, like a floating garden trug. I told him I was on a tour of *udkantsdanmark*. 'Ha!' he laughed, gesturing around us. 'This is *extreme udkants!*'

Nevertheless, it had also drawn two German tourists: a couple, who waited behind me in the queue in their van. The man told me that they were on a pilgrimage, visiting locations from the 'Olsen Band' films. The Olsen Band (or Olsen Gang) are great Danish *folkelig* icons, three ill-starred, fictional petty criminals who featured in a string of highly successful domestic comedies in the seventies and eighties. The films were remade with both Swedish and Norwegian casts, making them a bona fide pan-Scandinavian cultural phenomenon. I haven't seen those versions, but the original Danish films have a certain period charm, with a similar 1970s mainstream humour to the *Carry On* films, and with a Norman Wisdom 'little man' subtext. Some have gone so far as to interpret the gang's, usually unsuccessful, dealings with big business and the establishment as sociopolitical commentary and, accordingly, they were quite successful in East Germany, hence, I suppose, the pilgrims.

I stayed the night in Thisted, a proud, well-kept town beside the Limfjord, and then pottered back west, taking in what was, according to the national broadsheet *Jyllands-Posten*, Denmark's most boring town: Hørdum. Hørdum has become something of an emblem for the 'udkantisisation' of Denmark, having seen its train station and dairy close, its school shut down, and the last of its sixty shops disappear. It was quite the most dreary place; a charmless street of single-storey houses with corrugated roofs. Towns like Hørdum are the reason Danish researchers have warned that by 2050 only 10 per cent of the population will remain in the countryside. Currently around a quarter of the population remains, but the flow continues inexorably towards the cities – 75 per cent of new jobs in Denmark are created in Copenhagen, and the capital is responsible for around half of the country's GDP. Within the next couple of decades places like Hørdum will likely be ghost towns.

Returning south, I took a detour to Billund to complete my trilogy of Jutland's top spiritual sights after the Jelling stones and the Hindu temple, this time stopping off at Denmark's great secular place of worship, Legoland.

Here is a tip which could save you many times the cover price of this book: after five o'clock, admission to Legoland is free! Okay, the downside is that the rides are closed, but I couldn't get enough of the sprawling Lego citiscapes, with their desolate streets and eerily trundling cars. Towering over Copenhagen, I had an overwhelming urge to run amok like Godzilla.

It is an eccentric mix of subjects that the Lego builders have chosen to immortalise in injection-moulded acrylonitrile butadiene styrene bricks, ranging, seemingly at random, from Hollywood's Chinese Theatre to the Göta Canal. I particularly enjoyed the ever-so-subtle digs at the Danes' Nordic neighbours – the model of an exasperated, bearded Swede who stands, pulling his hair out in a rage, beside his broken-down Volvo, and the flashy Ferraris of nouveau-riche Norwegians on the streets of oil-rich Bergen.

If you visit Legoland hoping for a wholesome, non-commercial, Lutheran take on a theme park you will be disappointed. The first thing you see as you enter is a large bank, and from that point on it is all about being parted from your money via the myriad temptations of low-grade hot dogs, virus-coloured slush ice, greasy burgers and, of course, Lego kits. The world's largest Lego store is here. Pride of place goes to the company's new 'girly' range, called 'Friends'. Judging by the pictures on the boxes, Friends is hardly a shining beacon of Nordic gender equality: the figures seem mostly preoccupied with reclining in jacuzzis, making cupcakes and getting their hair done.

I was in search of a true Lego icon. If I am honest, the real goal of my Jutland odyssey was to buy my very own Lego Death Star. I had hoped that, here in the bosom of the Lego corporation, it might be a little cheaper than in Lego's flagship store on Strøget in

Copenhagen. Surely Legoland would offer a discount for the faithful who had made the pilgrimage through the Jutlandish hinterlands.

Finally, I found it. That receptacle of cherished memories and childhood dreams. On its front was a picture of the famous and magnificent orb of evil rendered with uncanny perfection in knobbly plastic bricks. Gingerly, breathlessly, I turned the box over in my hands trying to find the price, transported back thirty years by the familiar tinkling sounds as hundreds of pieces shifted around inside. A tear welled.

And then I found it: four hundred quid! For a box of coloured plastic! Do me a fucking favour . . .

Chapter 14

The happiness delusion

'We Danes are a hard pressed folk. No one pays as much
tax as we do. No one works so much, no one has more
physical illnesses as us, no one has more expensive cars,
no one has more impossible children or worse schools.'

Rasmus Bech, writing in *Politiken*, April 2012

Hr Bech might do well to check the figures for the Danes' working
hours (and he neglects to mention the awful weather), but, that
aside, he does a fine job of highlighting key elements of the Danish
happiness paradox. On the face of it, the Danes have considerably
less to be happy about than most of us, yet, when asked, they still
insist that they are the happiest of us all.

What is one to make of this? Are the Danes really as happy as
they claim? Or is this land of 12 million pigs telling porkies?

The obvious answer to this is 'Define happiness.' If we are talking
sombrero-wearing, heel-kicking, cocktail-umbrella *joie de vivre*, then
the Danes do not score highly, and I suspect not even they would
take their claims that far. But if we are talking about being contented
with one's lot, or (self-)satisfied, then the Danes do have a more
convincing case to present.

Over the years I have asked many Danes about these happiness
surveys – whether they really believe that they are the global happiness champions – and I have yet to meet a single one of them who
seriously believes it's true. They appreciate the safety net of their
welfare state, the way most things function well in their country,
and all the free time they have, and they are proud of the recent
international success of all the TV shows they have exported, but

they tend to approach the subject of their much-vaunted happiness like the victims of a practical joke waiting to discover who the perpetrator is.

On the other hand, these same Danes are often just as quick to counter any criticism of their country – of their schools, hospitals, transport, weather, taxes, politicians, taste in music, uneventful landscape, and so on – with the simple and, in a sense, argument-proof riposte: 'Well, if that's true, how come we are the happiest people in the world?' (this usually accompanied by upturned palms and a tight, smug smile). So I guess the happiness argument does come in useful sometimes.

I've mentioned my suspicion that this phenomenon has become a self-fulfilling prophecy for Danes: aware that they have a reputation to maintain in these international questionnaires, they pretend to be happier than they actually are. Anne Knudsen had another theory relating to why the Danes continue to respond positively to happiness surveys: 'In Denmark it is shameful to be unhappy,' she told me. 'If you ask me how I am and I start telling you how bad I feel then it might force you to do something about it. It might put a burden on you to help me. So, that's one of the main reasons people say things are all right, or even "super".'

Here's another convincing theory, posited by a Danish friend of mine: 'We always come top of those surveys because they ask us at the beginning of the year what our expectations are,' he said. 'Then they ask us at the end of the year whether those expectations were met. And because our expectations are so extremely low at the beginning of the year, they tend to get met more easily.'

Could *that* be the secret of the Danes' contentedness? Low expectations? It is true that, when asked how they expect the next year to pan out, the Danes do typically expect less than the rest of us, and when their low expectations are fulfilled, so are they. Happiness has never been an 'inalienable right' in Denmark, so it could be that the Danes appreciate it all the more when it manifests itself – their turbulent history of loss has made them grateful for any crumbs of joy that come their way. Perhaps Danish happiness is not really happiness at all, but something much more valuable and durable: contentedness, being satisfied with your lot, low-level needs being met, higher expectations being kept in check.

What do the Danes say makes them happy? A recent survey by a Danish newspaper brought these insights: 74 per cent cited being together with friends as their greatest source of happiness; family came second with 70 per cent; foreign travel was a perhaps unsurprising third choice; with sport taking precedence over eating or watching TV (yeah, right). Then again, another survey revealed that a remarkable 54 per cent of Danes do not fear death – perhaps *that's* their secret?

A few years ago, a professor of epidemiology at the University of Southern Denmark, Kaare Christensen, published a slightly tongue-in-cheek overview of what he saw as the possible reasons for the Danes' happiness, entitled 'Why Danes Are Smug: A Comparative Study of Life Satisfaction in the European Union'. His explanations ranged from the fact that the Danes might have been drunk when responding to questionnaires to their surprise 1992 European Championship victory (not only did they beat Germany in the final, but it took place in Sweden: a joyous confluence of multiple revenge fantasies). But Christensen and his team also concluded that low expectations were key: 'If expectations are unrealistically high they could also be the basis of disappointment and low life satisfaction,' writes Christensen. 'Year after year they are pleasantly surprised to find that not everything is getting more rotten in the state of Denmark.'

Christensen isn't the first to accuse the Danes of smugness, by the way: writing in her travelogue of the Nordic region, the eighteenth-century women's rights pioneer Mary Wollstonecraft had this to say on the subject of the Danes' – to her mind over-inflated – self-image:

If happiness only consists in opinion, they are the happiest people in the world; for I never saw any so well satisfied with their own situation . . . The men of business are domestic tyrants, coldly immersed in their own affairs, and so ignorant of the state of other countries that they dogmatically assert that Denmark is the happiest country in the world.

It is a thin line indeed between relaxed and smug. The Danes do have a remarkably relaxed approach to life which, I admit, I have sometimes interpreted as immense self-satisfaction, but they do have a great deal to teach us about not taking life too seriously. They are a remarkably chillaxed people. The Danish language is rich with phrases designed to encourage the reduction of stress: *Slap af* ('Relax'), they will say, *Rolig nu* ('Easy now'), *Det er lige meget* ('It doesn't really matter'), *Glem det* ('Forget about it'), *Hold nu op* ('Give over'), *Pyt med det* (essentially a combination of all of the above). It's not a bad way to approach life, I think.

Of course, there is another possible explanation: it may well be that these happiness surveys are so riddled with flaws and paradoxes that we ought not to take them seriously in the first place. As we have heard, renowned epidemiologist Professor Richard Wilkinson scoffs at the notion of gauging and comparing different countries' happiness levels, and believes that health statistics paint a far more accurate picture of societal well-being. But where does that leave the Danes? Danish happiness hardly seems to accord with any 'Well, at least we have our health' approach to life, because they so patently haven't. Their consumption of cigarettes, alcohol and sugar has made them among the unhealthiest people in Europe.

Yet another theory: when we spoke, Christian Bjørnskov mentioned to me that no Danish political leader has been assassinated for centuries. He believed that political stability is an important cornerstone of happy societies. This may well be the case, but he neglects to take into account the traumatic upheavals Denmark underwent during the nineteenth and twentieth centuries – the British bombardment and the loss of those precious territories (Norway, Schleswig-Holstein, Iceland, and so on); the occupation by the Germans during the Second World War; as well as the threat of Soviet invasion or even nuclear annihilation for much of the rest of the twentieth century. And, actually, Denmark has experienced a number of quite major domestic political upheavals – the resignation of governments; the rise of the right wing; the Mohammed cartoon crisis, and so on. Though it is true that they have not lost a prime minister and foreign minister to random assassins, as Sweden has in recent years, Denmark has had a far from frictionless ride for the last two centuries. The crucial point, though, is that the Danes still *feel* as if their history has been relatively placid. They are exceptionally adept at covering their ears to history and chanting 'la la la' until the nasty noises go away.

There is no doubt that democracy, a strong welfare state, equality of wealth and opportunity (particularly in terms of education), are all crucial to the success of any society and its people, and I do think that their excellent housing stock and well-designed furniture contributes a great deal to the Danes' quality of life – and I don't mean that flippantly, they do live extraordinarily well – but they are far from unique in these aspects.

Where they are unique, or at least supreme, is in their trust and social cohesion. Personally, I remain fond of my hypothesis that this tight-knittedness is founded in a survivalist reaction to nineteenth-century territorial defenestration – that they pulled together in the face of calamity and learned to appreciate, and make the most of, what they had left, including each other. The 'What was lost without will be found within' theory has a great deal to recommend it, and seems to explain so many of the Danes' idiosyncracies, from their disproportionate satisfaction in small pleasures (a game of handball, a can of crappy beer, an industrially produced sugary pastry), to their dislike of conflict and ostentatious display.

The Danes are a notably forgiving bunch, something which I think ties in with their underlying fear of conflict. Lord knows the Danes have been involved in – and lost – more than their fair share of military conflicts over the years. Has this left them with a strong and instinctive aversion to disputes or ruckus, I wonder? Certainly *hygge* acts as a useful prophylactic against social friction (as we've heard, it tends to put a block on controversial topics of discussion).

But the Danes are also extremely forgiving of public figures who transgress social or legal rules. Long before Lance Armstrong's mea culpa, the Danish 1996 Tour de France winner, Bjarne Riis, admitted to having taken banned substances over many years, yet he remains prominent in the sport. Christian Stadil, the high-profile new-age boss of Danish clothing company Hummel, wrote a corporate self-help book based on his theory of 'Company Karma' and garnered a great deal of publicity from his support for Tibet's women's football team, yet he withdrew that support in order to sell more T-shirts in China, and his shipping company was revealed to be (legally) transporting arms – an activity of which one imagines, the cosmos would strongly disapprove. Little fuss was made and Stadil continues to spout his new-age corporate philosophy in the Danish media. Another example is the former prime minister, Anders Fogh Rasmussen, who led the Danes into the wars in Afghanistan and Iraq and led the country's lenders to ruin with his introduction of interest-only mortgages. While Tony Blair and George W. Bush have become hate figures to large swathes of their respective populations, Rasmussen has sailed on merrily as a Danish elder statesman and remains head of NATO. His cowardly role in the Mohammed cartoon crisis is almost never referred to, or questioned, by the Danish media. The sense is that the Danes, conscious that they have an extremely limited talent pool when it comes to international statesmen, are very reluctant to attack their prime candidate.

And then we have the fat tax. Introduced in 2011 by the then ruling Venstre party, this levy on products such as bacon and butter was a quite spectacular and costly political cock-up. Though it was cloaked as a health initiative, the tax was a purely money-raising exercise and the Danes were having none of it. They are the fiercest bargain hunters on the face of the earth (spending less on their groceries per week than any other nationality in Europe, for instance, something I find especially dispiriting considering their groceries also cost more than anyone else's) and, as we have heard, simply drove across the borders to Sweden or Germany to buy these products. The country's crucial butter and bacon industries suffered significantly as a result and the tax was eventually scrapped, yet, when I questioned the Venstre party's health spokesperson about the fiasco she told me breezily, 'Oh no, we don't support that any more.' No heads rolled. There were no recriminations, no resignations, just a collective shrug. Now, you can view this as a healthy, even civilised, approach to mistakes, or as a negligent attitude towards accountability, either way, it certainly helps keep the ripples on the surface of Danish society to a minimum.

This might well be another of the keys to the Danes' happiness – and I suspect this applies to any kind of long-term happiness. Proper, deep, enduring joy usually requires a remarkable facility for denial, something which the Danes have in spades. I do not, of course, mean self-denial here. As we can conclude from their alcohol, tobacco, hash and sugar intake, the Danes deny themselves few pleasures. I am talking, for instance, about their denial of what it costs to be Danish – the literal cost, via their taxes and the cost of goods in their shops but also the spiritual costs in terms of their relative lack of ambition and dynamism, the denial of those sometimes necessary conflicts, and the loss of freedom of expression and individualism denied them by Jante Law and *hygge*.

The Danes are in denial about their poor health, too. In surveys they claim that they have above-average health, though the reality is quite the opposite. They are in denial about their creaking public services; in denial about the increasingly rampant gang criminality which has resulted in numerous shootings in Copenhagen suburbs; in denial about the realities of integration and of being part of a globalised world; in denial about the growing economic and geographical divide within their country and its consequences; and in denial about their various economic woes – the low productivity, their head-in-the-sand approach to debt, the massive public sector over-spend, and so on. I have read numerous articles in Danish newspapers of which the gist has been 'Well, things are going well for the other Scandinavian countries so they will probably go well for us, too,' in which no mention is ever made of Norway's colossal oil wealth or Sweden's manufacturing supremacy and major public-sector reforms. Denmark's economy is far, far weaker than its neighbours', and the country is facing far more serious problems, but the Danes are oddly reluctant to address their private debt levels or their gigantic welfare state.

The Danes have a number of other blind spots. Take their much-vaunted environmentalism. They are very proud of their ongoing efforts to make the world a cleaner place, with their sustainable this, renewable that, organic blah and recylable whatever. They have their windmills, their biofuels, their bicycles, their organic turnips, their punitive treatment of anyone who so much as looks at a set of car keys, and so on, and oh, don't they *go on* about it! Yes, but still, according to the Worldwide Fund for Nature's 2012 Living Planet Report, Denmark has the fourth largest per capita environmental footprint in the world, beaten only by three Gulf states and *ahead* of the US. It is also the EU's largest exporter of oil (Britain extracts more, but consumes most of it itself; Norway, of course, is not an EU member); the majority of its energy still comes from filthy coal-powered stations; and in Mærsk, Denmark's single most important company, they have the largest shipping company in the world. According to a 2008 UN report, shipping is responsible for twice the CO_2 emissions of aviation.* I am not necessarily saying that the Danes should wake up and smell the pollution, but they might want to clean up their own back yard before they try to rally the world's leaders to the cause of global warming at high-profile international summits.

And the Danes are in denial about actual, tangible things, too, like, say, the existence of Germany. Considering that Denmark has a substantial land border with Germany, and considering the relative sizes of the two countries and how important Germany is for Danish

---

* Similarly, while the Danes are generally appalled by the notion of capital punishment and the death penalty – it was abolished in Denmark in 1933 – can you guess which country provides America with most of its pentobarbital, the drug used for executions?

exports, it is remarkable how little attention German politics and culture receive in Denmark. It is as if the Germans weren't there, or the Danes would *rather* they weren't. During his fieldwork in Jutland, Richard Jenkins, noted that he never once heard a Dane make a joke about a German: 'Perhaps one has to recognise some affinity with the "other" for ethnic jokes to work. Or perhaps Denmark's shared history with Germany is simply not a laughing matter.'

Denial is always interesting because often the object of denial acts as a giant red, neon arrow accompanied by a klaxon alerting one to underlying issues. America is in denial about global warming because they are disproportionately responsible for the emission of greenhouse gasses. The British are in denial about their loss of empire because their pride cannot bear their irrelevance. The Chinese are in denial about human rights, because their economic success is founded on disregarding them. As for the French, well it would probably be easier to list the things they *aren't* in denial about.

After we had talked for a while about the benefits of economic equality, I asked Professor Richard Wilkinson if he thought there might perhaps be any downsides to the low Gini countries. Didn't the most equal societies also tend to be, you know, a bit samey, a little *boring*? All those lists of the best cities to live in are always made up of places with clean streets, cycle paths, and touring productions of *Phantom of the Opera*, like Bern or Toronto; it is never the really scintillating, stimulating places like New York or Barcelona. (Full disclosure: I have a great deal to answer for myself here. Every year I help compile *Monocle* magazine's Urban Quality of Life Survey, including the one that most recently claimed Copenhagen was the best city in the world in which to live.) As soon as I asked the question I realised that, compared with the social ills examined in *The Spirit Level* – crime, teenage pregnancy, obesity, cancer, suicide, and so on – a lack of decent street food and interesting graffiti were hardly serious complains.

'People do say that,' the professor replied. 'But the costs of inequality are very high indeed: the stress, the depression, the drug and drink problems, the tendency for narcissism.'

A surprising number of Danes agree with me, though: they also think their homeland is stultifyingly dull. Newspaper columnist Anne Sophia Hermansen, of the broadsheet *Berlingske*, caused a small kerfuffle recently when she expressed her feelings about what she saw as Denmark's suffocating monoculture. 'It is so boring in Denmark. We wear the same clothes, shop in the same places, see the same TV and struggle to know who to vote for because the parties are so alike. We are so alike it makes me weep . . . Here *Invasion of the Body Snatchers* is not just a 1970s horror film, but reality.'

Another prominent newspaper commentator, *Jyllands-Posten*'s Niels Lillelund, pinpointed a more serious side effect of the Danes' Jante Law mentality: 'In Denmark we do not raise the inventive, the hardworking, the ones with initiative, the successful or the outstanding, we create hopelessness, helplessness and the sacred, ordinary mediocrity.' He seems here to be echoing something else Mary Wollstonecraft observed. She wrote that the Danes' love of money 'does not render the people enterprising, as in America, but thrifty and cautious. I never, therefore, was in a capital where there was so little appearance of active industry,' later adding that, 'the Danes, in general, seem extremely averse to innovation.' As *The Economist* put it in their Nordic special edition, Scandinavia is a great place in which to be born . . . but only if you are average. If you are averagely talented, have average ambitions, average dreams, then you'll do just fine, but if you are extraordinary, if you have big dreams, great visions, or are just a bit different, you will be crushed, if you do not emigrate first.

Even the usually ebullient Ove Kaj Pedersen of the Copenhagen Business School was open to this line of criticism: 'I like Denmark, but I like to work abroad. I pay my taxes with great honour because I know for a fact that whenever I need something it will be there . . . every day I conclude the best place to live is Denmark, but for me this kind of social cohesion, these middle-class-oriented societies do not present the kind of challenges I am looking for. I want to be in the best places and you don't find the best places in Denmark when it comes to elite research and education. And why the hell can't you go down to the bookstore in the morning and buy the *New York Times* for five dollars? Or get a good cup of coffee for a cheap price?'

Most of us would probably conclude that expensive coffee and having to put up with another touring production of *Mamma Mia* are reasonable prices to pay for a fair, functioning society. Denmark – and the rest of Scandinavia for that matter – might not get your pulse racing like the Lower East Side or Copacabana, but in the long run a solid pension fund and reliable broadband will always win the day – as long as those plates keep spinning, and as long as the Danish miracle is sustained.

I had a standard question that I asked most of my interviewees: 'What are your fears for the future of Denmark?' One word cropped up more than any other in their responses: complacency. Many of my interviewees were worried that the Danes had had it too good for too long, that they were now content to sit back in their Arne Jacobsen Swan armchairs and watch the plates wobble and fall. Worryingly for the Danes, the latest OECD Better Life Index of life satisfaction saw them plummet to seventh place, behind Norway and Sweden, among others.

'There were a few years in the 2000s where there was this feeling that Denmark was the best country in the world type thing, and that complacency is a bad thing,' said Martin Ågerup.

'There's a downside to trust,' warned Professor Christian Bjørnskov. 'You tend to be too optimistic. We have this massive problem with the welfare state, but people seem to wish it will just go away, that somehow everything will be fine.'

'My fear is that we continue lying to ourselves,' said Anne Knudsen. 'Trying to make-believe that we are smarter and richer and more content and better educated than the next country . . . to the point where we end up, you know, *Greek*. I don't believe that is a realistic scenario, but it is a possibility.'

'We have a confusion in Denmark in terms of where should we go, what is the long-term sustainable version of the welfare state, version 2.0?' said Torben Tranæs. 'All the graphs about trends in Danish society and the economy have either gone up and then plateaued, or gone down and plateaued – the only exception is our weight.'

Danish society appears to have reached maturity, some would argue to a state of perfection, others to a perilous halt. The fear is that the next stage will be stagnation and decline. What happens when you develop a genuinely almost nearly perfect society in which there is nothing left to achieve, nothing to kick against, or work for?

'When you get up to this level, there are such small differences it gives this kind of confusion in terms of where are we heading,' said Tranæs. 'Is there another mountain we should try to conquer or . . .' He trailed off, as if unsure of what actually would happen next.

But I had one other question I always asked, which, in its way, was even more revealing. Whenever I asked my Danish interviewees whether they could think of a *better* country to live in, the answer was invariably a thoughtful silence. It was true, when the wind is howling and the taxman is knocking, they might sometimes hanker for Tuscany or Provence, but in the ultimate analysis, none could name a better place to live than Denmark. And, for all my moaning, as a parent I have to agree it is at least a fantastic place to raise kids.

The other Nordic countries might be alternative candidates, I suppose. The similarities between them are striking: the strong, extensive welfare states; the social cohesion, the interconnectedness and collectivism; the economic equality, and the masochistic licorice obsession – all are common to the people of the North.

This started me thinking: what would happen if you were to extract the very essence of Nordicness to create some kind of ultimate Nordic society? Would you end up with a society that was even more successful, even happier than the Danes'? Or could a country perhaps be *too* Nordic?

It turned out someone has already tried this.

ICELAND

Chapter 1

Hakarl

You could argue that Iceland shouldn't even be in this book – the Icelanders probably would. After all, their country was founded by people who wanted to *get away* from Scandinavia, and they went to a great deal of inconvenience to achieve this, so it hardly seems fair to drag them back again. Plus, it is located halfway to North America and has more trade with Germany, the US and the UK than with any of the Nordic countries. Besides, there are only 319,000 of them. I have no intention of dedicating chapters to Gothenburg or Aarhus, which have roughly the same number of inhabitants, so why Iceland? Why not Greenland or the Faroe Islands, both of which have equally strong, quasi-national identities? And in terms of gaining an insight into Nordic exceptionalism, the only aspect in which the Icelanders could be described as exceptional in recent years is their economic mismanagement, which isn't the kind of exceptionalism we are looking for.

There are, though, several compelling reasons why we are about to visit this idiosyncratic people and their mesmerising landscape. Genetically speaking, Iceland is more Scandinavian than Scandinavia. It was populated by escapees – let's be honest, outlaws – from western Norway, together with the Scottish and Irish sex slaves they picked up on their journey west. They still speak a version of Old Norse, a purer version of the Scandinavian languages of the past. Geneticists from around the world have long flocked to Iceland, so pure- (the uncharitable might say in-) bred are they. Also, Iceland was ruled by Denmark for 682 years and, as we'll see, it still has a close and somewhat complex relationship with its former masters in Copenhagen. Plus, it is a member of the Nordic Council, which pretty much settles the whole 'Nordic or not?' question.

Most of all, the chief reason Iceland is worthy of our attention is that its recent financial escapades are highly revealing of the latent dangers of the classic small, homogenous, tightly knit Nordic social model. A country can, it turns out, be too Nordic, and Iceland is that country.

First, a quick 'recent Icelandic economic history' primer. Between 2003 and 2008, Iceland's three main banks, Glitnir, Kaupthing and Landsbanki, borrowed over $140 billion, a figure equal to ten times the country's GDP, dwarfing its central bank's $2.5 billion reserves. A handful of entrepreneurs, egged on by their then government, embarked on an unprecedented international spending binge, buying everything from Danish department stores to West Ham Football Club, while a sizeable proportion of the rest of the adult population enthusiastically embraced the kind of cockamamie financial strategies usually only mooted in Nigerian spam emails – taking out loans in Japanese Yen, for example, or mortgaging their houses in Swiss francs. One minute the Icelanders were up to their waists in fish guts, the next they they were weighing up the options lists on their new Porsche Cayennes.

The tales of un-Nordic excess are legion: Elton John was flown in to sing one song at a birthday party; private jets were booked like they were taxis; people thought nothing of spending £5,000 on bottles of single malt whisky, or £100,000 on hunting weekends in the English countryside. The chief executive of the London arm of Kaupthing hired the Natural History Museum for a party, with Tom Jones providing the entertainment, and, by all accounts, Reykjavik's actual snow was augmented by a blizzard of the Colombian variety.

The collapse of Lehman Brothers in late 2008 exposed Iceland's debts which, at one point, were said to be around 850 per cent of GDP (compared with the US's 350 per cent), and set off a chain reaction which resulted in the krona plummeting to almost half its value. By this stage Iceland's banks were lending money to their own shareholders so that they could buy shares in . . . those very same Icelandic banks. I am no Paul Krugman, but even I can see that this was hardly a sustainable business model. The government didn't have the money to cover its banks' debts. It was forced to withdraw the krona from currency markets and accept loans totalling £4 billion from the IMF, and from other countries. Even the little Faroe Islands forked out £33 million, which must have been especially humiliating for the Icelanders. Interest rates peaked at 18 per cent. The stock market dropped 77 per cent; inflation hit 20 per cent; and the krona dropped 80 per cent. Depending who you listen to, the country's total debt ended up somewhere between £13 billion and £63 billion, or, to put it another way, anything from £38,000 to £210,000 for each and every Icelander.

Within weeks unemployment rose from its customary 2 per cent ('the retarded and refuseniks,' as one Icelander described them to me; up to that point anyone who wanted a job could have had one), to over 10 per cent. Inflation kicked in with a Weimar-esque vengeance. The cost of all those Yen mortgages and Swiss-franc loans – now illegal – more than doubled, leaving many with negative equity in their homes and cars. There were stories on the news about bottles of olive oil costing the equivalent of £130. Unsurprisingly, a third of Icelanders said they wanted to leave. As one *Times* headline put it, they had become 'The Little Economy That Couldn't'.

Arriving in Reykjavik for the first time shortly after the economic collapse, I wondered what it had been like to live in a society on the brink. 'It was like a bomb went off when the three banks fell,' Gísli Pálsson, a professor of anthropology at the University of Iceland told me. 'Yet everything sort of kept going: social services and even the banks. In the weeks after the crash there was extreme uncertainty. Would there be food shortages? There was a real fear of social breakdown. Some of it was scary. We have had a signifi-cant increase in crime in Reykjavik. People are installing alarms. There was a fire at the parliament, smashing of windows. There was extreme anger. At times there has been a kind of public depression, many people see no way out as they are losing their cars, their jobs and will lose their homes. I know many people who are in really bad shape. I owe a couple of million and I'm feeling the strain.'

In January 2009 came the so-called 'cutlery revolution': two thousand protesters clanged items of kitchenware together outside parliament and threw pots of *skyr* (the Icelandic yoghurt more usually employed as a stomach lining before the traditional Friday-night drinking binge). It was the first time tear gas had been used in Iceland since protests against joining NATO in 1949. The right-wing coalition, led by Prime Minister Geir Haarde and in power since the 1940s, were finally ousted. Haarde blamed the 'global financial hurricane', but eventually ceded power to a coalition led by the Social Democratic Alliance party's Jóhanna Sigurðardóttir, sixty-eight, ex-air stewardess, mother of two and grandmother of six, not to mention the world's first openly gay head of government. After further public protests, central bank chief Davíð Oddsson – a former PM – was replaced by a Norwegian economist, Svein Harald Øygard. Sigurðardóttir promptly announced 30 per cent cuts in spending, raised taxes, and tried to flog a few embassies.

The crash appears to have been a crime with no criminals. Haarde was eventually prosecuted for negligence at the Landsdómur criminal court, the first political leader anywhere in the world to be called to account for what happened in 2008. He faced up to two years in prison for his role in the widespread financial mispractice that had ruined Iceland, but was found not guilty. The president throughout all of this, Ólafur Ragnar Grímsson is, quite remarkably, still president, having been re-elected in 2012: the fact that he has consistently vetoed all attempts by the Icelandic parliament to repay the money they owe their foreign creditors might have something to do with his enduring popularity.

Reykjavik had the feel of a house the morning after a truly epic party. I had arrived just in time to catch the hosts emptying ashtrays into bin liners and rounding up the stray underwear. Those I spoke to seemed at turns weary, bewildered, angry and shell-shocked.

The city was once famed for its magnificent panoramas across the fjord to the mountains beyond, but these days the views were dominated by the large office and apartment towers that had erupted along the waterfront. Sparkling and new, they were also empty, like stacks of freshly robbed jewellery cases. Apart from those working on the extravagant harbour-front concert hall / opera house, Harpa, which they had started to build at the height of Iceland's economic hubris and which, I was assured, would have cost more to leave unfinished, the cranes stood silent on Reykjavik's building sites.

On the plus side, the nice lady in the tourist office told me that, thanks to the collapse of the krona, visitor numbers were up a tad, at a time when tourism had declined drastically in much of the rest of the world. Iceland had always been a famously costly destination – pre-crunch, *The Economist* named it the most expensive place to visit in the world – but with an exchange rate of 200 kronur to the pound (nearly double its previous rate), it had become, if not a bargain – they still have to import virtually everything apart from electricity and fish – then at least on a par with London. Getting *reyked*, as Reykjavik's infamous Friday- and Saturday-night pub crawl was termed, was now suddenly much more affordable, with beer around 600 kronur a pint. That explained why most of the voices I heard in the shops and restaurants in Reykjavik city centre were foreign. The streets, bars and restaurants were largely empty of locals.

There were other signs that all had not gone quite to plan recently: walking on the main high street, Laugavegur, I spotted in a shop window a T-shirt bearing the slogan 'Brown is the Colour of Poo'. It featured a picture of former British Prime Minister Gordon Brown, who had become a hate figure in Iceland after his government had moved to reclassify Iceland under anti-terrorist laws in order to freeze the country's assets. ('Interest-rate whores is all you were!' one Icelander grumbled to me.)

I had lunch on my first day sitting between a Chilean couple and a Frenchman, in a small fisherman's-shack restaurant, Sægreifinn ('Sea Baron'), amid the warehouses on the harbourfront. We sat, squeezed around communal tables on blue plastic fish-packing barrels, tucking into steaming bowls of *Humarsúpa* (langoustine soup – one of Iceland's culinary glories). *Hákarl* is another famous

Icelandic delicacy. *Humarsúpa* I would be happy to taste again, but I shall fight for as long as I remain conscious to avoid ingesting *hákarl* again. Apparently, the shark meat caught in these parts is toxic if eaten fresh but, rather than giving up on the whole eating shark business altogether, they eventually hit upon the idea of burying it in the ground for between eighteen months and four years until it has decayed to the point where it becomes, in the very loosest sense of the word, edible. This is *hákarl*.

I tried some at a bar in central Reykjavik. Clearly used to tourists 'just wanting a taste', a waitress brought me two small, sugar-cube sized chunks of unappetising-looking greyish meat in a sealed jar. 'Don't worry, it doesn't taste as bad as it smells,' she said, smiling. 'If you can get past the smell then that's the worst of it.'

She was lying. True, the smell from quite some distance away as she opened the jar was indeed abominable: redolent of a multistorey carpark staircase on a hot summer's day, with accents of urine and vomit. But that wasn't the worst of it. The burning, fishy-cheese flavour was much, much worse. I concluded that *hákarl*'s name was onomatopoeic. It was the noise one made upon upon eating it.

After that, whale sushi, guillemot and smoked puffin – all of which I tried during my time in Reykjavik – were relatively pleasant, but *hákarl* did get me wondering about the Icelanders. What kind of a people, when surrounded by some of the greatest, freshest fish on the planet, along with ice in which to store it, would decide they would rather eat toxic, putrefied shark? It seemed to demonstrate an extraordinary bloody-mindedness.

I began to explore the country's history. Though relatively short, it makes for unremittingly grim reading.

Early Iceland was a lawless, irreligious place peopled with Norwegian outlaws and their Scottish and Irish companions. Human sacrifices to appease the terrible forces that raged just beneath the surface of their meagre soil were not unknown. There was no executive authority, no king and no army, just a ragbag of laws mostly concerned with the apparently pressing issue of incest. In the thirteenth century, unable to control themselves, the Icelanders finally asked the Norwegians to intervene. King Olaf of Norway somehow managed to convert the Icelanders to Christianity, but theirs was always a half-hearted observance, at best.

Plagues, pirates, volcanic eruption and the sheer unrelenting hideousness of Iceland's climate pegged back its population to mere tens of thousands for most of the latter part of the last millennium. A museum diorama of these centuries would feature a smallpox outbreak here, a bubonic plague there, famine, choking clouds of volcanic ash over everything, and a carpet of dead cattle underfoot, with perhaps the odd beheading of a bishop or the arrival of an equally unfortunate wayward polar bear aboard an iceberg – which occasionally still happens. The most cataclysmic event was the 1783 eruption of the volcanic fissure of Laki, which had a major cooling effect on much of Northern Europe. A quarter of the population died as a result of the ensuing famine; Denmark, which by then had taken over Norway and Iceland, seriously considered evacuating the rest of the Icelanders to Jutland and leaving the cursed place to its 10 million puffins. In the early 1700s there were 50,358 people living in Iceland. A century later, there were 47,240. Virtually every other European country's population exploded during this period.

In the nineteenth century the Icelanders finally began to muster a half-hearted independence movement but, as we've already heard, they only obtained full independence thanks to the intervention of the most unlikely of liberators: Adolf Hitler. 'The 120,000 people of Iceland,' wrote The Times at the time, 'were completely undismayed that Adolf Hitler had bagged His Majesty Christian X, King of Denmark, and separately King of Iceland.'

The Danes were soon replaced by another quasi-occupying power, the US military, which maintained a base in Iceland until 2006. Iceland had been the poorest country in Europe, but all that changed with Marshall Plan money and massive infrastructure projects. Iceland began to flourish and grow in confidence.

In recent years Iceland has held its head high in the Nordic-exceptionalism stakes as the most developed country in the world according to the United Nations Human Development Index, as well as the fourth most productive country per capita in Europe. It ranked highly, too, on the Index of Economic Freedom; per capita gross national income had long been higher than the UK's; and at one point it was the fifth richest country in the OECD. Iceland had the highest birth rate in Europe, and has long been a model of gender equality. It was the first country in the world to have a female president, and a single mother to boot – Vigdís Finnbogadóttir, elected in 1980. Icelandic men live longer than any other men in the world, with an average life expectancy of 78.9 years, but the women are even more durable, living, on average, to the age of 82.8 years. Also, the Icelanders buy more books per capita than anyone else in the world, which has to be a good thing.

Since the *kreppa* (the crash), of course, all of the above achievements, as admirable as they were, have been eclipsed by the Icelanders' epic economic hubris. Iceland has become a single-issue nation.

Many books and articles have been written on what exactly happened to the Icelandic financial system in 2008–9, so I do not propose to go into great detail about it here, but I was interested in getting to the root of just *why* things had gone quite so awry for the Icelanders. After all, much of the success of the Nordic countries has been ascribed to three key factors: their homogeneity, their egalitarianism, and their social cohesion, all of which Iceland boasted in abundance, in some cases to a greater degree than any of its Nordic siblings.

But something, somewhere, went catastrophically wrong. Did Iceland lose its Nordic mojo? Did it have its head turned by distant sirens, or was it never really Nordic in the first place?

Chapter 2

Bankers

'We assume they are more or less Scandinavian – a gentle people who just want everyone to have the same amount of everything. They are not. They have a feral streak in them, like a horse that's just pretending to be broken.'

Michael Lewis, writing in *Vanity Fair*, April 2009

In 2009 the US economic commentator Michael Lewis wrote a now famous – and famously unflattering – article on Iceland for *Vanity Fair*, detailing everything from its deluded debt orgy to the rudeness of its men and, rather ungallantly, the plainness of its women. Iceland was, Lewis concluded, a macho, patriarchal, risk-prone society.

Lewis drew a direct causal link to the economic crash from the introduction of fishing quotas in the early 1980s. It used to be that Icelanders fished as everyone else did: they got on a boat and went out and tried to catch stuff. Some days they came home empty handed, others with a worthwhile catch. But, in 1983, following several bad fishing years due to atrocious weather, the Icelandic government decided to implement a quota system. Icelanders are famously risky fishermen, willing to go out in all weathers, and the system was intended to discourage this. The government awarded licences to all existing boats allowing them to catch a certain percentage of the total annual quota in proportion to the size of their boat. It was a controversial initiative: some argued that the government had no right to carve up a natural resource in this way. On the other hand, knowing they had a year to catch their quota, it was hoped that the fishermen would take fewer risks.

The real germ of the economic crisis is to be found a little later, in 1991, when the fishermen were given permission to trade the quotas and use future catches as collateral to borrow money. As one commentator put it, 'One decision two decades ago destroyed the country.'

Gísli Pálsson has been studying Iceland's fishing communities since the early 1980s and was the first academic to document the effects of the quota system. 'I do think there is a connection [between the 2008 crash and the quota system],' Pálsson told me. 'The owners of those first quotas became rich overnight. All the quotas ended up in the hands of maybe fifteen private companies. And the property rights were hidden, there was a mystification of ownership. Then the owners began to move their profits from these fifteen fishing companies into banking.'

Why on earth did no one object when these fishermen-come-bankers began to go rogue? There were frequent warnings from foreign economists and commentators. 'It is really difficult to explain. Critical discussion became silenced, including here at the university – this building was built by a fund from one of the millionaires,' Pálsson gestured to the room around us. 'Critics were marginalised as people who couldn't take pleasure in the success. These businessmen were very visibly offering funds for research, building public buildings, museums, festivals, whatever.'

'It's true, there was a lot of money trickling down through society,' journalist Bjarni Brynjólfsson, editor of the independent monthly magazine the *Iceland Review* – as well as a part-time fishing guide – told me later that day at his offices downtown. 'All the restaurants were full with bankers, but of course it was very unhealthy – it wasn't real wealth, it was all borrowed. You have to understand that these organisations [the banks] basically grew over our heads. I don't think the bankers in Iceland were doing very different things from foreign bankers, but I think they took up their methods raw, they didn't cook them at all, and then at the end they started doing some really funky stuff, like lending to each other. I was watching them closely and wondering how these guys could just keep on borrowing and borrowing, and they never seemed to sell anything except between themselves. They never put their own capital at stake.'

What happened in Iceland in the early years of this century seemed to me to be so very un-Nordic (tellingly, Finland, Sweden and Denmark all aligned themselves with the British in the dispute about the Icesave debts when British companies, local authorities and individuals, tempted by the high interest rates, deposited significant sums with the Icelandic bank, Landsbanki, only to see it all disappear when the bank went under). The concentration of business, media and political power in the hands of a few extreme ideologues, the blithe accumulation of surreal quantities of debt, the stretch Hummers and the private jets – it all seemed more redolent of Thatcher's Britain, or the US, than Scandinavia.

One night I dropped by one of Reykjavik's more flamboyant restaurants, a relic from the high times with shimmering flock wallpaper, perspex Philippe Starck chairs (the default choice for people who want to appear design-savvy but aren't), and a menu touting dishes featuring combinations such as foie gras and pineapple, and a hamburger 'New Fashion', with Tandoori sauce, camembert and parma ham. 'This, truly, is the ugly side of rampant neo-liberalist capitalism,' I thought to myself, leaving hurriedly. 'Not even the Swedes would put camembert and Tandoori sauce in a burger.'

The starkest contrast in terms of the Icelander's Nordic siblings is with their direct ancestors, the Norwegians. While they were nurturing their oil wealth with the cautious attentiveness of an orchid farmer for his blossoms, the Icelanders embarked on a crazy, magpie-like land grab of the most glittering foreign assets they could find – football clubs, hotels and department stores – combined with the most ill-advised borrowing since Antonio offered Shylock a pound of flesh as security.

'It was like we needed to do everything better and more shiny than any other nation,' one former bank employee, now unemployed, told me. 'It was like we had some kind of super race in Iceland which could bring to Europe and Britain a new model of doing things.'

'There is this Viking culture: everybody has grown up hearing how great the Vikings were,' Terry Gunnell, a British expat who has lived in Iceland for some years, told me. 'In the sagas, whenever an Icelander goes anywhere they are always taken straight to the king, no messing. They go to Norway, and the king of Norway says, "Hey, come back to my place!" They still feel that way: like Vikings, equals of anyone. They all grew up being told, "We may be small but we are equal to anyone." Iceland is the little man who sees himself as having a big voice. "You can't invade Iraq without asking us first," and so on.'

The Danes have a saying about the Icelanders which long predates the economic crisis, but which seems more apt than ever: 'They wear shoes which are too big for them, and keep falling over their shoelaces.'

Dr Elizabeth Ashman Rowe, lecturer in Scandinavian History at the University of Cambridge, also felt the Icelanders' Viking attitudes might be at the root of their contemporary economic misadventure: 'It is true that Viking-era Icelanders were a group of people who wanted their rights respected, they didn't want anyone telling them what to do and their system was one which rewarded people who were clever or bold. And that behaviour is echoed in the causes of the financial crisis.'

Perhaps this inbred sense of superiority was one of the reasons why all criticism of their banking sector was so easily quashed in Iceland. Any criticism from outside was dismissed as bullying, as was the case in 2006 when the Danish national bank published a report warning that Iceland's banks were on the path to oblivion. The Icelanders dismissed this as jealousy.

Eventually, though, reality bit. 'I started working for a bank in 2007 and already after three months there was no money,' Inga Jessen, a local woman I got chatting to in one of Reykjavik's many cool but half-empty coffee shops, told me. 'We didn't know when we were going to get paid. They started firing people. I remember one colleague would come to work every day and say, "Everything is going to hell!" and we were, like, "Yeah, right," we didn't quite believe it.' Inga finally lost her job managing large office buildings in Europe in late 2008.

By early 2009 Michael Lewis was describing Iceland as 'effectively bust'. He claimed to have heard Range Rovers exploding from his hotel room as the locals carried out insurance fraud on their now debt-ridden vehicles. He let rip with a scattergun of insults, calling the women 'mousy-haired and lumpy', and the men barbaric. 'Thursday, Friday, and Saturday . . . half the country appears to take it as a professional obligation to drink themselves into oblivion,' he wrote.

But who was to blame for the economic mess? While I was there the Icelandic media was reporting a wave of paint attacks by disgruntled Icelanders calling themselves *Skapofsi* ('Rage') on the property of some of those deemed responsible. These included the former CEO of Kaupthing Bank, Hreiðar Már Sigurðsson, whose home was redecorated with a Pollock-esque dash of red, as well as the Hummer of Björgólfur Thor Björgólfsson, the richest man in Iceland.

If you are looking for a poster boy for Iceland's economic misadventure, Björgólfsson fits the bill. As well as being Iceland's first billionaire, he is the grandson of Iceland's leading businessman of the early twentieth century, Thor Jensen, and son of one of the most 'colourful' entrepreneurs in Iceland's history, Björgólfur Guðmundsson, an ex-convict, ex-footballer, recovering alcoholic and, as of July 2009, bankrupt. Together with his son Guðmundsson made his money selling booze to Russia and used it to buy, among other things, West Ham Football Club (which he eventually sold in 2009), and a controlling stake in Landsbanki. Until the crash, many Icelanders saw Guðmundsson as a benevolent father figure, as they had his father before him: both doled out cash to social and cultural causes.

The Guðmundssons were among roughly fifteen families, collectively known as 'The Octopus', whose 'blue hand' had a grip on much of the Icelandic economy. Several of them have now left Iceland in shame, while others are keeping a low profile.

Retail entrepreneurs Jóhannes Jónsson and his son Jón Ásgeir Jóhannesson are also often mentioned in this context. As owners of the Baugur Group they controlled most of Iceland's media and retail sectors – including, in Britain, House of Fraser, Hamleys and, evidence of a rather literal approach to foreign investment, the frozen-foods chain Iceland. Baugur collapsed in early 2009 and finally began to lose its iron grip on Iceland's media (although, as is typical of the murky web of Icelandic ownership, at the time of writing Jóhannesson still owns TV channels and newspapers).

But most of the blame has been borne by the centre-right Independence Party, which had ruled Iceland since 1929, and primarily by its ex-prime minister, latterly chief of the central bank (and now editor of the country's main newspaper, *Morgunblaðið*), Davíð Oddsson, and his successor as PM, Geir Haarde.

Many of these politicians and businessmen were close associates: they went to the same schools and colleges (primarily Reykjavik's exclusive Latin School), and socialised together. And here is exposed Iceland's great Achilles' heel. In a country with only 319,000 people, everyone is pretty much guaranteed to know everyone else within one or fewer degrees of separation, and Iceland's ruling class does seem to have had an especially incestuous history.

'These loans [from Icelandic banks to their own shareholders to enable them to buy more shares] just serve as a nasty reminder of how corrupt things had gotten here,' one Icelander was quoted as saying in a UK newspaper shortly after the crash. 'This is such a small society, so businessmen, regulators, the media and politicians all end up in bed together.'

'If you want to understand how someone is hired in an Icelandic company, you start by looking at the political connection,' Sindri Freysson, one of Iceland's leading poets and novelists told me. 'If it's not that, then you look at the family tree, and if it's not that, then there is only one explanation: Alcoholics Anonymous! It is a close-knit society, but that allows for nepotism and cliques, which is all part of this economic problem. You will hire someone from your sports club, or who is in your family; there is a lot of that here and probably because we are so used to it, we don't call it corruption. It's very hard to avoid, and it is a problem when you come to bring these people to justice.'

It seems the very same social connectedness that encourages long-term stability, accountability, equality and prosperity elsewhere in the Nordic region has had quite the opposite outcome in Iceland.

As far back as 2001, the EU anti-corruption organisation Group of States Against Corruption (GRECO) warned that, in Iceland, the 'close links between the government and the business community could generate opportunities for corruption.' A good example of just how entangled government, media and business get in Iceland is the case of the vetoed media-ownership bill of 2004. Introduced to break up monopolistic ownership of the media by private companies (essentially it was targetting Baugur), the bill was sensationally vetoed by the president, Ólafur Ragnar Grímsson, who took the unprecedented step of refusing to sign it. It turned out that Grímsson's former campaign manager was now the director of one of the TV stations that would have fallen foul of the new law, and that his daughter was employed by Baugur.

Meritocratic ideals and democratic freedoms are always going to struggle in a country where the talent pool is the equivalent size of Coventry's (although, thus far, Coventry has yet to swindle Holland out of 4 billion euros). And if there is a limited number of doctors and teachers, that is also likely to be the case in terms of entrepreneurs, politicians and economists. That is why Icelanders are, by necessity, the world's ultimate jacks of all trades. Many of the people I interviewed had second jobs as taxi drivers or tour guides, and that multitasking extends up the social ladder: the former prime minster is often described as being a poet, for instance; his foreign minister was a physiotherapist.

One cannot overemphasise, I think, how very, very few Icelanders there actually are. If they were an animal species, they would be on the WWF's endangered list – the human equivalent of a yellow-nosed albatross. It is remarkable that they have been able to build any kind of a national infrastructure at all. 'Do they have heart surgeons, speech therapists or yoga teachers?' I wondered. Is there anyone who can translate Bulgarian, or such a thing as an Icelandic heptathlete? (Yes, as it turns out. Her name is Helga Margrét Thorsteinsdóttir.) And how on earth do the TV talent shows function? Presumably by now the whole nation has performed 'Hallelujah' for Simon Cowellsson at least once?

'We had X Factor,' said Brynjólfsson. 'But they pretty much ran out of people after the third season. It always amazed me when I lived in Hackney that you had a population there of, what, 1.5 million, but no cinemas. We have pretty much everything, but maintaining it all is a huge burden.'

Another aspect which differentiated Iceland from the other Nordic countries was a lack of a truly free, diverse press. You can't move for serious, independent broadsheet newspapers throughout the region, but in Iceland the press was either owned, or very closely influenced by, the neoliberalists, who effectively shut down any contradictory discourse.

'Four newspapers, twelve magazines, no press,' was a 2005 headline in the free English-language newspaper, the *Reykjavík Grapevine*, one of the few independent media voices in Iceland at the height of the economic boom. 'Every writer we got, as soon as they got some success, would be recruited by Baugur or Landsbanki for some kind of project,' complained a former editor.

'It had become a very unhealthy society in that these guys controlled the media,' said Brynjólfsson. 'Anyone who criticised them, they bought them up. I was fired [from celebrity gossip magazine *Se og Hør*] because I was critical of them.'

By the end, virtually all the media – from the state-run TV and radio, to private TV channels and newspapers – was under the control of people closely affiliated to the ruling Independent Party. Even the National Economic Institute was abolished in the late 1990s after publishing one too many reports questioning the direction in which the country was heading.

So, it would seem that a country can be too small, too socially knitted, too tightly tied for its own good. Strong social networks can, in certain circumstances, turn to incestuous corruption and the shutting down of democratic discourse. You can, it turns out, be too Nordic for your own good.

Chapter 3

Denmark

So where, I wondered, did this leave the country in terms of its place in the Nordic family?

For centuries Iceland's intellectual class were almost exclusively educated in Copenhagen, and even today the Danish capital is an important – perhaps still *the* most important – cultural metropolis for Icelanders. There are more flights from Reykjavik to Copenhagen per day than to any other destination, and more Icelanders live in the Danish capital than in any other place outside of the island. Many, perhaps even the majority of, Icelandic families, have Danish relatives.

The Danish language dominated the Icelandic education system for many years. Middle-aged Icelanders told me that, at school, most of their books had been in Danish, although despite this, they said they still found it easier to speak Norwegian or Swedish (which made me feel so much better about my own struggles with Danish). But for younger Icelanders – the generation that grew up with a US air base in their back garden and British programmes on TV – English is the dominant second language. 'I think Danish is a dinosaur for them,' said Pálsson.

For his colleague Professor Unnur Dís Skaptadóttir and her family Denmark still has a great deal of meaning. She too has relations in Denmark – in her case, a grandmother – and, as it does for many of her countrymen, Denmark retains a vestigial air of superiority and refinement. 'When I was growing up, anything cultured or good was Danish,' she told me. 'If it was good, it must be Danish. Wives would go to Denmark to learn to cook [as searing an indictment of Icelandic cuisine as one can imagine], it was considered the height of civilisation. People would use Danish words to show how civilised they were, even my mother's generation. she was sent to Denmark as a teenager to learn proper housekeeping. It was where good girls learned to behave.'

According to several Icelanders I spoke to, their respect for the Danes was rarely reciprocated, and even today they feel that the Danes look down on them. One Icelander I spoke to told a story of chatting up a Danish girl in a bar in Copenhagen: 'As soon as I told her where I was from, she was gone. I think they look at us as one step up from Greenlanders.' Another told me her brother had been out in Copenhagen once and overheard some Danes call him 'that retarded Icelander' in Danish, assuming he couldn't understand.

The Icelanders tend to respond to Danish slights with humour: 'People often make jokes speaking Icelandic with a Danish accent,' said Skaptadóttir. 'It is very funny. We don't make jokes about Norwegians speaking Icelandic, only Danes.' He did an impression of a Dane speaking English – a kind of indignant squawk. (To be fair, pretty much anything sounds funny spoken with a Danish accent, even Danish.)

This should not be misinterpreted: there is no real anti-Danish sentiment in Iceland. 'We love Danes,' one taxi driver told me when I told him where I lived. 'If any Icelander says he hates Danes then, well, you get jerks everywhere. We may look more like Norwegians, but if an Icelander meets a Dane, a Swede and a Norwegian he will get on best with the Dane. We have the same sense of humour, like the Brits. But Norwegians . . . oh my God, they are so boring. I think the Norwegians are, in a way, our little brother in solidarity against the Danes over the years.'

Iceland's ambivalent relationship with Denmark sheds an interesting light on the bizarre 'investment' spree embarked upon by Iceland's entrepreneurs between 2006 and 2008. Many of Iceland's most notable acquisitions were from its former colonial masters, Denmark. Along with Copenhagen's two main department stores, Illum and Magasin du Nord, Icelandic businessmen also bought the

Danish capital's most venerable and grand hotel, the Hotel d'Angleterre, along with Danish media companies, and Sterling, the Danish airline (bankrupting it within two years).

Judged on objective economic grounds, they couldn't have invested their money more stupidly if they had tried – department stores have long been considered the white elephants of retail, for instance, and both of Copenhagen's had been losing money for years – so one can only conclude that there must have been another agenda at play. Were these purchases a weird form of post-colonial revenge? Evidence that this might be the case came during a football match between Iceland and Denmark at around this time. In the middle of the match, the Icelandic supporters began chanting 'We're coming for Tivoli next': they were threatening to buy Denmark's historic amusement park, arguably the most sacred of all Danish cultural sites and its most popular tourist attraction. It was like the French chanting about buying Westminster Abbey at an England–France rugby match.*

'There was this strange attempt to colonise Copenhagen by Icelanders buying shops, banks, running a free newspaper – and the shops were the symbols of Danishness,' agreed Gísli Pálsson. 'Of course the Danish reaction was to say, "How can this go on? This is all going to collapse." To which we said, "The Danes have always treated us like this." There was a cultural war with that tinge of post-colonial tension. There has been a love/hate relationship for quite a long time.'

'The Danes were always asking me why we were buying Illum and so on,' Terry Gunnell told me. 'They were furious that the old colony was buying up these things, and were playing Monopoly with their institutions.'

In fact, Danish–Icelandic colonial history has undergone significant revision in recent years. While anti-Danish sentiment was usefully

---

* To give you an idea of how deeply Tivoli is enmeshed in the Danish consciousness, when one Dane spots that another's flies are undone, he will draw their attention by saying, 'I see Tivoli is open!'

whipped up in the cause of independence at the end of the nineteenth century, Icelandic historians have softened towards their old rulers. The Danes allowed the Icelanders to maintain their culture and language, in stark contrast to the Swedes' treatment of the Finns during the same period, for instance.

'Thankfully there is now an awareness that it was, in fact, the Icelandic farmer elite which was keeping us down more than the Danes,' said Skaptadøttir. 'The Danish king tried to initiate improvements, but the farmers wanted to maintain servitude until the beginning of the last century. When I was at school we were still being taught that the Danes were the bad guys but, these days, I don't think young Icelanders know anything about that history. And when I speak to Danes, they are completely ignorant of it, particularly the young. They don't even know where Iceland is. They were, like, "Do you mean Estland [the Danish for Estonia, pronounced similarly to the Danish for Iceland]?"'

'There has been a love–hate relationship between us for a long time,' said Pálsson. 'We were a colony, of course, and the economic system was bad for us: there were people who were jailed. The Danes suppressed singing and dancing here, but *they* kept on singing and having fun. Overall, though, the Danes didn't really treat us that badly. Still, Iceland takes immense pride in winning at football over Denmark, for instance, which they wouldn't over, say, England.'

Pálsson felt the Norwegians were the Icelanders' more natural kin: 'In many ways I think we are more like the Norwegians than the Danes,' he said. 'We have this emphasis on nature, roots, the past, the Vikings, Lutheranism, puritanism. The Danes are sometimes too playful, too much about *hygge* for our tastes.' He also pointed out an unexpected connection with Finland. 'Both of us feel marginalised; we are out of the Scandinavian domain. We have this myth about the Finnish male being depressed and drunk, and maybe we have some of that. Alcoholism is a growing issue.'

Danes, Swedes and Norwegians can generally understand each other's languages, but Icelandic and Finnish stand apart. When

Icelanders attend Nordic conferences, I am told they invariably end up in a corner speaking English with the Finns. (Perhaps this is why these two nations are the best English speakers out of all of them.)

'Icelanders always say they are like the Finns,' said Gunnell. 'It's the humour and the drinking, the darkness. They don't have a pub culture yet like the Danes do. They can't have one drink on the way home from work: if you try that they look at you like you're an idiot. They are bingers, like the Finns. This is a country where beer was banned because they didn't want everyone to be drunk, but you could buy spirits because they had a trade agreement with Scotland.

'There was a wonderful exhibition recently at the Culture House [the museum housing the sagas] about Icelandic culture. There was lots of stuff about connections with Scotland, the Hebrides, Ireland, Braveheart images, and so on. And tucked away in the corner was something to the effect of "Oh yes, and a lot of us came from Scandinavia." They like to play at being on the edge.'

As for the Danes, they are almost entirely oblivious to the broodings of the Icelanders over their colonial past. I have only occasionally detected a slight note of guilt among older Danes when talking about Iceland, but that was mostly that they felt bad about Icelandic schoolchildren still having to learn Danish. This isn't even true – Icelanders have to learn a Scandinavian language, and most choose Danish because of the close links between the countries.

'The more I live in Iceland, and teach about the people, the more I realise that whatever you can say about them, you can also say the opposite with as much conviction,' said Gunnell. 'The Icelanders have no problem with their paradoxes. There is a character on a popular satire programme here who is supposed to be the typical Icelandic little guy, with big sideburns, who has something to say about everything. He starts his speeches attacking something, and by the end is saying completely the opposite. That is the Icelanders.'

Chapter 4

Elves

Before travelling to Iceland, I made a vow to myself that there were two subjects that I would not mention: Björk and elves. I imagined that the Icelanders would have little patience for yet another foreign fool asking about these things, and thought it polite to refrain.

As it turned out, Björk did crop up occasionally (at one point I got very excited when I thought I had spotted her buying a knitting magazine in a local newsagents: it wasn't her). Generally though, it was more a case of having to steer the conversation *away* from the subject of the most famous living Icelander.

The Icelanders' belief in the existence of fairy folk, on the other hand, was too good to resist. It soon became apparent that elves are still an important part of what it means to be Icelandic, whether the Icelander in question believes in them or not. I started to conduct my own straw poll on their existence. I tended to ask the question in a jokey way, but the majority treated it quite seriously: many said with a straight face that they definitely believed they existed, and a couple claimed to have seen 'something' when they were children.

Every decade or so, the Icelandic people are asked about their feelings about elves, or the 'hidden people', as they call them, and the results are broadly consistent. In 1998 a poll revealed that 54.4 per cent said they believed in elves. Another, carried out as recently as 2007, revealed that 32 per cent believed the existence of the hidden people was 'possible', 16 per cent said 'probable', and 8 per cent were certain that elves existed. Many Icelanders even felt able to specify the type of elf they believed in: 26 per cent believed in flower elves; 30 per cent in house elves; 42 per cent in guardian angels. To put this into perspective, only 45 per cent of Icelanders believe in God.

According to first-hand accounts, elves look like humans, but wear traditional, home-made clothes, subsist largely on sheep-farming, and never, ever watch television. Icelandic elves live close to humans, inhabiting the landscape. But, if that landscape is disrupted in any way, the elves will set out to cause disruption.

In 1995–6 a University of Berkeley folklore specialist, Valdimar Hafstein, interviewed a number of what he called 'elf-harried' road-workers, who claimed to have had their work disrupted by the hijinks of the hidden people. It happens every year, apparently. Machinery mysteriously stops working, workmen are injured, or have fore-boding dreams, things fall down, the weather suddenly turns hostile (naturally, elves get the blame – how else would you explain sudden changes in the weather on an Atlantic island?). These incidents gathered momentum in the early 1970s, most famously with the attempts to move a so-called 'elf rock' to make way for the road from Reykjavik heading west. Following numerous incidents of an elf-orientated nature, a clairvoyant was called in to get their permis-sion to move the rock. He claimed to have succeeded in obtaining this, but shortly after, a bulldozer accidentally fractured a pipe that was supplying water to a trout farm: 70,000 trout died. Everyone blamed the elves (although I happened to notice in Hafstein's paper on this that the executive engineer of the project was also the presi-dent of the Icelandic Society for Psychic Research: I know that Icelanders are multitaskers, but this does seem a tad suspicious).

Then there was the 'elf hill' close to a Reykjavik suburb, which the local authorities attempted repeatedly to re-shape in the 1970s and 1980s, eventually being forced to give up. One worker was quoted as saying that he had a 'sort of fear of something' whenever he powered up his bulldozer, while TV crews found their cameras didn't work properly when they pointed them at the hill.

Hafstein speculates that the reason elf activity is usually centred on new building work 'demonstrates supernatural sanction against development and against urbanisation: that is to say, the supernaturals protect and enforce pastoral values and traditional rural culture'. It isn't clear whether he means this literally or that the Icelanders are projecting, but does add that they are working out 'pressing concerns of cultural identity, nationalism and social change'. They are, in other words, afraid of the modern world.

We've met Terry Gunnell already, but what I didn't tell you is that he is a senior lecturer in folklore at the University of Reykjavik. He has immersed himself in the ethnology of the Nordic countries for decades, so is quite used to foreign journalists sitting and smirking at him in his office as they ask questions about 'the little people'. He was quick to point out that everyone has their myths and superstitions.

'It is just a way of understanding the landscape, no different from how people understand the landscape in Birmingham,' Gunnell, in his forties with a ponytail, told me. My eyebrows duly raised, he continued: 'You don't let your kids play on the streets of Birmingham because of the danger of them being taken by paedophiles or terrorists or whatever, but how many are actually victims of these things? They are used to frighten your children. It is the same in Iceland. Don't go into the mountains because something will get you. Don't go near the waterfall because there are trolls there.'

Iceland, of course, offers an especially broad palette of potential kiddy death traps, more even than Birmingham. 'When your house can be destroyed by something you can't see; when you turn on the tap and you get the smell of sulphur and you know that not far below is magma, and you look up in the sky in the evening and you see these amazing lights, it instils a potent sense of nature's unfathomable power. When you can see the wind take the snow and make it into shapes, and you can be knocked off your feet by the wind, it's not surprising that you have the sense that nature has this power. You get the same kind of legends across Scandinavia and Ireland going back to the Viking times, and even the Bronze Age.'

But Iceland did seem rather especially fixated on its elves. 'Yes,' Gunnell admitted. 'The most common story is that someone played with fairies as a child. But the key thing is that a large number of Icelanders don't *not* believe.'

By way of an example, Gunnell described a scenario in which an Icelander is planning to build a jacuzzi in his back garden. To do so might require moving, say, a large rock. A neighbour might lean over the fence and say something to the effect of 'Are you really sure you want to do that? You do know that's an elf rock, don't you?'

'Most would rethink,' said Gunnell.

Just before the *kreppa* hit the fan, Iceland was planning to build an ambitious new opera house. The location had been decided: Borgaholt Hill, home, according to legend, to many of Reykjavik's elves. A proper, grown-up firm of architects, Arkitema and Arkthing, had been commissioned and, in deference to the indigenous paranormal inhabitants, had drawn up a design inspired by the subterranean dwellings of said elves. You wouldn't get goblins dictating the course of a road in Ireland, or major international corporations employing troll intermediaries to get permission to build power stations in Sweden.

'That's because Iceland didn't really make the jump into the twentieth century until 1940,' explained Gunnell. 'The money from the US base finally let them build roads and the cities started growing. The darkness was finally banished, but even up until the seventies, everybody had relations who lived in the countryside, where these myths were.'

I asked Gunnell about a story I had heard in connection with the building of the controversial Alcoa aluminium-smelting plant in eastern Iceland. Was it true Alcoa had employed someone to liaise with the elves to make sure the site wouldn't upset them? An 'elf and safety' expert, so to speak? (Stop me!)

'It is a beautiful story,' smiled Gunnell. 'The country was split about Alcoa. Some wanted to make money quick, others were worried about long-term environmental problems, flooding, and so on. The pagans were already cursing it. You had millions of dollars involved and protesters willing to use any means they could with the media to get attention. So a natural move by them would have been to invoke the elves. Alcoa got in first and hired their own expert.'

So it was a preemptive measure? 'Yes. I remember I was being interviewed on Canadian radio with another elf expert and the interviewer asked the expert whether all companies did this in Iceland, and the expert said "Oh yes," and went on to explain how much it costs, and how the fee depends on the size of the site, and so on. And I looked at him like, *what*?'

Gunnell agreed with Hafstein that the willingness of Icelanders to believe in disruptive spirits sabotaging modern developments indicates a deeper tussle between the old rural values of the landscape versus the modern age. But he had another theory about why Icelanders were so prone to superstition: 'Iceland didn't get the Pietism movement [extremist Lutherans who worked especially hard to stamp out pagan practices in the Nordic region]. There was a major effort to wipe out these myths in Norway in the seventeenth century. I have talked to elderly Norwegians about them: actually, one woman tried to chase me away with a broom when her husband started talking about these kinds of [paranormal] stories. He was daring to tell a foreigner about this "rubbish".'

Iceland's remoteness kept the missionaries at bay, and the Icelanders remained deeply superstitious (I haven't even mentioned the giant worm that lives in Kleifarvatn, a 1,000-metre deep volcanic lake; or that one that lives in Lagarfljót, another lake, in eastern Iceland; or that the Westfjords still have a reputation for witchcraft). While out driving the previous day, I had stopped at the Caves of Laugarvatnshellar, where I had read about the story of a shepherd who had sheltered from a blizzard there with his sheep one evening. Having settled down to sleep, the shepherd had found himself being dragged around by his feet. He managed to wrestle himself free and settled down once more to sleep, but it happened again. 'Someone' didn't want him to sleep there. So, he rounded up his sheep and struck out for a village a few miles away. It turned out that the blizzard lasted for two weeks. Had he stayed in the cave, the shepherd would have been snowed in and he and his sheep would have starved to death. All of this was reported, on a plaque on the cave wall, not as 'the legend of Laugarvatnshellar', but as fact.

But what of recent events? I hadn't really thought this through, but as I looked out of his office window at an icy Reykjavik, I wondered whether Gunnell perceived any connection between the Icelanders' willingness to believe in fairy folk, and their gullibility when it came to the preaching of the neo-liberal Icelandic economists and politicians.

Gunnell laughed, but then paused. 'Well, these are people who live very much for the moment, which is also connected to the landscape. You get this "Just get through the day" mentality. At Christmas time they would make prophesies about who was going to survive the winter – you would sit with candles and see who the wax ran to. You learn to take what you can from the landscape without thinking of the long term, just as with Alcoa. That's why, when you look at Icelandic farmhouses and compare them to farms in Sweden, there is pride in the buildings in Sweden, while in Iceland they are just buildings to live in. They don't care what they look like. And I suppose there was that same approach to all the borrowing: get what you can today and as for tomorrow . . . And, hopefully, you know, that same survival instinct, to just get through this day, might save them.'

As I was getting up to leave, I half-jokingly asked Gunnell if he had ever seen any elves. He shifted in his seat and looked away.

'My wife has certainly grown up with these beliefs and seen lots of things. I had to sleep on the floor of a youth hostel once because she said the room was full of people and I had to prove they weren't real.'

'But what about you?'

'It's not for me to say whether things are right or wrong.'

'That's not what I asked.'

He paused.

'I've seen hardly anything,' he said.

Chapter 5

Steam

I rented a car for a couple of days and headed out of Reykjavik. It was a drive unlike any other I had ever experienced. Finally, I got Iceland.

Within just a few miles of the outskirts of the capital, I found myself in a frigid moonscape of craggy, grey, moss-covered lava, and then, moments later, driving through the Scottish Highlands. This is how it is in Iceland: one minute you are amid heather-covered mountains kissed by heavenly shafts of chiaroscuro, the next you are crossing the Gobi. Turn a corner and you pass through the gentle, grassy undulations of Teletubby Land, before they give way to the granite mountains of Mordor, complete with twenty-storey waterfalls. Then, just as suddenly, you are on the moon (in fact, they rehearsed the Apollo moon landings here). The weather changes even more frequently.

I drove onward until the terrifying majesty of Vatnajökull hove into view. This is Iceland's largest glacier, 8,300 square kilometres and one kilometre deep. *Lonely Planet* tells me that it is three times the size of Luxembourg, which is only really useful if one has a decent grasp of the size of Luxembourg, which I don't. Even from many miles away your eyes widen at the scale of it as it sprawls over the mountains like a great, frosted muffin-top, its white icing oozing down the valleys.

Vatnajökull reaches the sea and crumbles into hundreds of icebergs at Jökulsárlón Bay. As they proceed at a dignified pace into the Atlantic, these bus-sized clumps of ice glow blue, as if lit from within. It is like watching dozens of really cool vodka bars pass by. I stood for over an hour, jacketless beneath a blazing blue sky, the only sounds a Stockhausen symphony of creaks, graunches and tinkles from the ice.

I picked up a piece of ice the size of a dinner plate. It was flawless, like glass, and I licked it. It just seemed like the thing to do.

At Gullfoss, Iceland's largest waterfall, the elements took a turn for the apocalyptic, with driving wind and rain augmenting the massive spray from the billions of gallons of water that cascade here every hour. It was quite a heart-stopper. I also made the pilgrimage to the geysers at Geysir and stood right beside the legendary Strokkur to experience one of the most thrilling natural phenomena in the world.

Typically of Iceland – where safety rules are for sissies – there is only a token low rope just beyond the edge of Strokkur, and no supervisors or safety attendants to save you from the scalding water's ejaculations. This means that, entranced by the steaming blue pool – around two metres in diameter and bringing to mind a giant nazar – the geyser virgin can find himself lured perilously close to the action; closer still as the waters commence bulging compellingly upwards. This, I discovered, is the first sign of an imminent eruption, but it lulls you slightly by sinking back down into its bottomless well. It turned out Strokkur was, literally, gathering steam before detonating 35 metres into the air in a great white column of scalding water. The first time this happened it sent me scurrying away in fear of my life, my arms flailing hysterically. To be honest, it had the same effect the second and third times as well. After the fourth and fifth (Strokkur erupts every four minutes or so) I felt confident enough to stand by nonchalantly as new arrivals went through the same shock-and-awe learning process.

As I drove from one once-in-a-life-time geological miracle to another over the course of the next two days, I couldn't help but reflect on the impact Iceland's landscape and climate must have had on its people. Theories about how the topography and climate of a country or region shape the character of the people who live there have been mooted since Herodotus's time (he claimed that Greece provided the optimum environment for nurturing the perfect human). A couple of millennia later, Baron Montesquieu assured *his* readers that *France*, in fact, had the ideal geography. Geographical, or climactic, determinism isn't a terribly fashionable theory these days for good reason: it has been used to claim that people from warmer climates are inherently 'lazy', for instance; but I did find myself drawn again and again to the idea that, for most of the Nordic peoples, for most of their histories, climate and geography have been the predominant long-term influences on their mentality and culture.

Standing next to Strokkur, I even managed to convince myself of a causal link between the geysers and the Icelanders' economic buccaneering. They had become so emboldened by the sheer fact of their survival on this fiery, bubbling, exploding island that they believed they could master any mysterious, destructive forces the world could throw at them, whether they be violent geothermal activity, ferocious climate, or the international money markets. If you can eke out an existence on this pyrotechnical lump of barren rock, few external challenges are likely to daunt you.

I was still perfecting this theory when I arrived at yet another of the country's spectacular geological sites, Thingvellir, a great granite scar across the land, 30 miles east of Reykjavik. This narrow canyon provided ancient Icelanders with a natural outdoor arena for their first parliament, the Althing, the oldest in the world. Since 930, they have gathered here to thrash out the legal and political destiny of their country, as well as to celebrate and commemorate. It is a sombre, forebidding place: between 1602 and 1750 there were 30 beheadings, 15 hangings, 9 burnings at the stake, and 18 women drowned here, mostly because they'd been found guilty of incest.

Oddly, though, this granite rift valley didn't present me with any more evidence for my geographical-determinism theory. Instead it struck me, as I sat in my car waiting for the rain to die down, that what we had here was a symbol for a very different theory about the Icelanders and their crazy debt spree.

My guidebook explained that this awful fissure is where Europe and America meet: the Eurasian and American tectonic plates are slowly drifting apart at this point at a rate of about a centimetre a year. This tectonic tug-of-war between east and west is, of course, the reason for Iceland's very existence, but it is also, I decided, sitting there in my fogged-up rental Astra with a smoked puffin sandwich on my lap, the perfect metaphor for what went wrong with Iceland in the first decade of the twenty-first century.

We have established that Icelanders are, essentially, western Norwegians with a touch of Celtic blood. So how come, when they were tempted with easy money from the international markets, they proved unable to exercise the strict fiscal self-control that their Norwegian ancestors have displayed with their recent oil wealth? Could it be that the Icelanders, for all their Lutheran, social-democratic, Nordic roots, had their heads turned by the free-market-capitalist American dream?

The Americans arrived during the Second World War and set up an airbase at Keflavík, just outside Reykjavik. As historian T. K. Derry put it, 'The war brought undreamed-of prosperity to the Icelanders – from high-priced fish exports, from construction work on airfields for the Americans, and from services of all kinds for American forces that at times amounted to as much as one-third of the native population.' Up until they left in 2007, tens of thousands of US airmen passed through Iceland. The influence on such a small population must have been considerable, not just in terms of the money spent and infrastructure built, but culturally, spiritually even. This has been the case wherever in the world the Americans have set up air bases: in the Philippines, Thule in Greenland, or Okinawa, Japan (where, for example, the influence of the American diet has seen the Okinawans go from being the healthiest, longest-living people in the world, to having the highest rates of obesity and diabetes in the country).

Could America be the real pernicious influence that turned the Icelanders into a nation of irresponsible high rollers? If so, how do you like them apples, Michael Lewis?

Terry Gunnell pointed out that, for the last half-century, American culture has had as great an influence on Iceland as anything from the east. 'I do think that's another card in the economic crash,' he agreed. 'They learned this notion of the American Dream. That anyone can get rich quick.'

As we've seen, the country's economic collapse has its roots in the fishing quotas of the early 1990s, but the Icelandic government led the country down several other US-style free-market paths. Income tax was reduced to the lowest levels in the Nordic region (22.75 per cent), there was whole-scale privatisation – including, most fatefully, of the banks – and the likes of Oddsson and Haarde became enthusiastic disciples of US neo-liberal economist Milton Friedman. The feeling was mutual: Friedman's son David once wrote: 'Medieval Icelandic Institutions . . . might almost have been invented by a mad economist to test the lengths to which market systems could supplant government in its most fundamental functions.' That was back in 1979, but his words would prove prophetic.

I had expected Iceland to be some kind of microcosm of Scandinavia. Icelanders look like Norwegians and speak Old Norse. They have a modern welfare state, high levels of education, equality, democracy, robust knitwear and the same hang-ups about the sale of alcohol, with their government-run alcohol shops staffed by the same species of disapproving elderly women as you find in Norway, Sweden and Finland. The young men smoke pipes, which I always find strangely reassuring. But the modern-day Icelander, with one foot in Scandinavia and the other in the Wild West, has evolved into something quite different from customary notions of what it is to be Nordic. Beaten and battered by the elements, cowed by the landscape, subjugated by a reasonably kind but still condescending colonial power, and then given a glimpse of a very different way of life by their American guests, the Icelanders have morphed into a curious hybrid.

As a result, their genetic homogeneity and small, tightly connected population didn't translate into trustworthiness, accountability, openness, a strong civil society, long-termism, individual self control – all of those things that have made the Nordic countries so successful. Instead, their genetic disposition towards high risk and a historic lack of Protestant inhibitions created the perfect climate for a corrupt, nepotistic, anti-democratic economic free-for-all. The same short communication links that enable quick decision-making, and which should have fostered trust and responsibility, still allowed for quick decisions, but also for certain people to bypass accountability and crush dissent. Deals were done outside of the usual democratic channels. Palms were greased, naysayers silenced, and it all happened so very quickly.

*

So what does the future hold for Iceland? The country finds itself sitting on the global naughty step with its pocket money confiscated. It doesn't have much of a manufacturing industry, and there aren't enough fish in the sea to pay back the money it owes. The Icelanders are looking, instead, to the fearful energy that rumbles beneath their feet.

The most famous tourist attraction in Iceland is the Blue Lagoon – the eerie, milky-blue, geothermally heated outdoor bathing pools in the middle of an otherwordly lava field forty-five minutes outside Reykjavik. I'd always assumed these lunar-like ponds were a natural phenomenon, like the coloured lakes of Flores in Indonesia; certainly the company that owns them does nothing to correct such assumptions. But in fact, the Blue Lagoon's warm waters and supposedly health-giving silica mud are the discharge from the nearby Svartsengi geothermal plant, which began operating in the 1970s (I guess, 'Come, bathe in an industrial waste product!' is not all that enticing a proposition for tourists). The waste is rich in salt, algae and, above all, silica, which is said to be good for various skin conditions. These days it is packaged and sold in the Blue Lagoon store as an upmarket face cream.

The air temperature was around freezing when I visited the Blue Lagoon, so I trotted briskly from the warmth of the communal changing rooms, throwing off my towelling dressing gown and plunging into the 38-degree water as quickly as I could. The water only came up to my thighs and so, to minimise contact with the chilly air, I was forced to adapt to an awkward crouch-walk, my toes wriggling in the gloopy silica mud that covers the bottom of the pool. It was also very crowded and much smaller than it looks in photographs, but, after duck-walking over to the the less occupied parts of the pool, I soon realised why there were fewer people there: the water was scorching hot, unbearably so in places. Looking down, I was taken aback to see that I had turned the colour of boiled lobster. I rapidly crouch-walked in the opposite direction. None of this seemed terribly relaxing to me.

The Icelanders have been exploiting the thinness of their earth's crust for centuries, and today virtually all of their homes are heated geothermally. With the hope of making fast money in the world of finance gone, the Icelanders are turning to their geothermal energy. Though the holy grail of being able to store electricity, or send it via an oft-mooted cable to the UK and Europe still eludes them, there is increasing optimism that clean tech industries might offer one way back from the brink for Iceland. Icelanders are also beginning to export their geothermal know-how to other 'thin-crust' areas like Indonesia and East Africa, and there are ambitious plans to triple geothermal output in the hope of attracting more companies like Google, which already has a base here.

The grand vision is for Iceland to become the world's 'green data hub', home to the servers housing all our digitised information. The IT industry currently accounts for around 2 per cent of the world's energy consumption, and the larger the demand for servers, the larger the demand will be for sustainable, non-polluting power to run and cool them. Already the Icelandic economy is showing signs of having turned the corner towards renewal: growth is outstripping the European average, unemployment is down, and the budget deficit is under control. Letting its banks fail turned out to be not such a bad call after all and, though it was morally questionable, it certainly helped that the Icelanders have so far simply refused to pay their multi-billion euro foreign debts. At least they avoided a national default.

I suspect it is going to take more than a few quietly humming computer servers to restore Iceland's morale. 'Very few people are proud Icelanders today,' the writer Sindri Freysson told me when we met in Kaffibarinn, back in Reykjavik. 'We are beating ourselves up for allowing this to have happened. The sense of national identity has been tarnished.'

Meanwhile, a thousand miles or so east, the Icelanders' ancestors were about to face an identity crisis of their own, a crisis on a far greater scale, and of a far deeper consequence, than anything merely financial.

NORWAY

Chapter 1

Dirndls

The lawns of Slottsparken are packed with picnickers and partying Norwegians. The sky is an unblemished blue and, as always in Scandinavia, somehow *higher*-seeming than any sky anywhere else in the world. In the near distance a stout figure in a top hat is waving from a balcony.

Today, here in Oslo, we are basking in a rare alignment of good fortune: it is *Syttende Mai* – 17 May, Norwegian Constitution Day, which this year has fallen on a Sunday blessed with spectacular weather; and last night Norway, represented by a Minsk-born violinist singing a pathologically catchy song inspired by Norwegian folk music, put to rest the country's *nul points* nightmares of the past with a landslide victory at the Eurovision Song Contest.

Oh, and let us not forget, these are the richest people on earth. Which is quite a cherry.

I have joined the crowds lining the streets of central Oslo to watch the annual parade of local schoolchildren meander through the city to the royal palace. King Harald V, in top hat and tails, his bearded Crown prince son Haakon, and sundry other spare parts from the Norwegian royal family, are greeting their people from the balcony with nods and waves.

They seem pretty satisfied with their lot today, the Norwegians, but elsewhere in Scandinavia Norway's Constitution Day is viewed with not a little condescension. The eminent Swedish ethnologist Åke Daun once described Norway's 17 May as a 'national delirium'. Talk to Danes and Swedes about the day and they will roll their eyes and chuckle as if to say, 'Those Norwegians aren't like us. Very nationalistic. Rather stuck in the past. Still, they've got all that oil so they can do as they please.' Some actually come right out and say all this, adding that the Norwegians are right-wing, reactionary, insular, nationalistic flag-wavers (this from Danes who, as we have heard, will stick their national flag in the cat's litter tray given the appropriate feline-orientated anniversary).

Part of the problem lies, I suspect, in how the Norwegians dress for their special day. They are a bit special, the Norwegians, and 17 May showcases this specialness in abundant ways magnificent to behold. It is the fancy dress party to end them all.

Soon after leaving my hotel at 9 a.m., I begin to encounter them en masse: men, women, children and, in some instances, their pets, all decked out in regional costume. These include heavily embroidered dirndls,* shawls, neckerchiefs and frock coats in black, red and green; shiny top hats; hobnail shoes with silver buckles; bright-buttoned breeches; crisp white blouses with pirate sleeves; horseshoe hats and natty knickerbockers – all of which eccentric get-up is collectively known as *bunad*. Babies wear lacey bonnets; dogs wear red-white-and-blue ribbons; taxis, trams and prams, too, bear the national colours. There are nautical uniforms and marching bands, and flags, of course, fields of them, big and small, held aloft and fluttering in the light spring breeze.

I should make it clear that we are not talking here about one or two enthusiastic odd bods in the crowd, like the ruddy-faced man at a royal pageant wearing a Union Jack suit, or dressed as Uncle Sam at a veterans' parade. A very large proportion of both those in the parade and spectators, are sporting some manner of elaborate eighteenth- or nineteenth-century rural garb.

'Yes, we are kind of special up here in the North,' a fellow bystander says to me, catching my look of concern as I arrive at the parade proper. I am especially surprised by the teenage girls freely, *proudly*, dressed like a cross between Heidi's grandmother

---

* A Norwegian friend of mine gets quite worked up when I call them this: 'They are not dirndls,' she says. 'They are gala costumes.' But they are close enough to dirndls, and besides, it's such a fantastic word.

and a holidaying Eva Braun: when I was a teenager I refused to leave the house if there was the slightest risk that my clothing might draw any attention from my peers. 'This'll be on TV live through the day and from parades all over Norway, and even in Norwegian communities in American and Canada,' continues the bystander, who is actually one of a minority dressed in civvies, adding with a big smile, '*Gratulerer med dagen!*'

'Make sure you dress smartly,' a Norwegian chef friend had told me when he found out I was travelling to his capital city on 17 May. I was glad for the advice. If they were not wearing one of the four hundred or so different traditional costumes from Norway's provinces (the most popular, according to a four-page spread devoted to the costumes in that day's *Dagbladet*, being the one from Telemark), most of my fellow spectators were dressed as if for a wedding: the men and boys in suits and ties, with shades and an excitable excess of hair gel; the women in posh summer frocks and heels; and the girls in their best new party dresses. 'I usually go to work in a hoodie and jeans, but I'll put on a shirt and proper shoes if I have to go out on 17 May,' the friend had added. It was the first time I had ever worn a suit to watch a public parade, but I was glad I had.

Of the Nordic peoples, only the Norwegians commemorate their national coming-of-age with quite such fervour, spending a total of around 30 million kroner on their *bunader* (individuals might spend up to 70,000 kroner – £7,000 – for one costume alone). Yet the historic reasons for such extravagant celebrations appear opaque. The split from Denmark and the writing of the Norwegian constitution in 1814, which is what they are supposed to be commemorating today, was only really the beginning of a long, slow, rather low-key effort to wrestle free from Sweden's grasp that did not culminate in full independence until 1905. And, even then, it wasn't so much a question of the Norwegians wrenching liberty from the tyrannical rule of Stockholm with their dirndls flying and all guns blazing. Theirs was an independence born of persistent nagging over many decades, followed by a few minor skirmishes on the streets of Oslo. In the end, Stockholm agreed to a referendum based on spectacularly bad intelligence: the Swedes thought the Norwegians would vote to stay with them, but they voted against.

One Norwegian conceded to me that 17 May was really not much more than 'a kind of "fuck you" to the Swedes'; in fact its roots stem largely from the end of German occupation in 1945. I learned all this later that morning, as I sat nursing the world's most expensive beer (a tenner) at an outdoor café table, and got chatting with a teacher from a school just outside of Oslo. 'It was really by chance that 17 May coincided with the Germans' surrender,' she told me. The actual date was 8 May, but that presumably gave the Norwegians just over a week to muster their bunting and burnish their buckles for what must have been a hell of a street party.

What of the other Nordic countries and their national celebrations? Only Finland and Iceland have been ruled by others for any significant period, so you would expect their national days to be more charged than those of Denmark or Sweden. Finland does celebrate its independence from Russia (in 1917), but in a typically Finnish, introspective kind of a way. The day plays out almost entirely in private homes and on television, something I suspect is only partly explained by the fact that it falls in December and so any marching would have to negotiate knee-deep snow, and more because that's just how Finns are. The Finns are special too, you see. Only the Icelanders, who share the Norwegians' penchant for fondly imagined nineteenth-century simulacra of medieval peasant costumes have anything to match, and Icelanders are basically self-exiled Norwegians anyway, so I am not sure they really count.

The Swedes consider themselves far too modern to indulge in this kind of public dressing up; besides, they have never been occupied, so have no such yoke-shrugging to celebrate. Their 'National Day' on 6 June is, by comparison, a contrived and half-hearted event being tied up with their break from the Kalmar Union in the sixteenth century. From what I hear, there is sporadic flag-waving on the day, but this has at times been hijacked by right-wing extremists, thus confirming many Swedes' fears that this kind of overt nationalistic expression brings the Nazis out of the woodwork. Some Norwegians accuse the Swedes of jealousy over the fact that they get to dress up and wave flags on 17 May, but I think it's fair to say that were the Swedes to adopt the Norwegian approach it would be a source of mortifying embarrassment for at least half the population. This kind of Nordic national romanticism still prompts uncomfortable memories of the Swedes' dalliances with the Nazis during the Second World War. The Norwegians, on the other hand, fought more determinedly against the Germans than any of their Scandinavian siblings, so have no such qualms about reviving this otherwise unfashionable iconography.

The Danes, meanwhile, would find the whole idea similarly preposterous, never having been yoked to anyone but the Germans for a handful of years during the Second World War (an occupation that was, let's be honest, no biggie in the grand scheme of things). As we have heard, you will not find a more fervent bunch of flag-wavers outside of Pyongyang, but, sadly for them, the Danes would struggle to muster any kind of a national costume beyond jeans and a cycle helmet.

So we are left with the Norwegians as the leading Nordic proponents of overt public nationalism in all its easily mocked glory. I rarely shy from the task of mocking easy targets but, as I mingle with the be-dirndled crowds on the streets of Oslo, gradually, quite unexpectedly, I begin to find my approach to the Norwegians and their 17 May celebrations transform.

For one thing, it takes some chutzpah to pull on a pair of knickerbockers, wrap yourself in a great, ivory-coloured cape, and stride out on to the streets of a twenty-first century European capital looking like an escapee from Middle Earth. It also demonstrates an enviable tribal confidence, a link to a less complicated, more innocent past, which most of us left behind when James Watt invented his steam engine and we all went off to live amid the bricks and smoke. In Britain, the few traces that remain of these kinds of folkloric traditions are easy fodder for the lazy comedian (or conductor Sir Thomas Beecham, for that matter, who once said, 'In this life, try everything once, except incest and folk dancing'). *Syttende Mai* may largely be a post-war revival of a national identity contrived in the late nineteenth century, a romanticised imagining of rural traditions that probably never really existed, but there is no doubting the sincerity of those who take part.

The overwhelming impression I had that day, standing on the broad, clean streets of Oslo, was of a country wholly at ease with itself, of a people basking not just in vast material wealth but in an equally valuable civil cohesion deeply rooted in a shared history: a solid national–spiritual capital, if you like. By stepping out wearing their intricate, expensive and, to some eyes perhaps, silly, regional costumes, the Norwegians were sending a signal to one another: 'I am like you. We share the same history, the same values, and I am prepared to expend vast amounts of money, go to significant sartorial lengths and risk public humiliation in order to demonstrate this.'

In the end, I spent a very happy couple of hours on the streets of central Oslo watching the traditional parade of children – a good number of them ethnically non-Norwegian – from kindergarten-age to teenagers, and I envied Norway that day. I envied its sense of togetherness, its unabashed pride and, yes, the capes. There should be more capes in the world. I would look great in a cape.

At one point, as a multicoloured gaggle of under-tens passed by in that distracted way that characterises the marching style of under-tens everywhere, I had to fight myself to stop from crying. Admittedly, this should be taken in the context of a man who has become pitifully prone to lachrymosity (Pixar films are virtually a no-go these days, and I can only watch major sporting events in private), but what on *earth* was this all about? As a Somali girl passed by, struggling proudly with a flag three times her height, followed by a Sikh boy in authentic *bunad*, it was all I could do to suppress a full-blown, snotting meltdown. And that really *would* have turned heads. It wasn't just the fact of their ethnicity that had so touched me, but that the Somali, Turkish, Iraqi and Pakistani kids had committed just as fully to the *Dungeons and Dragons* aesthetic as their 'pure' Norwegian peers. They, too, were proudly, unselfconsciously dressed up in their Hobbit Sunday best. And it doesn't get much more assimilated than that.

It wasn't so long ago, the 1980s in fact, that Norway was plagued by right-wing activity, with street marches, arson attacks on asylum centres, skinhead neo-Nazis parading on the streets of Oslo, and attacks on non-Western immigrants. But then, in 2001, members of a neo-Nazi group called the Boot Boys were found guilty of murdering a fifteen-year-old Oslo boy of mixed race. There was public outcry: a mass rally was held in Oslo attended by 40,000 people, and everyone assumed the far right had retreated to the wilds of the Internet. At around the same time, Oslo schools with large numbers of children of non-Western backgrounds who had wanted to march on 17 May had been the target of bomb threats and demonstrations by the same species of right-wing thug. In response, there had been a conscious effort by local authorities and civic groups to make 17 May an actively multicultural, inclusive event. It seems to have worked wonderfully, at least it did to me, on that morning.

Later that day, on NRK1 TV, amid live coverage of all the various other, often perplexing and arcane, 17 May rituals being acted out throughout rural Norway (in Tjøtta, in Nordland, some children were pushing an oil barrel down a dirt track on a shopping trolley and hitting it with hammers), I watched an interviewer in traditional costume ask an Iraqi woman what she thought it meant to be Norwegian: 'To be democratic, a socialist, pluralist. Maybe not so outgoing,' she said. Other commentators were keen to stress that anyone, immigrant or otherwise, could become a Norwegian, and that one of the nation's key values was 'not to feel threatened'. Another said that the Belorusian background of the previous evening's Eurovision winner set a good example for the 'New Norway': 'We should feel so proud to have so many accents,' he added.

While watching the TV, my eye was caught by a headline in one of the day's newspapers: 'Nothing Can Bring Us Together Like 17 May . . . And Nothing Can Split Us Like 17 May.' I scoured the article for evidence of the conflict alluded to in the headline. Were there some Norwegians who *opposed* 17 May? As it turned out, the controversy – and it was a major one: the article went on for five pages – concerned the *slight* alteration of the route of a 17 May parade in a town in Hadeland. It wasn't that some people wanted the parade stopped, or that they weren't interested in joining it, but that they were outraged that some local councillor had decided that it should no longer pass a particular old people's home. So much for my 17 May controversy.

After watching the morning's parade and having waved back enthusiastically at the far-off king, I sat on a grassy bank and watched as the younger children were hustled on to buses and coaches and whisked away from the city centre. Now, it seemed, the real party could begin. It was time for the high school graduates to let rip.

Throughout all of Scandinavia, *gymnasium* (high school), graduates celebrate by parading through their home towns on the backs of an assortment of open-aired farm vehicles, trucks and buses, clutching festively chinking carrier bags, and getting off with each other. In Denmark and Sweden, for some reason, they wear vaguely nautical-looking, peaked white caps, which make them look as if they are part of a sailing club. Graduation day often falls on an ordinary weekday and there can be a strange dissonance in seeing everyone else going about their daily business while a small section of society lets rip in the most spectacular fashion (I say the graduates 'parade', but no one really lines up to spectate). One afternoon while with my family on the beach near where we live in Denmark, a truckload of partying graduates arrived, promptly stripped off, and ran into the sea. In Britain or the US young eyes would have been shielded, there would have been loud tutting and the police might have been summoned, but in Denmark the other parents laughed and applauded as a parade of fashionably trimmed pubic topiary bounced past their children's eyes.

While the ever-sensible Swedes sensibly celebrate *after* their exams, in Norway they tie one off *before* their exams, which is either a mark of collective confidence or utter nihilism, I'm not sure. They also wear red dungarees along with their sailor's caps. The dungarees are festooned with flags and badges and, that year at least, worn with the shoulder straps hanging down. (One other odd thing, the graduates were handing out specially printed calling cards – *Russekort* – bearing their photos and a joke or two. The smaller children – those who had not been bussed hastily out of town – were scampering around trying to collect as many as they could. It was terribly sweet.) Soon the dirndls and capes were replaced by a sea of red dungarees swaying and dancing, occasionally intertwined, a tangle of scarlet limbs and, as time went on, a large number of them prone in the grass.

There was no skinny dipping that day in Oslo, but there was plenty of drinking. This was the fabled *helgefylla* (the Norwegian term for binge drinking) as the Independence Day revellers and the graduates caroused, sang and made merry amid the shiny glass yuppie towers of the redeveloped harbour area, Aker Brygge, home to some of the town's swankiest bars and most costly real estate. Here, beside the harbour, with the country's striking new opera house floating like a shard of ice in the near distance, the drinking started in earnest around lunchtime and kept right on through to the next morning. It seemed as if half of Norway was out in Oslo that day, with the express intention of having a jolly time of it. By mid evening the streets were awash with empty champagne bottles. The Eurovision-winning 'I'm in Love with a Fairytale' blasted from speakers balanced on window ledges on Frognerveien, where the cafés and bars were heaving, customers spilling boisterously out into the late-night sunshine. Women in heavy, ankle-length embroidered skirts danced with men in capes; kids in red dungarees danced with other kids in red sailor's caps. It was a great day to be in Norway.

A little over two years later, as I worked at home in my office one Saturday afternoon, I read a headline on my computer: a large bomb had gone off in central Oslo. Soon after, reports began filtering through that a gunman had shot a number of people – perhaps as many as fifteen – at a Young Labour summer camp on the island of Utøya, 24 miles north-west of the capital.

Chapter 2

Egoiste

'Innocence ends when one is stripped of the delusion that one likes oneself.'   Joan Didion

Even in midwinter the sun is so sharp it forces me to squint, reflecting off the snow it turns the landscape into a light box. The air is brisk and, as I make my way from the airport terminal, I catch the scent of fresh pine. The bus driver grunts when I ask if he is going to Oslo centre. I assume this is an affirmative but, as we drive, I scan the view anxiously for clues that we are heading in the right direction. We drive past the yacht harbours that fill the fjords surrounding Oslo and, between the regimented conifers, I catch glimpses of dayglo hikers bearing those high-tech walking sticks that make them look like they have mislaid their skis, striding in single-file along the forested hillside paths. I am reminded just how extraordinarily beautiful Norway is. It is perhaps the most beautiful country I have ever seen.

It is seven months since a 32-year-old Oslo man, the racist extremist Anders Behring Breivik, single-handedly doubled Norway's average annual homicide rate in one afternoon, killing a total of 77 people. One of his chief bugbears about non-Western immigrants – who were the indirect subjects of his attacks that day – was that he held them responsible for most of the violent crime in Norway. Well, not now they weren't.

From my seat in the bus nothing appears to have changed. What did I expect? Razor wire and police patrols? Hardly likely in a land where the then prime minister, at the memorial service to the dead of Utøya and the Oslo bomb, gave one of the most courageous speeches in defence of public freedom I have ever heard. Jens Stoltenberg had called for 'more openness, more democracy', at a time when most politicians elsewhere in the world would have used an attack of that nature to pledge revenge, exploit the anxieties of the electorate, garner greater authority and power, and then compromise civil liberties. His speech was a reminder that the political leaders of the North have often served as the moral compass of the world.

Wandering around the capital – mostly trying to find a restaurant I could afford, peering at the menus outside like some starving match girl – the atmosphere seemed to confirm my impression that little had changed. There were 'no barricades on Oslo's streets; no new security measures in this sturdy, restrained city; no X-ray machines on the Metro; no armed police patrolling its malls; no security checks at public institutions. You could still walk right up to the front door of the royal palace, which remained free of any kind of fencing or gates.

So, the furniture and fabric of Norwegian society appeared not to have altered, and it occurred to me later that day, as I caught the tram to Blindern, the stop for Oslo University, that merely to ask the question, 'How has Breivik changed Norway?' was to grant the man a far greater significance than will ever be his due. But the question needed to be asked, and that was why I had returned.

Though eventually judged to be quite sane, this crazed narcissist, the son of a Norwegian diplomat and a nurse, was clearly mad as far as the average observer was concerned, his psychological well-being apparently fatally fractured – assuming it had ever been whole – from an early age. The crack-up had been compounded by personal setbacks in adulthood, his life in retrospect seeming to have traced an inevitable parabola towards destruction of one kind or another (his suicide at some stage in the future would seem to be the natural end point). Breivik was the classic tragic loner, living with his mother, fuelling his racist paranoia by browsing Islamophobic rantings on the Internet, meticulously, nerdishly cutting-and-pasting them into a garbled 1,500-page manifesto detailing everything from his multiple, hate-filled delusions about the Muslim threat, to his preferred aftershave – Chanel Platinum Egoiste – a diatribe that he then mailed to 1,003 people across Europe.

What could the actions of a mentally ill man tell us about the country that made him? Nothing, presumably. Yet Breivik's attacks must have shaken the foundations of Norwegian society – the unprecedented scale of his slaughter would have ensured that – but there was also the inescapable fact of his ethnicity to deal with. This unthinkable act of violence had been carried out by a Norwegian, not a non-Western Islamic extremist, not a foreigner – as was the case with the various, thankfully small-scale, attacks in Sweden and Denmark in recent years – but a Norwegian born and bred: Europe's first anti-Muslim terrorist.

'The first picture I saw of him on 22 July was where he was wearing his Lacoste T-shirt with upturned collars,' one Norwegian had told me. 'And, you know, I thought, "I know him. I see him at football games, I've gone to school with this guy." He's so ordinary.'

I have to admit, and I am not especially proud of this, but there was the very slightest sense of relief when, in the hours after the first bomb had been detonated in central Oslo and the world's media had jumped to its default Islamic terrorist conclusions, the real identity of the perpetrator emerged and it transpired that he was as Norwegian as one could be. The relief that this was not the work of Islamic terrorists was, of course, entirely separate from any reaction to the crime itself, relating more to fears of the potential retribution such an attack might have inspired. An Islamic terrorist attack as heinous as this would have seen the political discourse on immigration and race blasted back to the Middle Ages. One presumes life would have become untenable for many Muslims living here, as was the case in the US in the wake of 9/11; and one assumes, too, that the attack would have been used by the mainstream right wing throughout Scandinavia to shore up their support, as also happened after 2001. In the few hours before Breivik's identity became known, various far-right websites and blogs had already begun to unleash their predictable and violent anti-Islamic sentiments, and several Muslims were physically assaulted in the Norwegian capital.

Certainly, the Norwegian Police Security Service had not foreseen such an event: in a report written just a few months prior to the attacks they stated that right-wing extremists did 'not present a serious threat to Norwegian society in 2011'.

One presumes it would have been at least marginally easier – only very marginally, admittedly – to come to terms with the attacks had the perpetrator been an outsider, someone from an established category of aggressor. Instead, it was a blond-haired, blue-eyed Norwegian 'patriot'. One of them.

The Norwegians had reacted to the attacks in various ways: horror, obviously; solidarity, mainly; revulsion at Breivik's opinions, of course. But some felt there had been too much discussion of Breivik's mental state and not enough about his views and the extent to which other Norwegians might agree with them. One Norwegian, commenting on an online article on the *Guardian* website about a Danish theatre production based on Breivik's manifesto, which premiered, rather tastelessly, during his trial, wrote: 'Here in Norway there has been very little discussion of what he said. The fact is that it's much less far from the mainstream than many are willing to accept – whilst most Norwegians are not racist, some hold deeply troubling views . . . Norway does need to ask itself some very serious questions about why the world's worst single-gunman atrocity happened here, in this apparently peaceful and harmonious country where nothing bad ever happens.'

Prior to 22/7, as the attacks are more commonly referred to in Norway, the country had the strongest mainstream right-wing party in all of the region, and one of the strongest in Europe: the Fremskrittsparti, or Progress Party. Though its popularity dipped following Breivik's attacks, in the last parliamentary election to take place in Norway, in September 2013, the Progress Party, led by the pugnacious blond Siv Jensen, won 16.3 per cent of the vote. Its triumph was all the more astonishing given the fact that Breivik was, for many years, a highly active member of the party. Until 2013, the Progress Party had been routinely shunned by the other political parties but, crucially, this electoral triumph was enough to make it a partner in the new centre-right coalition government for the first time in its history.

The Progress Party's unprecedented electoral success would appear to confirm the depictions of Norwegians I had heard from their neighbours as just a *shade* to the right of the Ku Klux Klan. Norway has accepted far fewer immigrants than either Denmark or Sweden, for instance, and has recently taken to repatriating denied asylum seekers at a rate of 1,500 or so a year. Coverage of the Breivik attacks had also mentioned numerous right-wing Norwegian organisations, activists and bloggers, highlighting what appeared to be a disturbing sub-culture of Islamophobia in the country, ranging from Facebook groups for people who refused to ride in taxis driven by Muslims, to those of the so-called Eurabian school, who believed their government was part of an early seventies conspiracy on the part of European oil-thirsty governments to allow Muslims to take over Europe in order to appease the OPEC nations (there are actually people who believe this, the fact that Norway is one of the largest oil producers in the world seeming to have escaped them).

On a previous visit to Norway I had read in *Dagbladet* that the Holocaust-denying British historian David Irving was going to be giving a talk near Lillehammer that week. Though the Norwegians proudly boast of having had a more active and successful resistance movement than the Danes, some Norwegians did collaborate with the Germans during the occupation of 1940–5, not least their then prime minister Vidkun Quisling, whose surname was famously adopted as an eponym for traitors everywhere. Norway's most celebrated literary figure, Knut Hamsun (kind of their James Joyce), gave his Nobel Prize to Goebbels, and wrote a famous obituary of Hitler in the Norwegian collaborationist newspaper, *Aftenposten*, calling him 'a reformist character of the highest order,' adding, 'We, his close followers, bow our heads at his death.' Hamsun's reputation never really recovered. *Aftenposten* remains the country's most popular daily newspaper.

Just how right wing was Norway? How had Breivik's actions altered the political landscape? Had the black shirts been tucked away at the back of the wardrobes, were the swastika neck tattoos being hidden by high collars, had the Islamophobic Internet trolls withdrawn to lick their wounds?

Chapter 3

The new Quislings

'Immediately after the terrorist attack everybody was still in
shock. Nobody could have anticipated anything like that
happening. It was too atrocious. Many of us had expected
violence to come from those quarters, those of us who had been
following these websites, and I had been the target of their
attacks having been dragged into it as a symbol of everything
that had gone wrong with Norway. But we hadn't expected it
to happen in that way. Maybe attacks on Muslims or on people
like me, high-profile defenders of pluralism, but not anything
of that kind.'

I have come to the University of Oslo, a bastion of the multicultural
intelligentsia that Breivik so loathed, to meet Thomas Hylland
Eriksen, one of Scandinavia's pre-eminent social anthropologists.

I had first met Eriksen during that 17 May trip in 2009, and we
had talked about Norway's Constitution Day and its meaning. Eriksen
often used to be trotted out on the day's TV coverage to bring a little
dissenting balance to proceedings as a member of Norway's pluralist
awkward squad. But he had changed his mind in recent years. 'I really
didn't use to like it,' he had told me of 17 May. 'But the content has
changed a great deal in recent years. It's far more inclusive these days,
almost a celebration of multiculturalism. So many minority kids take
part and are allowed to do the same as everyone else, for once. It's
often misunderstood but I find it heartening that it's now becoming
a ritual of inclusion, just like Australia Day in Australia. Most of the
people who are enthusiastic about Australia Day now are East Asian
immigrants who really have a stake in it.'

This time round, I wanted to know how Eriksen thought Breivik's atrocities might effect 17 May in the future. He was unsure: 'Because everyone wants a piece of it, you know. Lots of groups will try to appropriate it for their own purposes – they are already trying, even the Islamophobic right wing, who are portraying themselves as victims. They say the ultimate cause of 22/7 was multiculturalism. It's like saying the US had it coming to them on 9/11. It's a fairly tasteless thing to say, but they are saying it. They are just trying to deflect criticism from themselves that they have encouraged violence, not the kind of violence we saw on 22/7, but still violence, resentment, suspicion.'

Remarkably, the Norwegian right – the anti-multiculturalists and Islamophobes, in some cases the very bloggers whom Breivik had quoted in his diatribe – had indeed managed to turn the post-Breivik discourse on its head. They claimed that the media was now self-censoring when it came to discussions about immigration and Norwegian Muslims (who are estimated to make up about 3 per cent of the population), and that is was *they* – the right wing – who were suffering oppression. They were using Breivik's murders to their advantage. One prominent right-wing critic, Bruce Bawer, an American expat 'Eurabian' living in Norway, had written a now infamous opinion column in the *Wall Street Journal* shortly after Breivik's attacks making just this argument. And that morning I had read a Norwegian newspaper review of Bawer's latest e-book called *The New Quislings: How the International Left Used the Oslo Massacre to Silence Debate About Islam*.

Apparently, Eriksen was named in the book as one of these 'new Quislings', not to mention an anti-Semite. 'That's a first, you know!' Eriksen laughed, when I mention this to him. 'I've never heard that before.'

I asked him if he was afraid for his safety. 'No, I'm not easily scared. I get a lot of nasty emails, have done for years, but what can you do? You can't get police protection all day, and I don't really want it. After 22/7, of course, these personal attacks have taken on a slightly different meaning. People use these very violent metaphors of civil war, traitors and Quislings, and suddenly you feel less humorous about it. I used to see these people as quite comical but it's become very emotive.'

As we have heard, since I visited Eriksen that second time, Norway has had a general election. The comedians are now in power – the Progress Party being part of the new 'blue' governing coalition. The party started out in the early seventies as an anti-tax movement. Today, it is run on a hybrid right-wing/welfare-state platform of a type which can seem quite odd from a UK or US perspective, blending as it does calls for increased public spending, with emphasis on care for the elderly, together with more conventionally right-wing fear-mongering about non-Western immigrants. It is a similar template to that used by the Danish People's Party. Just don't ever make the mistake of mentioning this to the Progress Party, as I did when I initially tried to set up an interview with them (this prior to their 2013 election success). This was the response I received from their press secretary:

> We don't have any relations with any of these parties, we never have and we never will. I will tell you more about this when we meet. The only thing we have in common with the parties you have mentioned is that we have a 'frank' tone in the immigration debate. That's about it.

Well, that told me. Nevertheless, when I asked a Norwegian friend about the Progress Party, he said, 'Everyone knows that when it comes to being mean to immigrants, they are a lot more skilled at this than Labour. So if you want to be mean to immigrants, vote for them.'

Before Breivik, the Progress Party's rhetoric had been fairly extreme – a previous leader had claimed that all Muslims were terrorists, for example, and that they were 'on a par with Hitler in that they have a long-term plan to "Islamify" the world. They are well on their way to achieving this: they have travelled far into Africa and are well on their way in Europe, and we must speak out!' During a previous election – again, prior to Breivik's attacks – the party had issued leaflets showing a masked man with a gun and the words 'The perpetrator is a foreigner.'

I made an appointment to speak to the party's foreign affairs spokesman, Morten Høglund, and went along to the party's offices in a building behind the Storting (where there was, I might add, virtually no security).

How had Høglund felt when he discovered that Anders Behring Breivik had been a member of his party for seven years, chair of his local branch of the youth wing, not to mention the fact that his party was the only one in Norway not included in Breivik's blacklist of European political parties, thus placing it alongside organisations like the English Defence League (and Jeremy Clarkson) in the list of Breivik's good guys. 'He was one of you, wasn't he?' I said.

'It was disgusting. But he was upset with our party as well,' Høglund, a portly man, looking not unlike a provincial publican, replied. 'We have to think: do we give nourishment to elements when we talk about problems regarding immigration? But when we talk about Islam it is radical Islam, not Islam as a religion. We accept the freedom to believe any religion you want, the freedom to build a mosque.' (Something, it should be noted, that the Danish People's Party has consistently opposed.)

Back at the university the next day I met another of Bawer's 'new Quislings', Sindre Bangstad, a social anthropologist who has specialised in studying the lives of Muslims in Norway.

'Yes, I am apparently against freedom of speech,' Bangstad laughed, tightly. 'If you are public about anything involving immigration issues in Norway, this is what you risk. I do get regular hate mail, so it's not as if this is new to me. In his tract, Breivik sees universities as a soft target – this is in his instructions for potential solo terrorists – but,' he laughed dismissively, trying to lighten the mood, 'he seems to be convinced that the sociology department is much worse when it comes to Marxists.'

I had come to see Bangstad because he was an expert on the Norwegian Right. How much, I asked him, do Breivik's views represent those of ordinary Norwegians?

'Well, Breivik claimed he had 35 per cent of the Norwegian population on his side, but he is completely delusional about that.

There are, though, websites like document.no [a notorious anti-Islamic site] which are read by 50,000 every month. One of the worst groups, SIAN [Stopp islamiseringen av Norge] claims to have 10,000 Facebook followers, although, when they try to mobilise, only about thirty-odd people turn up. Many people would argue that a lot of the rhetoric you see on various websites these days is equally appalling to what was there before 22/7 and, if you look at opinion surveys, attitudes towards immigrants, Muslims and Islam in Norway haven't substantially changed. That's not to be expected either.'

But what of the man on the street? How racist are ordinary Norwegians? I mentioned to Bangstad that I was still routinely shocked by a fairly widespread brand of casual racism from the kinds of sources that should know better, not just in Norway, but in Denmark, and I'd seen it in Iceland too: broadsheet newspaper cartoons depicting Africans in tribal costume with exaggerated lips and bones through their noses, for instance; Asians with buck teeth and narrow eyes; comedy shows that mock immigrants' language skills; and the use of the word *neger*, meaning 'black person' and, for me (and, I know, for some black visitors to the Nordic region, too), uncomfortably close to 'negro', or even 'nigger'. I recently read a story about a Swedish town that, for forty years, had been nicknamed 'Negro Village' (*Negerby* – on account, I think, of some or other landmark: black chimneys perhaps), but was at last attempting to change its name to the more neutral 'Eastern Town'. The locals weren't having it though, and were sticking to the old name. It is the kind of attitude that can make the Nordic societies seem stuck in the 1950s, and not, for once, in a good way. But when you challenge them on this, their response is either genuine puzzlement that anyone might take offence – usually characterised by a kind of mock-innocent literalism: 'But they *do* have big lips!' – or accusations of overt political correctness.

'Norwegian racism is always a kind of racism that is not prepared to accept it being qualified as such,' agreed Bangstad. 'Because we're the good guys, and racism is what bad people do. Within the last ten years there was a public debate on whether one could use the Norwegian equivalent of *neger*, and people would get up and say, "I have the right to say this, why should I care about the sensitivities of African youths in Norway." A couple of weeks ago we had a case where a Swedish artist called Timbuktu contacted editors of a newspaper to complain about a cartoon of the tribal African with the big lips, and the basic argument again was "Why are you so offended?" And then it became a question of freedom of speech. "Here are all these politically correct people trying to prevent this."'

Ah, Scandinavians standing up for their right to print offensive cartoons. They have been here before, of course, with the Mohammed cartoon crisis of 2006, when the right-wing Danish newspaper *Jyllands-Posten* printed some boorish, wilfully unfunny cartoons of the Prophet Mohammed (with a bomb in his turban, and so on) to counter what they perceived as a mortal threat to their freedom of speech from Islamic rules on the two-dimensional depiction of their spiritual leader.

'Yes, quite,' Bangstad agreed. 'Of course, Norway was implicated in the Mohammed cartoon business; we actually got our embassy in Damascus burned down.'

'It's all rather depressing, isn't it?' I said. 'Is immigration from non-Western countries perhaps inevitably doomed to failure in the small, homogenous and traditionally isolated countries of the North?'

'Interesting question.' He paused. 'I mean, the way I see it, there are grounds for valid concerns over particular issues – homophobia, anti-Semitism, the treatment of women in certain sections of Muslim communities in Norway, but I don't necessarily see immigration from non-Western countries, or any other country for that matter, as a good or bad thing. Certainly it brings challenges, but I don't think they are insurmountable. I am certainly not among those from the radical Left – who you don't hear much from these days, admittedly – who campaigned saying "Let's have a million immigrants;" I am certainly not an advocate of that kind of head-in-the-sand approach. But if you look at the measures of success,

Norway seems actually to be dealing quite well with immigration from non-Western countries: if you look, for instance, at the figures on background of students in higher and tertiary education, particularly females.'

I had put the same question to Thomas Hylland Eriksen the day before. Did the Right perhaps have a point about non-Western immigration to Norway, and by extension Scandinavia? Were these kinds of societies inherently hopeless at integrating people so markedly different from themselves?

'Look, most Muslims are just like you and me. They want to live in peace with their neighbours, they want a peaceful life. You get dilemmas about hijabs and halal meat all over Europe and you need pragmatic solutions,' he said. 'We've got very good research on this which shows that second-generation immigrants have been very much "Norwegianised". They think like Protestants. When you look at the girls, they have replaced honour and shame with bad conscience, which is a very Protestant thing, and your relationship with God becomes an individual relationship, instead of it going through the community.

'You know, actually, Protestants and Muslims very easily reach a common understanding because they find out that they have a lot in common in how they see the world in questions of the sexes, fidelity and the idea that everything in this world is not random, that there is a transcendent mind behind things that gives life meaning. I sometimes think that, had the Pakistanis and Turks arrived in this country in the 1950s, it would have been easier for them to integrate because we were more rural, there was still gender segregation: in northern Norway, when the women were in the kitchen doing the dishes, the men would sit and smoke in the dining room, that was the norm for my parents' generation. If only they had arrived before we became so egalitarian and individualistic it would have been easier for them to relate.' Eriksen, a tall, bony, demonstrative man in his early fifties, laughed at the irony of this. Denmark was though, he said, a different matter.

'You know, Islam does seem a bit incompatible with the Danish way of life because, well, what do the Danes do in their leisure time? They go out and they drink a lot of beer and they eat dead pigs, and then they go home and have sex with strangers afterwards. And then they say to the Muslims, "Why don't you integrate better? Aren't you grateful for being in Denmark?"

'I always say this when people say to me, "Oh you're just another of these bloody multiculturalists who accepts everything, aren't you?" I say, well, no, but if you want to live in Norway there are a couple of things you need to make peace with: one is the cold and the darkness. If you can't cope with it, then go somewhere else. And the other is the equality of the genders, because otherwise you are never going to be happy because you will always feel there is something fundamentally wrong with Norway.'

Chapter 4

Friluftsliv

I had to leave Oslo, 'that strange city which no one leaves before it has set its mark upon them,' as Knut Hamsun puts it in the opening line of his masterwork *Sult* or *Hunger*. I had begun to feel increasingly nauseous at the sight of Breivik's self-satisfied grin on the television screens and front pages every day.

I had tried to find a few other distractions while I was in the Norwegian capital, but Oslo is, as I have mentioned, fiendishly expensive. According to a recent study by the Brookings Institution of the world's 200 richest cities, its residents are the second wealthiest in the world (just behind those of Hartford, Connecticut), with an average annual income of $74,057. They would need to be. This is the only city I have visited where the drivers of its public transport apologise to you for the fares. 'Sorry, this is Norway,' a tram driver said to me with apparently genuine remorse when I had appeared startled by his request for 50 kroner (£5) for the briefest of journeys.

At the Museum of Cultural History I had taken in the display on the Sami, featuring the usual Nordic tiptoeing around the subject of their oppressed indigenous minority. The Sami – 'Lapps' is, these days, a racist term – are effectively the sixth Nordic people, Europe's only nomads, whose territory spans the borders of northern Norway, Sweden, Finland and parts of north-west Russia, depending on where their reindeer roam. I learned that they probably number around 13,000 in Norway, their language was only officially recognised in 1987, and that, 'Some Sami still live in close contact with nature, but others spend their free time in front of the TV set and use their car even to visit a neighbour.' There was a small tableaux to illustrate the Sami's new, dissolute lifestyle, featuring a teenage bedroom with a computer and a mobile phone. Most odd.

Naturally, the museum had a copious collection of folk costumes, as well as a major exhibition on knitting patterns. In the rooms covering the country's more recent history, Aha's 'Take on Me' played in a continuous loop as I perused newspaper front pages from the past thirty years: Norway's first female prime minister (1981); the arrival of AIDS (1983); the first 7-Eleven (1986). Nowhere was there mention of the great lottery win of 1969 when the Norwegians first discovered oil. Odder still.

Even the most bewitching of knitting patterns can begin to pall after a while and, as the saying goes, 'When a man is bored with Oslo . . . he has probably been there for more than three days.' I am being unfair; Oslo is quite lovely and tries awfully hard to live up to its big-city billing, but for me it is the least interesting of the Nordic capitals. It can't compete with Copenhagen's dynamism and diversity; the scenic spectacle and architectural grandeur of Stockholm; or the edgy thrill of Helsinki's 'otherness', with its vestigial, Cold-War ambience. And Reykjavik has volcanoes and glaciers right on its doorstep, which is hardly fair. Oslo somehow feels like some other country's second city, which it of course was for many centuries.

It was time to see more of Norway, something natural. Time and again when talking to Norwegians about their Norwegian-ness they would bring the conversation back to the special relationship they have with their landscape, to their love of the *friluftsliv*, or 'open-air life'. Though the Swedes might argue (were they inclined to argue, which they are not), the Norwegians seem to have the strongest bond of all with their natural surroundings; their scenery is the source of their fiercest patriotic fervour. I suspect this might be because, historically, they have been distributed among it more widely than their neighbours. According to my *Encyclopedia of the Nations*, Norway is the least densely populated country in Europe, with eleven inhabitants for every square kilometre, three-quarters of them living within 10 miles of the coast. This has always been a country of peasant farmers and fishermen, with a decentralised population of small, isolated communities speaking hundreds of regional dialects. And because it was a colony for so long, and its capital city was a hub for the dissemination of foreign cultures, Norway has never looked to Oslo in the way that the Danes have to Copenhagen, or the Swedes to Stockholm. Denmark and Sweden have also reflected, and defined, themselves in and by each other, through their shared history of conflict and rivalry, but Norway has tended to mind its own business, separated by the great physical barriers of the mountains and the sea.

This decentralisation, coupled with a heightened respect for their natural surroundings, are two of the keys to understanding the Norwegians. Still, today, while Denmark struggles with its *udkants* problem and Sweden grows more and more centralised, in Norway people live out in the regions, way up north, in mountains, by the sea and on frozen islands. The contrast is striking when you cross from northern Norway to northern Sweden: on the Norwegian side there will be small towns with shops, perhaps a takeaway, decent roads and civic buildings, on the other . . . nothing. In Norway, the right to live wherever you want is enshrined in law: it is part of a strategy to maintain the populations in the north of the country, particularly those close to the strategically vital territories of the Barents Sea and Spitsbergen.

Elsewhere in the world, industrialisation led to urbanisation, but not so much in Norway: the fishing industry (which remains strong, and these days of course includes massive industrial salmon farms), and the oil industry, which is based on the west coast with Stavanger at its heart, have helped counter this trend. Thanks to the wealth generated by the latter, these days the Norwegians who live a long way from their capital live well, with decent infrastructure, cultural and sports facilities and impressive public buildings, like the Knut Hamsun Centre I visited in Oppeid, a village of around five hundred people. It is a stunning piece of contemporary concept architecture: a black tower with jutting perspex balconies, designed, I was told by my personal guide, to represent aspects of Hamsun's *Sult*. It cost the equivalent of £8 million of public money to build and would not look out of place in any modern capital city; but it only receives around 20,000 visitors a year, simply because it is so far away from everywhere, way, way up in the Arctic Circle.

One Norwegian I spoke to about this, Yngve Slyngstad, head of the country's oil-investment fund, likened the way the Norwegians are defined by their landscape to the way the French are defined by their culture: 'It is extraordinarily important for Norwegians to tell each other on a Monday morning that they have been out skiing, mountain walking, and so on,' he said. 'Norway has this fascination with having mountain cabins and ocean cabins, this fascination with nature.' Slyngstad also pointed out that an unusually high number of Norwegian surnames are connected to the landscape. 'Our names often come from actual physical places in nature, and it is not so long ago that people knew the places they came from ancestrally, and these were actual, physical places,' he said. 'My name refers to the place where the river bends and, exactly where the river bends, there was my father's farm, so there is this very strong identity and connection with nature. And if you live in cities, you only tend to reinforce it.'

One indication of this strong connection the Norwegians have to their landscape has been the remarkable success of two stupefyingly boring TV shows that aired in recent years. The first tracked the progress of a train from Oslo to Bergen through the mountains in real time for 7 hours, with just a fixed camera mounted on the front of the train. The tunnels must have been especially gripping. However, the unprecedented viewing figures for this show encouraged the national broadcaster, NRK, to go a step further and broadcast a 6-day, non-stop live transmission from a camera mounted on MS *Nordnorge*, one of Norway's Hurtigruten 'express' ferries, as it sailed from Bergen in the south, to Kirkenes, on the Russian border, in the north. Despite being billed by NRK with refreshing candour as 'Watching paint dry – live on TV', the programme was a massive viewing and cultural phenomenon, with half the population tuning in to watch: people hosted Hurtigruten-watching parties and, as the boat progressed further up the coast, crowds came out to light bonfires and wave from the shore, while smaller flotillas bobbed in the merry ferry's wake. The Hurtigruten programme was also streamed online and picked up 200,000 viewers in Denmark (a phenomenon the Norwegian media gleefully ascribed to 'mountain envy'), as well as viewers in other countries around the world. It ended up being one of the most popular Norwegian television programmes of all time, and all it was, was scenery . . .

But what scenery.

I look around at my fellow ferry passengers, who are mostly either playing cards, drinking beer or watching the TV screen mounted at the front of the boat. Haven't they *seen* what is passing by outside the window? My face is glued to the glass, as it has been for the past hour. Norway is passing by at a steady ferry pace, its landscape rendered with such clarity by the sharp Arctic light that I can make out every crenellation of the white mountain peaks, every facet of the granite rocks. The laser-etched scenery beyond my window appears to be being transmitted in the highest of high definition, that is the only explanation for the laser-etched scenery beyond my window. The mountain peaks look like the jaws of a shark magnified a thousandfold.

I am aboard the Hurtigruten, heading from Bodø to Nordskott, a microscopic fishing village, little more than a jetty and a handful of wooden houses, just inside the Arctic Circle.

Norway's fjords are staggeringly, CGI-ishly beautiful. No wonder *The Hitchhiker's Guide to the Galaxy*'s Slartibartfast won an award for designing them. Looking back, I can only conclude that it was the magic of this bewitching scenery, and my hosts' enthusiasm for it, which led me to take complete leave of my senses and – though it was February, and though all was snow and ice, and though this was the Arctic – allow myself to be persuaded to don a drysuit and wade into the waves in search of sea urchins. My friend, a Scot called Roddie, lives here with his Norwegian wife and children and fishes for these 'crows' balls', as the locals call them, selling them to top restaurants in the region. They were extremely good sea urchins, but it was fucking cold. Without gloves on my hands literally burned in the water.*

The landscape of Nordskott was, though, a feast for the soul. Each morning as I crunched through the snow to the fishing boat, I would stop for a moment amid the deafening stillness, the only sound my own tinnitus, and stare up at the mountains, my gast truly flabbered, thoughts of Oslo far from my mind.

* Visit Norway in the winter and you soon realise the single greatest challenge the Norwegians face every day is figuring out what to wear in order to stop the weather killing them. Their ability to plan ahead for the myriad extremes of temperature they will face during each day rivals the greatest of chess grandmasters. In Oslo I was forever finding myself either sweating buckets in my insulated jacket and overtrousers, and then trying to strip this cumbersome gear off while sitting in the confines of a tram (like some kind of downbeat escapologist act), or making sure no patch of skin was exposed while walking through the snow in temperatures as low as -15°C. Parents must spend an age getting their kids dressed for school.

Chapter 5

Bananas

Come and listen to a story 'bout a man named Jed,
A poor mountaineer, barely kept his family fed,
And then one day he was shootin' at some food,
And up through the ground came a bubblin' crude.
        The Beverly Hillbillies theme, by Paul Henning

To come to Norway and talk only of integration and immigration would be like visiting the Klondike in 1897 and preoccupying oneself with the plight of the Native Americans. For the vast majority of Norwegians, for the vast majority of the time, issues of Islamisation, immigration and populist politicians have been of little relevance because, over the last four decades, Norway has experienced a gold rush beyond anyone's wildest dreams, not least the Norwegians'.

The discovery in 1969 of what turned out to be gargantuan oil reserves in Norway's North Sea territories has shaped contemporary Norwegian society more than any other single factor – for the better but also, as we shall hear, for the worse. This black gold touches every Norwegian's life, pretty much every day. The success of modern Norway – of its welfare state, its virtually unparalleled standard of living, and its strong regional infrastructure, services and random, expensive and architecturally innovative museums – is to a great extent founded on oil.

This country of just over five million people now has the largest sovereign wealth fund in the world. And I don't mean per capita, we are talking in absolutes. It overtook Abu Dhabi's when it hit $600 billion in 2011, and continues to rise. The fund currently stands at £395 billion, or $617 billion, and is conservatively estimated to pass £1,000 billion before the end of the decade. To put that into perspective, the Norwegians could comfortably pay off all of Greece's national debt twice but, crucially, up until now, they have heeded their economists' warnings not to spend the money within their own borders, limiting themselves to using a mere 4 per cent every year and investing the rest elsewhere in the world.

I think it's fair to say that the Norwegians were not to the manor born. Norway has always been the downtrodden, economically disadvantaged poor relation of the Scandinavian triumvirate; a rural backwater whose population clawed their hardscrabble existence from barren soils – a mere 2.8 per cent of Norwegian land is farmable – and dangerous seas, often against the almost insurmountable odds presented by their climate and topography.

And then, one day, along came a man named Jed* and: Boom! Glug! Kerching!

The story of the Norwegians' transformation from dirndl-wearing peasants to dirndl-wearing Rockefellers has its beginnings in Holland, with the discovery of natural gas in Groningen, in 1959. This find prompted speculation that there might be more fossil fuel further north on the Norwegian continental shelf. Holland's Philips Petroleum requested permission to explore there and the Norwegian government moved quickly to assert its sovereignty over the shelf – at that time their territory only extended 12 miles out into the sea. Norway's claims raised eyebrows in London and Copenhagen, whose governments also felt they had dibs on part of the North Sea. And this is where the story of the Norwegian oil miracle takes an intriguing twist, one that has given rise to one of Scandinavia's most entertaining conspiracy theories.

In early 1965, representatives from each of the three governments met to thrash out a deal to divide up the North Sea shelf, a deal that was agreed and ratified at some haste in March of that year – greatly,

---

* Okay, he was more likely called Jan, and it took a couple of years to begin extracting the oil, but let's not slow the narrative.

it would transpire, to the Norwegians' advantage. If you ask Danes about these negotiations they will tell you, in all seriousness, that the Norwegians pulled a fast one. Press them on the point, and they will wave their hands vaguely as if to say, 'You know what the Norwegians are like.' Some will allude to the fact that the Danish foreign minister responsible for signing the treaty, Per Hækkerup, was a known alcoholic, and that he was drunk that day: 'Look at the line they drew,' they will say of the new North Sea bed's territorial borders. 'Notice how it suddenly drops down to take in the place where they found the oil!'

Having heard this rumour for many years from my Danish friends, I felt it was time I found out the facts, which are these: it is true that Hækkerup was an alcoholic, and, yes, that first massive Norwegian oil field, Ekofisk (which is still pumping the stuff out at quite a rate, and is predicted to continue to do so until 2050), was found right at the lower south-western corner of the Norwegians' newly demarcated territory, agonisingly close to Danish waters. It is also true that Denmark did have a justifiable quibble about who had sovereignty over that part of the North Sea, based on a technical issue to do with the depth of the ocean floor. It is also true that, for some reason, the usual cooling-off period relating to such agreements was not implemented. So why did the Danes sign so readily? It is not as if they didn't have ample historic precedents concerning the pitfalls of international border treaties.

The truth is, at that time no one really believed that there was oil in the North Sea, or that, if there was, it was extractable. Rather than argue the point, Denmark preferred not to risk annoying Norway with what it then deemed a petty argument about the sea bed: fishing rights were a far more pressing issue.

As for Hækkerup being drunk at the time he signed, there is no evidence for this but, well, alcoholics are not generally characterised by their sobriety during times of stress, are they?

'It was a coup,' Thomas Hylland Eriksen, admitted to me with barely disguised glee. 'It was cunning how they managed to expand the continental shelf area to 200 nautical miles. It was a guy called

Jens Evensen [a trade minister] who was the architect. The Norwegians got 70 per cent!'

Do the Danes perhaps regret having sent a possibly inebriated Social Democrat to negotiate their oil rights? One suspects they might well. Is this an issue between Norway and Denmark today? Absolutely not, at least not at any kind of political or diplomatic level. But the incident definitely features in the popular myth about the North Sea oil fields in Denmark, and continues to be recounted by older Danes as part of a narrative about being diddled out of their oil destiny by their country cousins, those tricksy Norwegians. It has also contributed to a slightly bitter, negative image of Norwegians among Danes as somehow having been rendered isolated and indolent by their misbegotten wealth; an image which also finds purchase among Swedes.

'Ak, they've never worked,' a male member of my Danish family, who wouldn't thank me for naming him so I won't, once told me. 'They have enough in themselves, they don't need anyone else.' The Danes pounce on any evidence of Norwegian indolence. They love to hear stories of migrant workers from Sweden manning Norwegian fish-processing factories, for instance, or waiting in their restaurants. 'I went to Oslo, and not once was I served by a Norwegian waiter!' is a common refrain among returning Danes (there are 35,000 Swedes working in Norway, tempted by wages of up to £30 per hour for semi-skilled work in shops, and so forth). One story in particular which has gladdened many a Danish heart concerns a number of Swedes working in a Norwegian processing plant, where they were reported to be employed to peel bananas. And it's true! I checked: the bananas are used in a popular Norwegian sandwich spread. Lazy Norwegians *and* exploited Swedes all in one joke. The Danes could hardly believe their good fortune.

In Sweden, meanwhile, resentment towards Norwegian high-handedness is growing. A recent sociological study questioned 3,800 Swedes about their neighbours, asking them, among other things, whether the Norwegians were bad at queueing ('Yes, very' said 59 per cent of Swedes – and I should point out, the Swedes queue for things with all the decorum of piglets jostling for a sow's teat); whether the Norwegians knew how to drive around roundabouts ('No'); and whether they ever parked in disabled parking spaces ('All the time!'). 'It is surprising how many negative things Swedes have to say about Norwegians,' the author of the study was reported as saying. 'They feel swamped by the Norwegians,' she added, warning that there was the potential for relations to turn ugly in border areas.

Back to the North Sea negotiations. In truth, the Danes didn't do too badly out of their own little patch of the sea bed. The so-called Dan Field began producing oil in 1972 and the country became self-sufficient in oil by 1991. At their output peak in 2004 the Danes were producing around 142 million barrels a year.

It is interesting to compare how the two countries differed in their handling of their respective oil bonanzas. The first barrels from the Norwegian Ekofisk field were produced in June 1971, and subsequent finds elsewhere in the newly delineated territory – some of the largest oil fields on earth at Statfjord, Oseberg, Gullfaks and Troll – came thick and fast, moving more northerly over the decade. By 1972 Norway had its own state oil company – the imaginatively named Statoil – which, by law, had to be a majority partner in any oil activities in the region (the law was later changed). The state took firm control over nationalised production and founded a wealth fund that it has since handled with remarkable self restraint. It has been able to ride out the global economic downturn and, in fact, the fund has increased by the equivalent of £30,000 per citizen since 2008.

The Danish oil field, on the other hand, became the sole preserve of one company, A. P. Møller–Maersk, the running of which was overseen until his recent death by Mærsk Mc-Kinney Møller, the son of its eponymous founder.

Quite how A. P. Møller–Mærsk won the sole concession rights to Danish hydrocarbon deposits for all eternity is rather opaque, but it seems to have involved a good few murky deals in smoke-filled rooms. Today, Mærsk is so central to the Danish economy – some estimates have it contributing over 10 per cent of GDP through its shipping and oil operations, as well as its supermarkets and various other activities – that one gets the sense that few politicians or journalists want to rock that particular boat, and the company has been able to renegotiate the terms by which it controls the Danish oil fields to its advantage ever since (most recently in 2012 when it extended the agreement until 2043) Some even claim the company effectively tells the Danish government how much tax it is going to pay each year, although – Mærsk lawyers please note – I don't believe this for a minute.

While Danish oil production peaked years ago, Norway's is still running at around 2 million barrels a day, or 730 million barrels a year. Statoil is the largest company of any kind in the Nordic region in terms of revenue and its current record profits. And, despite the perennial warnings that peak oil is imminent and that the Norwegians will soon find themselves on the slippery slope back to the fish-drying, sheep-shearing Dark Ages, they keep discovering massive new reserves: two gigantic puddles of the stuff containing up to a *billion* barrels-worth were found in the Barents Sea in 2011, and now, with the ice cap conveniently melting (I wonder how *that* happened?) the Norwegians also have the estimated 90 billion barrels of crude that lie beneath the Arctic in their beady sights. As if that wasn't enough to keep them going through the long, dark winters, Norway is also now the fifth largest producer of gas in the world; gas is expected to make up more than half of Norwegian petroleum production within a couple of years.

If there is a God, then he certainly exhibited a mischievous sense of humour in doling out the bling to Farmer Eigil and his be-dirndled wife. Scandinavia's much mocked little brother has done well for himself. Following that first discovery in 1969, Norway rose fairly rapidly to the top of the Scandinavian – and indeed, global – wealth rankings. Today it is the Dubai of the North. Croesus in a cape. The country now has the second highest GDP per capita in the world after Luxembourg, and Luxembourg is hardly a proper country.

I was fascinated to find out what kind of impact this windfall had had on a people more used to hoarding meagre resources through long winters and making the most of a life lived amid arid mountains, icy pastures and harsh seas. What had been the effect of the lottery rollover to end all lottery rollovers on the Norwegians' collective psyche, on the core of their character?

Chapter 6

Dutch disease

The Oil Fund is arguably modern Norway's greatest single achievement – the ultimate expression of Nordic self-discipline and control, and a paragon of responsible fiscal stewardship. This brilliantly managed, tightly controlled wealth fund is the envy of every oil-producing nation – not to mention every non-oil-producing nation – in the world.

The man ultimately responsibility for how that gigantic pot of gold is distributed around the globe is the CEO of Norwegian Bank Investment Management (NBIM), Yngve Slyngstad. I went to see Slyngstad in his Master-of-the-Universe eyrie on the top floor of the Norwegian National Bank building in central Oslo (where, as a result, perhaps, of Breivik's bomb, which was detonated just yards away, I noted they do actually have some security in the form of very natty individual, twin-door 'air locks' that make you feel like you are teleporting from the Starship Enterprise; every bank should have them).

'The purpose of the fund is to defend the consumption basket,' Slyngstad explained to me. My almost perfect ignorance of basic economic theory must have been writ large even at this early stage in our conversation, so he kindly explained what this meant. 'We have sold oil and gas to other countries, and sooner or later we will have to buy something and what we want therefore is to have the possibility of purchasing something a few generations from now that is at least equal in value to what we could have purchased today. So if world growth is good, we need to have a good return on the fund to protect our purchasing power in the future.'

The fund owns shares in over eight thousand companies, which effectively means that Norwegians own over 1 per cent of the world's listed companies, almost 2 per cent of Europe's and 0.7 per cent of Asia's.

I had read that the fund had recently begun to invest in what some analysts had seen as more risky propositions – property, for instance; they had bought some prestigious office buildings in Paris, for example. I leaned forwards, tapping the end of my pen on my chin. Why, I asked, was Norway taking a more risky approach with its pot of gold? (I didn't call it a pot of gold.)

Slyngstad, a trim fifty-year-old with a clean-shaven head and light-brown goatee, smiled sympathetically and explained that the oil fund was originally projected to run only for about thirty years. That point had long passed and yet they continue to discover new fields and new methods of exploiting existing ones, which means that they are able to make longer-term and riskier investment decisions: 'When the market was falling after 2008 we bought more than a thousand billion kroners worth of equities,' he said, a brave move at a time when not just Norway's investments, but all equities, were plummeting.

I wondered how Norwegians related to their fund. When it over-took Abu Dhabi's to become the world's largest, the Norwegian finance minister, Sigbjørn Johnsen, told a local newspaper that 'even if it is not a goal in itself to be the biggest, it is always nice to record that the fund is growing.' (I like to imagine him saying this while reclining in a jacuzzi, before downing the rest of his champagne and casting the flute over his shoulder.) Was all this money a cause for national pride, or was it considered vulgar to talk about it?

'Of course, we have been blessed and fortunate to have these natural resources, but I wouldn't say they we're proud,' said Slyngstad. 'If you go back two generations they were cautious about taking up all this wealth.'

How had the Norwegians managed to resist the temptation to spend their oil revenue, as Mrs Thatcher's government had in Britain in the 1980s, or some of the Arab states are doing so conspicuously at the moment?

'Two things: first is that the founding fathers of the fund were very clear about avoiding the Dutch disease. We could easily destroy the economy; we need to have an export-orientated economy that is able to survive without the oil, because if you are destroying your possibility to compete in the world, you can't be sure you will regain it later when the oil runs out.

'Traditionally, we have been a very poor country with a frugal consumption pattern, people living around the coasts,' he continued. 'Norway was not really part of Europe, to the extent that there was no European-style feudal system, people lived independently, not in towns and villages. People are connected to nature rather than to culture. It is a different mentality, right?'

As we've seen, this is a fundamental characteristic of Norway, and how its people differ from those of Sweden and Denmark. The Norwegians are used to subsisting on the bare essentials. As Slyngstad puts it, 'This is a country where, in the past, you didn't have enough to eat in winter unless you had saved it.' The Norwegians were mistrustful of indulgence or excess, ever-conscious of the need to save and hoard.

We talked a little about the current crisis in Europe. Slyngstad shared his surprisingly candid theory about how the other European nations had ended up in their respective economic quagmires. They were, he observed, simply fulfilling their own self-images.

'You go to Iceland and you kind of wonder, "What actually happened when they got all this unlimited cash?" They used it to fulfil their self-image as marauding Vikings, going around the world and taking assets. Vikings version 2.0. Norwegians could have done that with the oil fund, but we didn't because we perceived it as a wealth that was already there, therefore something to be protected. The Irish wanted to be English landlords, so they built these huge houses. And then you go to Greece and you ask, "What's their self-image?" I used to study philosophy, and Aristotle said, "Philosophy, what is that? Well the first premise is that you are not working." I am being a bit mean to the Greeks, but you shouldn't blame them for not working, they are philosophers, they have to sit there and think about life!'

The Greeks are a rather extreme example of a nation corrupted by cheap money, but the truth is the Norwegians have been somewhat corrupted too. To depict them as paragons of parsimony, untainted by their fantastic windfall, like the lottery winner who returns to his factory job and his usual place at the bar unaffected by the millions in the bank, is slightly misleading.

In his excellent book, *Petromania: A Journey Through the World's Richest Oil Lands* (unfortunately only available in Norwegian), the Norwegian author Simen Sætre documents how oil wealth rarely has a positive effect on any country in the long term. He does not believe his country has been immune to its corrupting influence either, pointing out that the Norwegians are working 23 per cent fewer hours per year than they were prior to the oil boom, taking more holidays (five weeks instead of four), and more sick leave (they top the European league in this), and retiring earlier (at 63.5 years). He quotes an OECD report on Norway which stated that the country's oil wealth had 'distorted the relationship between work and free time'.

Norway does seem to have been especially negligent of its capability to make things. It de-industrialised at a faster rate than most of its trading partners and today less than 10 per cent of its GDP is generated by manufacturing, compared with almost 20 per cent in Sweden. Oil and gas now make up over half the value of Norway's exports, fish and arms constituting the largest chunks of the rest, which explains why it has probably been a while since you bought anything branded 'Made in Norway'.

The country currently languishes in fifteenth place on the World Economic Forum's Global Competitiveness Index (the lowest of all the four main Nordic countries), but one statistic that stands out – even to an economic illiterate like me – as cause for special concern is the OECD's figure for gross domestic expenditure on research and development which, when considered as a percentage of a country's GDP, is a key indicator of future economic performance. Not only is Norway investing relatively little in its R&D – 1.71 per cent of GDP compared with 3.42 per cent in Sweden – but almost half the investment is coming from the government (compared with just over a quarter in Sweden). If these figures don't reveal a people who are resting on their laurels, then I'm an economist.

Perhaps the most troubling aspect of Norway's social structure is the fact that about a third of all Norwegians of working age do nothing at all. Over a million of them live on money from the State, the majority of them pensioners, but also a sizable number (340,000) on disability, unemployment or sickness benefits – proportionally the largest number in Europe. The picture is equally worrying for Norwegian children, who rank below the European average in terms of literacy, mathematics and sciences, with the trend worsening over the last ten years. With a striking lack of self-irony, the Norwegian media is often heard to complain that 'all young people want to do these days is be something in the media'.

The OECD has warned that the greatest challenge Norway faces is to maintain its population's incentive to work, study and innovate. Today, almost 10 per cent of Norwegian jobs are carried out by foreigners, mostly the kind of jobs – peeling bananas, gutting fish, washing hospital floors (according to Sætre almost half the country's cleaning staff are foreign) – from which Norwegians would run a mile. Recently, the *New York Times* spoke to an economist at Handelsbanken in Oslo, Knut Anton Mork, quoting him as saying, 'This is an oil-for-leisure program . . . We have been complacent. More and more vacation houses are being built. We have more holidays than most countries and extremely generous benefits and sick-leave policies. Some day the dream will end.'

Already many Norwegians are calling for more than 4 per cent of the fund to be spent each year, and there is increasing political pressure for this from the Progress Party. 'Why do we have to pay the world's highest petrol prices?' they ask. 'Why are our hospitals not the best in the world? Why did my post arrive at 9 a.m. this morning instead of 8 a.m.?' Up goes the cry, 'How can this happen in the world's richest country?'

'Wealth changes us, and we don't discuss it very much,' Sætre concludes at the end of *Petromania*. 'But how the oil wealth affects us is the most important question of our time.'

I contacted Sætre in New York, where he now lives, and asked him how the book had been received when it was published in 2009.

'I expected this to be a theme that all Norwegians were interested in,' he told me. 'But it turned out that Swedes were more interested. I felt the issues I tried to raise were largely ignored, especially by the older generation and people in the oil-producing areas, who were quite sceptical. Whenever I went to speak about the book, someone would rise from their seat and say that the oil had been a blessing for Norway. The attitude was often that I was spoiled, since I didn't appreciate the wealth the oil had brought to my country. I often pointed out that what I was interested in was not how bad Norway had become because of the oil, but that I rather tried to describe how Norway was changed.'

Sætre didn't want to paint too dystopian a picture of his homeland. Things are pretty great in Norway, and fears about what will happen when the oil runs out are being pushed further into the future. Eventually, though, it will run out, and an economy in which the public sector accounts for 52 per cent of GDP will no longer be viable. 'Norwegians will have to adapt to a new situation. Probably, the welfare state will have to be curbed, and people will have to get by with fewer government services. Another question is what the business community will do and what kinds of jobs people will get in the post-oil era, since the whole Norwegian economy is so tied to the oil. If these questions are handled the wrong way, there might be some tough times ahead for Norway, and this could lead to political unrest. I think the Norwegian institutions are solid enough to deal with this. I do, however, believe that I live in the best of times in Norway now, and that the wealth of the government is almost unreal, and this feels almost unfair, and I can imagine that it will go downhill from here.'

Sætre warns, too, of the colossal power of the oil lobby in Norway, with its anti-climate-change propaganda and the whitewashing of its industry's activities in countries headed by dubious regimes like Angola, Kazakhstan and Algeria. The oil industry controls Norway's foreign policy, Sætre claims, 'isolating us and making the country asocial'. As a result Norway has been sidelined from Europe and is becoming ever more protectionist. He points to what he perceives as the ever-increasing, pernicious influence of Statoil on life in Norway. The company is becoming a dominant element in the Norwegian cultural sphere, for instance, awarding massive grants to young artists and musicians. The only catch is, those artists and musicians have to sign a contract promising not to criticise the company.

Cultural censorship is by no means the most serious allegation aimed at Statoil. Greenpeace says that the company has completely undermined its reputation for good environmental practice with the acquisition of a controversial tar sands lease in Canada – tar sand oil being more polluting than crude, both in terms of its extraction and in its use. Though Statoil was awarded the lease having promised that its methods would be the least environmentally onerous, Greenpeace says their actions 'will certainly result in major greenhouse-gas emissions and environmental damage'. Statoil is very vocal on the subject of social corporate responsibility, but a few years back it was hit by what *Business Week* called 'the worse bribery and influence-peddling scandal in Norway's history', involving payments to Iranian officials. Really, it is hard to see how its ethical code differs from any other oil company.

I had talked a little about ethical issues with Yngve Slyngstad, head of Norway's oil fund. He said that they didn't invest in tobacco and followed the UN's advice on arms investments, explaining that their approach is to try to change companies' policies and practices from within.

'You cannot invest in eight thousand companies where there is no one to blame,' he said. 'What do you do? Wash your hands and say that's not our problem? Or do you sit down and say there are things we can improve here, and our role is to find ways to improve them?'

But what about the environmental impact of the oil itself? How did the Norwegians come to terms with that? Slyngstad took a deep breath.

'So, if it turns out that the cause of climate-change carbon emissions . . .' he caught my smile at that 'if', '. . . and it seems that most people are of that opinion, then at least as an oil fund we can see what we can do to make the companies aware of the issues.'

This, of course, is the elephant in the room as far as Norway's riches are concerned. It is universally acknowledged by most intelligent, independent observers that all fossil fuels, and oil in particular, are bad news for our planet – they are unsustainable, pollute the atmosphere, and it seems likely they are slowly making the planet warmer. Norway sources much of its own energy from clean, renewable hydro-electric power, thus absolving itself of direct consumer guilt. It is the wily drug pusher who refuses to touch its own product.

An even more uncomfortable issue for the Norwegians, one presumes, is the fact that they directly benefit from those geopolitical conflicts that push up the price of oil – the invasion of Iraq, for instance, or the Libyan Civil War. It is a great irony that a nation that is so often called upon to mediate in international conflicts – as Norway did in Sri Lanka, for instance – benefits the most from the various conflicts connected to oil production elsewhere in the world. I asked Slyngstad if there was any sense that their great fortune was tainted by the environmental and human destruction oil is responsible far in the world.

'You will receive different answers to that question depending which Norwegian is answering,' Slyngstad answered carefully. 'You would find someone of that opinion. I think the consensus view is that probably yes, this oil has this aspect of CO_2, but it's probably better than coal. But how about other renewable, sustainable energy sources? We have therefore put in place a specific programme to invest in new technologies.'

Obviously Slyngstad was never likely to criticise the source of his fund's gargantuan wealth. Thomas Hylland Eriksen, on the other hand, had fewer qualms.

'That's interesting,' he had said the first time I had interviewed him, back in 2009, and asked him about Norwegian oil guilt. 'I think you might be on to something, yes. We don't ever make any link from the pollution to our wealth; actually, Norwegians think they are very clean, but they pollute far more than the Swedes.'

The next time we met, post-Breivik, he had a new take on the subject: 'The mental conundrum is very similar to the situation we had on 23 July when we realised it was one of us who had committed the crime,' he said. 'We couldn't blame the foreigners. We've always been used to thinking of ourselves as a nation as part of the solution, and with the oil we suddenly became part of the problem, and we can't reconcile ourselves to that. Most people are really in denial. They say, "Well, you know, if we hadn't been involved in these tar sands in Canada," which is one of the filthiest ways of extracting oil you can imagine, "then someone else would have done it in an even less environmentally sustainable way." And you know, when you argue like that you can argue for everything, basically – "If we hadn't done it, someone else would have, and they are a lot badder than us."'

Does anyone in Norway ever suggest that you stop extracting the oil altogether?

'No. In fact we are pumping it up at enormous speed, much faster than anyone else, and I have always been struck by this because there is hardly any debate about this.'

And the impact on the Norwegians themselves? Is it making them soft and lazy, as the Danes liked to claim?

'Oh yes, of course it's done something to us. My evidence is mostly anecdotal because this is not really my area of research, but take the fish factories on the north coast – it's well paid but hard, cold work, fish-filleting. Most is now outsourced to China – the fish is flown to China, filleted, packaged in Findus boxes and sent back – but the rest is done by Tamils and Russians, not Norwegians. Norwegians move to London or Paris to be something "in the media",' he guffaws, 'and that's a real sign of decadence! No one wants to work in a factory, or be an engineer, everybody wants to be famous . . . One tends to take the world for granted. Nothing is at stake. It doesn't really matter if I show up for work tomorrow, things will chug on anyway. Sick leave is up, and has been since the nineties, and not because people get more influenza, but because they feel it doesn't really matter.'

Chapter 7

Butter

As we've heard, Norway has always been a somewhat peripheral, isolated, inward-looking place. In a sense, the geopolitical turbulence the region has seen over the centuries has played a lesser role in determining the psyche of the modern Norwegian than its beautiful, savage landscape has.

Denmark built, then lost, an empire, has always been the bridge with continental Europe, and wrangled ceaselessly with Sweden. Sweden ruled and lost Finland, waged wars deep into Europe, and, post-Second World War, has seen its manufacturing corporations conquer the world. Though it shares Norway's geographical isolation, in its own cursed way, Finland has also been forced to engage more with regional geopolitics thanks to its role as the rope in a tug-of-war between east and west, ruled first by Sweden, then Russia, bloodied yet defiant after countless conflicts, and it is the only Nordic country to have embraced the euro. You could argue that Iceland has also existed on the edges of Nordic history, although it was Icelanders who discovered America, and they have, of course, recently enjoyed a second rampage, this time out among the money markets of the world.

As for the Norwegians, they have always tended to keep themselves to themselves. Even within their own borders they spread themselves out as if they are trying to put as much space as possible between one another. And even on those justly celebrated occasions when the Norwegians have displayed immense courage and ingenuity in venturing out into the world – your Roald Amundsens, Fridtjof Nansens and Thor Heyerdals – they still appear to have taken great care to ensure that the venturing took place where there were likely to be few, if any, people.

The outside world can sometimes appear to be of little consequence to the Norwegians. They had their fish and their timber, and now they also have their oil and their dairy monopoly. They don't really need anyone else, except perhaps for a few Swedes to peel their bananas. My impression from a brief attempt once to seek help from the Norwegian tourist board for research on a magazine article seemed to suggest that visitors are politely welcomed rather than overtly encouraged, but they'd probably prefer it if you stayed on your cruise ship if you don't mind.

Why are the Norwegians so closed? Throughout the Danish and Swedish occupations they lacked not only self-determination, but to a large extent any sense of self or nationhood. After a long, drawn-out but not especially fiercely fought campaign for independence, self-rule finally came in 1905. What happened next presents us with a telling difference between the Norwegians and the Swedes, and their progress over the following century. The Swedes made a conscious, unified push towards the light, embracing technological and industrial progress, modernism, secularism and socially progressive politics, in the process becoming one of the most successful industrial nations of the post-war years, a manufacturing colossus, a paragon of what a modern, multicultural nation should be – and with great pop music and sexy tennis players to boot.

As Thomas Hylland Eriksen put it, 'Sweden went onwards and upwards into the future and modernism because, I think, they felt it was the only way. They had become a kind of syphilitic old country, they needed renewal. But Norway needed to find, and to an extent construct, an identity – hence all the weird costumes and national romanticism, which still continues.'

The Norwegians decided that they neither liked nor needed the modern world, they preferred their *bunad*, their folk dancing and their dried fish, and retreated back into the safety of their agrarian past to commune with nature and the sea. And then the oil came along, which has changed things to a degree, but if anything has only helped the Norwegians to maintain their traditional geographical population spread, their isolationism and protectionist trade policies.

'If you look at Europe horizontally, so to speak, you see Norway and Switzerland sticking up,' Yngve Slyngstad told me. 'They are not really part of Europe. Sweden and Denmark had a nobility and the feudal system, they were part of the European way of looking at the world, with small villages that expanded and farms with serfs, and so on, but we didn't have that in Norway, so the differences are much larger than you might expect given our common language.'

Occasionally though, this isolationism backfires on the Norwegians. There was much mirth in the rest of Scandinavia when, in 2011, Norway was reported to have run out of butter. A fad diet that recommended ingesting vast quantities of the stuff had swept the nation and cleared out domestic stocks. To protect its own dairy industry Norway imposes extravagant duties on imported dairy products and, as a consequence, the price of butter shot up. People began panic-buying, supplies of domestic butter produced by Norway's Tine Dairy monopoly ran out, and soon Norwegians began asking Danish friends to fill their suitcases with Lurpak when they came to visit.

'It's a disgrace and it is embarrassing,' harrumphed Torgeir Trældal, spokesperson on agricultural affairs for the Progress Party. 'The last time we received free food supplies from our neighbouring countries was during the Second World War.'

'I'd rather be a battered citizen of the EU with a mouth full of buttery cookies, than a filthy rich Norwegian chewing on unbuttered toast,' wrote one rather graceless Swedish journalist at the time, adding, 'There is an irresistible irony when a small country awash with oil money can't manage to supply its people with something as basic as butter . . . Our own home-cooked traditional saffron buns will taste that much better when we think that the Norwegians will have to do all their cooking with margarine.'

Unappealing as her *Schadenfreude* may have been, it offers a telling insight into the raw resentment and jealousy which festers beneath the surface of the supposedly harmonious Scandinavian tribal triumvirate. The Norwegians, however, remain unrepentant about their protectionism: recently they provoked great indignation in Copenhagen by arbitrarily imposing a 262 per cent import duty on Danish cheese – Norway's own form of post-colonial revenge.

Another revealing aspect of this are the numerous jokes at the expense of the Norwegians told by their neighbours, in which they always seem to play the role of village idiot – much like the Irish jokes told by the English, or the Poles in jokes told by Americans. Such jokes are racist, reductive, politically incorrect and colonialist. They must of course be condemned in the strongest terms by all right-thinking people and should never be repeated.

This is one of my favourites:

A Swede, a Dane and a Norwegian are shipwrecked on a desert island. The Swede finds a magic shell which, when rubbed, grants each of them a wish. 'I want to go home to my large and comfortable bungalow with the Volvo, video and slick IKEA furniture,' he says, and promptly vanishes. 'I want to go back to my cosy little flat in Copenhagen, to sit on my soft sofa, feet on the table, next to my sexy girlfriend and with a six-pack of lager,' says the Dane, and off he flies. The Norwegian, after giving the problem a bit of thought, rubs the shell. 'It's really lonely here,' he says. 'I wish my two friends could come back.'

These next two come courtesy of my son. That he heard them at his school in Denmark is testimony to the fact that Norwegian jokes are thriving. Interestingly, my Danish wife tells me that this is a relatively new development. When she was at school, she says, the role of the dunce in playground jokes was taken by people from Denmark's second city, Aarhus (meanwhile, a Norwegian friend says they used to tell these jokes about Swedes). Of course, back in the 1970s, the Norwegians' oil wealth was a distant fantasy. Could it be that Norwegian jokes have grown in currency as the Norwegians' currency has grown in value?

A policeman encounters a Norwegian walking through central Copenhagen with a penguin on a lead.

'You should take that to the zoo straightaway,' insists the policeman.

'Righty-ho!' says the Norwegian.

They meet again the next day, yet the Norwegian is still accompanied by the penguin.

'I thought I told you to take him to the zoo,' says the policeman.

'Yes, I did!' says the Norwegian. 'He seemed to like it. I was thinking we could go to the cinema today.'

And in a similar vein:

A Norwegian man buys a ticket from the girl in the kiosk at the cinema. A few moments later he returns to buy another. Then comes back for another. And another.

Eventually, the ticket girl asks him, 'Why do you keep coming back and buying new tickets?'

The Norwegian man, exasperated, says, 'Every time I try to go in, that man over by the door tears them in half!'

I asked Eriksen about the jokes the Danes told about the Norwegians. Were they bothered? 'Oh, we couldn't care less,' he laughed. 'They've got their pathetic little flat country. They are just jealous . . . Actually, we are very fond of the Danes – we see them as cosmopolitan and *hyggelig*. Even their flag is *hyggelig*. They even use it to sell stuff, on packaging. In Norway the flag is almost sacred. There would be uproar if someone put it on the side of a tin of ham.'

I think we can probably conclude that the Norwegians are not as stupid as the Danes and the Swedes like to make out. It is not easy sucking all that oil up from the depths of the North Sea, you know. Norway has topped the United Nations' Human Development Index in recent years (including at the time of writing), ironic given that the index was originally created as a way to assess countries on values other than wealth. Nevertheless, it means that Norway is officially the very best country in the world. Sort of. It is also the most gender equal and the most politically stable country in the world. Meanwhile, Norway has the lowest rate of imprisonment of any European country – just 3,500 of its citizens reside behind bars, compared with twice that many in Scotland, which has a similar-sized population.

And Norway is fighting back with the jokes, too. They never pass up a chance to ridicule the Danish language, for instance. Norwegians consider theirs to be the one true, pure Scandinavian tongue. It was an important element of the nationalist separatist movement in the nineteenth century, not least as a way to eradicate Danish influence. Around this time the Norwegians took the radical step of defining an additional Norwegian language, Nynorsk, based on rural dialects. Nynorsk was actually closer to Old Norse and traditional Norwegian dialects than the mainstream Norwegian language, Bokmål, which was, essentially, bastardised Danish. Nynorsk never came close to replacing Bokmål, but it is the official language for a little over 10 per cent of Norwegians, mostly in Western Norway.

In fact, Danish – in particular what the Swedes and Norwegians claim is its declining intelligibility, with the Danes apparently slurring and swallowing even more of their words, and employing even more glottal stops as time passes – is increasingly the butt of jokes throughout Scandinavia. As improbable as this may sound, one of the funniest TV comedy sketches I have ever seen featured two Norwegian comedians from the show *Uti Vår Hage* pretending to be Danes trying to communicate with each other (the sketch is in English and is listed on YouTube as, simply, 'Danish Language': it's had over three million hits to date). 'The Danish language has collapsed into meaningless guttural sounds,' begins one desperate 'Dane'. He enters a hardware store: 'I didn't even remember the Danish word for hello. I didn't understand anything, so I just repeated what he said. I had to take a wild shot and so I just said the word *Kamelåså.*' The sketch ends with the shopkeeper making a plea to the camera: 'If nothing is done, the Danish society will collapse! I want to direct an appeal to the United Nations and the international community. Please help us.'

Such fond ribbing is reserved for close neighbours. The Norwegians' attitudes towards immigrants from further afield remains conflicted, as was seen with the arrival of a group of two hundred Romanian gypsies in Oslo as the Breivik trial rumbled towards its conclusion. The Roma set up camp in the grounds of Sofienberg Church in central Oslo, provoking outrage among local politicians and the media. Certain Norwegian websites were reported as calling the Roma 'rats' and 'inhuman'. 'These people have no business being here, they should have been thrown out of Sofienberg Church and thrown out of Norway,' one local politician told TV2. 'We can't have a situation whereby Norway and Oslo serve as the world's social-welfare office.' As I write, the mayor is trying to ban begging to force the Roma out, and others are talking seriously about closing the borders to the country.

As usual, the then prime minister Jens Stoltenberg provided a voice of moderation: 'One of the things 22 July showed us was how important it is not to judge and brand people just because they belong to a certain group. These kinds of words and expressions can only lead to more hatred and conflict,' he said.

One can but hope such sentiments might eventually win the argument up here in the frosty North. It would suit the Norwegians so much better to show a little more openness and generosity of spirit. After all, for all their recent traumas, they have so very much to be grateful for. They have very similar advantages to the Danes in terms of social cohesion, equality, homogeneity and life quality, and if anything 22/7 seems to have brought them even closer together as a society.

'After 22/7 one really had the feeling, bloody hell, we are a family,' Eriksen told me. 'We are such a small group. The Prime Minister, the mayor of Oslo, the Crown prince, all these luminaries, they were not up there, they belonged to, and among us. The King spoke to us like a bereaved uncle, the PM spoke to us like our neighbour, and even the Crown prince gave this very strong sense of cultural intimacy. Because the differences between the top and bottom of society are so small, you meet. Everybody knows that if you live in this part of town and you go skiing in winter in the hills just outside town, you sometimes meet the Prime Minister. I know him a bit, like lots of people. I say hello.

'The point is that you can look at this sociologically – the chances of a Norwegian knowing the prime minister, or knowing someone who knows him, is twice as high as they would be in Sweden, where there are twice as many people. Or eight times as high as in Spain. You have this sense of really being connected with a big family. There is a high level of trust. One of the things you miss if you travel if you are Norwegian is to just sit on the tram and doze and know it's safe. That feeling.'

This feeling of unthreatened somnolence, of peace, stability and calm is, of course, central to the sense of security and quality of life enjoyed by the people of the North and, by extension, also to their happiness. But safety, functionality, consensus, moderation, social cohesion – these aren't the be-all and end-all of life, merely the foundations for a pyramid of needs. I would not be the first person to point out that Scandinavia might be a little lacking in a few of the things that you might hope to find further up that pyramid – the passion and spark, the flamboyance and *joie de vivre* you find if you venture further south, for instance. Where in Scandinavia is the emotion and the drive, the conflict and risk, the sense of a life lived on the edge?

I'll tell you where . . .

FINLAND

Chapter 1

Santa

Ask any journalist about their worst nightmare and it will likely be that they have conducted a fascinating, revealing, intimate interview with someone really, really famous and then come rushing home, for once actually excited about transcribing the conversation, only to discover that their tape recorder hasn't worked. It happened to me when I was interviewing the most famous man in the world.

I had travelled to the capital of Lapland, Rovaniemi, on the edge of the Finnish Arctic Circle, together with my ten-year-old son. It was July, the season of the white nights, with twenty-four-hour sunlight. One o'clock in the morning was just like one in the afternoon; deeply discombobulating. Finland was also in the midst of a rare heat wave. Together, the raging white light and the sweltering heat created a whole heap of cognitive dissonance as we arrived that evening at Santa Claus Village, 'The Official Home of Father Christmas', amid the pine forests 20 kilometres north of the city. We stood in our shorts and T-shirts, waiting in line to enter Santa's grotto, listening to Christmas carols, watching videos of reindeer gambolling in the snow, and trying to summon some yuletide spirit.

The Village is made up of a cluster of log cabins housing what is, essentially, a glorified outlet centre. It is staffed by elves who maintain a near-hysterical pitch of eagerness at all times. One of them showed us around Santa's post office, almost giddy at the sheer, unadulterated Christmassy fun of it all. (The only brief chink in her otherwise redoubtably bouncy façade came when my son asked why there was no pigeonhole for letters from children in Denmark. The answer is because the Danes believe Santa lives in Greenland, but the elf could never admit this, of course, so spent several minutes in an enthusiastic but, as she and I both knew full well, ultimately doomed search for the elusive Danish pigeon hole.)

On reflection, some might argue that taking a child to see Father Christmas in July is probably tantamount to child abuse, but my son seemed to enjoy it. And when we were finally shown in to see Santa, who was sitting on a throne in a kind of jazzed-up photographer's studio, and I saw how genuinely overwhelmed my eldest was by the experience, even my outlet-shopping-centre-induced cynicism dissipated. Slightly.

Santa listened attentively to my brilliant, original questions ('What would *you* like for Christmas?' 'What do you do for the other 364 days of the year?' and so on), and gave excellent answers with only a hint of a Finnish accent (to the first: 'That the children of the world have good health and education,' to the second: 'It's a year-round job!'), ho-ho-hoing in an only slightly forced manner at the conclusion of each answer. Just before we left, we had a chance to make our own wishes. My son asked for world peace. I asked for a Maserati. It could not have gone better.

But then I returned to my hotel room, casually pressed play, and instead of the Christmassy *Frost/Nixon* I had expected, my state-of-the-art Marantz digital recorder merely presented me with an insolent 'Error' message. After jabbing at its buttons frantically for 10 minutes in the manner of a laboratory chimp attempting to activate his food supply, I realised wearily that there was only one solution.

Usually, I would do what any good journalist would have done: try to remember as much as possible from the interview, and make the rest up; but as I had been recording for radio, this clearly was not going to wash. We would have to do a retake. Back to Santa's log cabin we went. I have to say, Santa was a true pro, finding space in his schedule within the hour, acting as if he had never met us, and answering as if my questions were just as original and brilliant as they were the first time he had heard them.

It was neither the first nor the last time I would have cause to marvel at the Finns' famed dependability in a crisis. (I might add that, while I was trying to get my voice recorder to work, the lovely PR woman for Rovaniemi who accompanied us on the visit had called the Finnish national broadcasting company and they had promised to bring me a replacement machine within the hour. I remind you, this was up in the Arctic Circle.)

Now is probably a good time to make my confession about Finland, our next destination in this Nordic odyssey: I think the Finns are fantastic. I can't get enough of them. I would be perfectly happy for the Finns to rule the world. They get my vote, they've won my heart. If you ask me, they should just change the word 'fantastic' to 'Finntastic'. Helsinki? Heavensinki more like.

I am not the only one in thrall to the home of the Moomins, monosyllabic racing-car drivers and Nokia. The Finnish school system draws educationalists from around the world keen to learn its secrets: according to international rankings, the Finns have the best education system in the world. They currently have the third most competitive economy, too. Within the last couple of years *Newsweek*, the Legatum Institute and *Monocle* magazine have all rated the country or its capital as the best place on the planet in which to live, bar none. Currently, Finland has the highest per capita income in Western Europe, and is the only economy in the eurozone to retain its AAA rating from those pesky ratings agencies. The Finns are perceived to be the least corrupt people on earth – they were joint-first with the Danes and the New Zealanders in Transparency International's latest survey.

Finns are solid, dependable. They also have a Sahara-dry sense of humour freighted with a heavily understated irony. During one visit to Helsinki while I was researching this book, I fell into conversation with a lugubrious Finnish film director late one night in a crowded bar. At one point I happened to mention the title I had in mind. He paused, his tumbler of vodka midway towards his mouth, fixed me with his heavy lidded gaze, and said, levelly: 'What do you mean, "*Almost* nearly"?'

The Finns are also the most courteous of all the Nordic people. Admittedly this is a close call, a little like saying that the orangutans have the best table manners of all non-human primates, but as an

Englishman living in this region you come to appreciate politeness wherever you find it. They are hardly David Niven, but Finns do wait for you to disembark from trains, stand aside to let you through doorways, and rarely ask how on earth you make a living from writing.

The more I got to know about them, and in particular their country's harrowing, conflict-riven history, the more my affection and respect for the Finns grew to the point where, these days, I am an unashamed groupie and cheerleader for all things Finnish. In conversations regarding the relative merits of any two countries – the vast majority of which, by definition, tend not to concern Finland – I will be heard to say, 'Ah, but you see, that *never* happens in Finland,' (if it's something bad), or 'They have far more of them in Finland' (if it's something good, like holidays, for instance).

So, though there will be elements of balanced reporting over the coming pages, bear in mind that I think Finland – or 'Suomi', as they call it (possibly from the Finnish for swamp, *suo*, although I find that very hard to believe) – is terrific.

That said, this wasn't my initial impression of this nation of Nordic outsiders, who straddle the cultural and tectonic rift between Western and Eastern Europe. In fact, the initial word on Finland could not have been much less encouraging. The 'Visit Helsinki' website was the first tourist board site I had ever seen that carried adverts for another destination (Minorca), for instance. I had heard the Finns were a modest people, but this was like hiding one's light under a bushel and then locking it in a cupboard, and whenever anyone asked about it, saying, 'What, this bushel here? No, no, nothing under there.'

Other reports were similarly off-putting. A Danish relative who had been to Helsinki on a business trip described a cold, grey pre-Glasnost Soviet-style city peopled by dour giants who turned into drunken maniacs at the first 'pssscht' of a beer can. His business contacts had taken him to a memorably grim strip club on the second floor of a suburban tower block. He shuddered at the recollection and refused to provide further details, other than to confess to waking up, literally, in a gutter the next morning.

Another old Finland hand told me that, of the top three most prescribed drugs in the country, the first was an anti-psychotic medicine, the second was insulin and the third was another anti-psychosis or antidepressant treatment. According to a report I read on an English-language Finnish news site, hundreds of thousands of Finns are hooked on the anxiety and insomnia drug benzodiazepine. More worryingly still, they have the third highest rate of gun ownership in the world (after the US and Yemen); the highest murder rate in Western Europe; and are famously hard and reckless drinkers as well as enthusiastic suicidalists.

Unlike Sweden or Denmark – both of which have given the world a good few film-makers, musicians, writers and lately, of course, TV series – Finland's cultural output has struggled to extend its reach beyond the Baltic. There is Sibelius, of course, an architect or two (Eliel Saarinen, Alvar Aalto), and the Moomins, but other than that and a few sports stars (all of whom seemed to specialise in loner sports like long-distance running and racing-car driving), Finns did not seem especially drawn to the limelight. The list of famous Finns on Wikipedia features such marquee names as:

Ior Bock – eccentric
Tony Halme – show wrestler
Väinö Myllyrinne – the tallest Finn

In preparation for my first trip to Finland, I acquainted myself with the work of their most acclaimed film-maker, Aki Kaurismäki (sadly not the director I met in the bar). His films, like *The Match Factory Girl* and *The Man Without a Past*, were so unremittingly morose they made Bergman look like Mr Bean. A typical Kaurismäki film presents a cast of, essentially, gargoyles, who toil in wretched jobs (coal mining, dish washing), exchange grunts and drink heroically. Eventually some of them shoot themselves to death. The end.

This would appear to mirror their auteur's outlook on life: 'I more or less know I will kill myself, but not yet,' Kaurismäki told a recent interviewer. I do hope he doesn't. I love his films and their strangely life-enhancing wretchedness, but tourist-board promos they are not.

Trawling the Internet for something remotely positive about Finland I found a website called 'You Know You Have Been in Finland Too Long When . . .' It included the following:

When a stranger on the street smiles at you:
a) you assume he is drunk
b) he is insane
c) he's an American

It would, then, be all too easy to form a picture of the Finns as an unhappy, often paralytically drunk hybrid of repressed, Swedish-style conformism and Russian barbarity, as many do. But persevere, I implore you. Get on a plane and go to Helsinki. The city is like a breath of fresh air, not least because the air is so very fresh. Its centre is small – you could walk across it in 20 minutes – but spacious, and refreshingly non-commercial, its streets are lined with linden trees, and there is a cosy harbour front, not unlike Oslo's, with islets and ferries, but lent a little frisson of Eastern exoticism by the onion dome of an Orthodox church and the splendid, dazzlingly white tsarist cathedral nearby.

At the iconic Fazer's Konditori (now Fazer Café & Restaurang), once the scene of revolutionary foment against the Russians, you can stuff your face with superb cakes, chocolates and ice cream (you can also foment against the Russians if you like, it's up to you). There are trams and cycle paths, stout public buildings (the muscle-bound caryatids fronting Saarinen's stern, rationalist Central station are fabulously camp) and listening posts dotted about the city with speakers that broadcast poems when you press a button, just in case you are out and about and found yourself in need of a couplet.

It all feels kind of Scandinavian, but not. There are the familiar state-run alcohol shops – over-lit, their tills staffed by the usual disapproving old ladies; the Finns dress like Scandinavians, with big puffy jackets, sensible shoes and expensive-looking spectacles; they drive cheap French cars; and are blond, unsmiling and considerably taller than me. There were audible gasps of disapproval when I crossed the road on a red light, even though there was not a car in sight. All is tidy, ordered, functional and extraordinarily ethnically homogenous, even by Scandinavian standards.

I soon learn that the Finns are even more obsessed with summer houses (*mökki* – they have 470,000 of them) than either the Danes or Swedes; that they are also big on parental leave after childbirth (the father and mother get a year to share between them); and that they are mostly atheistic, rarely setting foot inside their spartan Lutheran churches, just like the rest of Scandinavia.

One key characteristic of Nordic cities is the lack of people. Queues, jams and crowds are a rarity in the North; even the capitals can have a semi-deserted air if you are arriving from London or New York. Where *are* all the people? But Helsinki made Oslo look like Mumbai. There was no one there as far as I could make out. One morning I crossed the square to the east of the main station at the height of rush hour, stood for a while and counted fewer than sixty people. The shop displays were strangely muted too, the city's commercial signage was low-key, and there was virtually no billboard advertising. It was quite liberating not to be bombarded with messages imploring you to buy stuff at every turn.

Slowly I grew aware of other signs of 'otherness' that set Finland apart from the rest of the Nordic region. The language is the most glaring. Finnish bears no resemblance to, and has virtually no words in common with, the other Nordic languages. Most Finns speak Swedish, but few Swedes speak Finnish, and when Danes or Norwegians meet Finns they speak English. In Norway, Sweden and even Iceland, my second-rate Danish means I can understand most of what I see written around me, but in Finland my Danish was as much use as Klingon (which, now I think of it, Finnish resembles). On my first day of largely aimless wandering, I grew obsessed with spotting outlets of what I presumed was a highly popular Italian restaurant chain, called *Ravintola*. Virtually every restaurant in the city appeared to be part of the chain. Was it a throwback to some communistic government-run monopoly, I wondered? Turns out, *ravintola* is Finnish for 'restaurant'.

There isn't a great deal to see in Helsinki by way of sights or museums and, unlike Stockholm or Copenhagen, it has no twee medieval heart. The central part of the city, where most government and university buildings are situated, is dominated by cakey nineteenth-century Russian architecture (it looks like a mini St Petersburg and, during the Cold War, often stood in for the Russian city in movies). Most icing-sugary of all is the white cathedral. Devoid inside of both ornament and worshippers, as per the Lutheran Nordic template, it overlooks the only statue of a Russian tsar (Alexander II) outside of Russia. Beyond him is the western harbour, where ferries potter in and out depositing commuters from islands further out in the fjord.

I browsed in the produce market here on the quayside, its stalls laden with chanterelle mushrooms and wild berries (including the enigmatic, elusive cloudberry), before heading west through a park lined with grand cafés, bandstands and hotels – again, much like Oslo, but without all the Porsches. I stopped by the swoopy glass-and-concrete modern art museum, filled with angry sixth-form-style installations railing against capitalism and men. The National Gallery had chocolate-boxy nineteenth-century paintings of angels, children's funerals and melancholy peasants toiling through the tundra, all depicted in an unremitting palette of grey, ochre and black (although there was also that rare thing, a cheerful Munch self-portrait). The National Museum, meanwhile, was housed in a batty National Romantic building; a kind of 'spooky mansion' affair where I imagined a deformed baron might live with his organ-playing hunchbacked butler. Its various attractions included the world's oldest fishing net and a fragment of a Stone-Age ski. Here I learned that, two thousand years ago, Finland actually had quite a pleasant climate, comparable to Central Europe's today. Scant consolation now, I imagine.

The museum's tone was resolutely downbeat, the captions defining the Finns as much in terms of what they *weren't* – they were not Russian, nor Swedish, nor Vikings, and so on. A constant theme was the remoteness of Finland and its marginalised role in European history. Some Roman coins on display were said to have *'even* [my italics] found their way to Finland', for instance. The Industrial Revolution didn't reach these parts until the early twentieth century and, if the museum is to be believed, prior to that Finland didn't appear to have invented a single thing.

There was little mention of the Swedes, a curious omission given they ruled Finland for 659 years; meanwhile the Russians, who ruled for over a century after the Swedes were kicked out and continued to loom threateningly for almost another century thereafter, were generally painted in a positive light. The reforms of Tsar Alexander II were lauded for their effects in 'promoting the economy and the evolution of cultural pursuits', for instance, and there were numerous gifts from Russia on display, including portraits of the various tsars that once hung in Finnish government offices.

I also read about intriguingly named military conflicts, terrible battles that wreaked senseless devastation on the Finnish people over the centuries, such as the War of the Hats and the Greater Wrath. 'If only they'd put as much creativity into naming their restaurants,' I thought to myself.

Afterwards, I tried to find the main shopping area. I wandered for a while, stopping occasionally to enjoy the concert-standard classical musicians busking on every other street corner, but could only find a light smattering of shops. I asked a female passer-by where the centre of Helsinki was. 'You are standing in it,' she replied, puzzled.

'Yes, this is Ginza!' laughed Roman Schatz, a German actor and writer who has lived in Finland for twenty-eight years. We were walking in the same area together the following day, after a long and bibulous lunch. Schatz is one of Finland's most famous foreign residents, much loved for his gently sardonic take on the Finnish character. A newspaper columnist, TV presenter and sometime actor, he has written several books about the Finns and, judging by the number of greetings he received as we walked through the city centre, this tall, handsome German in his early fifties is fast approaching national-treasure status in Finland. He, in turn, seemed to hold his adopted homeland in equally high, albeit still slightly bemused, esteem.

'You know, I wouldn't trust a Swede, and I wouldn't trust an Icelander, but you can always trust a Finn,' Schatz told me while we had sat eating reindeer in a traditional restaurant just across from the cathedral. 'If you are hanging by your last thread over the chasm, you want the next person who comes by to be a Finn. If a Finn tells you they are going to bring you firewood on Friday, you can bet your sweet ass the firewood will be there on Friday because, fifty years ago, if the firewood wasn't there, you might die. Make a mistake in this country, and everyone will know you screwed up.'

According to Schatz, the Finns' 'can-do-will-do' attitude is reflected in their language: 'You know, there is no future tense in the Finnish language. While in English or German you might say, "I am going to do this or that," or "I shall have done that," a Finn would say, "How can you trust people who have different ways of talking about the future?" Either you do it, and consider it done, or not.'

Finnish nouns have no gender, in fact people have no gender – the word for 'he' and 'she' is the same, the masculine *hän*. A Finnish friend tells me that, increasingly, the Finns are just using 'it' to refer to everything: 'It is getting married in the morning,' 'It has been drinking vodka since breakfast,' and so on. There are no prepositions in Finnish and neither are there definite or indefinite articles: 'a book', 'the book' and 'book' are all just 'book', or *kirja*. (That said, Finnish does apparently have fourteen case-endings, so perhaps it is not all that straightforward.)

Schatz spoke Finnish almost perfectly, of course. 'There was a breakthrough moment when I was sitting with my wife, who is a psychologist, at our marriage therapist's, and I realised I had been discussing my marriage with two psychologists in Finnish. I thought to myself, "Hey, how cool is that!" He had a theory that the Finnish language – which some argue has its origins in the same group as Mongolian, Japanese and Turkish – directly informs the character of the people. 'Behaviours and value systems come from the grammar, the language. In Sweden, Norway, all of Scandinavia really, Germany and England we all speak languages that are dialects of one another, but in Finland the way of organising thoughts, the world, feelings, expressions, emotions is so completely different. It has taught me a new way to think. The Finnish language works like Lego, you can put any two pieces together and they always fit, somehow.'

When I first started to learn Danish, it often seemed to me quite shockingly direct – 'Give me a loaf of bread,' a Dane will command on entering a bakery – but Finnish makes Danish seem like the courtly French of Louis XIV's Versailles. 'If you want to say "She appears to pretend to sleep" in Finnish, you just need two words,' said Schatz, although why one would want to say that he did not explain. 'Finland is a very primitive culture, but that is a positive thing for me. They have a very simple approach to human life: are you thirsty, hungry, or do you want a blow job? Just ask. They have a good basic understanding of basic human needs, whereas countries like yours and mine, or France, have had centuries of urban neuroticism, which you might call "sophistication", and most Finns want that too now. But I am looking for the opposite. If a Finn tells you "I love you," you will have had to wait for ten years, but they will mean it.'

It is not just the Finns who take their time with this particular word: all the Nordic tribes seem to have a similar relationship to the word 'love' as the pilot of the *Enola Gay* had to the big red button next to his joystick – something to be deployed at the end of a very long journey, and only then if you are absolutely certain you are above the target. One woman I met in Helsinki, who worked in the Finish Foreign Office and was helping me with some connections, confided that she could say 'I love you' in other languages, but to say it in Finnish was more difficult because it seemed to carry so much more *weight*. My Danish wife has said something similar to me (at least, that was her excuse). Meanwhile, Swedish ethnologist, Åke Daun, has written that, to the Swedes, 'I love you' sounds 'artificially romantic, like something from a cheap romantic novel.' The word 'love' is just not bandied around in the North with the same ease as it is in the States, for instance, where it is perfectly natural to express one's love for what someone might be doing with their hair, say, or a particular muffin recipe.

'In Finland they show affection in other ways. Here, a husband can show his affection by repairing the washing machine,' said Schatz. 'It takes a while to understand, and like, the Finns. First impressions are that they are very uptight unless you give them alcohol and then they get very sexual or very violent. But I was twenty-five years old when I came here so that was okay with me.'

Far from taking offence, the Finns, by all accounts, can't get enough of Schatz's diagnoses of their personality quirks and foibles. 'They were isolated for so long, and are only now really coming out into the world, and they are fascinated by what others think of them. There is a joke about this,' he chuckled. 'They call it the elephant joke: a German, a Finn and a French guy are somewhere in Africa and they see an elephant. The German says, "If I kill the animal and sell the ivory, how much money will I make, I wonder?" The Frenchman says, "What a beautiful animal, a marvellous creature." And the Finn says, "Oh God, I wonder what the elephant thinks about Finland."'

Chapter 2

Silence

It is early evening and I am walking alone, and a little lost, through one of the shabbier parts of central Helsinki. The tenements here are built from porridgy concrete and are occupied at street-level by Thai massage parlours, sex shops and peep shows. Every Nordic capital has a nicely contained, almost stagey vice quarter like this, set-designed with the comatose junkie slumped on a bench, his trousers at half-mast and a needle sticking out of his thigh here, a heavily rouged African lady loitering on a street corner there; all of it set against a backdrop of shops with various by-products of the Polyurethane industry languishing in their dusty windows.

If one relied only on the British and US media's images of Scandinavia for one's view of this part of the world, with their images of sun-tanned children frolicking in pristine fjords, men with pipes sitting in austere wooden chairs, and women in arcane knitwear making spelt bread, this might come as a shock, but Scandinavia's urban sleaze districts are just as much a part of the scenery as the austere churches and cosy cafés. They are almost a kind of tourist attraction. In fact, the equivalent part of Copenhagen, Istedgade, actually *is* a tourist attraction.

I never usually feel threatened when I visit these parts of town (on those odd occasions when I have to pass through them to get somewhere else, you understand), but on this occasion there is a fist of anxiety in the pit of my stomach, for I am about to submit to something truly terrible, of my own volition.

I stop for a rethink. Oops, no, too close to that lady in the leopard-print top. I walk on and stop again. I haven't told a soul where I am going, so no one need know whether I actually go through with it

231

or not, I tell myself. Yet onward I walk, compelled by my morbid curiosity, egged on by the reckless freedom that anonymity affords, gripping a small piece of paper with an address.

I could just as easily head back to the library where I have spent the afternoon in a cosy corner researching, but if I leave Helsinki without going through with this, my Finnish experience will be incomplete. When I return home, people will ask if I did it, and I will be forced to admit that I wimped out. They will raise their eyebrows and I will have to bluster feeble excuses. Either that, or I'll have to lie, and what I am about to do is far too alien to me to get away with that. I need to experience it first-hand but to do so I must violate several principles that I have held dear for much of my life.

I am on my way to experience the archetypal Finnish pastime. Actually it is far more than a pastime, in Finland it is considered one of life's necessities, intrinsic to, and indivisible from, elemental notions of Finnishness. This ungodly act is simply something that Finns do, like the British and their DIY, or the French and their adultery. I have a Finnish friend who talks of virtually nothing else. The first time we met he raved about it for over an hour, and every time we have met since he has raised the subject again, always with the ulterior motive of trying to persuade me to have a go.

I am talking, of course, of the sauna. The Swedes like their saunas too, and Icelanders have their thermal baths, but the Finns take the appreciation of saunas to a whole new level. The sauna lies at the heart of Finnish social life and leisure time. There is one for every two of them in the country, more saunas than cars – over 2.5 million. The sauna is their prime meeting place, a venue for physical relaxation with family and friends of both genders. At the same time. Naked. Like a pub, or a village hall. But naked. And hot.

The Finns will tell you that their saunas are the hottest in the world, and that any non-Finnish sauna isn't really a sauna at all. They mock the tepid temperatures of Swedish saunas (anything under 80°C is a 'warm room', they will tell you), citing them as merely one more example of what they perceive as Swedish softness.

The Finns even have a Sauna World Championship, in which the sole requirement is to see who can sit for longest at the highest temperature. Last year a competitor died when the sauna he was competing in was turned up to 110°C. He was Russian.

Members of the Finnish parliament meet once a week in a sauna (I am assuming they also have a conventional parliamentary chamber) and, since the days when their Cold War president, Urho Kekkonen, ruled the country, there has been a tradition that the president invites foreign leaders to a sauna evening when they visit the country. (It is wrong that my thoughts turn immediately here to Angela Merkel, isn't it?)

Being raised in England in the 1970s I know that nudity is something shameful, embarrassing and to be avoided, when alone, if possible, but certainly at all cost when in the company of others. Meanwhile, the cumulative process towards human enlightenment resulting in our current apogee of civilisation has thus far been defined by the wholly admirable desire to *minimise* our physical suffering, pain, risk, danger, exposure and discomfort. Why on earth would you want to invite these things, to *wallow* in them, by sitting with your arse out in a big oven?

Rudimentary low-level vigilance has preserved me from experiencing a sauna up until now, but that is about to change. I am heading for the oldest wood-fired sauna in Helsinki, built in 1929. It isn't difficult to spot. Gathered outside like a nudists' picket is a group of men dressed in towelling robes and, in some cases, just towels, sitting or standing around a low wall by the entrance, smoking and drinking beer from bottles.

I walk brusquely past them and in through the front door, trying to look like the kind of fellow who knows his way around a sauna. A young man is sitting behind a glass window in a small kiosk. Affecting a casual tone, I say: 'I'd like to . . .'

Does one 'have' a sauna? Or 'take' one, or perhaps 'visit' one?

'. . . I mean a, you know, a sauna, please?'

'Do you have a towel?' the man asks. Damn, I don't. Now I will be exposed for the sauna rookie I am. No matter, he can rent me one he says. He gives it to me along with a key dangling from a rubber wristband and gestures to a door on my right.

Inside the timeworn, wood-panelled changing room I am greeted by a gaggle of saggy, white, wrinkled backsides. At least, I notice with relief, there are no women, which would have presented a whole other range of challenges. I find a hidden corner and begin to disrobe. I place my clothes in the locker and stand holding my towel. But what next? I have little idea. Should I wrap the towel around my waist, or would that – heaven forbid – appear prudish and Anglo-Saxon? Perhaps there are different grades of nudity depending on where you go in the sauna complex. Come to think of it, I don't even know which direction I am supposed to be going. I pretend to order my things once again, watching the others out of the corner of my eye while at the same time conscious of the risk of being caught perving anyone up. Eventually another sauna-goer walks past me, his towel tossed jauntily over his shoulder, his buttocks rising and falling like someone weighing up a pair of blancmanges, and exits through another door. I decide to follow him, my towel now over my shoulder.

Walking naked in public I feel immediately, cripplingly self-conscious. The more I try to concentrate on walking normally, the more awkward my gait becomes. We enter the shower room and I am horrified to see that, at one end of the room, a man lies naked on a massage table where he is being beaten with with a birch switch BY A WOMAN.

She is clothed and carries on without looking up, but, well, for heaven's sake! I bustle over to a shower and turn to face the wall. Having washed, I realise with mounting panic that I have lost the man I was shadowing. Where has he gone and, crucially, has he taken his towel with him? There are several towels hanging on the wall but is one of them his? What am I supposed to do now? I know that the Finns are obsessive about sauna cleanliness. Would a towel be considered unhygienic in the sauna itself? Or would it be considered unhygienic *not* to take a towel in with me? Would I need it to sit on, or are you supposed to experience a sauna bare-bottomed? Oh God! Why did I even consider subjecting myself to such indignities?

Another door, at the far end of the shower room, opens and a large gust of steam billows out. A man carrying a towel enters. Aha! I catch the door as it is closing and enter the sauna. The air is hot and wet and smells pleasantly of wood smoke without being smoky. Inside all is dark but then my eyes begin to adjust. Two sides of the room are taken up with concrete steps formed in a right-angle. Through thick steam I can make out two figures: the man I had been following, and another man, not dissimilar to the late American actor, Ernest Borgnine. He has a cannonball belly which, thankfully, shields his nether regions from view. The men are sitting as far away from each other as possible, which immediately presents me with another dilemma. Where should I sit? I notice that there are small wooden pallets stacked by the door. Are they for sitting on? I pluck up the courage and asked Ernest. He grunts something indecipherable but hostile in tone. It appears that merely by speaking I have already breached some aspect of sauna etiquette.

I smile weakly, take one of the pallets and sit in the middle of the sauna, precisely equidistant from the other men. I had been warned by my sauna fanatic friend that the higher up you sit in a sauna, the hotter it gets. Not wanting to appear the feeble foreigner, I choose a mid-range step, one step higher than the other two occupants, and sit down.

Within three seconds my face is burning. Trickles of sweat start to tickle all over my body. After about a minute, my lips are red raw and each breath burns my lungs, but there is no way I am leaving this room before one, or both, of the other men. Another man enters. He leans over and turns some kind of tap. An unearthly noise rumbles up somewhere in the bowels of the sauna, and steam fills the room. The temperature rises by a good couple of degrees and, as I sit there for another couple of minutes, I am mortified to notice that every new arrival thereafter opens the tap like this. Etiquette breach No. 2.

Time passes, very, very slowly. I grow resigned to my nakedness, almost at ease it with. It still troubles me, obviously, but the silence is far more vexing. Two more men enter, turn up the heat, and sit together. Clearly they are friends, but they do not exchange a single word.

Ernest Borgnine leaves. So does the other man. I now have an excuse to leave myself but, the truth is, I want to stay. The burning heat, the pumping heart, the floods of sweat – I am finding it all strangely compulsive. Ernest Borgnine returns, followed soon after by the other man. Of course! They have been for a cold shower.

Prior to coming to the sauna, I had given the whole cold shower / ice plunge aspect a great deal of thought and decided that there was no way I would subject my body to that kind of masochistic abuse. It is not so much that I have a low pain threshold, more that, as my wife will gladly tell anyone who'd care to know, I have zero tolerance for even minor discomfort; you'll find no woollen trousers in my wardrobe; pebbly beaches are a no-go. But, right now, a cold shower actually sounds rather appealing.

I go out, stand beneath the shower head, brace myself, turn the handle to full cold and am drenched in an icy waterfall more refreshing, invigorating and, strangely, soothing, than anything I have ever experienced. It is wonderful.

Back in the sauna I head straight for the top step, high above Ernest. It is scorchingly, bakingly hot. My head begins to swim. My vision goes speckly and I am forced to slink down a few steps, forgetting the wooden pallet, and branding my bum on the concrete when I sit back down. I muffle a yelp, take a deep, burning breath, and try not to look at the next two arrivals – Colonel Blimp and Tollund Man – as their sex vegetables swing by.

Increasingly short of breath and, I fear, close to cardiac arrest, I totter out, shower, dress and emerged into the brisk dusk of Helsinki feeling cleaner than I have ever felt, fiercely thirsty, and exhausted.

I am still sweating copiously an hour later as I sit drinking the most fantastic, crystal gold chilled beer of my life in a bar back in the centre of town, reflecting on the Finns and their sauna addiction. Against all the odds, I had enjoyed my visit, although my feelings about public nudity are, if anything, now all the more entrenched, and I can't say I'll be rushing back. But why are the Finns so obsessed by saunas? Is it some inherent masochism, or its close cousin, machismo? Do the Finns feel they deserve some kind of daily punishment? Or, is it just that, because it's so damn cold most of the time, they have an extra need for warmth in their bones? If so, whither Canadian sauna culture?

It certainly didn't seem to be doing much for them in terms of social interaction, so why pretend otherwise? It seemed to me that – at least from my brief experience, and I may have been unlucky, or unbeknownst to me, visited on the weekly quiet day – the Finnish sauna experience is characterised as much by the communal silence as it is by the heat. This may be the root of the sauna's appeal to the Finns. They are a famously non-verbal race.

'Foreigners in Finland are struck by the taciturnity of the males,' wrote US academic and Finnish expat Richard D. Lewis in his book *Finland, Cultural Lone Wolf*. The Finns, he says, dislike gossip or extraneous chitchat. Lewis is very much of the geographical determinism persuasion, believing that the Finnish climate and environment have directly formed the character of the people here: 'Low temperatures necessitate outdoor succinctness. One does not dally on the street at 20 degrees below freezing . . . A broad American smile in a Helsinki easterly makes one's front teeth ache.'

Finland's climate and topography must clearly have played a part in forming the Finnish character, but it also seems likely that the Finns' taciturnity is in some way connected to their homogeneity. Finland has very little ethnic diversity (only 2.5 per cent of the population are immigrants, compared with over a third in neighbouring Sweden). So, if you were to interpret Finnish society according to the famous high-context/low-context theories of US anthropologist Edward T. Hall, it would be considered a very high-context culture – probably one of the highest context cultures in the world.

According to Hall, a 'high context' culture is one in which the people share the same kind of expectations, experiences, background, and even genes. Such people have less need for verbal communication because they already know so much about each other and the situations in which they typically find themselves. In high-context cultures words take on a greater meaning, but fewer are needed. In a low-context culture, like London, where hundreds of different nationalities, races and religions are represented, there is a greater need to communicate verbally to be sure of making oneself understood. There is less common ground, fewer unspoken assumptions are made, more gaps need to be filled in.

This could be said, in varying degrees, of all the Nordic countries. They are all comparatively homogenous and thus high-context. Norwegian social anthropologist Tord Larsen identified a similar phenomenon in Norway where, because everyone is broadly similar, 'paradoxes and surprises are rare'. In such high-context societies as Finland and Norway, it is generally easy to predict what kind of people you are dealing with, how they are thinking, how they will act and react. The Finns barely need to speak to each other at all.

'Finnish small talk is minimalist in terms of communication, but can convey the same amount of information as a two-minute conversation,' agreed Roman Schatz. 'You can be with a Finn in silence for some minutes and all of a sudden they will say, "Give me the coffee," and you'll think, "Wow, that was blunt," but the thing is, we are friends, we don't need to verbalise everything like the English, with their "Would you mind awfullys," and their "Please thank you terriblys."'

Though the Finns' taciturnity may work among themselves, problems arise when they travel or have to work with foreigners. The men, in particular, can be simply *too* frank, *too* direct, sometimes to the point of rudeness. They find it especially challenging to engage in the social lubricant of small talk, something even Norwegians can manage if they put their minds to it.

'Finns distrust verbosity. If you speak for more than four or five minutes at a time, they begin to wonder what you are trying to hide,' writes Richard D. Lewis, adding that they belong to a reactive or listening culture, one which does not typically initiate conversations but prefers to watch and wait and see how things pan out before contributing. Lewis concedes there are historical as well as geographical influences at work here: 'Sandwiched between Swedish and Russian bosses in a cold climate, Finns had no incentive to open their mouths unless they were asked to.'

A Finnish acquaintance told me this story, which he said perfectly sums up the Finns' attitude towards the normal conventions of human interaction. He and his brother-in-law were driving in a blizzard in the countryside when their car broke down. They waited for half an hour before another car finally passed. It stopped and the driver got out to help them. He peered under the bonnet and managed to get their car started for them, all in silence. There was a nod or two of acknowledgement, but my friend swears not a single word was exchanged. The man drove off. My friend said, 'Wow, we were lucky there. Wonder who he was?' To which his brother-in-law answered, 'Oh, that was Juha, we went to school together.'

Another Finn told me that on her days off she loves to go walking up in the hills but she admitted that she prefers to walk alone and that if any friends or family offer to join her she gets vaguely irritated. 'If we go walking and stay overnight in one of the public cabins up there and find another group is also staying in them, I do get disappointed. I think most Finns would be. We would always prefer to be alone,' she told me. And she was one of the chatty ones. In contrast, most Danes would positively relish meeting other Danes in such circumstances; it would be another chance to find common acquaintances, share a can of Tuborg or two and sing some songs.

'I get headaches when I visit Helsinki for more than a couple of days – there are simply too many people, not enough personal space,' another Finnish woman told me. 'I went to Hong Kong once,' she said, shuddering at the memory. 'It was just too much. The people!'

Once, when flying over the country, I looked down as Finland passed by beneath me. I was struck by how, even in the midst of what appeared to be forest wilderness (75 per cent of Finland is forest wilderness, with another 10 per cent frigid lakes), I would occasionally spot a flash of sunlight reflected from the Velux window of an isolated house, or the smoke rising from a sauna, apparently many miles from civilisation. 'A Finn is at peace,' I thought to myself, strangely comforted by the thought, 'without a neighbour in sight.'

The Finnish reticence might also be interpreted as shyness. The Finnish for shy, *ujo*, doesn't carry the negative connotations it does in English, nor do the various other words for 'shy' elsewhere in the Nordic region. Up here in this part of the world, where modesty and equality are so esteemed, shyness is not perceived as a social handicap but, more often, as a quality demonstrating modesty, restraint, one's willingness to listen to others.

There are, though, varying degrees of Scandinavian shyness. In the category of 'really good to sit next to on a long-haul flight but not so great if you are sat next to them at a dinner party', the Finns are the heaviest dance partners conversation-wise, followed by the Swedes who share the Finns' fondness for silence; then come the Norwegians and Icelanders. The Danes are almost human in this context. Perhaps because they have a tradition of being a trading people and are closer to mainland Europe, they are more comfortable with small talk – the *hygge* imperative at work. As a result of this, the rest of Scandinavia eyes the Danes with some suspicion – they are the Slick Willies and blabbermouths of the region: 'They've a little of the south in their blood,' is how one Norwegian put it to me, quite seriously.

This description of the Danes as almost Latin in temperament – as fast-talking, party-loving, rule-bending, devil-may-care, maverick sophisticates – can seem a little far-fetched to those who have actually visited Denmark. On first acquaintance the Danes seemed to me to be pretty much like Germans, but with better furniture. Having now spent some time among them and their sibling tribes, I can see why the Danes have this image further north. Compared to a Finn or a Swede your Dane is a veritable Las Vegas cabaret host.

There is definitely a gender division when it comes to Nordic reticence: Scandinavian men are, broadly speaking, comfortable with silence, while the women are generally more willing to help put a foreigner at ease. Of course, this may well be down to my considerable personal charms, but in Finland I found the women far, far more chatty than the menfolk. That said, to give them their due credit, at least you know that, when the men have finally thought long enough about their contribution to a conversation, you will get their definitive opinion, unembellished with linguistic flourishes, unburdened by etiquette or politesse, an opinion not to be changed.

Still, one imagines that, as they glide through the salons of Paris, or venture out into polite society in London or Tokyo, the Finns must leave a good deal of bemused and offended people in their wake. They are said to share many traits with the Japanese – according to Richard Lewis they employ virtually no body language, are good listeners, non confrontational, and so on – but even the Japanese find the directness and abruptness of the Finns upsetting.

A digression: we have heard how the Scandinavians are not especially chatty, but they do have some mysterious, non-linguistic ways of communicating which, as with the high-frequency clicks emitted by bats, are virtually inaudible to the rest of us. This is their portfolio of seemingly insignificant subvocal utterances, which I am only just now learning to decode. The most common is the brief, sharp intake of breath, which is used in combination with a slight grunt, to indicate a kind of agreement; something along the lines of a 'yes, but'. With some Danes this can be quite pronounced, and the first few times I found myself on the receiving end I grew alarmed and wondered if the person I was talking to was having some kind of fit. Richard D. Lewis describes the Finnish version of this as 'sighs, almost inaudible groans, and agreeable grunts'. Every race and language has their affirmative 'uh-huhs', their quizzical 'hmm?s', and their verbal tics, but the Scandinavians seem to have turned them into a key mode of communication.

*

In some senses, the Finns can be considered über-Scandinavians. As we have discovered, the Swedes, Danes and Norwegians self-censor according to Jante Law – one must not boast about one's achievements or possessions, one mustn't think one is better than anyone else, and so on. The Finns take this kind of modesty to a whole other level, to the extent that many claim it has a negative effect on their export economy.

'We don't have the guts to go out there and bravely boast about how good we are,' the country's tourism director said recently. 'We stand in the corner with our hands in our pockets and hope that somebody will pay attention to us.'

Roman Schatz has a similar take on Finnish modesty. 'Take a screw. An American presenting a screw would say something like, "This screw is going to change your life! It will make you happy. It is the best screw in the world," and then bore you for two-and-a-half hours about the technical details of that screw. A Finn will just say, "Here is screw." Selling something is so much against the Finnish mentality. Only untrustworthy people *sell* or *market* things. But of course that doesn't work in a global context.'

Sometimes it doesn't even work in a Finnish context either. Heikki Aittokoski, the foreign editor of Finland's leading broadsheet newspaper, *Helsingin Sanomat*, told me he often felt frustrated by his colleagues' reticence. 'I like that Finns are low-key,' said Aittokoski, who had worked as a correspondent in Berlin and Brussels before returning home. 'But I have trouble at work when journalists are presenting ideas and good stories. They never say, "We should run this big." I keep telling them they can be proud of their ideas. I was looking for someone from another department who spoke good English. I found someone and asked her if it was true, and she said, "Well, I suppose. I studied it a bit." It turned out she majored in English! She was totally fluent.'

I began to wonder whether the Finns' pathological taciturnity was a symptom or the cause of many of the perceived negative aspects of Finnish society – the melancholy, the depressiveness, the violence, and so on. Or was it, instead, a manifestation of historical scars – too many conflicts and losses better left undiscussed – or, simply, a side-effect of the weather which, as Richard Lewis claims, in these parts is hardly conducive to frivolous chitchat.

The Finns' obmutescence seemed especially to go hand in hand with that other most famous Finnish characteristic, their drinking. But was the latter used as a cure for the former – medication to help deal with their self-imposed isolation – or were they mutually symptomatic? In other words, which came first, the spirits or the silence?

Chapter 3

Alcohol

Two Finns meet on the street. Hannu says to Jaakko, 'Fancy a drink?' Jaakko nods, and they head off to Hannu's house.

They drink the first bottle of vodka in silence.

As he opens the next, Hannu asks Jaakko, 'So, how are you?'

Jaakko replies, tetchily, 'I thought we were here to have a drink?'

Whenever I mentioned to people that I was going to be travelling to Finland, every single one of them, without exception, made some kind of nudge-wink reference to the Finns' reputation for drinking, whether it be a subtle dig along the lines of 'They like a drink, the Finns,' to warnings like 'You're going to be there on a Saturday night? It's Armageddon!', usually accompanied by the speaker gripping my elbow and maintaining eye contact just that little bit longer than strictly necessary.

This impression of the Finns is not limited to my social circle. An etiquette guide to foreign managers moving to Finland offers this advice: 'A word of warning: cocktail parties or drinks after dinner can be prolonged indefinitely by Finnish guests if you adhere to the practice of displaying an unlimited amount of liquor. Finns do not like to leave behind bottles that are full, or even half-full.'

Jean Sibelius was renowned for his three- or four-day drinking binges. Former prime minister Ahti Karjalainen was a noted boozer, once arrested for drink-driving and eventually sacked because of his alcoholism. A culture of extreme drinking also defines one of the country's chief exports after mobile phones and timber: death metal bands. And in Formula 1 the Finnish drivers always have a reputation for being big drinkers. One of them was once found guilty of the singular crime of 'drunk sailing', I seem to recall. To this day, Estonians run for cover, grabbing their children from their front doorsteps, when the ferry from Helsinki arrives and hundreds of thirsty Finns disembark to take advantage of the cheaper alcohol on that side of the Baltic.

Walking around Helsinki during my first few days there, I saw few signs of rampant dipsomania. The streets were not awash with vomit and broken glass. Cars drove in an orderly fashion, and I saw no ruddy-faced men in battered top hats tipping back suspiciously weighty brown paper bags and singing sea shanties.

The Finns' reputation for drink is perplexing given that, when you look at the per capita annual alcohol consumption figures for Europe, they are actually strikingly average drinkers. Most reports tend to place their alcohol consumption somewhere between 10 and 12 litres per person per year (that's the amount of pure alcohol were it separated from the drink itself), a mid-table ranking. The Swedes drink less, it's true, but their government spends more on anti-alcohol propaganda than any other in the world. The Danes and British both drink more than the Finns, as do almost two-thirds of the countries that featured in a 2010 OECD worldwide health report on alcohol. A study carried out in the mid-1980s into the drinking habits of the Nordic region revealed that all the Scandinavians were broadly similar in their approach to intoxication: only Icelanders actively *approved* of drunkenness. So where does the Finnish reputation for heavy boozing come from?

Matti Peltonen is head of the Department of Social History at the University of Helsinki. This large, thoughtful man in his early sixties has been researching his countrymen's relationship to alcohol since the 1980s. We met in his book-filled office in one of the university's palatial, nineteenth-century buildings in central Helsinki, where he explained the – surprising – original source of all the jokes about Finns and booze.

'It's the Finns who told the jokes first, otherwise how else would you know about them?' said Peltonen, blankly. 'We created this absurd myth ourselves.'

Negative national stereotypes tend to be promulgated by neighbouring countries – the British label the French 'devious', the Americans call the Canadians 'retarded', and so on – but Finland has saved everyone else the trouble by creating its *own* negative self-image. Peltonen has written of the Finns' 'tendency to go to extremes in order to discredit our own national character'. But why would they sully their own name in this way?

He blames the early twentieth-century Finnish temperance movement that grew out of a class struggle between the ruling classes and the emerging industrial working-class labour movements. The working classes couldn't be trusted with the vote because they were blotto most of the time, at least according to the establishment. By way of a response, those labour movements moved to self-impose mandatory abstinence in the form of prohibition, but the plan had a flaw of which both sides were well aware: in those days the Finns drank even less than they do now, around 2 litres per annum.

'To get a temperance law they had tremendous difficulties because everyone was temperate already. We were too poor to drink,' says Peltonen. 'The peasant movement at the time used this idea of temperance to become more accepted in society: "Look, we are representing all these temperate people so we should have more say in society."'

Their leadership happily fostered the myth that working-class Finns couldn't handle their drink – that they grew wild and uncontrolled under the influence – going as far as to claim that it was biological, something in their blood. They did so because they believed that, if the working-class could subsequently prove they were sober and responsible, they would be entitled to greater political rights. As they were largely sober and responsible to start with, this was something of a *fait accompli*.

The Finns grew so committed to curbing their imaginary drinking that in 1919 they did eventually manage to impose prohibition on themselves. That lead to the inevitable bootlegging and multiple deaths from home-distilled moonshine. Tellingly, Finland's first ever film, made around this time, was about a bootlegging farmer – already the self-image was being formed. For a long time after prohibition finally ended in 1932 Finland had a rationing system, with each adult allowed a personal alcohol quota; this was eventually replaced by the same kind of state-run alcohol monopoly that is found in Iceland, Norway and Sweden, in Finland's case with the dreaded Alko shops. This remains a humiliating way in which to treat ordinary drinkers, but at least in Finland the system is more relaxed than it once was – there are more alcohol shops now, and some of them are occasionally open. Still, it is not unusual for Finns in the remoter regions to have to drive a hundred miles to get their quavering hands on a bottle of 60 per cent proof Salmiakki Koskenkorva, the popular Finnish clear-grain, licquorice-flavoured alcohol.

The Finnish ruling classes continued their efforts to depict their lower orders as wanton boozers in the wake of the Second World War. The last thing the Finnish workforce should be doing was drowning their sorrows when there was a nation in need of rebuilding! As well as losing valuable agricultural land and prosperous towns to Russia following border changes, Finland was forced to pay heavy war reparations and desperately needed economic growth to pay for them. So, put down that bottle, Mika! Buck up, and get on with rebuilding the country! And thus the temperance movement granted itself an ongoing mandate for its state-sanctioned party-pooping.

When the Olympics were held in Helsinki in 1952, and the Finns began to emerge shyly on to the international stage, they were extremely self-conscious about others' perceptions of them. By this point they had become so convinced of their alcoholic tendencies that they were more anxious than ever to control their imaginary boozing – still well below 3 litres per capita per year, almost half that of their Swedish neighbours. The Finnish People's Moral Movement was formed by the state alcohol monopoly to try to keep their drinking under continued control. From then on booze would only be available in restaurants and the state-owned Alko stores.

'What would foreigners think?' Peltonen wrote in a recent essay about the Finns' paranoia concerning their supposed alcoholism at this time. 'An attempt was made to coerce Finns with this anxiety-producing uncertainty as early as 1948 . . . with the aid of the illustrated flyers distributed by the Moral Movement, in which Finns were depicted as club-wielding cavemen dressed in animal skins.'

Peltonen believes that the Finnish reputation for drinking got out of hand early on and has been allowed to run wild, unchecked, ever since. But I am afraid to say there is *some* truth to it. Admittedly, it is not a question of how much the Finns drink in total per year, but the way in which they drink that is at the root of their reputation. The Finns are bingers, or 'episodic' drinkers: they get more heavily drunk more often than almost anyone else in Europe. In a 2007 EU poll of almost 30,000 people, 27 per cent of Finns admitted that bingeing – consuming five or more drinks in one session – was their customary way of drinking alcohol (they were second only to 34 per cent of Irish people). It is not that the Finns drink any more than the rest of us during the year, but that they tend to guzzle it all down in one go.

It would appear, then, that the Alko stores are not having the sobering effect they are supposed to. To an Englishman, having one's government control the sale of wine, beer and spirits in this manner seems positively Huxley-esque, merely another way for the Bordeaux-quaffing ruling classes to subjugate the downtrodden masses. One might well argue that if you employ government alcohol monopolies to protect the health of those who are too ignorant to understand the consequences of overindulgence, or are unable to control their appetites, then why not have sugar and fat monopolies too? (Whole stores devoted to marshmallows and pork scratchings . . . perhaps not such a bad idea.) Besides, it is also *bloody annoying* if you want to buy a bottle of wine at such a time when you might actually want to consume it, say, in the evening, or at the weekends. In Sweden, Norway, Iceland and Finland it is quite normal for these stores to close at around 6 p.m. on a Friday night. Needless to say, they are closed all day on Sunday – in my experience, the very day when you are most in need of a drink.

Some alcohol monopoly stores do make an effort to present their goods as if they are a normal consumer product instead of, say, a treatment for venereal disease, but the worst alcohol monopoly store I ever visited was in Gamla stan, the historic quarter of Stockholm. There, the bottles were displayed in glass cabinets, out of reach of the animal urges of the tragic addicts who shopped there; on the Friday night I went, the customers had to queue for over an hour, utterly humiliated by their desperation for alcohol, just for the privilege of being able to hand over an absurd amount of money to a disapproving old shrew who would then disappear behind the counter for ten minutes to find them a tawdry bottle of Chilean plonk. It was like Argos, but for an even more wretched substrata of society. The American essayist Susan Sontag described Sweden's state-run alcohol shops – the *Systembolaget* (which translates, chillingly, as 'The System') – as, 'part funeral parlour, part back-room abortionist'. She wasn't far off.

Peltonen was having none of this though. 'There is no reason to feel sorry for us,' he said defiantly. 'Alcohol shops in Finland are better than [normal alcohol retailers] in Denmark because this is a monopoly: the government is a big buyer so they get better wines for less and the selection is much better. In the UK you can only buy cheap wine from Australia, the selection is not as good as Finland. We don't buy all those shit wines for under five euro.'

It seemed an odd state of affairs for a finger-wagging government to be supplying its people with *better*-quality booze for *less* money than customers paid in shops in supposedly permissive, intemperate lands. Could it be true? The Nordic government's alcohol monopolies do have massive purchasing power which, combined with an absence of profit motive means that, in theory, they should be able to supply a better-quality product for a lower price. This has not been my experience in Sweden, but a sommelier friend in Oslo explained to me how, because they have a fixed duty on wine rather than adding a percentage of the value of the bottle, better quality wines were actually far cheaper in Norway than they are in the UK. The more you spent on a bottle of wine, the better the bargain you got.

But still, as I left Peltonen's office I couldn't help feeling he was slightly in denial about the seriousness of the Finns' boozing. He had claimed it was 'difficult to prove' that it had anything to do with the country's violent crime levels and preferred to blame 'the pressures of Western life'. It was only a minority who binged, he said. Finns were drinking fewer spirits and learning to appreciate good wines in moderation. But the consequences of excess drinking in Finland are of growing concern. Alcohol is now the leading cause of death for Finnish men (three times as many die from alcohol abuse as do from lung cancer), and the second leading cause for women. According to *Helsingin Sanomat*, deaths from cirrhosis of the liver are rising faster among the Finns than among other European populations: for some as yet unknown reason, Finnish livers seem more vulnerable to the ravages of alcohol than those of other nationalities.

Though suicide figures are notoriously unreliable (Catholic countries tend to be more reluctant to declare a death a suicide, for instance), according to the World Health Organisation Finland has the highest suicide rate in the Nordic region: 17.6 people per 100,000 per year, compared with 11.9 for Denmark, which is the lowest scorer in the region (the US rate is 11.8, the UK's 6.9). Could this, too, be at least in part alcohol-related?

The damage to the Finns from alcohol is not only self-inflicted. According to the 2011 Global Study on Homicide carried out by the UN Office on Drugs and Crime, Finland's rate of intentional homicides is more than *double* that of Denmark, which has a similar-sized population – 2.3 deaths per 100,000 in Finland vs 0.9 per 100,000 in Denmark (the UK's was 1.2, the US's 5.0).

Yet it can sometimes seem as if the Finns are almost proud of their reputation for bingeing and violence (not so much the suicide). The Ostrobothnia region of Finland is considered by many to be the country's spiritual heartland. Perhaps tellingly, Ostrobothnians have long had a notable and celebrated reputation for violence – their knife-fighting horse thieves, known as the *puukkojunkkarit*, were legendary in the mid-nineteenth century as a kind of pissed-up cross between Robin Hood and Mack the Knife.

Ostrobothnia folk songs sing breezily of fighting and brawling. The lyrics of 'The Horrible Wedding in Härmä' (a town with a reputation for violence in Finnish folklore) speak of 'drinking and fighting going on – from the hallway to the head of stairs dead bodies were carried'.

This leads us, inevitably, to *sisu*, the Finn's cherished (by them) and envied (by the Swedes) spirit of endurance, stamina and manliness. The word evokes a sense of quiet, determined strength, of dependability; it speaks of the ability to display unwavering resolve in the face of insurmountable adversity, a kind of proactive stoicism, if you like. If a bus breaks down, the spirit of *sisu* dictates that the passengers get out and push, without complaint. *Sisu* is everything the Finnish male aspires to, the granite bedrock below the nation's topsoil. But is it also *sisu* when you empty a bottle of Stolichnaya, pass out face-down in the snow, your nose falls off due to frostbite, yet you refuse to go to Accident and Emergency? And is the Finns' binge drinking just another manifestation of this trademark national machismo?

And then it dawned on me: throughout all these discussions of what made a Finn a Finn, what was really being discussed was what made Finnish *men* Finnish. Finland's self-image as taciturn, strong, *sisu* boozers, is almost wholly male-orientated. Even the rampantly male-chauvinistic Italians allow for feminine elements in their self-image, but not the Finns. This is odd given the otherwise prominent role women have played in Finnish society since the Second World War as presidents and prime ministers; in the workplace; the first women to get the vote in Europe, and so on.

It is a cliché but, as with most clichés, there are elements of truth in the fact that the kinds of men who are prone to making bold claims for their machismo or virility, do so to mask weakness or insecurity. It doesn't require a quantum leap of speculative cod psychology to wonder whether, deep down, Finnish men aren't in fact just suffering from really low self-esteem. Could all this *sisu* business be a front? Is the Finnish male the virgin who boasts loudly of his sexual conquests at the bar? The short man who picks fights with 6-footers? The triathlete who . . . well, just the triathlete.

No, obviously that isn't the case. Absolutely not. Any Ostrobothnians reading this, put down your axes. But I do wonder if the modern Finnish male, despite being well aware of the health risks and antisocial consequences of his alcohol consumption (in one survey the Finns were the only nationality to rate alcohol as their greatest societal problem out of eleven other issues), continues his heroic consumption as some kind of ritual masculine display, or a collective drowning of masculine sorrows, or both. Perhaps they are drinking to forget all those historic humiliations under the yoke of the condescending Swedes or the high-handed Russians. Even the Danes had a pop at ruling Finland, although that was back in the fifteenth century and the Danes have forgotten all about it. Surely there isn't much to look back on with pride. Yet somehow the Finns manage.

The 1939–40 Winter War against the Soviets is, for instance, often cited as Finland's crowning *sisu* moment. Though it is true the Finnish army demonstrated astounding bravery, tenacity and fortitude in repelling the invasion of a Soviet military force more than five times its strength, and though they did this with virtually no help from Sweden, essentially the Finns still kind of, you know . . . *lost*. As courageous and indefatigable as they unquestionably were, the Mannerheim Line counted for little in the end. Arguably even more regrettable than the territory and reparations they ultimately ceded as a result of the defeat, was that their loss to Russia drove the ever-pragmatic Finns straight into the arms of the Germans. The Finns went on to fight against the Soviets, arm-in-arm with the Nazis, for three years.

It is easy to judge in retrospect, and we all understand that the Finns were fighting on the side they believed was best able to help maintain their freedom, but siding with the most thoroughly evil political system in modern history doesn't look that great from a historical perspective.

I am not the first person to wonder whether, because of this and other historic scars (perhaps most painful of all, the Civil War of 1918), the Finns actually might *hate* themselves. Finnish novelist Eila Pennanen concluded much the same in his celebrated 1956 novel, *Mongolit*.

I thought it was worth floating my 'Finnish men drink to soothe egos fractured by centuries of foreign rule and military loss' theory to Roman Schatz.

He wasn't that taken by it.

'I think that's a wimpish excuse served on a silver platter, frankly,' he said. 'Finnish men didn't start drinking because they felt ashamed of World War Two, Finnish men are damned proud about how this little country managed to defend itself against the Germans and Russians – and even one shot was fired against the British you know, somewhere in Lapland, I think. No, Finnish men were drinking long before that. Listen, if you sit here in November, all alone, it's dark and grey, you feel like having a drink. Then you feel a little better, and you think maybe if I have another drink I'll feel even better. In Finland you drink to get rid of all the shit from the week, to zero yourself and have a big convulsion and puke everything out and not remember it the next morning.'

Schatz has a radical solution to the Finnish drinking epidemic: 'Alcohol should be completely deregulated. If you did that you would have a hundred thousand people dead, that is the sober truth, but after that you would have the viable part of the population who could actually deal with it.' He was joking. Sort of. 'I am a liberalist so I believe that some people have the right to drink themselves to oblivion.'

He also mentioned something called the 'warrior gene', which had been identified in the Finnish DNA, and cast their relationship to alcohol in a slightly different light. I looked it up. In fact it's an enzyme, Monoamine Oxidase A, which works together with serotonin. According to research carried out by the US National Institute on Alcohol Abuse, there does seem to be some link between Monoamine Oxidase A levels, alcohol consumption and impulsive, violent behaviour. Research has shown that Finns have higher levels of the enzyme than other people and, apparently, it doesn't mix well with alcohol; inebriation seems to bring out the warrior in some Finns, making them even more up for it. It was a depiction that Heikki Aittokoski, recognised.

'I do notice that when I am out at a party, having a good time, at some point, somewhere around eleven-thirty in the evening, people start behaving aggressively,' he told me one day over lunch close to his office at *Helsingin Sanomat*. 'They get that warrior gene going, they start behaving like idiots, throwing punches, wrestling – and I am talking about "respectable" people – and for some reason I don't quite understand, it is accepted. The next day people laugh, "Did you see so and so?" and then forget about it. In the States they'd have an intervention and send them off to rehab. Here it's "That was kind of funny, he was pretty fucked up," but no more than that. We tend to accept behaviour you wouldn't accept in Sweden.'

The English actor Neil Hardwick, who has lived in Finland for forty years, agreed. 'Alcohol doesn't make them pleasant people, it makes them aggressive,' he told me. 'They are very serious and pragmatic about it: we work during the week, but now it's Friday, we're going to get drunk.'

Like Schatz, Hardwick ascribed the Finns' drinking at least in part to the weather and the winter darkness, or *kaamos*: 'February to June is just so long, and nothing happens. It's awful. Spring is so late and it really is very dark for large parts of the year. You never turn your lights off in the winter. You don't get used to it. I've tried vitamin D supplements and used a sunlamp, but it actually gets worse the longer you are here. Every year I wonder if I can get through it. I think that is why there is this sense that when you do get the chance to take your pleasure, you take it, for God's sake, because the summer is so short and the moments when you can enjoy yourself are few and far between. I think that explains that sort of intense hedonism.'

Sadly for them, around the world the Finns are defined by this 'intense hedonism' and the carnage that can ensue. It is not an ideal image for a progressive, modern democracy to project and so, in recent years, the kinds of people whose job it is to worry about Finland's international reputation have been trying to change it. During a five-year process, the Finnish government consulted everyone from the head of Nokia to schoolteachers on how they saw themselves and how they wished to be perceived by the world. The result was a 'brand vision' entitled, *A Mission for Finland*, which attempted to position Finland as the problem-solver of the world, plus an ad campaign emphasising the Finns' honesty and reliability, featuring the slogan 'Is there a Finn on board?' – their version of 'Is there a doctor on board?' the inference being that you can always rely on a Finn.

By chance I was introduced to one of the members of the branding committee, Paulina Ahokas of Music Export Finland, one evening during a fire-alarm-induced interval at a performance by Finland's leading modern dancer, Tero Saarinen, which we both happened to be attending at the Alexander Theatre (Saarinen's performance was astonishing, but also a little bonkers. It was so avant-garde that the fire alarm sounded for a good few minutes before the audience slowly began to realise that it wasn't part of the performance. Needless to say, the fire brigade was already there by the time we had been shepherded outside.)

'If you were designing a country today, from scratch, you would end up with Finland,' Ahokas told me confidently when we met at her office the next day. 'Finland is a miracle, but it's a story no one knows.'

Among other qualities, she cited Finnish society's equality of opportunity – 'The fact that we take care of everyone and everyone has a fair chance, regardless of their background'; the Finns' trust-worthiness – 'Ours is one of the most reliable handshakes in the world'; and even the weather – 'I love the snow, it brings light into the city in the winter. Rather that than the English damp.'

Then I mentioned the alcohol issue. It was a bit of a millstone in terms of one's international image, wasn't it? 'Well, it is a hindrance,' she said, then suddenly brightening: 'But there is a lot of joy in being crazy AND trustworthy!'

That Friday evening I ventured out into central Helsinki to try to assess for myself just how 'crazy' the Finns were in their cups. I started the evening at 8 p.m. in a bar on Tennispalatsi (where the basketball matches were held during the 1952 Olympics). The place was packed but subdued. By 9 p.m. it was absolutely heaving, a few drinks were being spilled, but nothing particularly untoward. I left around 10 p.m. and headed across the square, stopping off at another bar for further, serious-minded social-anthropological field work.

I left that bar at around 11.30 p.m. to find the streets rather more crowded, with gangs of teenage Goths roaming around in long black leather coats and silver jewellery, bellowing their mating calls across the square. They were quite staggeringly off their faces. Crescendos of breaking glass echoed all around and an army of bottle collectors swarmed over the rubbish bins (to encourage recycling there is a return-payment for bottles and cans in all the Nordic countries, so bin-rummaging is a common occupation among the less well-off. There have been times – usually when my taxes are due – when I have given this line of work serious consideration myself).

As Friday night turned into Saturday morning and the mood on the streets of Helsinki began to turn a little more threatening, I became aware of the black-clad private security guards stationed outside most bars and pubs. Truth to tell, though, it was no worse than in any other major city in Northern Europe, and certainly less scary than a Friday night in, say, Crawley or Leicester.

In Crawley I would fear for my life, in Helsinki I merely feared for their dress sense.

Chapter 4

Sweden

You have got to love a country that enters Lordi into the Eurovision Song Contest and wins, which consumes more ice cream per capita than any other European country (14 litres a year), and has more tango dancers than Argentina.* This is a special place, of that there is no doubt.

In his essay 'The Clash of Civilisations', the late Yale political scientist Samuel Huntington pointed out that Finland bestrides one of the world's key cultural fault lines, dividing the two civilisations of Christianity and Orthodoxy. In a sense, the Finns are forever torn between the history they share with Christian Europe thanks to the Swedish influence – the Renaissance, the Enlightenment, the Reformation, and so on – and that of the Orthodox world, with its tsarist and communist systems.

This might lead you to expect them to be somewhat schizophrenic, or culturally 'conflicted', which I suspect is true. In *Finland, Cultural Lone Wolf*, Richard D. Lewis sums up what he sees as the contradictory nature of the Finns thus: 'Finns are warm-hearted people, but they have a desire for solitude. They are hard-working and intelligent, but often seem slow to react. They love freedom, but they curtail their own liberty by closing their shops early, limiting their access to alcohol, prohibiting late baths in apartment buildings, and taxing themselves to death. They worship athletics and fitness,

---

* Finnish tango music is always in a melancholy minor key. One explanation for the dance's popularity, offered to me by a woman I got chatting to in Café Tin Tin Tango, is that if you can get Finnish men dancing long enough, they stop drinking. The tango takes some time to master.

but until recently their diet gave them the highest incidence of heart disease in Western Europe . . . They love their country but seldom speak well of it.'

Since 1947, when Finland was forced to cede 10 per cent of its territory to Russia, that east/west line has literally divided the country, but Finland has had to live with this duality for much longer: 'Finns in the early part of the twelfth century found themselves in the middle of a great power conflict, a situation that would persist – in hot and cold war periods – right up to 1945,' writes Lewis. 'The manner in which the Finns have dealt with this geopolitical balancing act defines to a large degree the history of the nation.' That's a long time to have been pulled in two directions. No wonder the Finnish psyche is such a tangled mess of deep-seated taboos, many of which seemed rooted in this duality of influence.

There is their complex relationship with the Swedes and their anxieties about the Russians; their fears about what the rest of us think of their non-verbal social inadequacies; the drinking and violence; the terrible Civil War; that awkward business with the Nazis; a 1947 partition every bit as divisive as the sub-continent's; the growing fear of Nokia going under and prompting another national near-bankruptcy like the one in the early 1990s, and so on.

You could argue that all the clichés of Finnishness – the drinking, the violence, the reticence, even the saunas – are really just symp-toms or side-effects of their taboos. The Finns are, essentially, defined by what they leave unsaid.

Prime among these cultural conflicts is their relation to the Swedes. A while back I got to know a Finnish father at the school my children attended. We would often meet at social functions to catch up and, as the evening went on, put the world to rights over a few glasses of wine. There was one thing I could never really understand about my friend though: he would often drop into the conversation the fact that he was a Swedish Finn. After the second mention I was, like, 'Yeah, right, you said already. And?' But it was important to him that I know this: he, the urbane, Swedish-speaking sophisticate from the southern coastal regions, was distinguishing himself from the other Finns, the woodsmen from the hinterland and the frozen north. He was from the Finland of Sibelius and Alvar Aalto, not one of the monosyllabic boozers from the forests.

Contact between Finland and Sweden predates records, but probably began via the stepping stones of the Åland Islands across to the south-west of Finland, which was about the only habitable part of the country for many millennia. The Swedes settled and started to trade with the Finns, who came from deep in the forests with their fur and their tar, and gradually 'conquered' Finland between 1155 and 1293.

The Finns have numerous grounds for resentment concerning the period of Swedish rule: the 1696–7 famine, caused by two particularly harsh winters, to name just one. Approximately a third of the population of Finland was left to starve by an incompetent Stockholm government. This has not been forgotten.

What is most remarkable about Swedish influence amid the higher echelons is the extent to which it continued long *after* the Swedes had relinquished power in the early nineteenth century. Barely had the 1809 Diet of Porvoo agreed the terms under which the Grand Duchy would be ruled by Russia, than the new Finnish ruling class – still mostly made up of Swedish Finns, it has to be said – were busy enshrining equal rights for Swedish speakers in its constitution. Swedish remained the only official language in Finland for more than half a century after the two countries divided; snobbery burnished Swedish culture for longer still. 'It was common practice for families with social aspirations to conceal a Finnish origin behind an adopted Swedish surname,' writes T. K. Derry.*

* Talking of Finnish independence, I had an insight into the different ways in which Finland and Sweden interpret the events of 1809 when I visited Helsinki on the 200th anniversary of the Diet of Porvoo. In Helsinki, the Finns were marking the bicentenary with an unmistakably celebratory tone to the extent that, according to one outraged Finnish ministry of education insider I spoke to, the Swedish government had apparently had the temerity to try to get the Finns to tone down their celebrations. In contrast, the rather downbeat title of Stockholm's commemorative exhibition was '1809 – A Kingdom Divided'. Clearly the loss still grated with the Swedes.

Today, though their prominence is waning, the 300,000 or so Swedish Finns who live in Finland still exercise a surprising amount of influence in the higher echelons of the establishment and in industry (perhaps the most famous case being Björn 'Nalle' Wahlroos, an outspoken banker and one of the richest men in Finland, who has come to symbolise a particular kind of free-market-capitalist Swedish Finn).

'It is difficult to gauge the influence of the Swedish minority,' Heikki Aittokoski told me. 'Probably only 10 per cent of them are old families with money, and of course they have lots of influence – this is centuries-old money and they have companies and employ thousands of people – but the majority of Swedish Finns are ordinary people. The bad boy is definitely Wahlroos. He is the most famous capitalist in Finland and every time he says something it makes the headlines.'

Swedish Finns have their own national assembly, the *Folketinget*; their own political party, the Swedish People's Party, which usually has a minister in government; their own national theatre, which is virtually as large as, and arguably more elegant than, the Finnish national theatre; and they even have their own flag, a yellow cross on a red background. Swedish remains an official language in Finland and is compulsory in schools. If a region has more than 8 per cent Swedish speakers, it must operate on a bilingual basis. Though only 6 per cent of Finland's population are Swedish Finns, there are still some places on the coast in southern and western Finland where they make up the majority, notably the self-governing, Swedish-speaking – but technically Finnish – Åland Islands, of which my chief recollections from a visit a few years ago are a morning spent visiting one of its main attractions, a snail farm, and being devoured by midges every evening. By law, in these Swedish-speaking parts of the country even the street signs have to be in Swedish first and Finnish second. Some parts of London have a sizable – perhaps even majority – French population; could you imagine Kensington Borough Council putting up street signs in French?

'There is still an ambiguity between the Swedish-speaking Finns and the Finnish Finns,' Roman Schatz told me. 'The Swedish Finns used to have a sense of superiority, but that isn't true any more. That is history. Finland has Nokia and cocktails and snowboarding now. We don't need them.'

I am told you can often tell Swedish Finns apart from 'proper' Finns by their physical appearance, but they do remain avowedly Finnish, with little desire to become Swedish, less still to move to Sweden. Finland is their home. Hence Finland's bilingual status remains rigorously enforced even, according to Schatz, among newborns. 'I was enrolling my son in a baby swimming group but they said they only had places in the Swedish-speaking one, the Finnish one was full. I said, "But they're babies! They don't speak any language." In the end, I had to claim that he was German Finnish and, by arguing that German was a sister language to Swedish, they let him in!'

'Sweden is the enemy you love to hate, and hate to love,' Neil Hardwick told me. 'I don't think the Swedish Finns run Finland, but they do run their own affairs in a cliquey way and they corner large sections of the cultural and educational budgets for Swedish-speaking projects. There is a tremendous amount of shadowy support for Swedish projects, a bit of an old boys' network.'

'Finns used to have – and still do to a certain extent – a huge inferiority complex with Swedes,' agreed Aittokoski. Then again, I suppose that's understandable. We all do.

The special treatment of the Swedish Finns particularly rankles with the fast-rising, right-wing True Finn party, which rocketed from 4 per cent to over 19 per cent in the polls in recent years and which, as I write, is the third largest political party in the country. As well as the usual anti-immigrant rhetoric (a key element of their success, despite the fact that Finland has even fewer immigrants than the other Nordic countries), the party also wants to eradicate the Swedish influence in Finland.

But Aittokoski – who is not a Swedish Finn – has a different approach to the issue. He sees their treatment as 'a prime example of how to take care of a minority'. Although the Finns have good cause for resentment towards the Swedes, for him the Swedish connection was a valuable bridge to the West during the Cold War.

Besides, erasing Swedish Finns from the history books could prove awkward, as many of Finland's greatest historical figures, not least the leaders in the fight for, and development of, Finnish nationhood, were Swedish Finns – like the country's national poet, Johan Ludvig Runeberg; its greatest composer, Jean Sibelius; greatest architect, Alvar Aalto (whose mother was Swedish); and even the greatest military hero, Marshal Carl Gustaf Mannerheim, after whom every Finnish town's main street appears to be named. Tove Jansson, creator of the Moomins: another Swedish Finn.

One person who I'd been told would have some interesting insights into Finland's complex historic relationships was historian Laura Kolbe. I met Kolbe, a petite, intense woman in her mid-forties, in her office at the University of Helsinki one day. I wondered if she agreed that the Finns had an inferiority complex when it came to their former masters.

'I think it's more that we envy their success,' she said. 'Sweden has been like a sun that just attracts everybody, a kind of magnet for success . . . and I think many Finns are grateful to the Swedes.'

I pressed Kolbe a little more on this. She sounded a little too magnanimous. Were there really no grudges? It didn't take much pressing . . .

'I recently stayed in Uppsala, and I started again to think about my relationship to Sweden. Do I love this country or do I hate this country? And I noticed it is a bit of both. I do feel that, if you look at the two countries today, it is unfortunate that they were separated in 1809 because both need the other to be completely fulfilled: the Swedes could get the seriousness, the dramatic, the feeling for real life from the Finns. They haven't been challenged enough, they've been complacent, lived a nice life in their suburban houses. You know, all the artists and writers in Sweden now are incomers. The best books and plays are written by people who are not Swedish by birth. It is a society that lacks a dynamic. And then of course you look at Sweden and you could say that their wealth is coming really from Finland protecting them, so there is – I don't think bitterness – but a realism. There is a little bit the sense that while we were holding up the wall, the Swedes were tending their gardens.'

I heard this from several Finns – the notion of the Swedes as slightly foppish; squeamish about getting their hands dirty; egging the Finns on to give the Russians a bloody nose as they fluttered their lacey hankies on the other side of the Gulf of Bothnia. Several Finnish males used the word 'gay' to me when describing their Swedish counterparts. As we will see, the Swedes did rather well out of their neutrality, both during the Second World War and in its aftermath.

'In Finland Swedes are commonly thought of as gay, the men at least,' said Roman Schatz. 'They are soft and pale, they don't have hair on their balls. In the Swedish army they don't have to cut their hair. They give them hairnets!' I checked up on this, and, rather wonderfully, this is a true story: in 1971 the Swedish army ordered 50,000 hairnets to contain their soldiers' then newly fashionable long locks.

Revealingly, in the 'masculinity versus femininity' section of Dutch anthropologist Geert Hofstede's hugely influential 1980 'cultural dimensions' study into the values of cultures around the world, Finnish society was deemed to be the most masculine in the Nordic region, while the Swedes were not only the least masculine in the region, but *in the world*.

Finland's adoption of the euro represented a major break from the Swedes who, of course have kept their krona. The Finns were proud to be the first country to adopt the single currency, thanks to the time difference. That said, the countries' slow-burn rivalry still gets a highly charged airing each year with an annual track-and-field event between the two countries, called the *Suomi-Ruotsi-maaottelu* (literally the 'Finland–Sweden match').

'It is abso-bloody-lutely nationalistic,' Schatz told me, rubbing his hands together in anticipation. 'The TV slogan in Finland for it this year is "It's not important that Finland wins, but that Sweden loses."'

Chapter 5

Russia

As all Pet Shop Boys fans will be aware (from the lyrics of 'West End Girls'), in April 1917 Vladimir Ilyich Lenin was smuggled from his exile on the banks of Lake Geneva and sent by train via Stockholm to the Finland Station in St Petersburg. The release of Finland from Russian control, which he had promised some years before, was only a matter of time.

Finnish autonomy, dreamed of since 1809, and prepared for with the nationalist Fennoman movement (motto: 'Swedes we are no longer, Russians we do not want to become, let us therefore become Finns!'), should have heralded a brave new age for Finland. As historian Laura Kolbe told me, 'During that time we were able to build up a national identity, the Finnish language, the mythologisation of the Kalevala [Elias Lönnrot's 1835 collection of Finnish folk poetry and myths, which were a great influence on Tolkien]. We decided who we were.' Instead the country descended into a self-sabotaging nightmare, the aftermath of which would linger for decades.

Communism was on the rise in Finland, as it was elsewhere in Europe. Radical Finns rallied behind the red flag, while the middle-class Whites were led by General Mannerheim, who had actually served time in the Russian army under the tsar. Though the resulting Civil War lasted fewer than four months, its psychological scars linger to this day. The Whites won; 37,000 people died. Many Reds and their supporters were executed or imprisoned, and though there was an eventual amnesty for them, for decades afterwards the whole miserable episode was largely swept under the carpet. It was the single most divisive moment in Finnish history. That may sound self-evident – *duh*, it was a civil war – but Finland's history does seem to have been especially bitter, and one imagines that the famed Finnish reticence would hardly have helped the healing process.

'It is still difficult to get any ceremonies on the Red graves,' one Finn whose family fought on the Red side told me. 'There are many unofficial Red graves out in the forests. Those divisions are not in the open, but if you go to any village in the countryside, everyone can tell you which family was on the Red side and which was on the White.'

Laura Kolbe says it took the Finns fifty years to come to terms with the Civil War. 'It's no longer a living memory, but still every Finnish family has a kind of relationship to it, either you were in the White part or the Red part. Today it's not like it was in the sixties, but yes, you carry a kind of traumatic relationship [to it] because it was really brother against brother, communists against bourgeoisie and farmers.'

'The whole Reds versus Whites thing is still very touchy,' agreed Neil Hardwick. 'After a while you can figure out who is on which side. It shouldn't matter, but it runs so deep. I used to call myself a communist, but you don't mention that these days, it's a silly word these days, but us old lefties, we kind of recognise each other, there'll be eye contact. But in the seventies the lefties were thought of as actually extremely unpatriotic – they would have sold the country to Moscow if they had the chance – but I never wanted anything to do with that.'

Perhaps the wounds of the civil war might have healed more easily had Finland not had the Soviet Empire breathing down its neck, the Politburo obviously being supportive of Finnish communists. Though Finno–Russian relations progressed well enough immediately following independence, as the Second World War approached, the Russian Bear once again turned its attention to its little neighbour to the west.

As with previous Russian interest in Finland, Stalin was probably never that serious about conquering the country, he just wanted a larger buffer zone to protect St Petersburg, now renamed Leningrad. He requested control of some of the Finnish islands that lay just beyond the city, as well as the Finnish port of Hanko. The Finns refused and the countries went to war in November 1939, a conflict which would prove to be the ultimate test of *sisu*.

The Finns faced certain defeat with only around 200,000 men and virtually no planes or tanks to defend the country against the 1.2 million-strong Red Army. Following a truly harrowing, permafrosted campaign that lasted three months and saw prolonged periods in which the temperature fell below $-40°C$, 26,000 Finnish lives were lost compared with 127,000 Russians. For a sense of how grindingly awful this conflict was, Pekka Parikka's 1989 film, *The Winter War* (a kind of Finnish *The Thin Red Line*), rams it home quite harrowingly during three hours of blood-stained snow, splintered trees, scorched trenches and severed limbs, the entire film played with virtually no emotion on the part of the actors (the one 'light' moment comes when the soldiers of Infantry Regiment JR23 on the Mannerheim Line somehow find the wherewithal to build a sauna).

As terrible as it was, in a sense the Winter War galvanised Finland, helping to bring together a divided nation and earning the Finns the admiration of the rest of the world. Their white-clad ski patrols, nicknamed 'the White Death' by Russian soldiers, became a Second World War icon. US war correspondent and ex-Mrs Hemingway Martha Gellhorn was in the country at the time and helped create the enduring image of the Finns as hardy and determined: 'The people are marvellous, with their pale, frozen fortitude,' she wrote in one dispatch.

Neutral Sweden did little to support its former territory during its conflicts with Russia, and even prevented the League of Nations and the Allies coming to Finland's aid in the early part of the conflict. Understandably there remains a residual bitterness among some Finns, not just about the blockade, or at being left to dangle by the Swedes during the War, but also at the way in which the Swedish economy flourished so brazenly, supplying both the Germans and British with raw materials, and from the sense of security that it enjoyed by having doughty Finland as a buffer against the Soviets for many decades afterwards. As one Finn put it to me: 'Sweden made hay while Finland held back the Soviet Union.' Was there any lingering resentment? After a very long pause he answered, with classic Finnish laconicism, 'That's a good question.'

Finland's limited success in resisting the Soviets – as I mentioned, the Mannerheim Line was eventually breached in early 1940 – was all the encouragement Hitler needed to believe he could defeat Stalin, and so the relatively brief Winter War was followed by the three-year Continuation, during which, despite initially declaring neutrality ('Don't mind us! You two carry on!'), the Finns eventually decided their best interests lay in joining the Nazis fighting against the Soviets under Operation Barbarossa. The Finns allowed over 200,000 German soldiers to fight in the north of their country and gave the Nazis access to various raw materials, particularly their nickel.

Though it is always easy to condemn such collaboration in retrospect, one can hardly help but view the Finnish alliance with Hitler with some scorn. And would the Soviets actually have invaded Finland anyway? Documentary evidence from the Soviet high command of the time suggests this was never on their agenda, rendering the alliance with Germany that bit less defensible.

Naturally, the Finns disagree. 'We fought together with Germany against the Soviet Union; but were not allied with Germany, that would have been different,' argues Kolbe. 'We were not collaborators in the same sense as the Netherlands, or Norway, or Denmark. We were a military brotherhood. We really prohibited Russia from occupying Finland, with the help of Germany.'

The ever-pragmatic Finns draw a fine distinction here: they were operating very strictly within their own, anti-communist, national interest to reclaim their territory and prevent a Soviet invasion: they were not assisting Hitler's Third Reich ambitions. The appalling atrocities that we now know were perpetrated by the Russians after they conquered Finland's neighbouring Baltic states (which are only now recovering from the Soviet era), suggest the Finns were wise to do anything they could to avoid becoming part of the Soviet

Bloc, however questionable the morality of their allegiances might appear from the vantage point of history. As a caption I read in the Rovaniemi history museum has it: 'The international situation forced Finland to seek support from Germany.'

In the last months of the war, though, the Finns did eventually turn on the Germans. The Germans took their revenge by burning every building, destroying every bridge and ripping up every road they came into contact with as they fled northwards through Lapland which is why, as my son and I saw when we visited Santa, Rovaniemi is today a soulless grid of concrete apartment blocks: everything had to be rebuilt from rubble during a time of unimaginable austerity.

As punishment for siding with the Germans, Finland ended up giving Russia 10 per cent of its territory. This included much of agriculturally rich Finnish Karelia; almost a hundred power stations; great tracts of forest; and, crucially in terms of its economy, the port of Vyborg. Finnish refugees fled back into Finland. It had, effectively, undergone its own equivalent of Partition, a national rupture which has these days been completely forgotten by the rest of the Europe.

Mannerheim somehow manoeuvred Finland out of the grasp of the Soviet Union; his second masterstroke was the rejection of Marshall Plan aid. Refusing American assistance was a classic example of Finnish obstinacy and bloody-mindedness. Though Finland was desperately in need of funds, its courageous self-sufficiency allowed the country to settle its debt to Russia while keeping it free of any ties to America. There would be no US bases, no membership of NATO, and so no threat to the Russians that Finland might be used as a stepping stone for any invasion from the West. In turn, Russia felt less need to strong-arm or invade Finland and so, instead of becoming another Estonia, the country benefitted hugely in economic terms from being a strategic pawn in the Cold War chess game.

Many attributed Finland's success at keeping Moscow at bay during the 1970s to one man: Urho Kekkonen. Initially as prime minister and then president for twenty-five years, he guided Finland along a diplomatic tightrope up until his resignation due to ill health, aged eighty, in 1981. There were times when Kekkonen toyed with dictatorship himself, dissolving parliament in 1961 to reassure the Russians that he was in control, for instance, but through various other Soviet-related crises – such as the so-called 'night frost' of 1958 when the Russians cancelled their orders to Finnish industry and withdrew their ambassador – he managed to preserve Finland's independence. 'If you want to know why we were the only country not occupied by Russia at the time,' one Finn told me, 'you need to understand this man's relationship with the Soviet Union.'

Today, Kekkonen occupies a quasi-mythological position in the history of his nation, with rumour and counter-rumour concerning his east–west allegiances, as well as his actions during the Civil War, still swirling around almost thirty years after his death in 1986.

'In all his speeches he always underlined the importance of good relations with Russia. We had it in our bones. Finland was forced to make its opinions more mild,' Kolbe said when I raised criticisms about Kekkonen's 'Active Neutrality' approach: what some see as his subservience to Moscow and his close relationship with Khrushchev (they were hunting buddies). 'The Soviet Union was so powerful, and there were ideological pressures to accept the Soviet version of history. It wasn't so much the Russians telling us what to say. I would call it "National Realism". It's easy for you to say we were pushed and pressurised: you, of course, had NATO.'

Kolbe had described Kekkonen as having 'excellent connections with the Soviet leaders', but many would take that further. Was he, in fact, a Soviet stooge?

'It was all very John le Carré, from what I understand,' Neil Hardwick told me of Finnish–Soviet relations in the sixties and seventies. 'He was very close to the Russians, and you never really knew which side he was on. Once, years ago, I was in a pub in London, in the theatre district, and there was this old guy in a rain-coat, very drunk. I kept looking at him thinking, "Hmm, I know him, who is he?" He noticed me looking at him and said, "Don't you know who I am? I am George Brown [former Labour foreign secretary in the Wilson government and a staunch anti-Soviet]." We got talking a bit and I said that I lived in Finland, to which he replied, "Ah, that Kekkonen, he worked for the KGB you know."' Whether this is true or not, what is little disputed is that the Finnish president was trusted by the Soviets (they awarded him their equivalent of the Nobel – the Lenin Peace Prize – in 1979), earning Finland the dubious nickname Kekkoslovakia.

Perhaps the single most perilous moment in Finnish–Soviet relations came in 1978. 'The Russians proposed a common military exercise between Soviet and Finnish troops,' remembers Kolbe. 'And our politicians, quite skillfully, said, "Maybe not, perhaps we can come and follow your troops and you can send yours to follow ours, but let's not mix." Throughout the Cold War we were close to a diplomatic invasion, a stealth invasion.'

This stealth invasion took many forms, some of which have an almost Ealing Comedy aspect to them. Several Finns when remembering this era had mentioned to me the extraordinary phenomenon of the 'Home Russian', a kind of Iron Curtain buddy system in which Finnish politicians and others in the establishment paired up with a Russian opposite number.

'The Soviet embassy was, of course, extremely powerful and every Finnish politician had a Home Russian, a Soviet diplomat who became a very close friend: you invited them to your summer house, to family get-togethers,' is how Kolbe put it.

The relationship was mutually beneficial: 'They gathered information on what we were doing, what the intellectuals and politicians were thinking, but everyone knew what the aim of these relationships was,' says Kolbe. The Soviets especially valued any information the Finns picked up in London and New York while on business there.

Neil Hardwick's arrival in Finland coincided with the height of the Cold War. When we met in the bar of my hotel I asked him for his memories of Helsinki during that time. 'Forty years ago it was very Eastern European and, basically, everything was forbidden except the things that were compulsory,' he laughed. 'Going out to a place like this would have been dreadful. You'd have had to queue up outside, there would have been a doorman, you'd buy your drink but you couldn't go from one table to another if you saw a mate. You couldn't just pick up your drink and walk over, you had to ask a waiter to take your drink for you. They covered the windows too, so that passers-by wouldn't be able to see people drinking.'

Russian influence on the lives of ordinary Finns was extraordinary. Once a week the national radio station broadcast a fifteen-minute bulletin, a kind of 'What's happening with the neighbours', according to Hardwick, filled with 'gentle Soviet propaganda'. He also explained how every home had to keep something called a House Book, in which were recorded the names, not only of everyone who lived in the house, but of every visitor. Come January, a member of the household had to queue at the local police station where the books would be checked and stamped. Failure to do this would result in a fine.

The Finnish media and publishing industries were ever alert to material that might displease the Soviets. 'What I have heard from older colleagues is that foreign policy in particular was a touchy issue,' foreign editor of *Helsingin Sanomat*, Heikki Aittokoski, told me. 'The foreign ministry was extremely active pressurising our people. Basically everybody knew that our independence depended on Moscow. Books were removed from libraries if they were anti-Soviet, for instance. It was big news when Gorbachev came to Helsinki and declared Finland was a neutral country. Today you think, "So what? Wasn't Finland already free?" But back then it was a big headline. He didn't say you are an independent country, he said "neutral", i.e. not a part of the Soviet Bloc – "You're free to go, do what you want to do."' (What Aittokoski neglects to mention here is that in 1991, when Gorbachev was kidnapped and deposed, his paper published a leader suggesting that this was a positive turn of events; it was still clearly wary of incurring the displeasure of the Politburo.)

All of this anxiety is entirely understandable. For much of the

Cold War, Russian tanks were lined up along the Finnish border awaiting the order to roll. And who would come to the Finns' aid if the Russians did invade? The neutral Swedes in their hairnets? The demilitarised Germans? Finland is an awfully long way from America. Instead, the Finns did what they were best at: they adapted to the prevailing realpolitik, swallowed their pride, put their heads down and got on with it. One imagines the taboos multiplied exponentially.

One would also assume that all the military losses, divisive internal conflicts and the subjugation of national autonomy to the multiple exigencies of pragmatism must have taken a severe toll on Finnish self-esteem. And then the collapse of the Iron Curtain in 1989 left Finland virtually bankrupt. With the Soviet Union in pieces it had lost its major trading partner. Exports plummeted and the economy shrank by 13 per cent within months. The nineties must, I imagined, have been just another long decade of wound-licking and humiliation to add to the many they had experienced during the previous century.

'Oh God, absolutely not. It's a success story!' said Roman Schatz when I put this to him. 'There have never been so many Finns on the planet as there are now. I don't see Finland's history as being full of suffering or occupation. They have managed to attract everything they needed to build up their own nation and culture since Finland became independent in 1917.'

They were the very definition of a pragmatic people. But what about the effect on their *soul* of the last hundred years? 'They have to be pragmatic,' Schatz argued. 'They are used to −40°C and they have bears! If you are used to dealing with 200,000 lakes, and winters that last for eight months, the Russians are nothing. I would call it a shrewdness, a survival instinct. For me Finlandisation [the name given to the self-censorship in matters sensitive to the Soviets] is a positive word, because that was the only way to deal with that situation.'

'There was never the feeling of being a victim,' agreed Kolbe. 'We were never occupied, so that was our success.'

I can't help feeling, though, that there is little romance in pragmatism; it is hard to muster any great stirring pride in realpolitik, hard to get passionate about men who trade secrets in the smoke-filled rooms of the Kremlin, titbits about London in the summer houses of Hanko, or packages of smoked salmon and vodka during Christmas parties at the embassy. It is unsurprising then that, for many years, Finlandisation was yet another taboo to add to the great list of things not to bring up in conversation with Finns.

And how does the Finnish media treat Russia today? President Putin recently threatened Finland with 'retaliatory measures' if it allowed a mooted deployment of NATO weapons, for instance. Do Finnish newspapers still maintain a respectful approach to the Russian leadership? 'No. I would say we have no inhibitions about bashing the Russians,' said Aittokoski. 'We're definitely no longer pro-Russian. There is always a latent threat if Putin's system turns out to be that of an evil aggressive power – obviously then we aren't that safe, because we are still close and deep down you can never feel comfortable because anybody who has read history knows you can never be entirely sure.'

Chapter 6

School

Finland's most lauded achievement of the Post Cold War era has been its education system, not that you would know it if it had been left to the Finns to broadcast the fact. Naturally, it took foreigners to point it out that Finland has the best schools in the world.

Every three years since 2000, the OECD has published what is widely considered to be the definitive ranking list of international educational systems. It charts the performance of fifteen-year-olds in maths, reading and science in 70 countries, and on every occasion Finland has been at, or close, to the top of the list in each of the three fields. *The Atlantic* recently called Finland 'the West's reigning educational superpower'.

For years, educationalists have been flocking to Finland from all over the world to discover its secrets. These are not immediately obvious. You might assume that the Finns are showering their schools with tax money faster than Nokia can earn it, but no: they spend no more than the OECD average on education per student; Finnish teachers are paid roughly in line with other Western European teachers, and actually around 20 per cent less than American teachers. You might also assume that Finnish schools have smaller class sizes, or that their children go straight from the womb to the classroom, or are sent home with stacks of homework as high as their hats, tested more often than pro cyclists, and that their Coco Pops are laced with a daily dose of Ritalin.

No, no and no again (admittedly, I have no analysis of their breakfast cereals). Class sizes are not unusually small by Nordic standards, twenty to twenty-three children. As happens in the rest of the Nordic counties, Finnish kids do not commence their formal education until seven years of age. Because such a large proportion of women work, and childcare is so cheap (fees are related to parental income), most children are in day care from a very early age, but only at seven do they finally sit down in a classroom for any prolonged amount of time. There is little or no testing before sixteen; comparatively little homework; no public listing of schools' performances; and children spend only an average of four hours a day at school. There's no hothousing here.

So far, so Scandinavian, but Finland outperforms its Nordic neighbours, too. One Danish friend sniffed when I raved about the Finnish education system, pointing out that it is not so successful at university level. There is some truth to this, but over 95 per cent of Finnish children still go on to some kind of further education beyond the age of sixteen. The Swedes, too, are miffed that their former territory is outperforming them in such an important marker of modernity and civilisation; they claim Finland has certain unfair advantages, in particular its extreme homogeneity and comparative lack of immigration.

It has to be said that even the Finns were a little perplexed at their domination of the first PISA ratings (the OECD Programme for Student Assessment). Initially they assumed it was a weird anomaly in PISA's system, and even today there are those who remain sceptical.

'The school system is good in the sense that everyone gets equal opportunities, but I don't go along with all this stuff about the Finnish education system being the best in the world: I don't believe these PISA studies,' journalist Heikki Aittokoski told me. 'The answer is simply that the Finnish school system is as good as other Western European ones, but we have a much smaller immigrant population and we don't have many poor students. Also 99 per cent of students speak Finnish or Swedish as their mother tongue, but if you go to Germany, say, then you have 10 per cent who speak Turkish. That's my theory anyway.'

'To that I would say, not only do the non-immigrants [Finns] perform better than non-immigrant Swedes, but the Finnish immigrants do better than the Swedish immigrants,' Professor Patrik Scheinin, Dean of the Faculty of Behavioural Sciences at the University of Helsinki (the department charged with fine-tuning the Finns' human development and learning), told me as we sat in his office in the northern part of the city centre. '*Everybody* does better. The Swedes' claims that PISA is explained by this don't hold up. There are countries with more immigrants than Sweden with better education systems, and ones with smaller immigrant populations who are doing worse.'

The most striking aspect of Finland's performance, beyond its general, all-round excellence, is the fact that the success is spread evenly among all of its schools: it is the country with the least amount of performance variance between school: there is just 4 per cent difference in performance between the best of them, and the worst. Other high achievers – the tiger-mum countries like Singapore, Taiwan and Hong Kong – stream off the highest-achieving students into special hothouse schools; they boast low levels of variation *within* schools but, when you compare performance *between* schools, particularly in different parts of the country, the disparities are great. In Finland, however, it doesn't matter if you go to school in a remote part of Lapland or a suburb of Helsinki, the chances are your child's performance will remain constant.

This might not seem that important, but in a recent survey by Gallup of internal migration, the Finns came third, behind New Zealand and the US, as the most likely people to move from one city to another over a period of five years. Scheinin thus believes this inter-school equality is crucial. 'Out of every hundred there will be several kids who do change classes, and if you put that together over nine years of schooling, it does make up quite a percentage. If you end up having a big hole in your maths [as a result of moving schools], you are in serious trouble.' The secret, he says, is a rigorously enforced, consistent curriculum, with children who fall behind given one-on-one tutoring (around a third of Finnish schoolkids get this extra help each year).

Equally important are the care and resources lavished on those doing the teaching. 'We have ridiculous numbers of teacher-training departments all over the place,' as Scheinin put it. In Finland, teaching has been seen as a prestigious career since the earliest days of the country's education system in the latter part of the nineteenth century, because teachers played a key role in the country's emergence as an independent nation. It is almost impossible to conceive of such a scenario when I recall the ragbag of psychopaths and social misfits who guided my own education, but Finland is a country in which teachers have long been national heroes, at the forefront of defining and disseminating their country's blossoming self-image. They were nothing less than the nation's intellectual freedom fighters.

'Back then it was about mind-building, identity-building, so they recruited teachers who would be pioneers, to carry the torch out into the country, so in that sense teaching has always had a certain glory to it ever since,' said Scheinin. Early on, Finnish education was essentially the teaching of survival skills, everything from woodwork to sewing. Teachers became known as the 'candles of the people', lighting the path to Finnish self-reliance.

Teaching remains an attractive career. Over a quarter of Finnish graduates see teaching as their top option. Unlike in the US or UK, where it is not unheard of for teacher-training applicants to be semi-literate, in Finland teaching attracts the brightest students.

'Think back to your teachers,' Scheinin suggests to me. I shudder. 'Exactly!' He laughs. 'Now would that experience induce you to go into teaching? No. But if your experience is of someone who is a nice guy, working well, diligent, trying hard, skilled, you might feel differently.'

In Finland, teacher-training courses can be more difficult to get on to than those in law or medicine. They are routinely oversubscribed by a factor of ten, sometimes much more. At the University of Helsinki a couple of years ago they had 2,400 applications for the 120 places on the master's programme. Ever since 1970, all Finnish teachers have been required to study to master's level with state support. 'All Finnish teachers have a research-based approach to their training. They are not just taught how to teach, they are taught to think critically about what they do,' says Scheinin.

Despite the historically important, heroic role teachers played in Finland's history, in truth, the country's education system was just as bad as ours until the introduction of the master's requirement for teachers. This was clearly a crucial element of their success.

'Give your teachers a master's-level education,' said Scheinin when I asked him what advice he would give other countries. But that would cost a fortune, I say. 'But can you afford *not* to spend the money? Either that or you have only those people coming to university whose parents are wealthy enough to pay for it – people who are less likely to choose teaching as a career and more likely to follow what their parents did. In Finland everyone can go to university. You want those smart working-class kids to be teachers. And, actually, the UK spends more but achieves less. The trick is to select the best possible students and fund them instead of using a hell of a lot of effort to train those who aren't so good and don't have the potential.'

Another theory about why Finnish kids do so well, particularly in the earlier stages of their schooling, is the simplicity of their language. The Canadian journalist Malcolm Gladwell famously speculated that Chinese children do well at maths because their number system is logical, clear, simple and monosyllabic compared with English and many other languages. Perhaps the same applies to Finnish. 'Once a child learns to read and write at age six or so, that skill is done once and for all. Of course vocabulary increases, but new words just slot in,' a Finnish friend told me when I put the theory to him. Does this simplicity give Finnish children a linguistic leg-up, I wonder? Doing away with the future tense must save a bit of time, for a start. Finland's Swedish-speaking schools do perform closer to European averages: Swedish is a more complex language and presumably takes longer to master.

There is one other, actually quite important reason why Finland does so well. That word again: equality. There is no two-tier, public–private education system in Finland. There *are* no private schools in Finland, at least not in the sense of private schools in the rest of the world. All schooling in Finland is state-funded. The message from Finland, then, is that equality starts at the blackboard.

So, the teachers are happy, PISA is happy, the parents are happy, and Finland's economy clearly benefits from having a labour force that can help it diversify away from selling stuff made out of trees. But what about the children? Are they happy?

Just before I travelled to Finland, the World Health Organisation published research into how different pupils from around the world enjoy their schooling – or not. To the surprise of many, Finnish children enjoyed school the least of all the nationalities asked. Back in 2006, the OECD published a similar report which revealed that Swedish children had more fun in school than Finnish kids and, though Finnish children achieved higher test results, Swedish youngsters were better at expressing themselves.

'If you look at [the question] actually asked it was, do you like school "a lot", and few said yes,' says Scheinin. 'Our research shows they think school is "okay" and, frankly, if you ask someone pre-puberty or in the midst of puberty whether they like anything, the most you are going to get is, "It's okay." Add to that the melancholy attitude of the Finns to everything . . . What we also saw from the WHO report was that the Finnish kids were among the most positive when you asked them "Do you think school counts?" Of course, if you compare them to countries where the alternative to school is to be on the streets, those children will be more positive [about any schooling].'

Many people pounced on the WHO report as evidence that the Finnish education system somehow fostered the social disengagement and resentment that had prompted two recent incidents in which Finnish students ran amok with guns at their schools. In November 2007, eighteen-year-old Pekka-Eric Auvinen shot his headmistress, the school nurse and seven students at his school in Jokela, thirty miles north of the capital. Then, in September 2008, Matti Juhani

Saari, a twenty-two-year-old trainee chef at the Kauhajoki School of Hospitality 180 miles north-west of Helsinki, shot ten of his fellow students dead at a college with a .22 caliber pistol.

In 2006 there had been another shocking, though thankfully not fatal, incident which had shaken Finland to the core. Unreported by the international media, in May of that year, another eighteen-year-old boy, Kalle Holm, burned down Finland's most sacred church, Porvoo's fifteenth-century cathedral, where Tsar Alexander I had granted Finland autonomy from Sweden in 1809.

I asked Scheinin for his theories on the two school shootings. Could they in any way be attributed to the Finnish education system? He thought not: he had a different scapegoat in mind. 'For centuries we have been looking at you [the British and Americans] – your literature, art, culture, and so on, have been models for us and now, especially with the Internet, Finnish youths have been watching the United States, role-modelling all the time. Think to yourself, why didn't this happen fifty years ago? There is a simple reason: you would have had to be bloody smart and crazy to have invented it yourself.'

'So, you're saying this is copycat behaviour inspired by Americans?' I asked. 'It's nothing to do with academic pressures, or the dark Finnish soul?'

'These days if you are in a small, dark minority you can find a network anywhere in the world, and the Finns have an aptitude for looking for role models,' he said. 'I don't know what your youth was like, but I had my dark moments. I think the problem is that you need to look at the communication between teachers, the school nurse, and psychologists. They tend not to communicate very well.'

As we have seen in Norway, random madmen with guns are indeed a tragic fact of life everywhere; Finland's two school massacres are probably more symptomatic of the fact that, as I mentioned earlier, the country is third only to the USA and Yemen in global gun-ownership levels. As one local told me, 'We are a hunting nation. We shoot 65,000 elk a year, sometimes in Helsinki there are bears, and there are wolves.'

A couple of days later I was in the Kamppi Mall in central Helsinki, stocking up on Moomin memorabilia. On the top floor I noticed a group of teenagers hanging out in front of a skateboarding store. Smiling broadly, trying not to seem like some shifty perv and making no sudden movements, I approached them, explained that I was researching their country's education system and was interested in hearing the views of 'ordinary' school-goers. Could I perhaps ask them some questions? Behind their long fringes I saw the two boys and a girl scan the area for an escape route, then glance, panic-stricken, at each other. Then they turned their gazes down to their Converse.

I should have realised that classic Finnish reticence, combined with universal teenage angst, was never likely to make for particularly spar-kling conversation. Most of their answers to my questions were communicated through shoulder movements, awkward shuffles, and grunts. None were especially quotable ('Generally, how do you feel about school?' 'Pschht, prffgh. It's okay.'). But, if I were to draw any conclusion from this brief non-interaction with Finnish youth, it would be this: Finnish teenagers are as pissed off and hormonal as any other teenagers.

Chapter 7

Wives

The future has never looked brighter for Finland. Not that they would ever let on, of course, but the rest of the world is beginning to take note. As well as the ongoing PISA success, its strong economy, and a generally exemplary standard of living, the world is finally cottoning on to the fact that quiet, shy, battered, bruised but indomitable Finland has a great deal of knowledge to share with the world.

Typically, on hearing of the accolades from the likes of *Newsweek* or the Legatum Institute heralding Finland or Helsinki as the greatest places to live in the world, the Finns shrug, frown, shake their heads and point out that they are still the poorest country in the Nordic region, still essentially five million woodsmen who have emerged from the forests and prefer to return there whenever possible, plus a few snobby Swedes. They are still the same old socially inept, self-destructive alcoholics they always were.

'It would be ridiculous to say Finland is heaven on earth,' says Heikki Aittokoski when I mention the *Newsweek* survey to him. 'It's a fine country, there are lots of things that work here, but I don't see it as a paradise.' Within hours of the *Newsweek* article being published, his newspaper, *Helsingin Sanomat*, had pounced on a mistake in the US magazine's calculations. Switzerland should have won, it claimed.

Another Finnish journalist reacting to the survey wrote: 'What about the suicides, depression, alcoholism and our cold, dark winters? ... Many of us feel that Finland is a Jekyll-and-Hyde country. We have both the positive and the negative in extremes, just like sunshine: the never-setting summer sun is offset by several months of dark winter.' It was an almost perfect statement of the Finn's chronically negative self-image.

When asked in a survey a few years ago to select eight adjectives to describe themselves, the Finns chose: honest, slow, reliable, true, shy, direct, reserved and punctual. Hardly descriptive of a confident, thrusting nation, is it? But whether they will admit it or not, there are signs that Finland's moment is coming at last, that the country is emerging from the shadow of its overbearing, bullying neighbours. The most recent World Economic Forum Global Competitiveness Index, which assesses which countries are in the best position for future growth, puts Finland in third place (this is particularly grati-fying as they bumped Sweden down to fourth).

But still it is left to outsiders like Roman Schatz or Neil Hardwick to sing the country's praises. 'I was once asked, if I could change three things about Finland, what would they be?' Hardwick told me. 'And I joked, "The climate, the inhabitants and the geographical location." These days I am hard-pressed to think of things I would change.'

I had visited Helsinki a couple of times and fallen in love with it but, aside from a day trip to Porvoo – an exceptionally pretty historic town a little outside of Helsinki – I had not seen much of the rest of the country. So I decided to take a trip through the 'real' Finland in the hope of forming a more nuanced picture of this mysterious land and its people. Having done so, I now have a good idea why the Finns are so negative and downbeat about themselves and their country.

After our visit to Santa in the Arctic, my son and I travelled down the 'spine' of the country and, from what I can make out, Finland is almost entirely forest. Viewed from our train window, it was little more than a monotonous green blur. The trains themselves were paragons of modernity: the tickets were cheap, with allocated seats (the second sign of a civilised country, after wine in the cinemas), and mostly empty. Best of all, unlike on Danish trains which can sometimes feel like you are in a Hogarth cartoon that's come to life, what with all the drinking, snogging, shouting and screaming, absolutely nobody speaks.

I was less impressed by the hotels – or rather, by their curtains. This may sound nitpicky, but in the land of the midnight sun you would have thought they would invest in thicker drapes. Instead, the dazzling white light floodlit our hotel rooms throughout the nights and, like Al Pacino in the deservedly forgotten movie *Insomnia*, I was driven to the very brink of insanity by being unable to sleep.* Every gap, every moth-hole, every chink in the weave of the fabric used in the curtains of my various hotel rooms on that trip allowed the sunlight to drill through my eyelids like the lamp in an interrogation room. And then there were the midges and mosquitoes. Venture anywhere in the Finnish countryside during summer and you will instantly become enveloped in a cloud of insects, like Charlie Brown's friend Pig-Pen.

Though they boasted wonderfully scenic settings, the provincial lakeside towns we stopped at on the way from Rovaniemi to Helsinki – Oulu, Iisalmi, Kuopio – were mostly charmless, featuring the same nondescript assortment of modern concrete blocks and H&M stores. Thanks to a combination of the Nazis' scorched-earth policy and the progressive social democratic housing policies of the 1970s (the latter described to me by one Finn as a symptom of their national inferiority complex: they were anxious to be seen as as modern as the Swedes), there was little of architectural or historical interest. It did eventually occur to me that the absence of old buildings might actually have been quite liberating for the Finns: perhaps it made them more open to change and progress. Architectural determinism, if you like. But still, I missed a sense of the past.

As far as I could make out, there was nothing edible outside of Helsinki either. The dining options were quite execrable – either crappy pizza, outdated Italian, or reindeer. Always reindeer. In these

---

* Pacino plays an LA cop who for some reason is sent to an Alaskan town to solve a murder. He eventually resorts to barricading the windows of his hotel with all the furniture in an increasingly crazed attempt to block out the sun. Then he goes mad and Robin Williams kills him. Apart from the Robin Williams climax, that was me in Finland.

towns the main pastime for the locals on a summer's evening appeared to be either cruising around in old American cars, or heading down to the harbour carrying crates of beer with the express intention of getting as drunk as possible very quickly.

On a balmy Saturday evening in Kuopio, we went for a walk to try to find something edible. As we followed the quiet crowds down to the lake, I began to feel a slight sense of unease, but could not put my finger on why. Eventually, my son spotted it. 'Where are the children?' he said. And he was right. There were none. It felt like a scene from *Chitty Chitty Bang Bang*. The citizens of Kuopio had presumably surrendered their children to their babysitters (hopefully not the Child Catcher), and were now intent on getting massively shit-faced.

Despite this dispiriting glimpse of life in the 'real' Finland, I remain a huge fan of the Finns. Got all their albums. And I am not the only one. Helsinki has just enjoyed a stint as World Design Capital; the Finnish economy is more export-orientated than ever before (accounting for almost 40 per cent of GDP); and Finland is recovering faster from the economic crisis of 2008 than virtually all the other eurozone countries. It comfortably holds the top spot in the OECD's latest list of gross domestic expenditure on research and development as a percentage of GDP with an impressive 3.87 per cent. Even more encouraging is the fact that relatively little of this is public money (24 per cent, compared with 46.8 per cent in Norway). Little Finland is also filing lots of patents – it is the 115th largest country by population in the world, but it ranks 13th in terms of patent applications according to the World International Property Organization.

Admittedly, there is the perennial fear that Finland still has an 'all-its-eggs-in-one-basket' economy, the egg in question being the beleaguered phone company, Nokia. At times Nokia has borne the weight of as much as a quarter of Finland's GDP, an astonishing burden for a single company. Things are not going well for Nokia. It has been usurped as the world's largest mobile phone manufacturer by Samsung and most ignominiously of all, was recently bought by Microsoft – a move, widely interpreted as a national tragedy. If such a thing were possible, today Apple could probably buy the entire country.

'We are desperately trying to diversify our industrial and economic base,' a spokesperson from the foreign ministry told me. 'We need a second Nokia because after timber and shipping it's all we have. We have a lot of small-scale innovators and invest really well in research and development, but we are a country of engineers, we lack marketing skills. We are very modest.'

One major advantage Finland has in terms of its labour market is that it is arguably the most gender-equal society in the world. Finnish women were the first in Europe to get the vote (1906); it is customary for half of parliament to be female; and the country has had both female prime ministers and female presidents. In 2011 over 60 per cent of Finnish university graduates were women.

'Finnish women are dominant,' Roman Schatz, a self-confessed fan of the species, enthused to me. 'Traditionally, on Finnish farms the woman was chief of everything under the roof, including the males, and the men were there to take care of everything outside. No Finnish man would ever decide anything without consulting his wife. Men do the dishes. We don't have housewives in Finland – no one can afford to live from one salary. Women don't stay at home and breastfeed, they have their own careers and banks accounts. It's great – my divorce only cost me a hundred euro.'

This gender equality extends to the corporate world, says Schatz. 'I've seen it happen so many times that two guys from overseas come to a Finnish company and are met by two men and a woman, and they assume the chick is going to make the coffee or take notes. Then, fifteen minutes in, they realise something is seriously odd here – the chick appears to be senior to the other guys. Do not underestimate the Finnish woman. We have more women with high-school diplomas and more women with degrees, the highest percentage of women in parliament.'

'Finnish women are tremendous,' agrees Neil Hardwick. 'I got so used in England to women pretending they were a bit sillier when they were in the company of men so as not to frighten them off, but here women take the initiative. It is a very matriarchal society.'

I am not sure where the Wife-carrying World Championships fits in to all this. My son and I stopped off to catch the action, which takes place every July in the small, one-street town of Sonkajärvi, slap bang in the centre of the country. As far as I can make out, this hilarious competition is held primarily for the benefit of Asian TV news crews, who love nothing more than an eccentric Finnish sporting event (see also the Air Guitar Championships in Oulu; the various dwarf- and mobile-phone-throwing competitions; Oulu's Garlic Festival; the Swamp Soccer World Championships, and so on). It takes place at the local school's running track amid a country-fair atmosphere with craft stalls, tombolas and beer tents, and started in the mid-nineties, concocted from local legends of rogues and brigands who supposedly stole other men's wives. Today the event attracts competitors from around the world or, at least, from Estonia – the Estonians win most years. I was a little disappointed to discover that the competitors don't have to be married, or even a couple; you can borrow someone else's spouse, although I suppose this is in keeping with the spirit of the contest's origins.

The race itself turned out to be a kind of Japanese-game-show-style steeplechase, with the men and their female cargoes racing in a time-trial relay around a 200-metre course featuring various hurdles and water hazards. It was hard to tell whether this was a serious athletic event or pantomime: some competitors wore fancy dress (Asterix and Obelix, the Smurfs), others had clearly trained with some dedication.

There were interesting variations on how to carry the wives: some male runners favoured the straightforward piggyback, some employed a fireman's lift, while others opted for an undignified arrangement – like something rejected from an early draft of the *Kama Sutra* – in which the woman was slung, head pointing downwards, over the man's shoulders, her legs straddling his neck and her face bouncing off his backside. The latter was especially ill-advised when it came to the water hazard as the 'wife' would find her head submerged for some moments while the man waded slowly to the other side.

The crowd, dressed in cut-down jeans and sandals with socks, bellies bulging beneath T-shirts (also the men), watched the proceedings in near-silence, slowly munching their way through bags of fresh peas and downing plastic beakers of beer.

In the beer tent after the first race, I caught up with one of the organisers (he may have been the mayor, I never did find out).

'Who won?' I asked him, trying to make polite conversation.

'Who cares?' he said, and drained his glass.

I noticed that by far the toughest part of the race was not the actual carrying of the wives, or even the obstacles (although both would have defeated me), but the fact that, after each major hurdle, the wife was passed like a baton to another member of the team, and before this could happen the previous member of the relay had to drink a bottle of fizzy water. This sounds innocuous enough, but it would appear that when one is gasping for breath having run as fast as one can over 80 metres carrying an adult female, and then wading up to one's waist through ice-cold water, a bottle of water takes on barrel-like proportions. Several men were almost defeated by it altogether, spewing frothing liquid out of their nostrils as they drank before regurgitating it all on the track. This undignified Strokkur-esque ejaculation at last prompted some kind of a response from the largely silent spectators. They loved this bit. Some almost allowed themselves a slight smile. Here in the Finnish boondocks, watching a man's head explode due to an over-hasty intake of carbonated water passed for a pleasant summer afternoon's entertainment. And I can't really argue with that. We had a great time.

The prominent role of women in society – whether in govern-ment or enduring an undignified circuit of a running track with their faces rebounding off Pappa Smurf's backside like a rubber door-knocker – is one of the many ways in which, superficially, Finnish society appears to resemble its neighbouring Scandinavian lands (though not the wife-carrying – I think it is fair to say that is uniquely Finnish). But there are lingering doubts about whether Finland really is Scandinavian, or even Nordic for that matter.

As we have seen, in some senses Finns are almost über-Scandinavians, with their high-context homogeneity, reticence, openness and trustworthiness, their welfare state, and fondness for booze and salty licquorice. As Roman Schatz says: 'They uphold a society which is surprisingly pluralistic, surprisingly liberal – you can belong to any minority you want, sexual, political, religious, and they leave you in peace. Freedom of speech is 100 per cent; nobody gets in trouble for saying anything. It is a really open culture.' All very Scandinavian, but Russia's political and cultural influence should never be underestimated and, in more recent years, Finland has increasingly looked across the Baltic to Estonia and towards the EU for trade, comradeship and cheap alcohol.

It will be interesting to see what effect the rise of the nationalistic True Finn party will have on Finland's relationship with its neighbours in the coming years. The party wants to sever ties with Europe; it also has a clear fellowship with the right-wing parties in Norway, Sweden and Denmark, and no great affection for Russia, so perhaps Finland will embrace its Nordic-ness to a greater extent in the future.

'I think they think of themselves as more Scandinavian than European,' said Neil Hardwick. 'But that is changing. I don't think the Finns feel any connection to Denmark. Norwegians are outdoor people, like them, with their mountains, skiing, and loads of money, but Iceland isn't really on the map.'

'Some people do think of themselves as Scandinavian; some don't and aspire to be European,' says Aittokoski. 'I want to be both. I want to represent the Nordic model and the Northern European way of doing things. Scandinavia is a good group to be included with.'

My basic understanding of Finland's history had led me to expect a much more insecure, culturally superficial nation. Instead I found a people possessed of a steely reserve that was more than just stamina or *sisu*, more than mere macho tolerance for pain and endurance; the people here have demonstrated a bottomless reserve of resilience, resourcefulness and pride, as well as an agile political pragmatism honed over many centuries. I came expecting neurotic, post-colonial victims with a fragile sense of culture, instead I discovered a rare, quiet heroism.

'You should never describe us as victims,' Laura Kolbe had said to me. 'Our national culture has been about a kind of building up of the heroic element of our losses and wars. There has always been a consensus to make the future together better, and that is the heroic element. Our wars have forced the nation to unite. Our history has been very dramatic compared with Sweden's, which has been the calm, beautiful, rich, industrialised, modern nation where nothing has happened since 1809. Little Finland has all the time been going through wars, changes, revolutions, the humiliation of the 1990s . . .

'But,' she added with a broad smile. 'It's never boring here.'

Which leads us nicely to our final destination . . .

SWEDEN

Chapter 1

Crayfish

It is a Friday evening in Stortorget, Malmö. Around me a crowd of thousands stands pressed tightly together beside long tables, their arms interlinked, swaying in time to a song sung in Swedish to the tune of 'My Bonnie Lies Over the Ocean'. The tables are cluttered with empty bottles and cans, the detritus of the largest crayfish orgy in the world, which is now reaching a crescendo of salty sucking and slurping.

The traditional Swedish crayfish party – the *kräftskiva* – is one of the Swedes' few self-sanctioned days of public disorder, a rare moment of unguarded merriment when they permit themselves to unleash their (otherwise dormant) Viking spirit. It is held every year in mid-August, as the last hurrah of summer before the murk of winter draws in. And there is no point in tiptoeing around this: everyone is absolutely shit-faced. Including me.

Bearing in mind my experience in Kuopio, the absence of any children when I arrived in Malmö's main square should have given me warning that, an hour or two hence, I might find myself ruddy-faced and country dancing with an elderly lady I had never met before. The lady in question is clutching an empty schnapps bottle in one hand, while I'm wearing a conical paper hat and a plastic bib decorated with cartoon crustacea. *Skål!*

'*Helan går, Sjung hopp faderallan lallan lej!*' The folk band on stage have picked up the tempo now, playing what is best described as 'hoe-down' music, with banjos, harmonicas and violins. The Swedes are famed for their vast canon of drinking songs and everyone gathered here seems to know the words. Several revellers have climbed on to the tables and are dancing gingerly, but with enthusiasm, arms in the air, silly hats akimbo, their shirts still tucked firmly into their shorts. It is time for me to crawl off to a darkened room.

This is Sweden.

This is so not Sweden.

We have finally arrived at the central piece of our Nordic puzzle – the hub, the crux, the Rosetta Stone by which so much of the cultural, political, social and inter-relational history of Scandinavia can be deciphered. This is the country which has done more than any other to define how the rest of the world sees Scandinavia: as modern, liberal, collectivist and – *kräftskiva* parties aside – more than a little dull. We have reached the largest, most populated (9.3 million), by just about every measure the most successful, occasionally the most infuriating, and undoubtedly the most influential country of them all (sorry Denmark, but deep down, you know it's true): Sweden.

As Finnish historian Laura Kolbe had said to me, Sweden is like a sun, a magnet, at times perhaps a kind of black hole (albeit one with sleek sofas and excellent day-care facilities), to which all Nordic people have turned their faces in admiration, been drawn to (or, in some cases, consumed and then spat out by), at some time or another over the last half-millennium. It is the elder brother, the head boy, the role model. We have arrived at, as *The Guardian* once put it, 'the most successful society the world has ever known'.

Over the centuries, all of its Nordic siblings have felt the wrath of an aggrieved or threatened Sweden, as indeed has a large swathe of Central Europe, though these days the famously peaceable, supposedly neutral Swedes prefer not to dwell on their bloodthirsty rampages. The Finns, the Norwegians and the Danes all have cause for residual resentment and envy towards their goody-goody, high-achieving neighbours. And sure enough, for all the brotherly front these four nations show to the world, with their Nordic Unions and Councils, the open borders, and the Scandinavian cliques that form around swimming pools from Phuket to Gran Canaria, the deeper you dig, the more of them you speak to (and the more inebriated they are), the more the outsider will detect a persistent, niggling animosity towards the Swedes. It may be comparatively low-level, the vestigial wounds of centuries of tension, rivalry and betrayal, but it is there, trust me, and the Swedes are always the focus. It is there in the grudging way the Danes react to Swedish economic success and the global domination of IKEA (it hardly helps that the Swedish company insists on naming its least dignified products – door mats, and so forth – after Danish towns). It is there in the relish with which the Norwegians tell you of their banana-peeling immigrant Swedish workforce. And it's there when the Finns murmur about 'homo' Swedish men and the Winter War.

To the rest of us, of course, a Swede is a wholly benign, admirable thing. The accomplishments of twentieth-century Sweden are legion and, mostly, noble: from its rationalist, respectful secularism, to its industrial might and economic success and, of course, its compassionate, all-embracing, shining beacon of a welfare state. For much of the last hundred years, Sweden has been seen, and has very much seen itself, as the social laboratory of the world: a heroic blond collective intent on pioneering better ways of living, abiding by higher, more modern moral codes, and writing really catchy four-minute pop songs.

How we lap up news of their free schools and foundation hospitals, their harmonious 'middle-way' consensus politics, and their economic and gender equality. The latest Swedish innovation to grab the attention of the British media are the *Kunskapsskolan* (Knowledge Schools), with their free-form, open-plan style of education with no classrooms, where children set their own academic targets and draw up their own timetables. If my school had been run on that basis we would have gone the full *Lord of the Flies* within the first morning, but when the British media sees that Sweden has them, it wants them too.

Right now, the Swedish model has the attention of the world's policymakers and politicians. From David Cameron to François Hollande, and even Barack Obama, many a moderate Western political leader has fantasised about emulating Sweden's mixed economy and consensus-driven politics. This serene Nordic swan always seems to achieve its goals with minimum fuss and discord: whether it be implementing progressive labour laws, orchestrating an economic recovery following a banking misadventure, or being very, very good at tennis, the Swedes never break a sweat.

The boldest of Sweden's recent social experiments has been in the field of multiculturalism. Over the last forty years Scandinavia's largest country has welcomed more immigrants than any other European land. Today, almost 15 per cent of the Swedish population was born outside of Sweden (compared with just over 6 per cent in Denmark, the next-largest immigrant population in the North), and if you include the next generation, almost a third of the population was born outside of the country. That's an astonishing statistic for a country which, up until the late nineteenth century, was made up of homogenous, isolated rural communities, and whose foreign policy has for the last two centuries been characterised by insularity and neutrality. Although, as we will see, this development has not been without its consequences.

In the last few years the world has also looked to Sweden for tips on how to cope with its various banking and economic crises, Sweden having endured a similar credit-induced rollercoaster decades ago. In 1985, after the government had deregulated the credit market, the Swedes made the most of the so-called 'Santa Claus' credit with which they were showered, and paid the price when their housing bubble inevitably burst. By the early 1990s Sweden was in crisis: unemployment quadrupled and the budget deficit soared. But the government moved quickly to tidy up the mess, implementing major public sector spending and tax cuts while preserving the core of its welfare state; reforming and privatising services to a far greater extent than even Mrs Thatcher had dared; encouraging schools to opt out of the state system; allowing patients to choose any doctor, including private ones, and charge the state, and so on. Perhaps most importantly, they put the banks on a short leash from which they have never been released. This positioned the country well to cope with the fallout from the recent global economic crisis and so, once again, onward sails Sweden, seemingly oblivious to the earth-quakes around it.

Like Denmark's similar 'bumblebee' model (high taxes, large public sector, extensive welfare state), Sweden continues to defy the warnings of many economists, warnings which have been sounding in one form or other since the Second World War. Sweden is, if not booming, then at least doing very well for itself. As I have already mentioned, it is fourth on the World Economic Forum's latest Global Competitiveness Report, and tenth on the UN's Human Development Index, ahead of Denmark and Finland. Norway takes first place – its extravagant oil wealth ought to ensure its position as the richest Nordic country in absolute terms for many decades to come – but Sweden's industrial output continues to dwarf that of all its neighbours. Its great strength lies in fostering large-scale international corporations, like Tetra Pak (the world's largest food-packaging company), H&M (the second largest clothing retailer in the world), industrial engineering firm Atlas Copco, Eriksson, Volvo, and that global chain of marriage graveyards, IKEA. In fact, almost half of the largest companies in the Nordic region are Swedish.*

Less happily, unemployment has been running at a comparatively high rate for some years: it is currently at 7.3 per cent (and Swedish unemployment figures are about as reliable as Joan Collins's age, so it is likely a good deal higher in reality). Most seriously of all, youth unemployment is far higher than in any other Nordic country (approaching 30 per cent). Nevertheless, both Sweden's GDP and its growth figures continue to outstrip others in the region. Government debt is declining too – in stark contrast to the rest of the continent: it represents 35 per cent of GDP, compared with an average of 90 per cent of GDP in the eurozone.

As well as selling us spangly boob tubes, awkward-to-open milk

---

* Please, though, a moment's silence for SAAB. It enriched the tapestry of the motoring world over the years, but fell victim to American corporate mismanagement and its own wilful quirkiness. When news of its demise was announced, a million architects and graphic designers sighed deeply and turned to their Audi brochures.

cartons and Ödmjuks (my personal favourite IKEA product-range name – it's for a tea set), Sweden also boasts several notable cultural exports in recent years. These include its domination of the world's airport bookstores with the whole Nordic Noir movement – chiefly, the 35 million-selling Henning Mankel and the 60 million-selling Stieg Larsson. Sweden is also the world's third largest exporter of music (after the US and UK). There is a raft of Swedish composers and producers who seem to share an uncanny flair for overproduced, tinny teen pop. All those brilliant, shimmering, infuriatingly catchy Katy Perry, Pink and Britney songs – they were all written by Swedes.

And, Sweden also has a bald prime minister, which is absolutely a step in the right direction as far as I am concerned.

I have visited Sweden many times over the years, mostly Malmö, but also the capital and elsewhere, and gotten to know quite a few Swedes socially, but, as with the Norwegians, my image of them was still largely defined through the eyes of my Danish friends and family. I shouldn't have hoped to get any kind of balanced view of a country from its great historic rival, and didn't.

'I went to Sweden once,' I remember a Danish friend saying to me, before adding drily, 'I think . . .'

I asked another how a recent trip to Gothenburg had gone. 'Sweden was great,' he said. 'In the seventies.' Ouch.

The abiding view of the Swedes from their neighbours to the south is of a stiff, humourless, rule-obsessed and dull crowd who inhabit a suffocatingly conformist society, and chew tobacco. The Danes love to tell each other stories of Swedish prissiness, drone-like obedience, or pedantry.*

---

* The truth is, when I first moved to Denmark, the Danes' descriptions of the Swedes as being cold, stiff and not a little Germanic was not far removed from my initial impression of the Danes, although I obviously didn't mention this at the time. I have since come to the conclusion that it is probably quite healthy for the Danes to have an even more formal, rule-obsessed neighbour to the north with whom to compare themselves favourably, and I see no need to disavow them of their self-image as beacons of chillaxery and fun.

A Danish friend told me this anecdote just the other day:

'A group of Swedish colleagues met every Friday afternoon to share a bottle of wine as an end-of-week treat. After several weeks, one of the party suddenly stood up and said, "I really think we should declare this bottle of wine as a tax perk." There was some discussion among the rest of the group and it was agreed, they must declare the 5 krona tax to the appropriate authorities.'

Here is another, from a friend who was visiting some Swedes he knew in the suburbs of Stockholm:

'I was waiting on the station platform to catch the train into the city when this Swedish guy in a suit came up to me and said, "I am sorry, but that's where I stand". The platform was only about a third full, but he had his special place where he waited for the train every day, and I was occupying it. I moved.'

The only alternative to the Danes' withering description of the Swedes tends to come mostly from an equally slanted, overly credulous international media. British and American newspapers and magazines long ago decided that Sweden was a paragon of progressive social policies, mixed capitalism, groovy furniture and sourdough bread-baking hipsters with beards and fixies, and they are sticking to that line no matter what.

I wanted to dig a little deeper into this Stepford Wife of a country. Surely no race could be as pedantic and humourless as the Danes made the Swedes out to be, nor as perfect as the left-leaning media claimed. The truth, presumably, lay somewhere in between.

Chapter 2

Donald Duck

A deceased, badger-haired, New York Jewish–American political essayist might not be the most obvious first source for revealing insights into Sweden, but Susan Sontag lived there for twelve years back in the sixties and seventies during which time she made a handful of, by all accounts not especially good, sub-Bergman-esque films and, more interestingly from my point of view, wrote a fabulously bitchy, poison-pen farewell to the country upon leaving.

Sontag did not find the Swedes a companionable race. 'Silence is the Swedish national vice. Honestly, Sweden is full of prosaic, graceless mini-Garbos,' she wrote, adding for good measure that the Swedes were clumsy, mistrustful and 'devoted to rules', not to mention being misanthropic alcoholics: 'The Swedes want to be raped. And drink is their national form of self-rape,' she wrote, pulling the pin from her polemical grenade before hurling it over her shoulder as she boarded her Pan Am flight to JFK. Even Swedish neutrality turned out to be less a high-minded gesture of humanist principle and more a manifestation of collective paranoia (not to mention hypocritical – more than half of Swedes were pro-German during the Second World War, Sontag pointed out).

Perhaps the lack of success of her films tainted her view of her hosts, but Sontag even managed to turn what many perceive as one of the Swedes' great strengths into a negative: 'I am convinced that the Swedish reasonableness is deeply defective, owing far too much to inhibition and anxiety and emotional dissociation . . . I find it little short of pathological.' Their porn was of the wrong sort, too, it 'degrades sexual feeling . . . like illustrations for some male gynaecologist's encyclopadia . . . numbing to men.'

Oh, and they overcooked their vegetables.

Above all, Sontag appears to have been bored to the very brink of insanity by her reticent, unexpressive, timid Swedish hosts. I know quite a few Swedish people and, in truth (and with the caveat that I haven't met all 9.3 million of them), I find them not so much boring, as reserved (unless there are crayfish and schnapps close at hand, of course). On the plus side, they do listen to you with a selfless attentiveness, rarely interrupting even when you are clearly spouting drivel, and they laugh at your jokes (either out of politeness or pity, I don't know and, frankly, does it matter?). As one guidebook on the Swedes put it: 'The more you talk, the longer they listen – and the quieter they become.' They are the perfect audience for a flatulent blow-hard such as myself. I like them.

Unlike the Danes, who will proclaim themselves the happiest people in the world to any passing academic, journalist or be-mused Chinese tourist who is only trying to get an ice cream on Nyhavn, the Swedes don't hold themselves in terribly high regard. A few years ago the Swedish Institute of Public Opinion Research asked young Swedes to describe their compatriots. The top eight adjectives they chose, in descending order of relevance, were: envious, stiff, industrious, nature-loving, quiet, honest, dishonest and xenophobic

The bottom three (out of thirty) characteristics, i.e. those *least* exhibited by the Swedes, were: masculine, sexy and artistic.

A book written by the founder of Stockholm's Cross Cultural Relations Centre, Jean Phillips-Martinsson's *Swedes as Others See Them*, adds a few more Swedish descriptors: taciturn, serious, stiff, boring, superficially friendly, unsociable, punctual, inflexible, arrogant and overcautious. Another word that crops up regularly in analyses of the Swedes is 'shy'. One US psychiatrist who spent time observing the Swedes in the 1960s reported that they blushed more often than other nationalities. What were they so embarrassed about, I wondered.

One explanation is their often-cited, unusually heightened fear of appearing foolish. My first reaction on reading this was, well, you might want to rethink naming your children 'Hans Hansen', 'Jens Jensen', 'Sven Svensson', and so on (and, while we are at it, we need to talk about that whole business with your soldiers and their hair nets), but, as leading Swedish ethnologist Åke Daun put it in his book *Swedish Mentality*: 'Before expressing one's views on a controversial issue, one tries to detect the position of the opposite party . . . Swedes seem to reflect a great deal on what they would like to say, how to say it and when, how other people might react, etc., before they actually say it – if they decide to do so at all.'

This fear of being ridiculed is reflected in one of the key words by which the Swedes define themselves: *duktig*. It literally translates as 'clever', but this is a specific type of Swedish cleverness: it is a diligent, responsible kind of clever; punctual, law-abiding, industrious clever. We're talking Japanese-style responsible competence, rather than show-offy clever; not clever like knowing who won *Strictly Come Dancing* two years ago, more filing-in-your-tax-forms-on-time-without-any-rubbings-out-clever.

Of course shyness goes hand in hand with the familiar Nordic aversion to conversation. In *Fishing in Utopia*, a melancholic memoir of the Sweden he lived in during the seventies, British journalist Andrew Brown writes: 'I have never lived in, nor could imagine a place where people talked less to each other.' My first thought on reading this was that clearly he has never spent time in a Finnish sauna, but, as with their former eastern territory, a possible explanation for Swedish taciturnity is the familiar 'high-context society' theory: each Swede knows what the other is thinking and this similarity in outlook, expectation and aspiration means that, though communication might be easier, they are also able to judge each other to within an inch of their lives. Åke Daun again:

'Swedish homogeneity provides little of the security felt with good friends. On the contrary, homogeneity can easily lead one to overestimate one's ability to interpret, to understand the behaviour of others. This makes it risky to give off the "wrong" signal: for example, by wearing expensive, elegant clothes when one holds socialist values.'

Thomas Hylland Eriksen, the Norwegian anthropologist, said something similar to me when we talked about the relationship between the Norwegians and the Swedes: 'They have much more of a culture of conflict-avoidance in public life. They pull back, you know, they try to avoid controversy, to avoid strong disagreements, and there's a lot of understatement. There are a lot of cultural problems when Norwegians deal with Swedes. We always make fun of the Swedes because they are so formal, and stiff, and never really say what is on their minds because they want to keep a nice polite ambience.'

It was becoming clear that Malmö's crayfish festival was an aberration. Sweden was beginning to sound like some kind of sci-fi dystopia where everyone could read each other's minds and people no longer had the privilege of private thoughts, compelling them to suppress any emotion, opinion or urge which might run counter to the prevailing ethos. As Indian anthropologist H. S. Dhillon wrote: 'Anyone who gets heated in a discussion is taken to be an anxious and neurotic figure.' The result, according to Daun, was that 'Swedes seem not to "feel as strongly" as certain other people.'

If Daun was to be believed, Swedish shyness and self-effacement even extended to the country's maternity wards and funeral parlours, in what have to be the most extreme examples of Nordic inhibition I have yet encountered. During childbirth, Daun says 'Swedish women try to moan as little as possible, and they often ask, when it is all over, whether they screamed very much. They are very pleased to be told they did not.' He quotes a midwife as saying that in Swedish society 'it is forbidden to express strong feelings, and giving birth is a situation in which it is natural to give vent to strong feelings.' At funerals, meanwhile, Daun warns that, while mild sniffling is just about acceptable 'cries of despair are embarrassing and are remembered long afterwards'. This doesn't mean the Swedes are unaffected by or unsympathetic to bereavement, he stresses: 'Rather, they lack the skills to deal with strong feelings and are afraid of doing the wrong thing, of behaving clumsily.'

This desire to avoid causing friction extends from Swedish politics (to the extent that dissenting voices can be undemocratically silenced, as we will discover), to the corporate world, famously characterised by its consensus culture. Swedish companies tend to have a flat structure with little overt hierarchy. Everyone can have their say; management and workers consider each other equals; democracy and equality rule. This can have problematic side effects, particularly when it comes to decision-making. A Danish friend of mine is the CEO of a Swedish company and their overriding instinct to get everybody on board with all decisions drives him mad. 'If we want to change the board members, we have to check that it's okay with the receptionist,' he says, exaggerating only slightly. Hiring Danes to kick butt is quite common practice in Swedish companies, apparently. Swedish managers are just too consensus-orientated to push through unpopular decisions.

'We have this ritual of making employees come together, asking what they think,' one Swede told me. 'You can't just change something, it has to be prepared and discussed. Swedes don't get annoyed, or disappointed, if they don't get their way: it is part of the game to compromise.'

This sounds like a recipe for procrastination and stagnation, doesn't it? So how come Swedish companies have had such huge, global success in recent decades? Because these kind of organisations require large numbers of people to move in the same direction over the long term, they do not tend to benefit from headstrong management. In contrast, the Danes excel at small-to-medium-scale businesses which need to be more agile and reactive; apart from a handful of examples, Danish companies struggle to achieve a truly international scale.

When they are not striving to be perceived by their fellow countrymen as *duktig*, the Swedes will seek to impress each other with how *lagom* they are. *Lagom* is another key Swedish watchword. It literally means 'according to law, or accepted custom' but it used to suggest 'moderate', 'reasonable', 'fair', 'acting in a common-sense way', 'rational'. Though it clearly resonates with Lutheran doctrines, its etymology is said to go much further back, to the Vikings. Legend has it that when they shared a horn of mead around the campfire, those gentle, caring-sharing Vikings would always remember to take care not to drink too much before passing the cup on to their neighbour (before going out and ripping a monk's head from his neck). *Laget om* loosely translates as 'pass around'; over time this is thought to have transformed into *lagom*, which has today come to imply a kind of self-imposed, collective restraint.

Lagom defines many behavioural aspects of Swedish society, from consumption patterns, which are resolutely inconspicuous (at least outside certain pockets of central Stockholm where Swarovski crystal-covered iPhone covers and pastel sweaters are *de rigeur*), to their system of government, which has tended to rely on compromise, moderation and consensus. *Lagom* is clearly related to Jante Law, the fictional Danish social manifesto that defines Swedish society (where they call it *Jantelag*) as much as, if not more than, in Denmark. The Swedes are even more afraid to pop their heads above the parapet, even less likely to boast or brag of their achievements, even more prone to understatement and modesty.*

---

* I have a theory – possibly one of my more far-fetched ones, but it is a favourite – that *lagom* and Jante Law lie behind one of the more curious, yet abiding, Scandinavian cultural imports: Donald Duck. Every time I use the bathroom in someone's home in Denmark or Sweden and see the inevitable pile of well-thumbed Donald Duck comics – *Anders And* in Denmark, *Kalle Anka* in Sweden – beside the toilet; or when I switch on DR1, the flagship Danish TV channel, at primetime on a Friday night and see their hour-long *Disney Fun* show featuring sixty-year-old Donald Duck cartoons; not to mention when I heard that, traditionally, the most-watched 24 December TV

Though, as I discovered in Malmö, the Swedes have by far the best drinking songs in the region, it takes a fair bit of alcohol before they show their more gregarious side, and you usually have to wade through a good deal of strictly observed social protocol to reach that point. Swedish dinner parties are especially stressful affairs for the uninitiated – something women's rights pioneer Mary Wollstonecraft appears to have spotted back in 1796 when she observed:

> The Swedes pique themselves on their politeness; but far from being the polish of a cultivated mind, it consists merely of tiresome forms and ceremonies. So far, indeed, from entering immediately into your character, and making you feel instantly at your ease, like the well-bred French, their over-acted civility is a continual restraint on all your actions.

So here's a primer, just in case you ever find yourself having to deal with Swedish over-acted civility.

Firstly, to remove, or not to remove is the question all foreigners must ask themselves on arriving at the threshold of a Swedish home. To *ask* your hosts whether you should take off your shoes is to imply a reluctance to do so; the polite host might not want to impose, but will then secretly despise you for sullying their floors.

---

show in Sweden every year is a Donald Duck Christmas special from 1958, I have pondered on this strange affection for the ill-starred, trouserless fowl. Donald Duck's approach to life seems to go so wholly against the Scandinavian grain; he is greedy, selfish, quick-tempered and behaves rashly but, crucially of course, he always pays the price for his frailties with his inevitable defeat, loss, humiliation, and small yellow birds circling his head. In the same way that audiences gain a vicarious thrill from a comedian joking about taboo subjects, I am convinced that Donald Duck performs a similar kind of safety-valve function for the modest, even-tempered, law-abiding Scandinavians. They would never dream of making such a scene about, say, three cheeky nephews eating their cake, or allow themselves to be so goaded by a pair of chipmunks that they smash up their own home in a squawking fury, but they find peace, a displaced catharsis, watching such episodes unfold in cartoon form.

Discard them automatically, though, and you could find yourself circling a soirée in your socks while everyone else is in shoes, which would be embarrassing. One Swedish etiquette guide advises: 'Never, ever wear shoes inside another person's home. Unless, of course, others are doing so,' adding that Swedes simply know when to remove their shoes and when not to. 'Look directly at your host, shake his hand, then look down at everyone's feet. Do not leave the entrance hall before ensuring that your feet are in the same state of dress or undress as everyone else's.' But what if you arrive alone and the party is out of sight? Simple: you are doomed.

In truth, Swedes will likely cut foreigners some slack in the footwear department, but there is one golden rule which you will not be forgiven for breaking: be on time. You should not be too early – no one appreciates that – but equally you should absolutely never arrive later than five minutes after the time you were invited. In Sweden, the concept of 'fashionably late' is akin to 'fashionably flatulent'.

Assuming you survive the entrance-hall trial, when you arrive at the party proper make sure to circumnavigate the room, shaking hands with each of the other guests in turn, introducing yourself in the manner of the Queen at a post-Royal Command Performance line-up. (They do the same in Denmark, except in Sweden they are more likely to announce both of their names instead of just their Christian names.) Actually, I rather like this formality, even though I instantly forget the other guests' names. My advice: when you meet them later during the course of the evening it is always worth risking 'Erik' for men, or 'Maria' for women. Most Swedes seem to be called one or the other. (In Denmark, try 'Sebastian' or 'Helle'.)

As you mingle before being called to the table, feel free to ask how much people earn, how long they were in education for, and make very clear your stance on how racist the Danes are, an attitude that will instantly endear you to your Swedish hosts. If you find yourself seated to the right of the hostess, bad luck. The other assembled guests will now be rubbing their hands in anticipation of the short toast you are expected to give, greatly relieved that it is not they who must stand up and be modest and witty in complimenting the hostess without provoking her husband. Following your toast, each guest must raise their glass and make, and hold, eye contact with the other diners in turn, all the while keeping one eye on the hostess. When she sips from her glass, the rest of the guests are free to do likewise.

This is merely the preamble to the meal. I could fill a book with what is expected of you during and after your meatballs and *Jansons frestelse* (potato gratin with anchovies – a great Swedish invention), but you get the idea. Just one more warning: I made this grotesque error just the once, but after the bewildered looks and nervous mimicking of my misstep by compassionate hosts keen to make sure I didn't feel humiliated, I learned my lesson. Never touch glasses when you toast. Despite what you might have been led to believe from the various carousing scenes in Hollywood Viking movies over the years, in Scandinavia this is considered unforgivably proletarian.

If you suspect my primer is not quite comprehensive enough (and you are right, but truly it would take a lifetime of pain to fill in the gaps), the best source on how to navigate the frigid depths of the Swedish psyche is Åke Daun's book *Swedish Mentality*. Formerly head of Stockholm's Nordic Museum and the Ethnology Department at the University of Stockholm, Daun is considered to be one of the greatest Nordic ethnologists of his time. He has been called the 'guru' of Swedishness, and his book is a masterpiece of character analysis: never have I read a text which so perfectly – or, indeed, so brutally – skewers a nation.

Daun describes the Swedes as a race of wallflowers wracked with insecurities; they would rather take the stairs than share a lift, he writes. Their more scintillating habits including visiting the country-side, eating crispbread, speaking in a low voice, and avoiding contro-versial subjects in conversation. 'What is remarkable is the weight Swedish culture attaches to "orderliness",' he continues, adding that punctuality and thorough organisation are among the characteristics Swedes value most highly. Mmm, *sexy*.

Swedish Mentality was written in 1985, and I wondered whether things might have changed since then. Fearing that Daun might no longer be with us, I held little hope of tracking him down for an update but, happily, I was wrong. Daun, who is in his late seventies (and will be played by Max von Sydow when this book is made into a movie), is very much alive and well and living in a well-to-do part of central Stockholm. Indeed, when I contacted him via email, he had just won the prestigious Gad Rausing Prize worth SEK800,000 (about £73,000), awarded by a fund bequeathed by the Tetra Pak billionaire for outstanding work in humanistic research. Very kindly he invited me to his home to talk further.

Do the Swedes really avoid getting into lifts with people? It sounds so extreme.

'Yes, it's true. We don't know how to talk to people we don't know,' Daun chuckled. 'That's really interesting, because most people like to talk. In southern Europe it's the best thing in life. I have a French colleague and when she came to Sweden she was convinced it was forbidden to talk on buses. She couldn't find any other explanation.'

'We do tend to give a "special" impression to foreigners,' Daun continued as we sat in the dimly lit drawing room of his large, high-ceilinged apartment. 'We are not so talkative, but in Sweden that is something good, you are being polite: "I am going to listen to you." But after a while the American, or whoever, will start to wonder, "Doesn't he have his own opinion, something to offer to make it a conversation?" because in America, they think that shy people are stupid.'

Daun traces the Swedes' preference for isolation back to their pre-industrial past. Up until the mid-nineteenth century, Sweden was very sparsely populated. The late-nineteenth-century agricultural reforms, which merged farms together into larger units, only exacerbated the isolation of farming families and communities: 'You didn't meet many people at all, mainly your own family and neighbours, and everything was equal. They had problems, but similar problems. There was no need to talk about it. You could visit your neighbour without saying anything, knock on the door, and sit down for a while. You might say, "It's rainy today," but everything you could have said had been said so many times before.'

I found this image of Swedish farmers sitting in companionable silence strangely touching, but presumably the industrial revolution must have altered things. Not so, said Daun. By that stage the Swedes were highly adept at insulating themselves from others, and remained able to do so even in urban environments. 'That's why, in Sweden you might have observed that they just walk into people as if they don't exist,' he added.

At last, an explanation for the breathtaking rudeness I had routinely experienced while visiting Sweden: the unapologetic barging, the oblivious blocking, the complete absence of common courtesies that had left me impotent with rage on so many occasions. When waiting for trains to Copenhagen Airport at the city-centre station, for instance, you could always tell the Swedish passengers who were continuing across the Øresund Bridge towards home because they would barge into the carriage while passengers were still disembarking as if it were the most normal thing in the world. I had experienced many similar instances of this kind of civil discourtesy in Denmark, but the Swedes rivalled the Hong Kong Chinese as the rudest people on earth, and their rudeness was all the more confusing as it ran so very counter to their otherwise respectful, orderly, timid image. Someone once described Scandinavian manners to me as a manifestation of a kind of perverse equality: I have just as much right to walk/drive/cycle here as you. I think there is something to this – either that or perhaps for most of the time it's simply too cold to hang around being polite.

One Swede I spoke to recounted this anecdote, which could so well describe me on several occasions in my Scandinavian life: 'I was at a café and there was an Englishman sitting at one table. A Swede passing on his way to the toilet knocked over the Englishman's briefcase but continued without apologising or putting the case upright again. The Englishman said nothing, but when the Swede came out of the toilet, he screamed across the café: "THE WORD IS SORRY."'

'I understand it is unpleasant for you,' Daun said, simply, after I had finished venting on this subject for longer than was probably polite. 'But for us it is normality.' Clearly, though, the rudeness and isolationist tendencies of his countrymen had troubled him too. For years Daun had passed the same few people on the streets of his neighbourhood without acknowledgement, but recently he had decided to run an impromptu sociological experiment.

'There was an elderly gentleman, very elegantly dressed, and I would meet him every day, and we'd pass each other without looking up. Finally, one day I went up to him and said, "Well, we have been walking here for years looking at one another, shouldn't we be able perhaps at least to say hello?" And he was so happy.' The two men ended up becoming friends and inviting each other to dinner and, thus encouraged, Daun approached other neighbours, who were equally surprised, but similarly receptive. 'It's so great. People love it!' he said, clapping his hands together.

Daun's missionary work on the streets of Stockholm was a heart-ening sign of hope that, deep down, there might exist some traces of humanity within the Swedish psyche and, as I left his apartment and elbowed my way on to my silent bus back into town, I came up with an idea for a social experiment of my own, which I planned to carry out among the unsuspecting people of Stockholm that very afternoon.

Chapter 3

Stockholm syndrome

My plan was to spend the rest of the day – perhaps longer, should I survive – going about Stockholm behaving as un-Swedishly as possible, the theory being that, by acting in diametric opposition to Swedish social norms, I would be better able to identify and observe said norms. By provoking the Swedes I encountered with behaviour entirely antithetical to theirs, I would be able to measure the extremes of their mentality; by pushing them to the edge of their tolerance, I would gauge, definitively, just how shy, reticent, rule-abiding, stiff or square they were, and thus locate the Swedes' precise position on the Scandinavian social-autistic spectrum. Hopefully, by understanding them better, I might come to view them more sympathetically. I would be a guinea pig for the world, an anthropological budgerigar being carried down into the coal mine of the Swedish psyche. Anything could happen in the next five hours: awkward silences, avoided gazes, assault, arrest, deportation . . .

My first stop was the Nobel Museum on the almost painfully picturesque historic city-centre island of Gamla stan. Frankly, the whole Nobel hullabaloo has always irritated me. As you know, Alfred Nobel made his fortune by inventing dynamite, initially for the mining industry, but later for the munitions used to slaughter thousands in the Crimean War, and countless millions thereafter. And yet, somehow, one idle day while drawing up his will in his retirement home on the Italian Riviera, Nobel felt his life's bloodstained legacy warranted, of all things, a peace prize in his name – it is akin to King Herod sponsoring a beautiful-baby competition, or a demolition man handing out architecture prizes.

Over the years, the various Nobel juries have certainly picked some real humdingers. Henry Kissinger, for example, the man who, as Christopher Hitchens pointed out, betrayed the Iraqi Kurds, supported apartheid, and gave the go-ahead for 'the deliberate mass killing of civilian populations in Indochina'. He got the peace prize in 1973. Obama's win in 2009, though less controversial, was a trifle absurd too, not least when you discover that Gandhi never got one (but Al Gore did). The peace prize is awarded by a committee chosen by the Norwegian parliament; the other prizes – for literature, chemistry, physics, medicine and economics – are give out by a Swedish committee. No one really knows why Nobel felt they should be split in this way, but at the time of his death Norway was ruled by Sweden, and perhaps he judged it to be the least warlike nation of the two.

As you would expect of an institution in which is assembled the glittering sum of all human endeavour, the Nobel Museum was hushed and reverential. The perfect place, then, to take out a bag of crisps and crunch them loudly, and slurp a can of coke while standing beside a 'no eating or drinking' sign. Here was a true test for Swedish tolerance if ever there was one. I rustled, crunched and gulped for all I was worth in full sight of two members of staff and numerous other visitors, but there was no response from any of them. This was frustrating, not least because I had to continue eating the entire bag of crisps for far longer than I would otherwise have wished – Swedish crisps are really awful – and, combined with the fizzy drink, this generated substantial and unpleasant frothy burps. But from this early probing of Swedish social norms, I could conclusively deduce that the Swedes were even more conflict-shy than they were rule-abiding.

I left the Nobel Museum shortly afterwards and came to a pedestrian crossing. A handful of people had gathered at the kerb, waiting for the light to change to green so that they would be permitted to cross, even though there were no cars nearby, or in sight for that matter. The Danes behave similarly when faced with the terrible quandary of a clear road and a red man, and for years I mocked their sheep-like behaviour. 'I don't need a light to tell me how to cross the road,' I used to scoff loudly, stepping boldly from the pavement as my wife grabbed my elbow in desperation, casting nervous glances while the waiting pedestrians murmured their disapproval. Over time, I am ashamed to admit, I have come to observe the red light more and more. My rebellious streak has been tamed by the sheer weight of Scandinavian social collectivism, but on this occasion, looking briefly both ways, my head held high, I crossed while the light remained red. An aggressive act in Denmark, I imagined this would be even more provocative in Sweden.

A woman to one side of me, who obviously wasn't concentrating, took my action as a subliminal prompt, and began to cross the road too, but at the last second she looked up, saw the red light, and hurried back sheepishly on to the pavement. I believe I heard a 'tut' from one of the others in the group, but I can't be sure. Anyway, I made it safely to the other side of the road, turned to the group, and raised my palms in a 'See, I survived!' gesture, but they were all still looking up towards the red light in expectant obedience.

Next stop was a park bench close to the theatre, where I sidled up to a woman who was eating a packet of gummy bears. I looked at the packet of jellied sweets, hoping she might offer me one. Sensing the intensity of my gaze, the woman shifted buttocks awkwardly, but carried on eating. I continued to stare. Nothing. Eventually the woman glanced up. I made a face which was intended to communicate my desire for one of her sweets but, clearly deeply alarmed, without speaking, the woman rose and walked briskly off. Oh dear.

I didn't talk to anyone at all at one of the world's greatest history museums. I was too busy staring up in wonder at the great warship *Vasa*, King Gustav II Adolf's ill-starred flagship, which was launched on 10 August 1628 and promptly sank in Stockholm harbour a few moments later. Most countries would prefer to leave such a conspicuous national embarrassment out of sight on the harbour bed, but not the self-flagellating Swedes, who raised the *Vasa* in the early sixties and put what is clearly an absurdly top-heavy (even I could see that) galleon on display in a purpose-built museum.

I am glad they did. A staggering sight awaits as you enter the exhibition hall and are confronted with the 20-metre-high stern of this mighty ship (which is an even more incredible 53 metres high above its keel), its oak timbers heavily carved and darkly stained like some great cathedral. The *Vasa* took two years to build, sunk in not many more minutes, and now stands as a striking testimony to kingly hubris. How must he have felt as he stood in all his royal pomp beside the dock and watched the *Vasa* slowly keel over and disappear beneath the gentle waves? ('And how many hits would that have on YouTube today?' I wondered.)

Stockholm is exceptionally beautiful, Scandinavia's most impressive capital – like Edinburgh crossed with Venice. At least, that's how it looks on the waterfront, but behind the granite grandeur lies a grim concrete zone not unlike Croydon. As Andrew Brown writes, central Stockholm 'was almost entirely rebuilt and dehumanized in the Sixties'. It is soulless and brutalist. Why this should be the case is slightly mysterious: Sweden emerged from the Second World War entirely unscathed. There was no bombing here. As I sat on a bench outside the Kulturhuset, I wondered to myself, 'Why did they choose to rebuild Stockholm in Soviet-style concrete blocks?' What did this say about how the Swedes – or their city planners – saw themselves?

A man with a Kindle sat down next to me. 'Is that one of those electronic books?' I asked cheerily.

The man nodded.

'So, like, wow, that's real *Star Trek* stuff, isn't it? Do you like it? Would you recommend one?'

'It is good if you are travelling,' said the man without making eye contact, and went back to his reading. A few moments later, some deeply dormant notion of humanity apparently roused, he stopped reading, and turned to me. 'I like it because you can take lots of books with you,' he said and, satisfied that he had performed his duty as a good citizen, returned to his reading.

It was a promising sign that the Swedes were capable of human interaction given a little prompting and, thus encouraged, back in my hotel I loitered for a while around the lift until I was sure a Swede was about to use it. The first target was a woman in her fifties with a large vertical suitcase that she was pushing on wheels. I waited until she was about to enter, then swiftly moved in front of her to take up position in the lift. She backed off immediately and made a slight nod to indicate that I should continue in the lift alone. It was a small lift, but there was room for two if I backed into the corner, which I did. 'Don't worry, we can both fit in!' I chirruped. But she had suddenly found something much more interesting to look at in the lobby (oddly, my hotel, the Berns, was offering dildos for sale in a glass cabinet – perhaps it was these she was drawn to), and moved away.

As Åke Daun had suggested, lifts seemed to be ripe environments for exploring the Swedish psyche so, on several more occasions over the next few days, I attempted to share one with locals. Learning from my first experience, I made sure my victims were properly ensconced in the lift before I slipped in and attempted to engage them in human dialogue. The responses to my opening salvo, 'Hi, how are you? Lovely hotel, isn't it?' were almost uniformly monosyllabic. One bulky, late-middle-aged man in a suit simply ignored me while looking straight ahead; a younger woman smiled nervously and backed away looking at her shoes; only a couple in their late twenties went further, answering in the affirmative that yes, it was a nice hotel, before returning to their hushed conversation, at which point I realised they were from one of the Baltic states.

My next Swede-taunting arena was public transport. One of Stockholm's major tourist attractions is a glass viewing pod which is hauled up and over the top of a spherical sports arena, the Stockholm Globe, affording its occupants a nice view of the city. It was a short metro ride out of town and, as I went to board the train, there was the usual two-way rugby scrum between the passengers who were disembarking and those who were intent on boarding. In most other countries it would have been considered a disgraceful display of counter-productive selfishness, but here in Stockholm no one batted an eye.

I grabbed the arm of one man, a businessman in a suit with a record bag slung over his shoulder who was attempting to force himself on to the carriage before it had emptied.

'So sorry to trouble you,' I said. 'But I wonder if you could help me with something.'

Anger, bewilderment and impatience scudded in quick succession across his face, culminating in an irritated, quizzical look.

'I am doing some research into Swedish behaviour and I noticed that you were pushing on to the train before the other passengers had got off. I was wondering why you were doing this, when it's kind of obvious that everything would work better if the passengers on the platform stood aside?'

By now we were the last passengers on the platform and the man was looking anxiously over my shoulder into the carriage of the soon-to-depart train.

'I . . . I, what do you mean? I have to go.' Head down, he barged past me into the carriage, bristling. 'You can dress yourself in the morning, presumably, so why can't you behave reasonably towards other people?' I felt like shouting after him. But didn't. Even I know it's wrong to shout at other people when you are a guest in their country.

The train stopped at the next station. It wasn't my station, but I decided to continue the experiment. Sure enough, the small group of people waiting on the platform began to steam on to the train before I managed to disembark. I spread my arms wide, to push some of them back in a Jesus-like gesture of compassionate instruction.

'Hello! Shall we let people get off first?' I said in a raised voice (not shouting), pushing two of them back off the train's steps. Two others barged past regardless, but a couple of the crowd did seem genuinely embarrassed and backed off. My achievement here was admittedly of a more pyrrhic order as, having made such a song and dance about getting off the train, I could hardly then get back on, so had to wait twelve minutes for the next one. Still, I felt I had struck a blow for common commuter decency.

On the next train, a Romanian man passed through the carriage and placed cards on the empty seats next to the passengers. On the cards was written:

I am a poor man with two children.
They have leukaemia and I need money for their treatment.

Several people left coins on the cards for the man to collect on his return sweep through the carriage, including the woman sitting opposite me. In my new Daunian spirit of social interaction, I asked her why she had done this, considering that Sweden had an excellent, free health service.

Once she had digested the extraordinary fact of a stranger talking to her unbidden, the woman replied that if the man didn't have papers to live in Sweden then he would not be eligible for the treatments.

'But you don't *really* think he is saving for his children, do you?' I said.

'No, but for me just the idea of him begging is beneath human dignity. That's why I gave.'

Now it was my turn to feel chastened and embarrassed by such very modern, very Swedish compassion. Time perhaps to quit bugging the locals. I was losing enthusiasm for my ground-breaking anthropological research anyway. Trying to get the Swedes to be more polite was like picking on Italian men for being vain, or Japanese women for being shy. The poor creatures could not help themselves and besides, what had the Swedes ever done to me?

I did, though, attempt to strike up the odd conversation in cafés and restaurants over the next few days, in a desperate attempt to disprove the stereotype. Most Swedes responded to my opening gambits, answering my questions but making no effort to keep the conversational plate spinning. Of course, we cannot entirely discount the idea that it was me, personally, from whom an entire nation was recoiling, but I was trying my utmost not to be creepy.

In the meantime, I was also on the constant lookout for any chink in the Swedes' goody-goody armour, for any hint of vice. There were precious few, save for their inexplicable addiction to chewing tobacco, which is sold in small round pots (like boiled sweets) at every 7-Eleven. (I once interviewed the country's leading chef, but was distracted the entire time by the bulge in his lower lip as he rested his *snus*.)

Oh, I nearly forgot, there were also the people masturbating at the National Museum. One afternoon I accidentally found myself visiting a special exhibition there entitled 'Lust and Vice', billed as an exposé of the Swedes' 'predilictions and perversions from past to present'. Though I was there for the Strindberg seascapes, I reluctantly decided that I should take just a quick peek in order to plumb the sordid depths of my hosts' sexual psyche. For research.

The exhibition ranged freely and frankly through the history of Swedish mucky pictures from the last few centuries. There was a vast, 9-foot painting by Julius Kronberg which apparently caused quite a kerfuffle when it was unveiled in 1876, depicting two men leering at a nude ginger-haired woman; there were various blurry art-masturbation videos; an entire wall of naked women pleasuring themselves; more photos of blurry-handed men; a few bare-bottomed nuns, and so on.

What to make of it all? The Swedes have a global reputation for being sexually liberated but many commentators, visitors and even the Swedes themselves say this is largely unwarranted; what some perceive as Swedish 'sexiness' is attributable to a number of factors, none of which have much to do with where they put their genitals and how often they put them there.

Firstly, there was the decriminalisation of the Swedish porn industry in the 1960s, a move that mirrored one by the Danes around the same time and which had the effect of turning the Swedish and Danish porn industries into global leaders. Then there is the Swedes' apparently relaxed approach to nudity – in saunas, on the beach, and so on – which, again, has very little to do with actual 'copping off'. There is a wonderfully awkward television interview between David Frost and the soon-to-be Swedish prime minister, the late Olof Palme, from 1968 (awkward only on account of Frost's creepy, self-satisfied manner, I should add; Palme comes across as a thoroughly decent, intelligent politician), in which the latter is asked about the Swedes' reputation for sexual liberation. Palme calls it 'overinflated', describing the Swedes as 'a people with a deep moral sense and great inhibitions in the sexual field', but adding that they also had a 'very normal, healthy attitude towards sex'.

Sweden's great strides towards gender equality may also have confused casual observers into believing Swedish women were especially free and easy in other areas (Agnetha Fälstkog's low-cut jumpsuits probably didn't help matters), but these measures were implemented primarily to get more women into work, not into bed.

If anything, the National Museum's exhibition revealed a country that was, historically, rather puritanical about sex, but at least it made a change from the usual Nordic museum experience. By now, towards the end of my travels, I had become familiar with the stylistic clichés and thematic tropes of museums in this part of the world. The eerie, whistling-wind sound effects with which they augmented all their prehistory sections, for instance. (If the museums of the region are to be believed, most prehistoric Scandinavians spent their lives trudging, alone, across windswept heaths before accidentally falling into peat bogs and dying.) It had also become a minor hobby of mine to spot their politically correct, pro-Viking propaganda, and Stockholm's Historiska museum did not disappoint on that front either.

'The Vikings are probably best known for their warlike rampages. But there was so much more to them than that,' claimed one of its captions. And it wasn't just the Vikings they seemed keen to rehabilitate: Scandinavian history museums specialise in presenting this kind of politically correct, positive spin on virtually every mildly controversial issue, from their bloodthirsty ancestors to issues of gender, race and disability. This is not necessarily meant as a criticism. Though it might not always be apparent, I am a great enthusiast for political correctness: it may be counter-fashionable these days, but it seems to me just another manifestation of politeness and, as I believe we have established, I want more politeness, not less. That said, attempting to blame the Swedes' drinking on the Italians, as one caption in the museum did, seemed a step too far: 'Gambling and strong drinks are nothing new. During the first centuries AD, Roman habits spread to the people of the north.' Ah, I *see*, it's all the fault of those loose-moralled swarthy types from the south!

One must also tiptoe around the subject of diversity. 'In today's Sweden we constantly meet different ways of believing,' explained another caption charting the country's late-twentieth-century immigration. 'Sometimes there is fear, but more and more often there is also understanding. The satellite dishes and broadband of the suburbs are directed at the whole world. There is room for the whole world.'

Was this true? I had seen relatively few black or Asian people in Stockholm. During an afternoon wandering around the upmarket district of Östermalm, literally the only person of colour I had seen was emptying the bins outside McDonalds. I was surprised by how unintegrated, how *un*-multicultural the city centre had been considering Sweden had by far the highest level of immigration in the region.

Yet an exhibition at the Historiska museum had featured photographs from Sweden's most notorious immigrant estate, Rosengård in Malmö. Rosengård is known throughout Scandinavia for its social problems, racial tension, squalor and violence, and is genuinely feared by the Danes who live just twenty minutes away across the Øresund strait. They talk with palpable horror of Rosengård – of the lawlessness, the Islamic extremism, the shootings, the arson. You'd think they were describing a suburb of Mogadishu.

It was time to pay a visit, and to take a closer look at Sweden's great, multicultural experiment.

Chapter 4

Integration

'I don't go there after dark,' my taxi driver tells me as we drive away from Malmö Station on a bright, sunny spring morning. 'A driver I know was very badly beaten and robbed there recently. It's Sweden's Chicago, you know.'

This is one of the wealthiest, most developed and safest countries in the world, but it is not the first time I have heard such tales about Malmö's Rosengård estate, where we are heading. In the eyes of Danish right-wingers, Rosengård and its near 90 per cent immigrant population have come to symbolise all that is wrong with Sweden's open-door immigration policy. If you believe the rumours, it is a crime-ridden hellhole, a sink-estate-of-no-hope where the country herds its Somali, Iraqi and Afghani immigrants, denying them any hope of a decent life or income.

At the extreme end of this political spectrum are the likes of Anders Behring Breivik and the ranting Eurabian bloggers who claim that Europe is facing a second Siege of Vienna. They say Rosengård is a no-go area for non-Muslims, a place where white people and even the emergency services are not wanted – a hotbed of the kind of Islamic extremism which has already implemented Sharia Law in this small pocket of the city and intends to roll it out across the continent. At the less extreme end of the spectrum, Norway's Progress Party and their Swedish equivalent, *Sverigedemokraterna* (the Sweden Democrats – slogan: 'Security and Tradition') cite Rosengård as evidence that the people of a hundred or more different faiths, races and nationalities who live there cannot cohabit harmoniously with ethnic Swedes. What happens to traditional Swedish values when the 'real Swedes' are outnumbered a thousand to one they ask.

Rosengård has something of a bad rep then, not helped by a number of media-friendly, headline-grabbing episodes over the last ten years – riots, arson and sniper attacks. It doesn't matter that some of these crimes were committed by 'ethnic Swedes', or that there are also regular shootings and occasional riots in Denmark's most ethnically diverse quarter, Nørrebro in Copenhagen; the Danes dismiss these as mere inter-gang warfare. 'It's just the bikers and the drug gangs taking pot shots,' Copenhageners will say, metaphorically ruffling the miscreants hair. Similarly, the indigenous mafia-style organised biker gangs that terrorise provincial Danish towns and run many, if not most, of the drug operations in the country, are rarely, if ever, referred to by the Nordic Right. Despite the fact that attention shifted to Stockholm in the spring of 2013 following several days of serious rioting, Malmö's reputation for exemplifying the rotten core at the heart of the great modern Scandinavian experiment endures.

So I had come to see Rosengård for myself. How bad could it be? After all, this was still Sweden, the country where mothers leave their babies sleeping in prams outside of shops, and people in the suburbs leave their front doors unlocked; home of the three-point safety belt; the country where everyone is required by law to drive with their headlights on at all times.

Continuing the road safety theme, my arrival in Malmö had begun with a perfect parody of Swedishness. Before starting his taxi, my driver had blown bashfully into a dashboard-mounted breathalyser, explaining that the car wouldn't start unless his breath was entirely free of alcohol. It was, and, eventually, we headed away from the cobbled squares and tranquil canals of Malmö's historic centre, arriving after just a few minutes amid a very different landscape of tower blocks, ring roads and strip malls. This was Rosengård.

Actually, Rosengård didn't look all that bad. Though it may well hold less appeal on those evenings when the cars are burning and molotov cocktails are being hurled, or if you are living ten people to one damp, cockroach-infested apartment, on that sunny April day it looked like every other modern Scandinavian high-rise housing project that I had seen from Helsinki to Oslo, including Copenhagen – no better, no worse. From the outside, the tower blocks appeared to be well-kept; many had new façades; there were plenty of trees and greenery surrounding them; little razor wire, few CCTV cameras or walls topped with shards of glass. Having lived in South London, I know just how grisly low-cost, high-rise housing can become once the local authorities have relinquished responsibility for its upkeep, but Rosengård was a world away from its equivalents in Brixton or Kennington.

The taxi driver dropped me outside the main shopping complex, a bland, low-rise affair housing various discount stores, a chemist and a supermarket. It wasn't terribly attractive, but Scandinavian shopping malls never are, even when they are located in the most exclusive of residential areas (I always assume this is on account of some deep-seated, Lutheran notion that shopping for pleasure is shameful and wrong).

I had an appointment with the man with perhaps the toughest communications job in all of Scandinavia: Dick Fredholm, Head of Public Relations for the City District of Rosengård. His office was just behind the strip mall in a newly built council building.

I asked him, first, what Rosengård had done to deserve its dubious ghetto reputation. 'Well, we don't use the word "ghetto",' he said, briskly. 'It's not paradise on earth, but it has no more problems than city districts of Stockholm or Gothenburg. The last major riots were four years ago. It's much quieter now, we've had lots of infra-structure changes. Everyone says Rosengård is proof that immigration has gone bad, but we say this is where integration *starts.*'

Fredholm, in his late thirties, dressed casually and sporting a perky quiff (looking like a member of Morrissey's backing band, if that helps), was friendly enough but, perhaps understandably, also wary. He listed a rose garden project, a new cycle track and a swimming pool as recent local improvements, adding that the area was begin-ning to attract corporate investment – I passed a large office for Ricoh on my way out of the area later that day. As for crime, he claimed that, because most of the residents were Muslims, there was little alcohol-fuelled crime or drink-driving, and 'they don't beat each other up on a Saturday night.' He also name-dropped Zlatan Ibrahimović, Sweden's best footballer of recent years, who was born in Rosengård.

Malmö's Social Democratic mayor for the last decade and a half (he retired in 2013), Ilmar Reepalu, was similarly upbeat when I met him the following day, back across the water where he was holding meetings in Copenhagen's town hall: 'I have just seen a study that shows that if it was a suburb of Stockholm, Rosengård would be one of the safest parts of the city,' he told me proudly. He laid the blame for Rosengård's problems on the private landlords who own most of the large apartment blocks there. They were built as part of Sweden's extraordinary Million Programme; between 1965 and 1974, the Social Democratic government constructed over a million new homes, many of them surplus to requirements. According to Reepalu, the problem was that housing planning in Sweden is a very slow, long-term business, often outpaced by economic and demographic changes.

'From 1971 to 1981 Malmö's population declined by almost forty thousand, but they were still building four thousand flats a year, so there was lots of empty space. In the early 1990s they began to be filled by immigrants from the former Yugoslavia, who worked here in the shipyards; by the end of that process there were ten people in every flat.' This was the beginning of the dark days for the estate as landlords essentially left the apartments, and their residents, to rot. Basic amenities broke down, the fabric of the buildings deteriorated, and overcrowding from the next wave of arrivals from the Middle East exacerbated the problem. Eventually the local authority bought and repaired some of the buildings, the mayor told me, but then in the early nineties, Sweden's economy tanked, unemployment quadrupled and the central bank's interest rate hit 500 per cent. The central government passed a law preventing any more homes passing into public ownership as part of the cost-cutting, privatisation strategy and Rosengård was left to fend for itself.

I was intrigued to hear from Fredholm that Rosengård's most

notorious group of apartment blocks, Herregården (where unemployment runs at 90 per cent), borders Almgården, a predominantly white, working-class housing complex which has one of the largest proportions of voters for the anti-immigration Sweden Democrats. The party polled 36 per cent of the votes cast in Almgården in the last election, compared with just under 6 per cent nationally.

Malmö's first major riots took place in Herregården back in the early 2000s. At the time the apartment blocks here should have provided homes for two thousand people but in reality they housed eight thousand. 'People were living in the hallways,' Fredholm told me. 'The only reason to go to Herregården was either to buy drugs, or if you lived there.' The buses stopped running to the estate for a while and, in 2008, when one of the building's landlords closed down a mosque that was operating from the basement, it was the scene of the worst riots in the city's history.

In other words, the two polar opposites of Swedish society lived cheek by jowl with one another right here in these two low-income housing districts – the immigrants and asylum seekers on one side, the right-wing working class on the other. After my meeting with Fredholm, I took a walk to check them both out.

I passed the shopping centre again, where I was assailed by the characteristic Scandinavian culinary aromas of ketchup, vinegar and stale cooking oil. I crossed the main road and passed Rosengård School, a modern, open campus with jolly pastel-coloured buildings and low fences.

As I walked further, beyond the school, it occurred to me that the chief reason this part of Malmö felt so soulless was not because of the clusters of tower blocks, which were surrounded by reasonably pleasant gardens and recreation areas, but due to the broad, busy ring roads that encircled them. Each group of apartment blocks was isolated by non-stop, four-lane traffic, the roads lined sometimes with wide pavements, sometimes with no pavement at all, and often entombed in steep embankments like medieval ramparts. This tended to make the distances between the residential areas quite large and difficult to negotiate on foot. At one point I had to climb a steep muddy bank and push back the branches of low trees to arrive at the road I wanted to cross. The road itself was busy with fast-moving traffic which I was forced to cross in stages, pausing perilously at the halfway mark before dashing across to the opposite pavement. 'City planners have a great deal to answer for,' I thought to myself as I picked the leaves out of my hat. Then I thought again: perhaps the isolating nature of the urban layout here in Rosengård was intentional. Perhaps someone *wanted* to fragment these communities and keep them apart.

I passed a small allotment, an oasis of humanity amid the traffic, and stopped to talk to a couple of older men – from their accents I'd guess they were Turkish – about their vegetables. I don't really understand spoken Swedish, and they didn't speak English, so the conversation mostly consisted of us all smiling and pointing at plants, but it provided a welcome human interlude amid this dystopian landscape.

I was heading for the local mosque and Islamic centre, the dome and minarets of which I could make out in the distance. I couldn't help notice that, in this supposed Islamic ghetto, the mosque was located within sight of two churches. Both the churches were locked, but their grounds were open and there was no apparent security. I could walk right up to their doors. It did not appear to me as if anyone was living in fear because of their religious beliefs here, at least not the Christian community.

'This is how it looked in 2003,' the founder and head of the mosque, Bejzat Becirov, told me when I complimented him on how well-kept the building and its grounds were. He showed me photographs taken after the centre suffered the worst of several arson attacks in recent years (there were two more in 2005, plus a shooting on New Year's Eve in 2009 in which Becirov was injured). In the photos it resembled the scenes of devastation we are used to seeing on a weekly basis from Tikrit or Kabul, with gaping, charred walls and a foreground of rubble. Who destroyed the mosque in 2003 is still unknown (as we will discover, the Swedish police are the antithesis of the Mounties). The most likely culprits are right-wing ethnic

Swedes, like the Malmö sniper Peter Mangs – on trial as I write for shooting dead three people and injuring twelve others in a series of attacks on immigrants in the city over the last nine years – but it is not beyond the realms of possibility that the attacks were carried out by local Muslim extremists disgruntled with the mosque's moderate approach.

Becirov, who came to Sweden from his native Macedonia in the 1960s, opened the mosque in 1984. Being a 'Western' Muslim, he was proud that Sunnis and Shiites worshipped side by side here. Becirov was even broadly tolerant of the Danish Mohammed cartoons: 'I did not personally approve of them, but we live in a democracy.' (Improbably here, I found myself holding a *more* extreme stance on the cartoons than an actual imam: I thought the cartoons were childishly provocative and, perhaps worse, about as funny as dental pain.) The mosque was partly funded by Colonel Gaddafi's World Islamic Call Society (the late dictator's attempt to prove his Islamic credentials to the rest of the Arabic world), but Becirov, in his early seventies and dressed in a suit, was keen to impress upon me the moderateness of his congregation, showing me photographs from open days attended by local dignitaries, including the city's leading rabbi, and even the US ambassador (not to mention, Siv Jensen, leader of Norway's Progress Party). As if to prove there were no extremists hiding about the place, Becirov took me on a tour of – literally – every corner of the building.

In his view Rosengård's chief problem was its poor housing: 'There are twenty people in some apartments, cockroaches . . .' but also the more recent arrival of non-Western muslims, often from conflict areas or far-away areas of rural poverty. 'Not the same traditions. They are very slow to integrate – perhaps take twenty years. They have no language, criminality grows.'

I left the mosque and walked across a rather boggy, desolate park to the cluster of tower blocks that made up Almgården, the white, working-class sub-estate a few hundred metres away. As if a switch had been flicked, I was back in mainstream Sweden again. There were no head scarves, no Arabic signs in the shop windows, no Halal burgers. The occasional tattered Swedish flag fluttered from a balcony. There were lace curtains. Overweight women with orange highlights walked small white dogs. I asked one how it was to live here, mentioning that I had heard about the friction with their immigrant neighbours. 'What, Herregården?' She exhaled impatiently, as if to say 'I have more to worry about than them', and moved on. Another man I met was more interested in telling me about the broken lift in his building, and how no one was doing anything to help the people who lived around there.

As I waited by a kebab stand behind the estate for the bus back to central Malmö, it struck me that the people of Almgården probably faced precisely the same problems as their immigrant neighbours in Herregården – poor education, few opportunities, little hope, and no money – yet each was fearful and resentful of the other, their animosity as much a barrier as the city planning which defined and divided their everyday landscape.

Chapter 5

Catalonians

The awkward truth for Sweden's multiculturalists is that immigrants and asylum seekers do appear to be responsible for a disproportionate amount of crime in the country, particularly violent crime, and particularly rape. In *Fishing in Utopia* Andrew Brown writes:

> It is one of the known unspeakables of Swedish life that the crime rate among immigrants and their descendants is at least double that in the native population . . . Immigrants are more than four times as likely as Swedes to commit a murder, and more than five times as likely to commit a rape.

Even some of the liberal, left-wing muliculturalist Scandinavians I spoke with were occasionally willing to concede, off the record, that newly arrived, uneducated immigrants, particularly those from rural parts of Islamic countries, are simply not equipped to deal, for instance, with the way Western women dress and behave.

The equally awkward truth for the right-wingers opposed to immigration – by which they usually mean Muslims – is that one major factor in immigrant crime is the very Scandinavian welfare model, which the right-wing parties are often fighting just as hard as the Social Democrats to maintain. The Scandinavian welfare-state model was not designed with non-Western immigrants in mind. Unlike, say, the immigrants who came to the UK in the 1950s, immigrants to the Nordic countries often lack the language skills and qualifications required to make best use of the safety net and, even when they do acquire these things, they face prejudice among potential employers and society in general. By effectively shunting newly arrived immigrants off to places like Rosengård, where they are given just enough money to live on but face often insurmountable obstacles to progressing further in society,* the system creates convenient ghettoes for their ongoing 'clientification' (as the process of making new arrivals wholly dependent on welfare provision is known). This is in stark contrast to the US, for instance, where immigrants generally have to work hard to survive and, in doing so, create lives and businesses with little state support – those employment and earning opportunities, of course, being the very things that draw them to the States in the first place.

One proposed solution to the problem is to have a two-tier system, with different welfare provision for new arrivals, more stringent rules for applications, and so on. Denmark has taken this path over recent years, but in doing so has provoked outrage from human rights organisations, the EU and others, and suffered irrevocable damage to its international image. Sweden did clamp down on immigration in the wake of its economic problems in the early 1990s, but it has still been running at record levels (roughly 100,000 new arrivals every year), above even 1970s figures. The country has also taken in around 30,000 asylum seekers each year, compared with 3,000–5,000 in Denmark, a figure which is striking enough in absolute terms, but which makes Sweden the third highest destination for asylum seekers in the world in per capita terms (Britain is seventeenth, the US twenty-fourth, Denmark a surprisingly high sixteenth).

Åke Daun had both positive and negative reflections on the future of Sweden's immigration experiment. I had asked him my usual question: weren't the homogenous, isolated, introspective people of Scandinavia inherently unpromising candidates for the large-scale integration of immigrants? He told me about some research conducted twenty-five years ago by the European Values Study. It canvassed

---

* Not having a name which ends in '-son', being one such obstacle. In 2006, *Svenska Dagbladet* reported that people with foreign-sounding surnames were changing them to more Swedish-sounding ones in order to stand a chance of getting at least a job interview.

around 16,000 people in 16 countries about their points of view on a range of subjects. 'One of the "agree or disagree" statements they were asked about was "I don't like to be with people who are different from me in terms of their values, opinions, and so on",' Daun explained. 'And I think it was 43 per cent of Swedes that said "Yes, I don't like to be together with people who are different from me." When I first saw that, I thought, well that's not bad, less than half. But then I saw the responses from the other countries and the difference was immense. In the other Nordic countries it was about 10 per cent, even Spain was only 22 per cent. I thought, this can't be true, it must be a statistical error, so twenty years later, in 2004, when I was invited to contribute a question to the same survey, I asked for this one again and this time the answer was 41 per cent, so no change really.'

Despite this, Daun did seem moderately optimistic about his country's multicultural future, pointing out that, for all the troubled youth of Rosengård, there were many young immigrants who were making great progress through the education system. 'There is no alternative, whatever we think, the world will be more and more international with mixed populations, also in Scandinavia,' he said.

'I don't buy your idea,' Henrik Berggren, one of Sweden's leading historians and social commentators told me when I put my hypothesis of the awkward ethnographical fit between Swedes and immigrants to him during a later visit to Stockholm. 'Obviously you're right that our history is one of a homogenous country, but if you compare Denmark and Sweden, modernity has been a very, very strong force in Sweden. And in terms of immigration – and you can call it an illusion if you want to – there is this idea that we are a modern society, a modern people, we don't have prejudices, we are forward-looking. You can say that's a self-deception, and just ideology, but at some point self-deceptions come true, they matter.'

In other words, the prevailing Social Democratic doctrine that immigration is a good thing, the *right* thing, has become a kind of self-fulfilling socio-political prophecy. But what about Daun's survey? The Swedes did appear to be dramatically less inclined to rub along with people who were different from them, didn't they? 'You can do those surveys, but you have no idea if people are telling the truth,' Berggren said with a dismissive wave of the hand.

We talked around the subject of immigration for some time in his office in a converted shop in a quiet residential area of Stockholm, but I could sense Berggren, a large, owlish man possessed of a daunting intellect, becoming more and more uncomfortable with the conversation.

Eventually, he held his palms up and said, 'Look, I really dislike the idea of being on the defensive and saying we are these wonderful good people, please don't portray me in that way.' He laughed. 'I'm just saying that, honestly, I just don't think you are right. I really can't say that Swedes are more inward-looking than, for God's sake, *Catalonians*, or, come on, Flemish people! I mean give me a break, seriously, come on. Take a walk around Stockholm, talk to people. I mean, you know. No!' He took a deep breath. 'I am not trying to make you out to be a fascist for asking these questions, but I just don't see immigration as a problem. I am sorry if I sound pious, but I have heard so many times before that Sweden is heading for problems, that there's going to be catastrophe, so if I sound preachy or self-righteous . . .'

Actually, I did feel a bit of a fascist for asking my next question, but did he not think that, with more than a third of Sweden's population either born overseas or from foreign parents, might it at least be the time to consider stopping *further* immigration?

'I think you are putting the question in the wrong frame,' Berggren said, more evenly now. 'Firstly, they are here, so we are going to have to get on with it. But we are going to need immigrants in this country; what we need is a system for working immigrants. It would help build a greater multicultural society. I agree, not all of the people seeking asylum can come to Sweden, but there are very different types of immigration.

'I am more worried about unemployment. I worry about all these regions which are being depopulated, where people can't get jobs, there's not enough energy or businesses, and the infrastructure is not good. It's not like Norway with all the oil money. That, I think, is really worrying. I worry about the Sweden Democrats, I worry about the people who are resorting to voting for them. Economic inequality, schools, all that is a worry, but the ethnic composition of the population? I don't think that is the main issue here. What you do with the people you have here, that is much more important.'

Chapter 6

Somali pizza

Berggren wasn't the only one worried about the Sweden Democrats. Prior to the most recent election, Sweden's far-right party had been judged so far beyond the pale that the major newspapers had refused to run their campaign adverts, and some of the TV political discussion shows had not invited the party's representatives to participate. The channels defended their position on the grounds that the right-wingers had not won sufficient votes in previous elections to justify their presence, but previously the Green Party had been allowed to participate despite being even less popular. The other political parties also refused to have anything to do with the Sweden Democrats to the extent that, when one of their representatives was finally allowed to go on TV, a left-wing party representative who was booked for the same show refused to have their make-up put on in the same room.

Berggren did not especially agree with the Swedish media's censorship of the Sweden Democrats, but pointed to the beneficial effects the Danish People's Party had enjoyed from their coverage on Danish TV. Thanks in part to the media attention it received in the run-up to Denmark's 2001 general election, the DPP became the third-party power broker in the Danish coalition government, and went on to use their position to get numerous draconian immigration proposals passed into law.

'In Denmark, it seems to me things are being said in the public realm which aren't being said in Sweden. You have two choices: isolate that which you do not like, or bring it into power and make them responsible to the voters,' Berggren said. 'There's a lot to be said for the latter, but of course you get these parties where that doesn't work, and I think in Sweden we have seen [what's happened] in Denmark. We have seen that inclusiveness doesn't work, and we have decided not to do that.'

I find the Nordic Right's bigotry and falsehoods as distasteful as anyone, but I did find the phrase 'We have decided not to do that' a little troubling here. What exactly was it that 'they' – presumably Sweden's media and political elite – had decided not to do? They had decided not to allow the representatives of what, at the last election, turned out to be almost 6 per cent of the population, from participating in the public debate. This has prompted gleeful accusations from the Danes that Sweden is in denial of its problems as well as being guilty of infringing on freedom of speech.

'This Danish point of view on freedom of speech is quite ridiculous,' Stefan Jonsson, formerly a journalist on *Dagens Nyheter* and now a professor of ethnic studies, told me when I met him in his office at Stockholm University. 'They [the Sweden Democrats] think the media has to be a mirror that reflects society, but the media doesn't work like that. There is always an evaluation of what kind of news to promote.'

This was a new one on me: journalists 'promoting' the news? Weren't we supposed to report stuff, reflect society, tell people what was happening? Not in Sweden, apparently. In Sweden things were different.

'It is extremely naive to think that all ideas should be given the same space and importance,' said Jonsson, who has written several books on multiculturalism. 'The Sweden Democrats are quite a different party from the Dansk Folkeparti [the Danish People's Party] because it has its roots in the Swedish Nazi party. It's well documented, everyone knows that. It is clearly a party that has been explicitly racist and represents a viewpoint which is counter to a free society, which has nothing to do with democratic society . . . the more you debate with extreme parties like them, the more legitimate, and larger, they become.'

Jonsson had recently participated in a discussion with a Danish journalist, Mikael Jalving, in the Danish newspaper *Berlingske*, on the subject of their two country's differing approaches to freedom of speech. Jalving had written a book – *Absolut Sweden: A Journey in a Wealth of Silence* – in which he claimed that, by suppressing discussion about immigration and not allowing the Sweden Democrats their say, the Swedes were making the subject taboo and inadvertently fuelling extremism (something you could argue was borne out by Anders Breivik). Jalving described the Øresund Bridge as a 'mental Berlin Wall', with the two nations on either side diametrically opposed on how to approach the issue. 'When you read what is written about Denmark in the Swedish media,' he writes,

> it is almost all about one topic – immigration: that we are racist or xenophobic, or how we have been criticised by the EU or UN. Though Swedes think that they are hypermodern, open and rational, they are hiding themselves behind some taboos. Beneath the surface there is masses of conflict and extremists which are not heard about in Swedish society. This includes, for example, the growing gang criminality, nazism, ultra-feminism and problems with Muslim immigration – and no one is talking about this officially.

The Danish newspaper editor Anne Knudsen agreed with her compatriot: 'In Sweden you have a surprising level of vindictiveness in the political discourse,' she told me. 'Of course, the Sweden Democrats are awful, but the mainstream really *hates* them; there is this hatred of people who do not share their tolerant opinions. I shouldn't say totalitarianism, but . . .'

But Jonsson was adamant, the Swedish way was best: 'Immigration is perhaps the most important topic in Europe today,' he told me. 'And I think that most Swedish intellectuals, journalists and publishers have been very responsible, in contrast to Denmark where, in the name of free speech, they have openly permitted and legitimised the DPP and a certain kind of racist depiction of Islam.

'Since the 1950s, Sweden has been one of the most internationally open countries in terms of its foreign policies and foreign aid. Sweden got this reputation as the conscience of the world, and I think that ideology has a real effect on the ideology of Swedes towards people who are different from them. It created a climate of tolerance and curiosity, and certainly a sense of being in a position of privilege, which brings a kind of responsibility to help. Integration has worked better in Sweden because we have had this powerful idea of internationalism.'

Jonsson was resolutely upbeat about Sweden's comparatively large-scale immigration: 'It has worked. There are a huge number of integrated second-, third-, fourth-, fifth-, sixth-generation immigrants in this country, and I think in the long run the conditions for integration aren't terribly unfavourable. It is economic suicide not to integrate immigrants and not to invite people from elsewhere to come and work here. The Swedish economy is booming. People have moved around throughout human history. With some patience, and stable economic circumstances, it works; and if it doesn't work it has to be made to work, and that is a political task, it is for politicians to make it work.'

I had a great deal of sympathy with Jonsson's advocacy of silencing right-wing Scandinavian parties. I would prefer never to have to listen to another self-satisfied snake-oil salesman from the Danish People's Party scaremongering on television about *de mørke mennesker* or *de sorte* ('those dark people', 'the blacks') again.

The Danish People's Party's rhetoric on Muslims over the last ten years has made Enoch Powell's 'Rivers of Blood' speech sound like a nursery rhyme. Prominent members have, variously, claimed that Islam is not a religion but a 'terrorist organisation' and compared Muslims to Nazis; they have received suspended sentences for waving banners depicting Muslims as rapists and gang members; and claimed that Muslims were infiltrating Europe with the ultimate intention of killing us all. Just today, for instance, I read in a Danish newspaper this quote from the party's integration spokesman, Martin Henriksen: 'There is a tendency for unpleasant situations to occur when many Muslims are gathered in one place,' he said (remind me again, Martin, how many people visit Mecca during Ramadan? How many arrests are there? And your job is what, exactly?). Concerned for my blood pressure, my wife used to make me leave the room whenever the party's founder and former leader, a shrill, elfin woman called Pia Kjærsgaard, appeared on the TV screen. Kjærsgaard's bon mots have included 'There is only one civilisation, and it is ours', and the claim, in a party newsletter in 2001, that Muslims 'lie, cheat and deceive'.

One expects bile and lies from these kinds of people, but what has been even more dismaying has been the way in which their bigotry has infected the broader political discourse in Denmark, to the extent that even centrist parties routinely generalise negatively about immigrants and Muslims. One of the most pernicious aspects of this is the widespread use of the terms 'new-' or 'second-generation' to describe Danes, Swedes, Finns or Norwegians who hold legitimate passports for their countries; in many cases were born in those countries; pay taxes in those countries; vote in those countries; and contribute to those societies in so many ways, yet who are, you know, not *really* one of them. People who are, well, how to put it, a bit *darker*. Could you imagine anyone in the US referring to people as 'second-generation Americans', or even British politicians talking of 'New Britons'?

On the other hand, 'leave it to the politicians' – which is essentially what Jonsson is saying – sounds pretty feeble and, like it or not, the Danish People's Party, and to a lesser extent the Sweden Democrats, do speak for a significant proportion of their respective populations. And what of freedom of speech? Shouldn't the right wing be allowed to make fools of themselves like every other politician? Isn't the electorate grown up enough to make up their own minds? That was certainly the case with the buffoonish leader of the British National Party in the run-up to the last general election.

The simple fact is that trying to pretend the Sweden Democrats do not exist has not worked as far as their popular vote is concerned: the party was more successful than ever at the last election, scoring 5.7 per cent of the votes, enough to win them twenty seats in parliament.

It was time to put my money where my liberal, free-speech mouth was, and go and meet the Sweden Democrats in their new lair.

'We would lower immigration by approximately 90 per cent,'

Sweden Democrat spokesman Eric Myrin told me when I met him in their plush new offices close to the Swedish parliament (the *Riksdag*). 'Especially when it comes to asylum seekers and close-to-kin immigration, which is one of the biggest groups coming in today. Basically, if you own a pizza shop you can bring more relatives from Somalia to make pizzas, and there is no stop to it now.'

Ah, the well-known scourge of the Somali pizza chef. Like his smooth-talking leader Jimmie Åkesson, Myrin was young and smart and spouted his anti-immigrant rhetoric as if it were the mildest statement of fact. I had come expecting to meet pale, sinister-looking men in long black leather coats and round wire glasses (and, actually, there was someone precisely fitting that description sitting in the corner, monitoring our conversation), but Myrin was dressed in dark jeans and a jacket, like any other aspiring middle-way Scandinavian politician.

Myrin continued in this vein, ranting about segregated public swimming pools and lax sentencing, and claiming that Swedish courts allowed immigrants to beat their children 'because it's their culture to beat their kids'.

'Immigrants pick on Swedes for no reason whatsoever because they know they can dominate them, because they are more aggressive. They are more prone to violence than the Swedes. I experienced it in school, and my friends experienced it.' He claimed that immigrants had a 'completely different way of regarding human life.' But didn't the Swedes also have quite a track record of being a bit 'fighty'? Was he not not familiar with the Thirty Years War, for example?*

'Yeah, yeah, of course we did wars, but—'

'You rampaged across Europe.'

---

* Under the notoriously bloodthirsty Gustaf II Adolf, Sweden fielded what was at the time the largest army in the world – 90,000 soldiers – and commenced a three-decades-long campaign of slaughter and rape across Central Europe that is said to have resulted in a greater number of deaths, proportional to the population of the time, than the two World Wars combined, or the plague. One Swedish journalist proudly told me that Austrian grandmothers still warn their grandchildren, 'Be nice, *mein Kind*, otherwise the Swede will come and get you.'

'Sure, yeah, things change.'

'And,' I added. 'I might be a bit cross if I was, say, an Iranian refugee, and the Swedish authorities herded me into a ghetto with no chance of getting a job or building a future, and people like you branded me a threat and a menace. I might not react all that well either.'

'If you come to Sweden you have absolutely no reason to be pissed off at anything. If you come to Sweden you get everything, you get health care, you get education. You can learn Swedish, you have every single opportunity.'

Sweden accepts around 100,000 immigrants a year, he told me, aghast. But I happened to have taken a closer look at the figures, and knew how many actually *leave* Sweden each year. Was Myrin aware of the figure for emigrants? I wondered.

He shifted in his seat. 'It's about fifty thousand.'

'So, actually, net immigration is fifty thousand.'

'Yes, well, it's not just about figures,' he said. 'It's about who they are.'

'But the Swedish economy is doing well, you need the labour force, don't you?'

'They've been saying that for forty years, and every year we have had unemployment at 10 per cent.'

'Which would suggest there is a fixed level of unemployment, irrespective of the level of immigration . . .'

There seemed little point in getting bogged down in statistics – Myrin was hardly likely to have a Damascene epiphany and run off to join the Social Democrats in the office next door – so I asked him about the media's exclusion of his party in the run-up to the last election.

'Yes, the media has been extremely anti our party, with editorials talking about sending us to concentration camps and stuff,' he said. 'They do not allow us to advertise. We have been stigmatised; politically, no one will cooperate with us.'

I wondered out loud if this perhaps had something to do with their infamous election ad, which was banned in Sweden but is, of course, available on YouTube, thus rendering the ban not only futile but lending the film an illicit thrill. It depicted a herd of hijab-clad women barging past an elderly ethnic Swedish woman to reach a table where money was being handed out by politicians, the implication being that the latter were suffering financially in Sweden's welfare redistribution. Or, perhaps it was because the party was, as Jonsson had pointed out, originally (and under a previous name) formed by neo-Nazis, and that from time to time photographs surface of their members in Nazi uniform. Had Myrin ever dressed up in a Nazi uniform to mark Hitler's birthday, as members of his party had been exposed as doing? I wondered.

'We don't really have a neo-Nazi past in that sense,' he bristled. 'We've had members we didn't know were Nazis, but the party has never been racist.'

I left the *Riksdag* deeply depressed that so many Swedes had voted for the kinds of people who believe that foreigners are intrinsically more violent and aggressive than they are. I was beginning to sympathise with the Swedish intelligentsia's conspiracy of silence.

On a positive note, there is always a chance that the Sweden Democrats might disappear without trace by the next election, although that is looking increasingly unlikely. Their popularity began to slip in the polls almost immediately after the election as it rapidly became apparent they hadn't the first idea of how to operate as a grown-up party on a national scale, but as I write, in mid-2013, in the last few months they have surged once more and are now approaching the 10 per cent mark. This is despite a number of scandals that have vividly exposed the party's racist underbelly, not least an incident that saw one of their MPs, Lars Isovaara, being disciplined by the leadership after falsely claiming that he had been robbed by immigrants (he had left his possessions in a restaurant) and then oinking like a pig and spitting at a security guard whom he believed to be a Muslim. It does not require a great leap of imagination to assume this is how most of his colleagues in the party would like to behave if they thought they could get away with it.

The historic precedent is hopeful though: a previous right-wing party that had even greater success in Sweden in the early nineties disappeared as quickly as it had emerged.

We can but hope.

Chapter 7

The party

Sweden is a totalitarian state: discuss.

No, really, I am serious. I was beginning to think that the Danish newspaper editor Anne Knudsen was on to something when she had used that word, albeit tentatively, to describe Sweden. My dictionary defines totalitarianism as 'a form of government that includes control of everything under one authority, and allows no opposition,' and for much of the twentieth century Sweden was effectively a one-party state, the party being the Social Democrats. They regulated every aspect of their dutiful, acquiescent citizens' lives, doing their utmost to ensure adherence to the prescribed modern, progressive social norms. Of course Sweden was no Soviet Union – its wealth was generally distributed much more fairly, and the goods and services offered to its citizens were of a far higher quality. It is not as if Herr and Fru Svensson had their property confiscated and were sent to work in the salt mines with half a turnip to gnaw on. Instead of potato queues and Trabants, the Swedes were rewarded for their collective compliance with a kind of modern, secular Valhalla.

They called it *Folkhemmet* (the 'People's Home'). It was the most generous, progressive and extensive welfare state in the world. *Folkhemmet* ensured its citizens never went hungry or homeless, that they were cared for when they were sick, and provided for when they grew old. For much of the twentieth century the Swedes enjoyed full employment, some of the highest wages in the world, ample national holidays, and unprecedented economic prosperity. Not much to kick against there. Perhaps, then, 'benign totalitarianism' might be a better term.

I was rather pleased with myself for coming up with this notion of benign totalitarianism, until I discovered that the great Polar author Roland Huntford had described Sweden in precisely those terms as long ago as 1971, painting a picture in his book *The New Totalitarians* of the country as a socialist dystopia in which personal freedoms, ambition and humanity had been sacrificed to the Social Democrats' ideals. 'Modern Sweden has fulfilled Huxley's specifications for the new totalitarianism,' he wrote. 'A centralised administration rules people who love their servitude.'

In the 1980s, the German author Hans Magnus Enzensberger had spotted something of this too, describing in his book *Europe, Europe* how the Swedish government regulated 'the affairs of individuals to a degree unparalleled in other free societies', and had gradually eroded not just its citizens' rights, but also somehow crushed their spirit: 'It really looked as if the Social Democrats . . . had succeeded in taming the human animal where other quite different regimes, from theocracy to Bolshevism, had failed,' he writes. 'Anyone who opposes the Social Democrats tends to apologise for his stance, often without noticing it.'

Enzensberger was referring to the extraordinary levels of conformity and consensus he had observed during a general election, but also the fact that the Swedish Social Democrats had enjoyed a virtually unchallenged stranglehold on power for most of the twentieth century. They made General Franco look like a dilettante, the Soviet Communist Party mere fly-by-nights. The Social Democrats grabbed the keys to the *Riksdag* in 1920 and held on to them, virtually uninterrupted, from 1932 to 1976. They lost power briefly, but then took it back for another fifteen years before the end of the last century. It was not until 2010 that a non-Social Democratic government – the current Moderate coalition, led by bald role model Fredrik Reinfeldt – was voted in for a second term.

Hand in hand with the unions (until recently, if you joined one of the larger Swedish unions, you automatically became a member of the Social Democratic party), and together with a small group of industrialists, the party set wages and ensured that Swedish industry was almost completely free from labour disputes (at least up until the national strikes of 1980). As payback for such a compliant workforce, the government implemented some of the most stringent labour market regulations in the world (still to this day it is inordinately difficult and costly for Swedish companies to sack anyone); the most generous unemployment benefits; and by 1975 had made it compulsory for union representatives to sit on the boards of all companies. True to the totalitarian template, Social Democrats dominated the judiciary, ran the state television and radio broadcasting monopolies, and guided Swedish culture through the influence of extensive government arts funding. 'At the turn of the century, the majority of bishops, generals, directors general, university professors and ambassadors were Social Democrats or sympathisers,' writes veteran Swedish journalist Ulf Nilson in his book *What Happened to Sweden?*

There were few aspects of the Swedes' lives that their government did not strive to control, including their pay, how they raised their children, how much they drank, what they watched on TV, how much holiday they took, and their views on the Vietnam War. And the Swedes, it seems, were the most willing of puppets, 'world record-holders in docility', as Enzensberger puts it.

One famous, and in its way really quite magnificent, example of the Swedish population's malleability is that, when the government decided, on the night of 3 September 1967, to switch from driving on the right to driving on the left, they promptly did so without so much as a honked horn. It was also decided that the formal Swedish mode of address, *ni* (their equivalent of the French *vous*) was undemocratic and should cease to be used (the laid-back Danes let their equivalent, *de*, drift out of common usage). In a similar vein, the Swedes have been mulling over abolishing gender-specific pronouns – the Swedish equivalents of 'he' or 'she' (*han* and *hon*) – the concern being that they contribute to negative gender stereotyping. The idea is that everyone should be referred to as *hen*, regardless of their gender – one Stockholm kindergarten recently made *hen* the mandatory pronoun. Elsewhere, I recently read – and I am not making this up – that members of Sörmland

County Council had passed a motion, so to speak, to insist that men working for the local council should urinate sitting down, with the ultimate aim of making their public toilets genderless.

Reading about all this you get a sense of the almost *religious* fervour with which the Social Democrats went about dreaming up and implementing their radical policies. They do seem to have been on a kind of modernist crusade. No figure epitomised this self-righteous, finger-wagging approach more than the Social Democratic prime minister of the seventies and eighties, Olof Palme.

'To the outside world, in so far as it noticed him, he stood for everything about the country's pious, leftist internationalism,' writes Andrew Brown. 'Within the country, he symbolised the arrogance and sense of entitlement of the Social Democratic estab-lishment better than anyone else. They had inherited a poor, patri-archal, and formal society, and turned it into a rich, feminist, and fiercely egalitarian one.'

Olof Palme was born into an aristocratic, land-owning family but, after travelling in the United States and being shocked by the inequality he discovered there, he returned to Sweden in the late 1950s and joined the Social Democrats. He became a protegé of Tage Erlander – the longest-serving prime minister Sweden has ever had – eventually replacing him in that post in 1969. Under Palme, Sweden's welfare system expanded exponentially in the fields of health care, childcare, housing, care for the elderly and much more, and taxes rose to cover the costs and redistribute Sweden's fast-growing wealth. Palme was famously proactive, some might say 'preachy', on the international stage, cleverly spinning Sweden's neutrality into a posi-tion from which he would moralise at length on international conflicts, marching alongside the North Vietnamese ambassador to Sweden in protest against the American war there, and welcoming three hundred deserters from the US military (prompting Henry Kissinger to wonder aloud why the Swedes had not been roused to make similar protests against the Nazis in 1940).

After his American epiphany, Palme strove to foster a man-of-the-people image; even when he became prime minister he still lived with his wife, Lisbet, in a humdrum terraced house in Stockholm, eschewing the fripperies of power such as limousines and body-guards. These 'man of the people' poses would turn out to have fatal consequences.

At around midnight on 28 February 1986, as the Palmes were walking home from the cinema, an unknown assailant fired several shots at them, injuring Lisbet but killing Palme. The shock to this peaceful nation of having its prime minister gunned down in the street is hard to overestimate, indeed Palme's murder still resonates among an entire generation of Scandinavians. As historian Tony Griffiths writes: 'Sweden suffered a collective nervous breakdown.'

The trauma was compounded by the fact that the Swedish police were exposed as hopelessly amateurish in the aftermath of the assassination, failing to set up roadblocks on the night and taking for ever to charge someone over the murder. Eventually, a junkie, Christer Pettersson, who had previously served time for killing a man with a bayonet but had been released after serving just a few years, was found guilty of Palme's murder. He was later acquitted on appeal and the case remains technically unsolved to this day. Rumours have since swirled that the assassination was the work of either the CIA or the KGB (indeed, it is indicative of the fine-edged, some would say hypocritical, foreign policy line Palme walked that both had motive enough), although Petterson, who died in 2004, confessed on several occasions and is generally believed to have been guilty.

Historian Henrik Berggren has written a highly acclaimed biography of Palme. I probably should have realised that anyone who spends years writing a biography is likely to have a positive approach to their subject, but for some reason this didn't enter my head when I shared my thoughts about Palme: from what I had read about him, I said, he seemed at worst a kind of preachy ideologue, at best naive.

'I don't think he was naive at all,' Berggren replied. 'He was actually quite unusual for a Swede in that he was rather hard and pragmatic, a wily politician, actually. He was like Bobby Kennedy, someone who could be very moral, but totally ruthless in pursuing his political thoughts. Palme did two things: he thought the Vietnam war was a total catastrophe and used his position as PM of Sweden to maximise critical impact on the US; at the same time he was very concerned about Swedish neutrality and defence and wanted us to be able to defend ourselves against the Soviet Union, so he upheld connections with the US to get technology, and with NATO. Some Swedes have a very tough time dealing with the fact that Palme was both. The right wing say, okay, he didn't collapse our relationship with the US, but that could have happened, he was playing with fire, while the left call him a total hypocrite . . . He was part of a whole generation – like Trudeau [Pierre Trudeau, former PM of Canada] – of aristocratic radicals in the sixties who came from the technocratic class, were self-confident, a bit arrogant, but embraced radical ideas.'

When I was in Stockholm I also caught up with Ulf Nilson, the veteran journalist who has been a correspondent and columnist for Swedish newspapers since the 1950s. As Nilson will proudly tell you, he has met every US president from Johnson to the latest Bush along the way. He knew Palme personally and agrees with Berggren that, beneath the ideology, he was a most pragmatic politician.

'We were actually fairly good friends,' Nilson told me. 'I travelled all over the world covering him and every time we met he would say, "Your father was a stonecutter," approvingly. To him, I was noble, from a noble family, because he had this romantic idea about the pure worker. He was actually an aristocrat, from a slightly noble family. He wanted to convert everybody but of course he used his power in millions of dirty ways – he was, after all, a politician. They've got to dirty their hands, otherwise they can't exist.'

Nilson calls himself a 'Swedish dissident'; he is no fan of the Social Democrats and never has been. He left Sweden in 1968 and hasn't lived there since, but visits regularly. I wondered what he thought about my Swedish totalitarianism theory.

'In a sense it is totalitarian,' he agreed as we sat in the canteen at the offices of the newspaper for which he is a columnist, *Expressen*. 'Of course, you can't compare it to Nazi Germany or North Korea, it isn't as bad as that, but there is a creeping totalitarianism which is defined as conforming, to do like others. Nobody really questions the kind of society we have, that's what I dislike so much about Sweden. Indoctrination is what you would call it.'

Åke Daun would seem to agree, writing in *Swedish Mentality* that 'All deviance from group norms and common group patterns is potentially threatening to the individual.' But when I asked him about Swedish totalitarianism he rejected my theory: 'I don't buy that description, no. We didn't experience it as something that was coming from the top. It was a modern state and that's how a modern state should be organised, in all its details.'

Rather than totalitarianism, both Berggren and Daun perceived a different force at work in Sweden over the last hundred years: modernism. 'Swedes are not interested in history,' Daun told me. 'Swedes look at their country as modern.'

Henrik Berggren compared his country's approach to the UK's: 'The way Britain deals with modernity is fascinating. You are not modernists. This is the great difference. I find it very appealing that in Britain the argument "this is modern" is not going to trump everything else the way it does in Sweden. But, on the other hand, you realise that at some point you need to make a push into the modern. Britain resisted that and has been stuck with a lot of old, not very well-functioning, systems.'

But still, how did the Swedes allow one party to exercise such immense power and impose such radical policies for so long, relieving them of such a large chunk of their earnings in the process? I am aware that a transparent democratic process took place every few years in which they *elected* the Social Democrats, but as they slowly watched their rights and freedoms being eroded, and felt the long tentacles of the state rummaging around for any remaining tax kronor hidden in their underwear, did the Swedish people never once say 'Enough is enough'? Or, were they like the proverbial frog in a pan of cold water, oblivious to the incremental temperature change as they were brought slowly to a rolling boil?

As a child, when I read about the Berlin Wall I used to wonder,

'It must have taken the East German authorities ages to build it, how come the Berliners didn't rise up and stop them?' Had the Swedes experienced a similar kind of collective torpor when faced with the gradual, but unprecedented, expansion of their centralised state and its interference in their lives? Did they never feel the tentacles?

Chapter 8

Guilt

If an animal kingdom simile is required – and when is it not? – then perhaps more apt than than likening the Swedes to frogs would be to say that they were the most diligent of worker bees, happy to toil for the good of the hive. But what made the Swedes such perfect subjects for benign totalitarianism?

Historically, several factors paved the way: the alleged Viking egalitarianism; Lutheranism, with its emphasis on collective sacrifice, social justice, equality, self-control and denial; a comparatively weak feudal system; high levels of centralisation from the sixteenth century onwards; and the emergence of the trade union and cooperative movements. Above all, Sweden had a far larger landless peasant population than, say, Denmark, and a far greater concentration of wealth in a small number of rich landowners – it was a society ripe for what you might call, if you wanted to annoy some socialists, collective social vengeance.

So the hungry, dutiful populace was ready to be shaped and guided by an unholy trinity: the extraordinary and lasting accord between the Social Democrats, the Swedish Trade Union Confederation (LO) and the Employers Association (SAF). The role of the latter was especially remarkable. Its core was made up of fewer than twenty families, prime among them the industrialist–banking family, the Wallenbergs. These three entities – the Social Democratic government, the unions and the company owners – would cooperate to a remarkable degree over the coming decades on matters such as wage levels, childcare provision, women's rights, employment law, economic policy, and even foreign policy, allowing some of the most progressive social innovations the world has ever seen to be imposed upon a broadly accepting (baa!) Swedish public. As T. K. Derry writes of Sweden's history of industrial action, 'The Swedish record is quite outstanding: with a total labour force approaching four million it experienced five years in which the average loss of working days was no more than five thousand, and in one of these years the figure fell to four hundred.'

Modernity became the golden carrot dangled in front of Sweden's citizens by its ruling powers. Initially led by the four-time prime minister, Per Albin Hansson, then by his successor, Tage Erlander (who held the post for a total of twenty-three years), and then Palme, the Swedes were encouraged to cast off their old ways and move as one towards the light. If something was deemed modern, it was good. A rational, enlightened country such as Sweden had no need for folklore and buckled shoes, for rituals and community customs. Trade unions were modern. Collectivism was modern. Neutrality was modern. Economic and gender equality were modern. Universal suffrage was modern. Divorce was modern. The welfare state was modern. Eventually multiculturalism and mass immigration were deemed modern. Spending an hour every Sunday morning listening to a second-rate theology graduate wearing an over-sized ruff that looked like a slide projector was not modern. Neither, for that matter, was nationalism – the Swedish national anthem does not once mention the word 'Sweden'.

For me, the most extraordinary role in this supposedly socialistic, redistributive society was played by the company bosses. Even when Sweden skirted perilously close to outright socialism with the mooted Wage-earner Funds (effectively a way for the workers to eventually take over the means of production, a concept *Tribune* magazine called at the time 'one of the purest socialist proposals that has ever found its way into an election manifesto'), these wealthy, reclusive capitalist families were right there, if not actually holding the reins of power, then at least advising the driver. The Wallenbergs, Sweden's most prominent and powerful old-money family (equivalent in many ways to Denmark's Møller–Mærsk shipping dynasty, and comparably significant to Sweden's GDP) became so intertwined with the country's government that, at one point during the Second World War, Jacob Wallenberg, who had by that point inherited the company with his brother Marcus, handled national trade negotiations with the Nazis. Later the Wallenbergs were business partners with the government in founding Sweden's ambitious nuclear programme. At its height, the company employed almost of a fifth of all private sector workers (around 180,000 Swedes).

All three factions in Sweden's ruling triumvirate benefitted hugely from the country's extensive collaboration and trade with the Nazis during the Second World War. The Swedes had been selling iron to the Germans since the fourteenth century and clearly saw no reason to stop.

'Until the time of Stalingrad, [Sweden] seemed to be neutral, firmly on the Nazi side,' writes Andrew Brown. 'Swedish volunteers went to fight in Finland against the communists, and German troops and supplies were allowed to transit the Swedish railway system. After Stalingrad, Sweden was decisively neutral on the winning side. This was long and very bitterly resented, especially in Norway.' Ulf Nilson agrees, describing his homeland as 'an extension of Germany's war industry' up until at least 1943.

Thanks to this ruthless pragmatism Sweden, the serene swan, sailed through the 1939–45 conflict – during which its GNP rose by 20 per cent – and in the decades that followed its wealth grew to match that of the US in per capita terms. But its reputation was permanently tarnished by its often personal connections to Nazi Germany (Hermann Göring was married to a Swede, for example). As Norway's King Haakon put it at the time: 'There must be no more talk of Sweden as the big brother.'

I bring up the Second World War here not to rub the Swedes' noses in it (okay, perhaps just a bit), but because their post-war economic and social miracle would not have been possible without the devastation and subsequent rebuilding of much of the rest of Europe. Sweden's neutrality left it unscathed, placing it in a prime position to exploit Europe's rapid, Marshall Plan-fuelled growth. As a result, for some years afterwards, Sweden had the fastest-growing economy in the world after Japan's.

The Swedes seem to have taken a collective, unspoken decision to avoid reflection on their conduct between 1939 and 1945, but the writer Sean French, who is half Swedish, feels that in burying their guilt about their betrayal of their Nordic neighbours during the Second World War, and about their extensive trade with the Nazis to the direct cost of Allied lives, the Swedes have paid the price in the longer term: 'After the war, the agreement that they would go for growth, retain a national consensus and, tacitly, bury the past, worked very well. But it's left a kind of scar . . . And in order to achieve that success it gave up division: so there's agreement, or apparent agreement, on everything.' Though you could argue that Sweden is no longer fully neutral, participating as it does in international peace-keeping missions, French also points out the brazen hypocrisy of a country which has a 'huge commitment to peace and neutrality while at the same time fostering a huge arms industry', Sweden is the world's eighth largest arms exporter.

As historian Tony Hall writes in *Scandinavia: At War with Trolls*, 'The collective weight of Swedish shame built up slowly – shame for not helping the Finns was replaced by shame for turning their backs on the Norwegians, for not standing up against the Germans, for sending some Balts to certain death – until shame and guilt seemed to be the natural state of the Swedish conscience.'

I asked the historian Henrik Berggren about the Swedes' war guilt, or lack of it. One of my more outlandish theories was that the Swedes' ostentatious political correctness, in particular with regard to their openness to immigration and multiculturalism, was a manifestation of this repressed guilt: they realised they had let us all down, and were now trying to make up for it. Surprisingly, for once he agreed with me.

'Yes, it is war guilt, I think so,' he said. 'Because prosperity in general in moral people does tend to create a sense of guilt. If you have a lot and someone else has a little you get guilty anyway, if you are of the Protestant persuasion.'

'Or if you have gotten rich off the back of others' misery.'

'Quite. I think the war really, as you say, compounds the guilt very much. I think Sweden felt we had a little bit of a mission trying to deal with this. I mean, I think we apologised to the Norwegians and the Danes, but it was very superficial, token stuff.'

Looking beyond the Second World War, if we can ignore the Swedes' role in Hitler's expansionism then, considering they achieved such a consistently high standard of living, admirable levels of gender and economic equality, and built a compassionate welfare state, is it really a problem that their country might have veered towards just a *teensy* bit of totalitarianism from time to time?

Well, yes. Particularly if, for instance, you were one of the sixty thousand Swedish women – mostly working-class – who were forcibly sterilised or coerced into being sterilised between 1935 and 1976 during the country's unfortunate eugenics misadventure.

As early as 1922 the Swedes had an Institute for Racial Biology, in Uppsala. A leading Swedish politician at the time, Arthur Engberg, wrote: 'We have the good fortune to belong to a race that is so far relatively unspoiled, a race that is the bearer of very high and very good qualities,' adding that it was about time they protected said superior race. Such views led to the sterilisation of 'lesser' specimens in a programme which, according to one commentator, was 'second only to [those of] Nazi Germany'. The two regimes shared the same goal: the purification of a race of tall, blond, blue-eyed people. In 1934, laws were strengthened so that women deemed 'inferior' were sterilised against their will, along with male juvenile delinquents. Even in 1945, after the world had become aware of what the Nazis had been up to, 1,747 Swedes were sterilised, and in 1947 the figure had *increased* to 2,264. 'How could men like Per Albin Hansson* . . . and Tage Erlander condone, indeed order, this shockingly undemocratic, cruel, and unfair program?' asks Ulf Nilson in his book *What Happened to Sweden?*

---

* Still a national hero in Sweden, Hansson allowed the movement of around a million Nazis through the country's territory during the Second World War.

'The answer is quite simple,' he continues. 'They really thought that by eliminating the inferior unborn, a cleaner, healthier race would gradually be produced.'

During the sixties and seventies the Swedish state also became notorious around the world for the large numbers of children it took into care, sometimes for apparently spurious, even ideological, reasons. When it was revealed that Sweden's Orwellian-sounding Child Welfare Board had proportionately taken more children into care than any other foreign country, journalist Brita Sundberg-Weitman wrote: 'This is a country where the authorities can forcibly separate a child from its parents to prevent them from giving it a privileged upbringing.' According to the UK-based Tetra Pak heiress and publisher of *Granta* magazine, Sigrid Rausing, the Swedish state 'created a society of conformity and concrete, state surveillance'; 'took excessive numbers of children into care'; created schools that were 'joyless and mediocre'; and secretly monitored communists. The Swedish state was, she writes, 'a repressive machinery where individual rights were potentially sacrificed to powerful social norms'.

Nor would the totalitarian question have been academic for those Swedes unfortunate enough to be diagnosed with HIV at a time when their government was seriously considering forcible quarantine for people with the condition. Or, today, if you are transgender and want your new gender to be recognised, but aren't prepared to be sterilised as Swedish law currently requires, despite a ruling by the European Council pointing out that this violates human rights. Or if you are a Swedish mother and want to stay at home with your young child, but find yourself accused of being old fashioned, a traitor to feminism. Or, simply, if you find it a disincentive to offer up more than three quarters of your wages to politicians in the form of direct and indirect taxes (as the saying goes, 'Swedish people are born free but taxed to death').

Opponents could have disagreed, of course, put their heads above the parapet, but that is not the Swedish way. As the authors of *Modern-Day Vikings*, Christina Johansson Robinowitc and Lisa Werner Carr write: in Sweden 'life can be difficult for those who do not "cooperate".' Until relatively recently, a Swede who felt they had been denied their basic rights had little recourse for appeal in the Swedish courts, which were unable to address claims against Swedish law. While social rights were elevated, civic rights were comparatively weak, particularly at the height of Social Democratic rule – individuals had to go to the European Court of Human Rights if they felt they had a significant case against the authorities.

'The individual was more and more dependent on the state and municipal administration, the unions, the associations, and the officials. In other words: the system,' writes Ulf Nilson.

Henrik Berggren – who will hate me for placing him again in the 'defender of Sweden' role here, but he does a convincing job – concedes that the Swedish state still has extraordinary influence over the lives of its citizens, but argues that it exercises its powers with transparency and compassion: 'Yes you are transferring an enormous amount of power to the state, but it depends how the state uses that power. Now, most of the time the state has used that power benevolently, and has respected human rights and things like that. It does not follow logically that you are going to sterilise people because you have a welfare system. The problem is that you transfer so much power to the state that a certain idea can gain a power and momentum.'

Everything I read about the Swedish Social Democratic government of the last century suggested an organisation that was driven by one single, overarching goal: to sever the traditional, some would say natural, ties between its citizens, be they those that bound children to their parents, workers to their employers, wives to their husbands, or the elderly to their families. Instead, individuals were encouraged – mostly by financial incentive or disincentive, but also through legislation, propaganda and social pressure – to 'take their place in the collective', as one commentator rather ominously put it, and become dependent on the government.

Berggren has a slightly different spin on the Swedish state and its role in its citizens' lives: rather than meddling and controlling, in his provocatively titled book *Är svensken människa?* (*Is the Swede a Human?*)

he and his co-author Lars Trägårdh argue that the real aim of the Swedish government was to *liberate* its citizens from each other, to set them free and allow them to become fully autonomous, independent entities in charge of their own destinies. Far from being the collectivist sheep their neighbours perceive them to be, Berggren and Trägårdh argue that the Swedes are 'hyper individualists' – more so even than the Americans – and that they are 'devoted to the pursuit of personal autonomy'.

I found this theory a little confusing at first: the idea that the most collectivist, conformist, consensus-orientated people in Scandinavia were in fact driven by a rampant, American-style individualism sounded, frankly, wrong.

'The point we are making is not to be confused with being unconventional, or to do with independent thinking,' explained Berggren. 'We are talking about autonomy in terms of not being dependent on other people.

'The Swedish system is best understood not in terms of socialism, but in terms of Rousseau,' he continued, generously assuming that I knew the slightest thing about Rousseau. 'Rousseau was an extreme egalitarian and he really hated any kind of dependence – depending on other people destroyed your integrity, your *authenticity* – therefore the ideal situation was one where every citizen was an atom separated from all the other atoms . . . The Swedish system's logic is that it is dangerous to be dependent on other people, to be beholden to other people. Even to your family.'

But isn't family a *nice* thing?

'Yes, dependence is sort of the natural condition of human beings. So I think that's where you get some of the negative aspects that come from giving so much power to the state,' admitted Berggren. Nevertheless he generally felt that when it came to the Swedish state's role in people's lives, the ends justified the means. He gave an example.

'When I talk about this to US college students, halfway through they say, "But that's horrible, you are saying you become dependent on the state," and I say, "But look, okay, when you go to college how do you pay tuition?" And they say, "We have to apply for finance." I ask them, "Well, what are the conditions for you to get financing?" "Well, it depends on my family." "Ah, so if you have rich parents then they have to pay for you. But what if you have parents who don't agree with what you want to study? It sounds like you are pretty dependent on your parents." This is not the kind of problem we have. We can study anything we want to. It's a small example, but it's telling.'

Sweden's 'statist individualism', as he terms it, enables the very purest form of wholly independent love to blossom between two people. Wives don't stick around because their husband keeps the joint bank account pin code in a locked drawer in his desk, and husbands don't hold their tongues because their wife's father owns the mill. 'Authentic love and friendship is possible only between individuals who are independent and equal', he and Trägårdh write. So the Social Democrats are, in effect, über cupids.

Berggren pointed out that this is completely counter to the way they do things in Germany, for example, where state support is funnelled through the family and thus perpetuates the institution of the family, with the father at its head as the breadwinner. 'Sweden is set up differently. The main objective is not to be dependent on your family, the wife shouldn't be dependent on her husband, the children should be autonomous when they are eighteen, old people should not be dependent on their children taking care of them, and therefore to a large extent the state steps in and provides these things.'

'But,' I wondered, 'doesn't this just replace one dependency with another – the state – which takes us back to those concerns about totalitarianism?'

'We are not arguing that people are totally independent, because they are dependent on the state. One take is your totalitarian take, but I don't buy that. I think its a rather even trade-off. You can get an awful lot of autonomy by accepting a democratic state is actually furnishing you with the means to be autonomous in this way, and reach a certain self-realisation. I wouldn't take it to its extreme, too far and you do end up with a totalitarian state.

'For Americans and Brits the state is such a bogeyman, such a horrible menacing thing, and in the States now they can't even have a health system because they are so scared of the state. But the point here is not that the state is saying this is *how* you should live your life, but it is providing you with the support structure. Society is unequal and people don't have the same opportunities, but we are trying to lift everybody to the same level so they can achieve the same kind of freedom and self-realisation which only a small group could do previously.'

It seems to me that the problem with this form of social engineering is that it takes many of the Swedes' underlying characteristics, particularly their love of being alone and isolated, and really lets them run with it. Thus, today in Sweden most students live by themselves – not for them *Young Ones*-style squats; the Swedes have the highest divorce rate in the world (although some might look upon this as a positive, of course); the highest number of single-person households; and more of their elderly live alone than in any other country. It also reinforces the generally accepted notion – in Sweden – that one should be able to solve one's own problems. Swedes don't like to ask favours of each other: they keep their problems to themselves and suffer in silence. Being *duktig* is one facet of this: if you are *duktig* then you don't need any help, and as *duktighet* is the ultimate ideal for Swedes, to ask for help – or even to give it – is a kind of low-level social taboo.

Why are the Swedes so hell-bent on achieving self-sufficiency and independence? Why did these radical social changes – childcare, divorce, secularism – take hold in Sweden to such a great extent?

'I think that positive experiences of self-sufficiency played a part,' writes Daun. 'Self-sufficiency as a value may have existed for a long time, but because of a number of social changes it could only be expressed concretely in the 1960s. The same kinds of social changes in other countries – for example increased frequency of women wage-earners, better birth-control measures, diminished power of Church and tradition, less informal social control – have not had anything like the same impact. We may thus assume that Swedish couples, even before the 1960s – possibly long before – have related to each other with a greater emotional distance than have their counterparts in many other places in the world.'

In Sweden, self-sufficiency and autonomy is all; debt of any kind, be it emotional, a favour, or cash, is to be avoided at all cost. The Swedes don't even like to owe a round of drinks.

'Many Swedes seem to have a strong need for independence. It can express itself in a desire to be alone, to "avoid people", but also to avoid "being indebted",' writes Åke Daun. In one study cited in his book, 70 per cent of Swedes said that they could endure being separated from their friends for quite a long time. When the supposedly loner Finns were asked the same question, only 41 per cent said that they could sever contact with friends, and almost twice as many said that they become unhappy or depressed during such times of comradely separation. Daun's conclusion: 'Close and deep friendships are more important to Finns than they are to Swedes.'

Greta Garbo's 'I want to be alone' was no schtick. She meant it.

Swedish autonomy also seemed to me to be much more passive than the kind of independence the Americans strive for. It is not about achieving something, striking out on your own, grabbing life by the lapels and wringing every ounce of potential from it, it is about being able to get your teeth seen to on a regular basis, for spouses to be able to take separate holidays, or for pensioners to be free to decide what to have for dinner. As the authors of *Modern-Day Vikings* put it, 'The American wants the freedom to do, the Swede wants the freedom to be.' Of Olof Palme Andrew Brown writes witheringly, 'When he died, he left a country where no one was poor and no one had room for optimism.' In other words, in eradicating social ills, the Social Democratic party also smothered its people's motivation, ambition and spirit.

'I know why you say this, and this is at the heart of the book, you are perfectly right,' Berggren said when I expressed the same concerns about Scandinavian sameness – the stifling conformity, and so on – as I had to Richard Wilkinson when he and I had talked about Denmark. 'This is the point. I think there is a conformity involved here. It is usually much easier to be eccentric in a diverse society. I don't think Sweden will generate the kind of thinking that comes out of specific groups who develop a strong sensibility of the self, and own values and things like that; here it's a rather general conformism.'

So, Sweden is probably not a society in which eccentrics, oddballs, contrarians or nonconformists are likely to flourish. But there is one rather large segment of society for whom Sweden has been, and continues to be, a kind of paradise.

Chapter 9

Hairnets

Women's rights were a key element of the Social Democratic social revolution, as well as being central to their economic plan. Though women's suffrage came later to Sweden than the other Nordic countries (1921; the Finns like to remind their 'modern' neighbours that *their* women got the vote in 1906), and all the countries of the North can justifiably claim to be paragons of feminism, Swedish women have subsequently seen their position in society advance even more comprehensively thanks to a raft of policies concerning gender equality, childcare and positive discrimination.

For some years Sweden had a dedicated Ministry of Gender Equality (recently amalgamated with the Ministry of Education) charged with overseeing legislation aimed at eliminating discrimination in the workplace, bringing more women into the labour market and making sure that every advert for cleaning products featured a man with a mop and a bucket rather than a woman. Partly as a result, Sweden now has some of the most generous parental leave allowance in the world, with sixteen months' leave on 80 per cent of wages guaranteed by law, to be taken whenever the parents feel like it up until the child is eight years old. Two months of this are assigned exclusively to the father. 'Daddy leave', as it's known, was introduced in 1995 and today 85 per cent of Swedish fathers take advantage of it.

Newsweek magazine recently ranked Sweden second on its list of the best countries in the world in which to be a woman (after Iceland, where presumably the women have now removed all sharp objects from the reach of their men); and Save the Children placed it at number three on its 'best places to be a mother' list, after Norway and Iceland (with Denmark in fifth place). The latter ranking probably has much to do with the fact that Sweden has the cheapest childcare in terms of percentage of average wages in the Nordic region: it costs a little over a hundred pounds per month to park your little bundle of joy in a crèche (compared with five, or even ten, times that in the UK). By age twelve to eighteen months over 82 per cent of Swedish children are in day care, or *dagis* as it is known. The highest figure of its kind in the world.

The Swedes have never quite plucked up the courage to have a woman prime minister (unlike their Nordic peers), but almost half of Sweden's MPs and currently more than half of government ministers are women, making the British government look positively Arthurian. Swedish women's rights organisations are, however, still quick to remind us that they remain woefully under-represented in the higher echelons of the corporate world, and that women's pay still lags behind men's.

Meanwhile, Swedish men are reputedly the least chauvinistic in the world. A 2009 survey by the University of Oxford revealed that Swedish men help out more with household chores than men of any other nation. You might think the Swedish male's softer, more caring side would be another quality for the pros column, but not according to former Miss Sweden Anna Anka. In a newspaper interview she once described Sweden's 'velvet dads' – those stay-at-home fathers identifiable by the baby sick down their fronts and whip marks on their backs – as 'nappy-changing sissies'. She believes Swedish men could benefit from rediscovering some of their Viking forefathers' machismo.

This, as Finnish men will again point out with glee, has been one downside to Sweden's feminist revolution. As if all those Swedish soldiers clutching their make-up bags when the Russians rattled their sabres wasn't enough of an embarrassment for Swedish manhood, the shift in the gender balance towards greater equality seems to have emasculated them even further. Divested of their roles as the bread-winning protectors of the fairer sex, Swedish men have now been gelded to the extent that they struggle even to engage in the most basic interplay of the genders. Flirting, courting, pitching woo, call it what you will, this has now become a political minefield. I am told that Swedish men have been cowed by their ascendant womenfolk into discarding any pretence to gallantry or courtly manners. I have also heard this argument made in relation to Danish men, and one assumes it applies in Norway, too. According to the many Danish women I have spoken to about this (the poor creatures, we must assume, having been magnetically drawn to my unbridled British masculinity), courtly manners have no place in Scandinavian society. Their men have lost touch with their masculinity and in doing so relinquished their role in the art of seduction.

This is hardly the men's fault. In my experience old-fashioned chivalry is about as welcome among Scandinavian women as chastity belts. Hold a door open for a Danish woman in a department store in central Copenhagen, as I used to do before I knew better, and you risk a look either of baffled suspicion or outright hostility ('Don't you oppress me with your gallantry!'). The kind of gentlemanly manners expected in the UK or US bewilder and amuse Scandinavian women. At a restaurant with a group of Danes during the first year I moved here, I made the mistake of standing up when one of the female diners returned to the table. The conversation stopped and all those gathered stared at me expectantly. I tried to explain why I had done this in the middle of dessert but realised that, actually, I didn't really know (later, one of the other guests told me that they had all thought I was going to make a speech). Early on in our relationship, my wife found it hilarious that I would automatically walk on the outside of the pavement when I was with her, and always tried to outmanoeuvre me.

'I went into a meeting here at the office the other day, and I had a bad toe, and there were all these young men sitting around and not one of them offered me a seat. And I am their boss!' Danish newspaper editor Anne Knudsen told me. Her two sons have been brought up to show such courtesies, she said, but she did concede that there is an entire generation of Danish men who have been taught otherwise. 'A lot of men of my generation say they are afraid of taking on those old-fashioned roles. They come from that generation where they were slapped down for these kind of things and constantly taught that they were not good enough. The new generation just hasn't been brought up to know about it. They're just badly brought up.'

Meanwhile, foreign women who date Danish men wonder what they have done wrong when the men suggest sharing the bill at the end of the evening, and neglect to pay them compliments. Don't blame the poor man, that's how they've been raised, I tell them, laying my cape over an approaching puddle.

'It turned out he was actually quite keen on me,' said one English girl who dated a Dane (and eventually married him, I am happy to say) and was mystified by the fact that he would pass through doors in front of her, fail to get up when she entered a room and never give her gifts. 'But for ages I assumed he was either gay or somehow backward.'

You could argue there is another, more serious, cost to Sweden's state-led radical feminism than lots of misguided foreign men holding doors open like so many freelance concierges. The social and economic pressure on women to return to work soon after childbirth means that Scandinavian children tend to be enrolled in day care at a younger than average age (in Denmark almost a quarter of six-month-olds attend some kind of regular day care), and for more hours per day. Some observers have claimed that separation from the mother at a young age lays the foundation for a whole host of neuroses and anxieties in later life, as well as exacerbating the inherent tendency of Swedes towards independence and isolation. Could this 'abandonment' be one of the explanations for all those single-person households, for instance?

In his book *Suicide and Scandinavia* US psychiatrist Herbert Hendin observed that the Swedish approach tended to encourage independence in their children at a very early age. Swedish children were, he said, taught that to be dependent on another person – even one's own mother – is a failing. 'Children are encouraged to separate from their mothers early on, socially and psychologically,' agrees Åke Daun in *The Swedish Mentality*. 'They deny the existence of any such need and mask it behind an ostensible self-reliance.'

Ulf Nilson has also written of the pressures that Swedish women feel to conform to social norms by depositing their spawn at the kindergarten on their way to the office every morning: 'Feminists start to more or less criminalise women who want to stay at home with their toddlers rather than leave them in the nurseries.' But Daun suggests that the women are not so much pressurised into leaving their children as *escaping* from them. He quotes research that shows that, although Swedish women say they are forced to go back to work out of economic necessity, the truth is they are going back to their jobs because they find them more satisfying than staying at home with their children. As lovely as they are, newborns also possess an almost limitless capacity for being tedious; they can be challenging in all the wrong ways. So this desire to escape is quite understandable, but might it be just ever so *slightly* possible that the way in which Sweden has so wholeheartedly embraced day care from such an early age has had a negative effect on its children and, by extension, in the long run, Swedish society as a whole? Could this be part of the reason why Sweden suffers from comparatively high rates of juvenile delinquency and petty crime, for instance?

Few would go as far as Hendin and claim that Swedish mothers did 'not experience the same joy in being together with their children as mothers in certain other cultures' (after all, a certain class of English mother thinks nothing of packing her progeny off to boarding school at the age of eight), but he isn't the only one to have questioned the indecent rapidity with which Swedish society moves to separate its young from their parents.

Writing in the mid-1980s, child psychiatrist Marianne Cederblad commented: 'In Sweden we have . . . extreme expectations from an early age regarding self-sufficiency in children, and parents see the defiance of children during their refractory periods as positive and desirable.' In a similar vein, Daun quotes a proposal on after-school care written in the seventies by the National Board of Health and Welfare as stating its responsibility was to 'support the children in their release from close dependence upon adults'. I think it is safe to say the 'earth mother' is not a common Swedish archetype.

Am I the only one who finds it slightly chilling that the Swedish state believes it has an active role to play in the severance of children from their parents in what amounts to an institutionalisation of childhood? Shouldn't the process of a child's independence from its parents be a gradual, natural one, rather than something systematically imposed from birth by some or other ministry? One instinctively recoils when one hears about children being guided towards 'taking their place in the collective', as one commentator put it. Or am I just being old-fashioned or, probably worse in Scandinavian eyes, warped by my Anglocentric attachment to the primacy of family?

'I'm not really uncomfortable with that,' says Henrik Berggren when I voice my concerns about the Swedish childcare model. 'I can see why you might be, but I think that the idea of emancipation of women is very strong on all fronts. Look at Germany where women have to choose between work or having children and they can't do both.'

Some would argue that you can't.

'Well, right, but I see a lot of women doing it.'

But, if I may play the bigoted, chauvinistic dinosaur for a moment longer (a stretch, but I'll give it a go), I also see a lot of families struggling and the children paying the price.

'Well then, you should ask the fathers, what are they doing to help?' says Berggren. 'There is an American sociologist, David Popenoe, who wrote a book in the eighties which was really critical [of Sweden], and said essentially what you are saying – Swedish mothers were bad leaving their children in day care all day, that it was an inhuman horrible society. He is a very nice guy, I like him a lot, but he is a traditional American conservative who likes family values. He revisited Sweden a couple of years ago and wrote this really interesting piece which said "Okay, I have some problems with this idea of the family, but when I look at children in Sweden and the United States, studies show that in Sweden children spend much more time with their parents than they do in the US, and children are better, happier, every statistic is basically better." He doesn't like divorces – on that point Sweden is bad – but on all other points Sweden is a family-values society. It's a society that takes far better care of its children than America does.'

UNICEF agrees; it recently awarded Sweden more first places in its child well-being survey than any other country (Denmark and Finland were second and third), including in the categories of 'material well-being', 'health and safety', and 'behaviours and risks'. But, tellingly in terms of my isolation theory, Swedish kids performed notably poorly in terms of 'family and peer relationships' – they were ranked fifteenth – and not all that well in 'educational well-being' (eighth place – that'll be all those schools where they write their own timetables).

Of course no one has the patent on parenting, and there are many, many approaches to raising children. Who is to argue that the Swedes haven't hit upon the optimum strategy? Not me. I took my son to see Santa in the middle of summer, so I am hardly in a position to judge.

And who is to argue with the goal of gender equality? Sweden's economy has undoubtedly benefited from encouraging more women into the labour market and, as time passes, their presence there reinforces this as the norm. If I were a woman I know where I'd want to live.

Chapter 10

Class

I think it is fair to say that in the rest of the world, as far as they are thought of at all, the Scandinavian countries are broadly perceived as democratic, meritocratic, egalitarian and classless, populated by vaguely outdoorsy, blond, liberal, bicycle-riding folk who live in tastefully lit middle-class homes with Bang & Olufsen TVs in their living rooms, mid-range German estate cars in their driveways (Passat, not Mercedes), who holiday in Spain and slip a couple of notes in a Red Cross envelope every month. When we picture the people of the North we do not see a rigidly stratified society made up of, say, men in flat caps toiling at coalfaces, a bloated, self-satisfied bourgeoisie standing on their shoulders and an aristocracy in white suits and Panama hats playing croquet. We don't visualise stately homes and terraced houses, hunting parties and working men's clubs. And we wouldn't for a moment imagine that Scandinavia's government cabinets are made up of groups of men who attended the same costly private schools, the same universities, and belong to the same Pall Mall private members' clubs.

Put it another way: picture a posh Danish person. How about a working class Swede? I mean an actual, proper white-trash, trailer-park Sven. A Norwegian chav? A Finnish aristocrat? Don't be ridiculous. Though, as we have seen in Denmark, social stratification definitely exists in Scandinavia, notions of class are very, very different up here in the North. To the Scandinavians, having a House of Lords as part of your legislative process, for instance, would be deemed as archaic as using Spinning Jennies to make your clothes, or commuting in a pony and trap. I don't think they would ever be able to fathom the concept of Debrett's. They find the extremes of poverty and wealth, deprivation and privilege you find in the States downright horrifying. Scandinavian class structures tend to be far more subtle, income and status differences far less marked.

Walk through Copenhagen's Central Station, or cycle into central Stockholm during rush hour, and you will be hard-pressed to tell the difference between those commuters on their way to a cubicle in an open-plan office, and those heading for the corner office on the top floor. That man on the mud-splattered mountain bike with one bicycle clip and a battered cycle helmet might just as easily be the head of the Central Bank as a deputy headmaster or office clerk. That woman in the herringbone-print H&M dress with the expensive-looking leather shoulder bag could be going to make lunches for schoolkids, or on her way to the Prime Minister's office. Visit a Swedish or Danish company to interview the MD or CEO, as I have done on occasion, and more often than not you will be greeted by someone dressed in the classic Scandinavian corporate uniform of dark jeans and a jacket worn without a tie, an ensemble designed to give little indication of his position or power in the company (it can sometimes seem as if the entire male population of the Nordic region over thirty is sponsored by Gant). Watch the live feed from the Danish parliament, meanwhile, and you will see MPs dressed in jeans and the kind of knackered knitwear usually found lining a dog basket; every day is dress-down Friday at the folksy Danish *Folketing*.

Informal dress codes are to be expected from such paragons of economic equality. Social forces such as Jante Law and *lagom*, as well as the Scandinavians' deep-rooted instinct for consensus and conformity, their democratic systems, universal free education and redistributive tax systems all ensure they can look each other in the eyes as equals, no matter where they were born or what job they do. This is rightly a source of immense pride in the region. In Danish it is expressed as seeing one another at *øjenhøjde*, literally 'eye level'; you regard those you meet as social equals, regardless of their job, wealth or status (a major downside of which is the crappy service you receive in cafés and restaurants throughout the region. I don't mean to imply that one should look down on those who work in the service industry, but surely one has the right to expect one's waiter or waitress to, like, *bring you stuff* without making it seem like a total inconvenience).

Where was I? Ah, yes, my point. All may seem clever and classless and free, but there is an elephant in the democratic, meritocratic, middle-class Scandinavian living room; it is wearing velvet robes, an ermine stole and a crown, and is glaring evidence that the class system is alive and well in all three Scandinavian countries. I am talking, of course, about the absurd, anti-democratic carnival that is the monarchy.

For once I am choosing my geographical terms carefully – the other two Nordic countries, Iceland and Finland, are of course republics, so we are specifically talking about the Scandinavians here – and you may be able detect just a hint of republicanism in my tone here too, but, well, *come on*, you guys! This is all so very disappointing. Those of us who look to the North for inspiration for a better way to live expect so much more from you than the timorous idolatry of a portly man in epaulettes or a woman in a tiara waving from a balcony. That's the kind of nonsense us class-ridden, post-colonial, socially desiccated Brits cling to; this is not the cut of social democracy's jib!

What are these ridiculous figureheads still doing squatting in your prime city centre real estate? Why do you persist with these Ruritanian mannequins, swanning around their summer palaces, waving from their yachts and occasionally deigning to lend their patronage to the soft-sexy issues *du jour* – environmental sustainability, polar bears, the Olympics – in the name of 'work'? I am conscious that, as a guest in this part of the world, let alone an Englishman, it ill behooves me to criticise my hosts in this way, but really, what *are* these preposterous feudal throwbacks doing here in these otherwise exemplary egalitarian democracies? I bet they can't believe their luck, the Scandinavian royals. One hopes they wake up every morning in perpetual fear of torches and pitchforks, but I fear the mob may never arrive at the gates of Amalienborg or Oscarshall because, by and large – and here's the truly upsetting aspect of the whole sorry situation – the Scandinavians are actually rather *fond* of their royal families.

The Danes are the most fervent royalists of them all and, to be fair, their royal family – the Glücksburgs – is the only one which has anything like a legitimate claim to being an authentic, indigenous monarchy, with a history stretching back a thousand years to the time of Harald Bluetooth. But the jingoistic Norwegians love their king almost as much as the Danes love their Queen Margaret. According to a recent poll, King Harald enjoys between 60 and 70 per cent of public support. Harald must be a remarkable individual, either that or the Norwegians have very short memories, as their royal family is only a twentieth-century concoction, sired by Danish stock. Back in 1905 a newly independent Norway chose a Dane for their new king: Carl (Haakon VII), the second son of the then Danish king Frederick VIII, with his English wife Maud as queen – an ironic state of affairs given that the country had broken free of Danish rule less than a century earlier.

The Swedish royal family's legitimacy is even more tenuous. The current king of Sweden, Carl XVI Gustaf, is descended neither from noble Viking blood nor even from one of their sixteenth-century warrior kings, but from some random French bloke. When Sweden lost Finland to Russia in 1809, the then king, Gustav IV Adolf – by all accounts as mad as a hamburger – left for exile. To fill his throne and, it is thought, as a sop to Napoleon whose help Sweden hoped to secure against Russia in reclaiming Finland, the finger of fate ended up pointing at a French marshal by the name of Jean-Baptiste Bernadotte (who also happened to be the husband of Napoleon's beloved Desirée). Upon his arrival in Stockholm, the fact that Bernadotte had actually once fought *against* the Swedes in Germany was quickly forgotten, as was his name, which was changed to Charles XIV John. This, though, is where the assimilation ended: the notoriously short-tempered Charles XIV John attempted to speak Swedish to his new subjects just the once, meeting with such deafening laughter that he never bothered again (there is an echo of this in the apparently endless delight afforded the Danes by the thickly accented attempts at their language by their current queen's consort, the portly and unintentionally comical French aristocrat Henri de Monpezat). On the subject of his new country, the forefather of Sweden's current royal family was withering: 'The wine is terrible, the people without temperament, and even the sun radiates no warmth,' the arriviste king is alleged to have said.

The current king is generally considered to be a bit bumbling, but can at least speak Swedish, usually stands where he is told, and waves enthusiastically. At least, that was the perception until 2010, when the long-whispered rumours of his rampant philandering were finally exposed in a book, *Den motvillige monarken* (*The Reluctant Monarch*). Sweden's tabloids salivated over gory details of the king's relationships with numerous exotic women, visits to strip clubs, Dominique Strauss-Kahn-style sex parties, and his fraternising with members of the underworld. Hardly appropriate behaviour for the chairman of the World Scout Foundation. (The exposé followed on from revelations that the father of the king's German-Brazilian wife, Queen Silvia, was a member of the Nazi party. Awkward.) These days, whenever I see Carl Gustaf performing his official duties I can't shake the feeling that he would much prefer to be trussed up in a dominatrix's cellar.

The Scandinavian royals are often conflated with their Dutch bike-riding counterparts, but that is misleading. You won't catch Queen Margaret down the bottle bank, or cycling to work at a soup kitchen. The Scandinavian royals still enjoy all the traditional trappings of monarchy – the gilded carriages, the Aston Martins, the yachts and the multiple, taxpayer-funded homes. They are also robustly protective of their 'downtime'. In a recent exposé in Denmark, the Crown prince and princess, both of whom are enthusiastic riders, skiers and sailors, were revealed to be dedicating about six hours a year to official duties (I can't remember the exact figure, but I am sure it was thereabouts). Remarkably, this appeared to have virtually no impact on their popularity, nor on their under-the-counter sponsorship deals – the Princess reportedly delights in her complimentary £20,000 handbags, for instance.

This in the country that welcomed Lenin, gave birth to Scandinavia's cooperative movement and still marks 1 May with a gigantic piss-up in the main park in Copenhagen! The Danes would probably laugh at the deification of the Thai king by his subjects, or scoff at the deference Americans grant the office of president, but, and I speak from bitter personal experience, if you make a disparaging remark about, say, Queen Margaret's awful dentistry, or point out that it is a slightly rum state of affairs that her entire family still has immunity from prosecution under Danish law, or that democratically elected government ministers must back out of her presence following official audiences, and you will be rounded on like a rat in a kennel.

So, whither the Scandinavian republican movement? you might ask. I know I did. In terms of popularity, in Norway and Denmark republicanism is right up there with Sharia Law and spicy food, but there are hopeful stirrings in Sweden. Ten years ago Swedish republicanism was a minority cause, with perhaps 7,500 members. Today it has three times that – still not much in a country of over nine million, but it's a start. Ironically, the boost came not from the exposure of the king's sexual adventures, but from the supposedly 'fairytale' wedding of his daughter to her fitness instructor.

'With the scandal I think people actually felt a little bit sorry for the king and his family. But in the run-up to the wedding there was this discussion about how much the state had to pay, which turned people to the republican cause,' Magnus Simonsson, spokesman for the Swedish Republican Association told me when we met in central Stockholm. 'The day before the wedding there was a survey which was one of the first to show that less than half of the population supported the monarchy.'

I mentioned to Magnus my terrible disappointment that Sweden had a monarchy at all. 'Don't you realise,' I said, perhaps a touch too imploringly, as we sat together on a bench in the entrance hall of the building where Simonsson worked as an advisor to a government minister, 'you're letting *all* of us down! If you still have your monarchy what chance have we got of getting rid of ours?' He edged away from me slightly and gently explained that part of the reason that Sweden had tolerated its royal family for so long was that the country's move towards democracy and universal suffrage had been a gradual, peaceful one. It is a similar story in Denmark. 'By the time of the late seventies most people didn't feel there was a need to get rid of the king because he didn't do much and didn't cost much,' he said.

In a country where the taxes are almost as ferocious as Denmark's, you would imagine the cost of the royals would be high on the Swedish republicans' agenda.

'No, for us it's not about money – a president would cost money, too – it's more about democracy. The head of state is not elected, but he does have powers. The King meets with ministers sometimes, which is ridiculous, and he is chair of the foreign affairs committee, opens parliament and sometimes does get involved in politics. When the law was changed to allow women to become head of state, he was against it – he said that it was too heavy work for a woman.'

What about the tourist industry, which is one of the excuses people often give for maintaining the monarchy in the UK? 'Well,' said Simonsson, 'I don't know any people who go to Belgium because Belgium has a king, do you?'

Though he is convinced it is 'just a question of time' before Sweden gets rid of its royal family, I fear the Bernadottes will be around for a while yet. Several of the Swedes I spoke to loosely defined themselves as republicans, but despite this few could summon much energy to oppose them: 'I tolerate them, I don't like to engage myself in such an unimportant thing,' said Ulf Nilson. 'I don't like him [the King], he says stupid things but we kind of like that, I suppose. I've met her [the Queen] many times, she's a lovely lady. Monarchy is illogical of course, but they don't mean a whole lot.'

'I am not a royalist, no,' Åke Daun had chuckled. 'It's a little thing. They have no power; they don't decide anything. It is something beautiful, nice to see; be careful with it, don't touch it.'

Berggren was at least prepared to nail his colours to the mast: 'I'm a republican, basically, and it's definitely an intellectual nuisance, but

I tend to agree with Engels that it's a distraction. Historically there has been an alliance between the people and the king against the aristocracy in Sweden. This may in truth be baloney, but there has been this idea that we need a strong king to oppose the aristocracy.'

Mattias Frihammar, a professor at Stockholm University, has studied the relationship of the Swedes to their royals for some years. When I visited him in his office there, I asked how he thought his fellow countrymen squared this antiquated, anti-democratic institution with their self-image as modern meritocrats.

'Sweden is not as egalitarian as it claims,' he told me. 'We have rich and poor, powerful and powerless. Everybody knows it is a big difference which family you are born into – if you are born into the Wallenbergs it is an advantage. We are told people are born equal, but that is bullshit. I think we are very good at hiding inequalities. For example, abolishing the formal and informal ways of addressing people – that's a way to hide inequalities. The Swedes are more banal royalists. They accept the way it is, but they don't call themselves royalists. They might say, "I don't like the idea of the monarchy as a way of arranging society, but I don't have anything against the king personally." And as he gets older he gets more and more popular. If you compare it to Denmark, the Queen of Denmark is really a personality, she is a charming person. Our king is not very personable and he is not good with words or at talking to people. He says the wrong things always, and in a way he becomes like this relative that you accept.'

Frihammar pointed out that, while the Danes hang on every word of their Queen's New Year's Eve speech, the Swedes pay not the slightest heed to their king's equivalent speech, given on Christmas Day.

'The Danes are more engaged in their nationality, their national community, and I think that is because they are a small country and they have larger neighbours like Germany and Sweden. Denmark is the little sister or brother and their royal family played a greater symbolic role during the Second World War, for example, also in Norway – they became national symbols.'

We talked a little about the extraordinary turn of events in Denmark in 2004 which saw a pretty but unremarkable young Tasmanian student, the aforementioned Mary Donaldson, whose main interest up to that point seemed to be spending time hanging around singles bars, transformed into Crown Princess Mary, international style icon, screamed at by strangers as a red-carpet deity, literally overnight.

'People use this soap opera to reflect on their own lives,' Frihammar explained. 'They ask themselves, is it okay to pick up a girl like that? Is it okay to let our daughter party all night like the Swedish princess? They are on a pedestal, in this glamorous, fairytale world. And it can happen, they might pick you. It keeps that dream alive.'

Chapter 11

Ball bearings

Writing about what the five Nordic tribes really think of each other is a bit like discussing someone else's marriage – you never *really* know how one feels about the other, deep down, how they talk to each other when they are taking their make-up off and brushing their teeth at the end of an evening. I only know how Danes, Swedes, Norwegians, Icelanders and Finns talk to an Englishman about each other, and it has to be said that the main topic of conversation on that front is how annoying the Swedes are. None of their neighbours seem to like the Swedes very much. Historic enmities still simmer, resentments linger, the Swedes still have a habit of getting up people's noses. The Swedes, meanwhile, tend to remain aloof to the regional resentment.

'We really like the Danes, they are lovely people,' Åke Daun told me. 'There are Danish characterisations of the Swedes, saying we are more efficient and hard-working, more serious and so on, while we think the Danes are charming, warm, lovely, a little chaotic. We envy their lack of alcohol restrictions.'

'The Danes have always been seen as the more easygoing, cosmopolitan, less working, more drinking, more frivolous people; less, shall we say, industrious than Swedes,' Jonsson, the multiculturalism expert from Stockholm University told me. 'We go to Copenhagen to breathe Europe, to have a beer. It's looser, freer, more European, and you also have this more open attitude to drugs and alcohol, but more recently people are shaking their heads that Denmark has become a fascist country, at war with Islam, extremely eager to send aircraft to bomb Libya.'

Leaving aside the notion of the Danes really 'knowing how to have a good time' (clearly he has never spent an afternoon in a sports hall in Slagelse watching a women's handball match – neither have I, actually, but the *thought* . . .), Jonsson, Daun and many of the Swedes I spoke to seemed oddly oblivious to how disliked the Swedes are. I suspect they might be taken aback by the extent to which the Danes bad-mouth them to anyone who'll listen.

'They are so stiff and *boring*,' is the common Danish description of the Swedes, 'and they don't know how to handle their beer.' 'They didn't win back Skåne,' one Danish friend told me, referring to the still traumatic (to the Danes, at least) year of 1658 when the Swedes wrestled the Danes' southern province from them. 'We *granted* them their freedom.' (I once heard a Danish radio talk show in which the host only half-jokingly suggested that Sweden's traditional August crayfish party season would be a good time to reinvade the south and take back their former territory.)

I asked Henrik Berggren about Swedish–Danish relations, pointing out that the Swedes could afford to remain aloof from the Nordic trash-talk as they have, by just about every measurement, ended up richer, and more successful than their neighbours.

'Yes, we were the winners,' he agreed. 'The big brother, definitely. But there is more animosity in it than we understood at first. When I was growing up we had a very positive view of the Danes and Denmark. They were like us – welfare state, modern – but by God they were a lot more fun than us. Danish women! Christiania! Smoking hash! I think a lot of Swedes felt like the Danes had it all, plus a bit more *joie de vivre*. But with this whole Danish anti-immigrant thing the perception of Denmark has changed drastically into "God, we don't understand this. Where did this come from?" And it's kind of funny because I think it's kindled a kind of Swedish nationalism in a sense that before we felt a bit inferior to the Danes, but suddenly now we can get on a moral high horse.'

And boy don't the Danes know it: they are mightily tired of the Swedes' sanctimony towards their immigration policy and their condescension regarding the rise of the anti-Islamist Danish People's Party. The Swedes haven't just got on their high horse over what they perceive as Danish racism and xenophobia, they are standing on its back, riding round the circus ring juggling fire and playing kazoos. Oh, how long they have waited to repay all the slights about their Nazi past and 'cowardly' neutrality, the jokes about the hairnets and the armament sales. And they have seized their chance.

In truth though, if we can set aside the typical younger brother resentment of a patronising older sibling, the Danes don't have very much reason to resent the Swedes, and neither do the Norwegians, who certainly these days have enough money to rise above ancient bitterness. As for the Finns, they probably do have grounds for anger, but guys, I think it's time to move on. For all the moaning about the Swedes, I remain convinced that there is greater fellow feeling up here in the North than between any of the other countries in Europe. I am not aware of much grudging affection emanating from the Belgians towards the French, for instance, or from the Swiss towards the Italians, are you? For all the bickering, the Nordic region is hardly likely to go the way of the Balkans. As Stefan Jonsson pointed out to me when I got a little carried away on the subject of inter-Scandinavian rivalry, 'This isn't Israel–Palestine, you know.'

The fact that the Swedes have appeared fallible in recent years ought to have helped temper neighbourly jealousies a little. They are facing similar problems to the Danes in terms of having to curb their welfare state and keep their provinces from dying a slow death, and have even greater challenges in the areas of integration and globalisation. The truth is that the great Swedish social democratic adventure hit the buffers a couple of decades ago when the country's economy tanked and the then government introduced quite radical privatisation programmes, reduced taxes and began to tackle the welfare state. Yet the rest of the world has still not really cottoned on to how much Sweden has changed – in the US, right-leaning politicians still cite Swedish society as an example of socialist extremism when really it is no such thing. The Sweden we came to know and politely admire while secretly being glad we didn't live there, is, these days, an uncertain place in a state of political flux.

According to Stefan Jonsson, his country has reached a crucial crossroads. 'There is huge confusion in Sweden. I think it is a society on the edge of cracking up. Mentally it is disintegrating, questioning what it is. Questioning social democracy. Many are now wondering what to salvage, whether this is sustainable, and what will come if it is not sustainable.'

This sounds dramatic – we are still talking about Sweden here, after all – but to pluck out one sobering statistic, as I write Sweden's ratio of tax revenue to GDP is 47.9 percent – the fourth highest in the world (with Denmark third). To give you an idea of what kind of an indicator this is of the economic well-being of a country, Zimbabwe is second and Kiribati first.

'I am not optimistic for Sweden,' agrees Ulf Nilson. 'We have to open up this rigid system; the welfare state is too bureaucratic. Too many people are invested in the system. Tax strategy is the obvious key to it all. I live in France and there, if I earned 100,000 kroner a month, they take maybe 30,000 of it. Here they take 50,000, but there is no doubt that French healthcare is better. So are we being taken for a ride? Yeah, we are being taken for a ride. The fact that we have thousands of people who could work living on the dole is of course not good. That dependence system is no good. I have left Sweden and become a millionaire by work. You could never do that here. I feel I have escaped, I was lucky.'

As always, Henrik Berggren remains a lone voice of optimism: 'The system is doing rather well. I've lived through all these prognoses that it isn't going to work because people aren't motivated to work, and so on. Do you see a society decaying around you? Be honest. We might be a bit rude, but . . .'

One deeper issue did trouble me about Sweden's long-term prospects: in rejecting their Lutheran principles to embrace consumerism and the various temptations of the modern world, had the Swedes perhaps thrown the puritanical baby out with the globalisation bath water? Put differently, consider all those old agrarian principles of self-sufficiency, caution, modesty, equality and parsimony, the instinctive urge to compromise, to cooperate and share – the very characteristics that laid the foundations for the Social Democratic experiment. Are these characteristics not inevitably, *fatally* eroded by increased wealth, consumerism, globalisation and urbanisation? Is the country's great modern, urban experiment not de-stabilising the very foundations on which that modernity was constructed?

Åke Daun answered this with the breezy 'Oh yes, I think so, yes' of an elderly man who has seen it all before and has resigned himself to the world going to the dogs.

Andrew Brown appeared to agree, too: 'Whether prosperity can survive without the memories and disciplines of poverty is a question I don't know the answer to.' In his book *Fishing in Utopia* Brown points to the marked rise in crime in Sweden since the 1970s, in particular rape (in recent years Sweden has seen the highest number of reported rapes per capita in Europe); to the McDonald's fever sweeping the country, with the result that he begins to notice obese people in the streets of Stockholm for the first time; to the changing media landscape ('A generation of flamboyant gangsters and businessmen, not always easy to tell apart, moved through the newspapers'); to a new openness about alcohol, symbolised by the slick rebranding of Absolut Vodka, once a resolutely unglamorous state-owned alcohol producer ('Drunkenness came back into fashion'); not to mention the loss of two-fifths of industrial jobs since the mid-seventies. All, he says, are signifiers of a country which is, essentially, making one final circumnavigation of the plughole.

I don't believe this is the case, but Sweden does appear to be sitting on a demographic time bomb. It is the only country in the world in which people over eighty years old make up over 5 per cent of the population (the global average is 1 per cent). Almost 20 per cent of Swedes are over sixty-five, making Sweden the oldest country in Scandinavia, and the eighth oldest in the world. The World Bank predicts that by 2040 a third of Swedes will be over retirement age. But Sweden, as you would expect, is well prepared (unlike, say, Italy, which is truly screwed in this regard). It has a highly developed state pension system which is expected to be able to cope with future demographic challenges; the IMF ranked Sweden seventh globally for its current elderly care and its future preparedness in terms of looking after an aging population.

In the final analysis, perhaps we shouldn't be so worried about Sweden. As Henrik Berggren pointed out, people have been writing off his homeland since the seventies, and even after the early nineties, when the Swedish model did appear to have been fatally undermined by its economic imbalance, it recovered quickly and strongly. Sweden still has one of the highest-achieving economies in the world chiefly because it overhauled the old Social Democratic structures and transformed itself into a rather unique type of mixed economy, and introduced both some marked liberal economic tendencies and strict fiscal and banking controls.

So Sweden is probably safe economically for the time being. Politically it has endured the assassination of its prime minister and its foreign minister (the latter, Anne Lindh, was stabbed to death in a Stockholm department store in 2003; as it happened, the day after I had visited). But how resilient is it culturally? One thing that often surprised me during my travels in Sweden was the dismissive attitude of many Swedes I spoke to about their country's cultural output. I've always thought of Sweden as being home to heavy hitters like Strindberg and Bergman, as well as all those massively popular authors like Astrid Lindgren, Henning Mankell and of course Stieg Larsson. From Jenny Lind, the Swedish nightingale on whom Hans Christian Andersen doted, to ABBA and Robyn, Sweden has also sent forth great popular singers and songwriters into a grateful world.

Nevertheless, comments such as this one from Åke Daun were not untypical: 'Culture is not a big thing in Sweden. We are technically creative, not artistically.' He suggested that Sweden's self-image was more invested in being a successful manufacturer of ball bearings, zippers and safety matches.

'It's true, you run out after Bergman and Strindberg,' agreed Stefan Jonsson. 'Culturally and intellectually the international contribution of Sweden is quite limited, but the typical Swedish intellectual believes the country is big enough for him to have a career, and not so small that he feels he needs to go outside and bring things in. Its the tragedy of being a mid-sized country.'

When I tentatively mentioned the country's paucity of cultural titans to Henrik Berggren, he reacted with his customary patriotic vigour.

'From what objective standpoint are you saying this? That sounds rather typically British, to be honest, a rather snotty British attitude to the world: "I can sit on my island and I can judge all cultures . . ."'

Oh dear. Honestly, Henrik, that's not what I meant.

Though, you are right, I probably am a snotty Brit.

Epilogue

When faced with the happiest, most trusting and successful people on the planet, one's natural instinct is to try to find fault, to X-ray the fissures. It is an instinct I may not have been entirely successful in resisting over the course of this book, but I hope that any Nordic people who might read it will forgive me. Put it down to jealousy, if that helps.

The fissures and flaws are definitely there, though. This region has its own set of problems and challenges, weird personality kinks and frailties, just like the rest of us. But ultimately its success is still hard to argue with. As Paul McCartney once said when a journalist suggested that *The White Album* might have been better as just one disc instead of two: 'Yeah, well, you know, it is still *The White Album*.' Of course there are downsides even in almost nearly perfect societies: there are historical skeletons in every closet, and yes, countries with homogenous, monocultural tendencies do tend to be a little too safe and dull, and insular. Looking to the future, the Nordic countries are also facing some serious challenges – aging populations, creaking welfare states, the ongoing integration of immigrant populations, and rising inequality. But it's still Scandinavia. It is still the enviably rich, peaceful, harmonious and progressive place it has long been. It's still *The White Album*.

Though I set out to redress the rose-tinted imbalance in the reporting on the Nordic region in the Western media, as well as to get a few things off my chest, I hope, too, that I have shed light on some of the more positive aspects of Scandinavia – the trust, the social cohesion, the economic and gender equality, the rationalism, the modesty, the well-balanced political and economic systems, and so on. Right now, the West is looking for an alternative to the rampant capitalism which has ravaged our economies, a system which might avoid the extremes of Soviet socialism or American deregulated neo-liberalism. Really, as far as I am concerned there is only one place to look for the economic and societal role model of the future, and it is not Brazil or Russia or China. The Nordic countries have the answer. Even little Iceland is recovering, with higher growth than most of the rest of Europe. Up here, even when they get it wrong they soon figure out how to get it right without any blood being spilled.

I hope, too, that in my own clumsy, reductive, probably at times racist (is it racist if the target is rich people?) way I have demonstrated the fascinating diversity that exists here; that though they may look alike at first glance, the Nordic peoples are wildly, fascinatingly different from each other. They have different genetic roots, different mentalities, different histories and different economic systems. Some have oil and gas, others have trees or hot air. One has the euro, another is outside the EU altogether, and I haven't even touched on the diversity *within* these supposedly 'homogenous' countries – Sweden's striking north–south divide; the hundreds of regional dialects in Norway; the Sami, and so on.

And there is an element of the Nordic happiness phenomenon that I have not yet mentioned, at least not explicitly. One of the keys to happiness, experts tell us, is autonomy in one's life – the luxury of being able to decide your own destiny and achieve the fulfilment of self-realisation. It is no coincidence that the region that is consistently judged to have the highest levels of well-being and life quality, and the happiest, most fulfilled people, also has the greatest equality of educational opportunity and, according to a London School of Economics study comparing the incomes of fathers and sons over thirty years, among the very highest levels of social mobility in the world. The four main Nordic countries occupied the top four places on the list.

To achieve authentic, sustained happiness, above all else you need to be in charge of your life, to be in control of who you want to be, and be able to make the appropriate changes if you are not. This cannot merely be a perception, an empty slogan like the American Dream (the US came way down on the LSE's social mobility scale, incidentally). In Scandinavia it is a reality. These are the real lands of opportunity. There is far greater social mobility in the Nordic countries than in the US or Britain and, for all the collectivism and state interference in the lives of the people who live here, there is far greater freedom to be the person you want to be, and do the things you want to do, up here in the North. In a recent poll by Gallup, only 5 per cent of Danes said they could not change their lives if they wanted to. In contrast, I can think of many American states where it would probably be quite an uncomfortable experience to declare yourself an atheist, for example, or gay, or to be married yet choose not to have children, or to be unmarried and have children, or to have an abortion, or raise your children as Muslims. I don't imagine it would be easy being vegetarian in Texas, for instance, or a wine buff in Salt Lake City come to that. And don't even think of coming out as socialist in any of the fifty states. In Scandinavia you can be all of these things and no one will bat an eye (as long as you wait and cross on green).

Crucial to this social mobility are the schools. The autonomy enabled by a high-quality, free education system is just as important as the region's economic equality and extensive welfare safety nets, if not more so. In Scandinavia the standard of education is not only the best in the world, but the opportunities it presents are available to all, free of charge. It is the bedrock of Nordic exceptionalism.

Some might argue that the reality of Nordic autonomy is that you are free . . . to be Nordic. If you are a Muslim who is looking to build a mosque, or an American who wants to drive a large car, espouse your deeply held Creationist beliefs and go shopping with your platinum card on a Sunday, or even if you are English and choose to conduct yourself according to archaic forms of baroque politeness, you are likely to experience varying degrees of oppression and exclusion should you come to live in this part of the world.

This is true. Scandinavia is struggling to integrate its non-Western immigrants in particular. In Sweden over the past two decades, average household incomes for non-European immigrants have actually *declined* compared with those of native-born Swedes. They now bring in 36 per cent less money per month compared with 21 per cent less in 1991. But it is comparatively early days yet. Immigration didn't really begin in this part of the world until the late 1960s and, unlike Britain, its immigrants did not arrive from former colonies already fluent in the language and familiar with the cultural norms. It's going to take a generation or two for things to change. And the Breiviks will not win. They never do. Immigration will continue in the North – it has to for many reasons – and integration will continue to improve. I am confident of this, although they might want to think about dropping all this 'second-generation Dane' nonsense and start occasionally giving the jobs to the applicants whose surnames don't end in '-sen'.

Back in the sixties, Susan Sontag wrote that Sweden was in desperate need of some kind of revolution, something to cause a rupture of the established social order and behavioural norms. Well, Sweden has had its revolution, and so has the rest of the Nordic region. It may not have taken the form Sontag had in mind, but the hundreds of thousands of immigrants to Scandinavia are challenging and revitalising these societies, turning these sometimes monotonous monocultures into kaleidoscopic multi-ethnic models of diversity. It has been a bumpy ride so far, but there are hopeful signs that the real issues are being addressed and that one day things might smooth out.

I didn't mention it but the day after the Malmö crayfish orgy, the city's annual festival continued with more al fresco feasting – mainly of Turkish, Indian, Arabic and Chinese food – but this time the streets of the city were packed with the most multiethnic crowd I have ever seen on the streets of a Scandinavian city. The atmosphere was terrific that day; it felt to me like there was a genuine sense of community and that, contrary to much of what I had heard about Malmö in the Danish media, this was a city at peace with itself.

But of all the countries of the North, and ironically given the inflammatory rhetoric of its right-wing politicians over the last decade, I would argue that Denmark seems to be leading the way towards a properly integrated, multiethnic Nordic society. Danish immigrants are less segregated than those in Sweden; traditionally they have been more spread out among the provinces, and they mix more with the indigenous population. This has meant that the Danes have been confronted more directly with the challenges of integration, but they have also made more progress.

As that great voice of reason and wisdom, the Norwegian anthropologist Thomas Hylland Eriksen said to me, 'In Denmark there are ghettoes, but you also have the Turk on the street with his tobacconist shop; and they drive the bus, they are placed in villages so they have to deal with the neighbours, and are very much more part of society.' No one is claiming this process has not been difficult, but once this initial, often fraught, occasionally violent getting-to-know-you phase is over, I like to hope that things will settle down. As Richard Jenkins writes in his study *Being Danish*, 'A multiethnic Denmark is not an option to be accepted or rejected; it is an existing fact of life, for better or worse, [but] integration is much less problematic than the rhetoric of politicians on the national scene would have us believe.'

It is going to take time – Britain has had over half a century and still isn't there yet – but let's hope that human nature and Nordic pragmatism will triumph over fear and prejudice.

Speech over.

I have one more hope. A heartfelt plea to the people of the North.

Every once in a while, a Nordic politician or member of the Nordic Council issues a clarion call for the Nordic countries to integrate further, to come together to form a proper Nordic Union, to unite economically and militarily, with a joint army, joint foreign policy and even a joint currency. Something along the lines of the EU, but without the squabbling and corruption.

A former Danish government minister, now chairman of the Danish delegation to the Nordic Council, Bertel Haarder, told me that greater pan-Nordic cooperation is inevitable and to be welcomed. 'It is already happening,' he said. 'And the Arctic is going to be one area where it will be vital in the future.'

The Swedish historian Gunnar Wetterberg also believes the combined 26 million people of the North could have a greater influence in the EU, and rightfully demand a seat at the G20. He has pointed out that the Scandinavian countries were unified once before, in the fourteenth century, when the threat of German traders brought the Norwegians, the Swedes and the Danes together under the rule of the Danish Queen Margaret I – the Kalmar Union. In the end Scandinavia did not take to being ruled from Copenhagen, but that was mostly because the Danes slaughtered most of the Swedish nobility. I don't think they would do that again.

The short-lived Scandinavism movement of the nineteenth century raised the possibility once again. In an address to a Scandinavian scientific congress, the great Danish physicist H. C. Ørsted said: 'Let 6 million Scandinavians place their entire weight on one scale, and surely it shall not be found too light.'

Today we have the aforementioned Nordic Union. It has opened up trade between the five countries, coordinated effective 'soft power' cooperation between them in terms of overseas aid, and has worked hard to paper over historic conflicts and foster cultural ties between the member states. Now that the Nordic people are not 6 million as they were in Ørsted's day, but 25 million, a proper union would carry even more weight. Could the next step be full unity – the five countries, Denmark, Sweden, Iceland, Norway and Finland coming together in a properly integrated economic and military Nordic Union?

Though there has been increasing discussion about this in the Scandinavian media in recent years – with some suggesting a Federal States of Scandinavia as a northern alternative to the faltering EU – it is still relatively unlikely. Just in case, though, my plea to the Nordic people is this: please don't.

For if you ever really did band together in such a way then, truly, the rest of us would not stand a chance.

Acknowledgements

As you can probably imagine, my Danish friends and family are an exceptionally patient, tolerant, supportive and, above all, forgiving group of people. To them I would like to say, firstly, thank you for all your support and for listening to my various theories about your society and, secondly, sorry if I have been a little hard on your compatriots at times. If I promise to keep my mouth shut from now on, is it okay if I stay a little longer?

I would also like to thank my British publisher, Dan Franklin at Jonathan Cape, for all of his support during what has been an unusually long gestation period for this book and to Kris Potter for his work on the cover.

Norwegian anthropologist Lindis Sloan was kind enough to check through the Norwegian chapters for me (thanks, too, to her husband Roddie for the unforgettable sea-urchin-safari experience). Samppa Rouhtula was similarly helpful in terms of the Finland chapters. Needless to say, their generosity does not mean that either Sampa or Lindis are in any way responsible for any errors or wild inaccuracies to be found within these pages. They are entirely my own work. I didn't have the nerve to ask any of my Swedish friends to check the Swedish chapters, which explains why there are probably so many mistakes in them. And why I will very likely soon have significantly fewer Swedish friends.

I would also like to thank – in no particular order – either for granting me a useful interview or simply for listening patiently while I explained to them my latest theory about the region in which they were born, and about which they know far more than I ever will: Laura Kolbe, Bertel Haarder, Tor Nørretranders, Roman Schatz,

Thomas Hylland Eriksen, Anne Knudsen, Henrik Berggren, Karen-Marie Lillelund, Cecilie Frøkjær, Professor Richard Wilkinson, Christian Bjørnskov, Mike from Trelleborg, Dr Elizabeth Ashman Rowe, Åke Daun, Ove Kaj Pedersen, Mogens Lykketoft, Torben Trænæs, Martin Ågerup, Bent Dupont, Annegrethe Rasmussen, Richard Jenkins, Sree Abhirami Upasaki, Stefan Jonsson, Professor Gísli Pálsson, Terry Gunnell, Sindri Freysson, Bjarni Brynjólfsson, Inga Jessen, Professor Unnur Dís Skaptadóttir, Morten Høglund, Sindre Bangstad, Yngve Slyngstad, Simen Sætre, the Finnish and Rovaniemi tourist boards, the Finnish Foreign Ministry, Heikki Aittokoski, Matti Peltonen, Paulina Ahokas, Neil Hardwick, the wife-carriers of Sonkajärvi, Dick Fredholm, Ilmar Reepalu, Professor Patrick Scheinin, Bejzat Becirov, Ulf Nilson, René Redzepi, Santa Claus and his elves.

Index